TENTH EDITION

THE ECONOMICS OF POVERTY AND DISCRIMINATION

Bradley R. Schiller

American University

PEARSON

Prentice Hall

Upper Saddle River, NJ 07458

Library of Congress Cataloging-in-Publication Data

Schiller, Bradley R.
  The economics of poverty and discrimination / Bradley R. Schiller. — 10th ed.
    p. cm.
  Includes bibliographical references and index.
  ISBN-13: 978-0-13-188969-9
  ISBN-10:   0-13-188969-9
  1. Poor — United States.   2. Poverty — United States.   3. Discrimination — United States.   4. Economic assistance, Domestic — United States.   I. Title.
HC110.P6S27 2008
305.5'690973 — dc22

                                                    2007019236

AVP/Executive Editor: David Alexander
Product Development Manager: Ashley Santora
Project Manager: Mary Kate Murray
Marketing Manager: Jodi Bassett
Marketing Assistant: Ian Gold
Senior Managing Editor: Judy Leale
Production Editor: Suzanne Grappi
Permissions Coordinator: Charles Morris
Manufacturing Buyer: Michelle Klein
Design/Composition Manager: Christy Mahon
Cover Design: Jayne Conte
Composition: Aptara, Inc.
Full-Service Project Management: Aptara, Inc.
Printer/Binder: R. R. Donnelley/Harrisonburg
Typeface: 10/12 Times Ten Roman

Credits and acknowledgments borrowed from other sources and reproduced, with permission, in this textbook appear on appropriate page within text.

Pearson Education LTD.   Pearson Education Australia PTY, Limited
Pearson Education Singapore, Pte. Ltd   Pearson Education North Asia Ltd
Pearson Education, Canada, Ltd   Pearson Educación de Mexico, S.A. de C.V.
Pearson Education–Japan   Pearson Education Malaysia, Pte. Ltd

10 9 8 7 6 5 4 3 2
ISBN 13: 978-0-13-188969-9
ISBN 10:   0-13-188969-9

BRIEF CONTENTS

CONTENTS

PREFACE

The landscape of poverty and discrimination keeps changing. The landmark welfare reforms of 1996 (the Personal Responsibility and Work Opportunity Act) became fully effective in 2001, when the legislated time limits on welfare eligibility first took hold. In the first five years of welfare reform welfare caseloads plunged. Some observers credit tougher eligibility conditions for the caseload decline; others point to the strong expansion of the U.S. economy in those same years. After the economy started slipping in spring 2001, the debate over cause and effect took on a more urgent tone. Would a slumping economy reverse the caseload declines of 1996–2001, or did welfare reform lay a more permanent foundation for financial independence? Evidence since then suggests that welfare reform did instill more permanent changes in the incidence of welfare dependency. Welfare caseloads have stayed low while labor force participation has increased.

The poverty population didn't decline as dramatically as the nation's welfare population. Between 1996 and 2001, welfare caseloads fell by more than 50 percent as nearly 6 million people left welfare. During those same years, however, the poverty population declined by only 3.3 million. This suggests that welfare reduction isn't synonymous with poverty reduction. While most welfare leavers moved up the economic ladder, a good many others remained in or near poverty.

The financial and economic turbulence of the last decade has also sparked broad interest in issues of inequality. The rise and fall of the dot.coms, the roller-coaster rides of the stock market, the revelations of corporate malfeasance and executive largesse have all heightened awareness of how unequal incomes can be. This heightened awareness has fostered more inquires into the nature and causes of inequality. These new inquires go beyond explanations for *poverty* to broader questions of how relative incomes are determined. This tenth edition pursues these questions, offering more insights into both the *structure* of the income distribution and increased attention to the *movement* of individuals within that structure.

Completely new to this edition is a broader, *global* perspective on poverty and inequality. Global poverty is gauged in terms of *absolute* deprivation, not the relative standards of American affluence. Despite such low thresholds, however, *billions* of people around the world are counted as "severely" or "extremely" poor. Chapter 4 examines the incidence and distribution of this *global* poverty and related inequalities. Alternative approaches for achieving the United Nations' Millennium poverty-reduction goal are also assessed. This new chapter not only heightens awareness of an acute global problem, but also helps put America's social problems into a comparative perspective.

This tenth edition also continues to pursue the injustices that contribute to both inequality and poverty. Chapters 11 and 12 examine the nature of discrimination and its gender, race, and class manifestations in both schools and the labor market. The latest

Supreme Court cases on college and secondary-school admissions are assessed in the context of the evolving judicial record.

MULTIDISCIPLINARY APPROACH

All of these changes more than just justify a fresh look at poverty, discrimination, and related topics. That is the purpose of this new edition. Once again, an effort has been made to incorporate the latest research findings from diverse disciplines, including economics, sociology, political science, gerontology, anthropology, law, and public health. Although my own training in economics gives a unique structure and perspective to the text, the discussion ranges far beyond the conventional boundaries of academic disciplines. This is particularly evident in expanded discussions of the urban underclass, the increasing feminization of poverty, the renewed IQ controversy, the behavioral constraints on welfare reform, and public attitudes on poverty, race, and inequality.

INTERNATIONAL PERSPECTIVES

The new Chapter 4 provides an explicit foundation for a global perspective on poverty and inequality. Other chapters reinforce this foundation with international comparisons and references.

CURRENT AND CUSTOMIZED DATA

As always, this text uses the latest available data to depict the landscape of poverty and discrimination. Once again, special, customized tabulations from the U.S. Census Bureau augment the published reports available to the general public. These additional tabulations give the text a unique perspective on several key issues.

LOGICAL ORGANIZATION

Despite many changes, the basic organization of the text remains the same. The logical progression moves from concepts of poverty and inequality to their measurement. Then the discussion moves into causation and, finally, to policy options.

The central focus of the text continues to be on the phenomenon of poverty, with discrimination examined as a potential contributing cause. The text begins with a conceptual discussion of poverty and inequality, highlighting the differing views of causation. Three distinct causal perspectives are introduced in Chapter 1, namely Flawed Character, Restrictive Opportunity, and Big Brother. These competing "explanations" of poverty and inequality are referenced throughout the text in order to accentuate disparate views of why poverty persists and what role public policy should play.

Chapter 2 focuses on the nature and dimensions of inequality. A unique feature of this chapter is the emphasis on income mobility, that is, the movement of individuals across different rungs of the economic ladder. This discussion highlights the critical distinction between equal *status* and equal *opportunity*.

Chapter 3 tries to quantify the dimensions of poverty. The seemingly mundane task of counting the poor has become increasingly controversial, as evidenced by the National Academy of Science's 1995 report and the continuing debate over poverty standards and census methods. Chapter 3 summarizes the key dimensions of this debate and emphasizes how our perceptions of poverty depend on the yardstick used. Data for 2005 are used to illustrate both the official poverty count and the impact of various adjustments.

Chapter 4 is the new one on global poverty. After surveying the depth, the extent, and the distribution of global poverty, the chapter assesses the importance of foreign aid, economic growth, and institutional reform for alleviating world deprivation.

Chapters 5 through 12 address the major causes of poverty. Each chapter focuses on a cluster of related causes, drawing on a broad range of research. Points of controversy are emphasized and analyzed in the context of the best available evidence. The intent is not to advocate one point of view but to encourage critical thinking on central issues in the poverty debate.

The more prominent policy options for eliminating poverty are examined in the final five chapters. Welfare reform gets a lot of attention, in keeping with the historic 1996 reforms. Chapter 14 is devoted to social insurance programs. In addition to Social Security and Unemployment Insurance, the chapter includes an extended description of child-support enforcement and assurance. In each case, the theoretical and historical foundations of the policy option are reviewed, with an eye toward assessing its antipoverty potential.

The potential of employment and training policies to reduce poverty is examined in Chapter 15. The debate over whether economic growth creates "good" jobs or "bad" ones is reviewed, as are a host of skill-training programs. The impact of the Earned Income Tax Credit (EITC) on labor supply and on income gets more space in this edition.

The renewed debate over affirmative action is the central focus of Chapter 16. The discussion reviews the history and experience of equal opportunity initiatives in both employment and education. The inherent conflict between affirmative action and reverse discrimination is examined in the context of legal milestones and the California, Texas, Michigan, and Kentucky experiences.

The ultimate objective of this book has not changed through ten editions. Its goal is to lay the foundations for a clearer understanding of poverty and discrimination and for a keener perspective on related public policy. Until we know why people are poor, or what kinds of programs are effective in combating poverty and discrimination, we cannot expect these problems to disappear.

REFERENCE MATERIAL

The theoretical and empirical foundation of the text has been strengthened with new data, new research studies, and an expanded bibliography. Scores of new citations are strewn across all the chapters. The bibliographies at the end of each chapter have been updated, as has the list of relevant web sites. This reference material will allow both instructors and students to update data and extend textbook discussions.

WEB RESOURCES (www.prenhall.com/schiller)

FOR INSTRUCTORS

The following supplements are available to adopting instructors. For detailed descriptions, please visit: www.prenhall.com/schiller

Instructor's Manual - ISBN: 978-013-1889705
  Steven Rock of Western Illinois University

FOR STUDENTS

www.prenhall.com/schiller contains valuable resources for both students and professors, including access to homework exercises and web links for each chapter which keeps the text material current.

ACKNOWLEDGMENTS

As with previous editions, I have benefited from the feedback of students and instructors who have used this text. I am particularly grateful for the detailed reviews provided by:

Marlene Kim, University of Massachusetts, Boston
Jennifer VanGilder, Ursinus College
Steven Rock, Western Illinois University
Rudy Fichtenbaum, Wright State University
Jeff Ankrom, Wittenburg University
Keith Bender, University of Wisconsin, Milwaukee
Gail Hoyt, University of Kentucky
Tom Larson, California State University, Los Angeles
Mitch Renkow, North Carolina State University
Susan Christopherson, Cornell University
Tiffani A. Gottschall, Washington & Jefferson College

I am also grateful again to the many personnel at the U.S. Bureau of the Census, the U.S. Bureau of Labor Statistics, and the U.S. Social Security Administration who provided the data—much of it unpublished—to update this edition. My research assistant, Eamon Monahan, also proved to be adept at ferreting data from sundry sources.

Bradley R. Schiller
American University

FEEDBACK

The author and product team would appreciate hearing from you! Let us know what you think about this textbook by writing to college marketing@prenhall.com. Please include "Feedback about Schiller 10e" in the subject line.

   If you have questions related to this product, please contact our customer service department online at www.247.prenhall.com.

CHAPTER 1
VIEWS OF INEQUALITY
AND POVERTY

Amerca is a very rich nation. With only 5 percent of the world's population, America produces more than 20 percent of the world's output. While half of the world's population struggles along with less than $2,000 per year in per capita income (about $6 a day), the average American enjoys roughly $40,000 in annual income. While a third of the world's population has never used a telephone, Americans are carrying around cell phones with camera, video, paging, Internet, and voice mail capabilities. Americans spend billions of dollars on diet and exercise programs to rid themselves of the vestiges of overeating while billions of people around the world go hungry every day. The typical American family has a kitchen outfitted with a microwave oven, a conventional oven/stove, and a refrigerator with built-in freezer. In Indonesia, Ethiopia, Kenya, Haiti, and Pakistan most families have no appliances and often no kitchen at all. The running water, hot showers, and indoor toilets that are taken for granted by the average American citizen are still considered luxuries by most people on this planet. With one doctor for every 500 people, Americans fret over a health care "crisis." In Ethiopia, there is only one doctor for every 88,000 people, and life expectancy is only 42 years (versus 76 years in the United States). Few people around the world associate the word *poverty* with America.

THE CONTINUING CONTROVERSY

Within the United States, however, poverty is still a hot issue. Public opinion polls indicate that Americans regard poverty as one of the most important problems facing the nation. In fact, many Americans think the poverty problem is getting *worse* every year. In the ocean of American prosperity, people still see spreading pools of poverty—the homeless persons who wander the streets, the welfare families who crowd into substandard housing, the farm workers who can't afford indoor plumbing, and the aged who need public assistance to provide food and shelter. Although even these Americans might be better off than most of the people in Haiti, Angola, Madagascar, Yemen, or Bangladesh, their standard of living is far below the American norm. In fact, it is so far below that we feel justified in calling them "poor."

WHAT TO DO?

To most observers, such impoverishment in a land of evident abundance is both inexplicable and unacceptable. With total output exceeding $14 *trillion* per year, America unquestionably produces enough to assure every citizen material comforts. But that enormous economic pie isn't sliced evenly. Some people get huge slices, while others get only crumbs.

TABLE 1.1   How the Government Should Help

When asked in a Gallup opinion poll "In what ways do you think the government should help the poor?" the following responses were offered:

Suggested Help	Percent of Respondents
Better education	38
More skill training	29
More jobs and job opportunities	16
Financial aid; more money	12
More housing	11
Better health care coverage	10
Better child care	7
More social programs and services	6
Tax breaks; lower taxes	5
Better jobs	3
More opportunities	3
Raise minimum wage	2

Note: Total adds to more than 100 percent due to multiple responses.

Source: Adapted from the Gallup Organization, "Social Audit" opinion poll, 1999.

There are many ideas about how to remedy this problem but no consensus on even the most general policy approach. In every election year, political candidates offer a slew of proposals for reducing poverty, but the electorate remains ambivalent about what should be done. Only 65 percent of American adults think the federal government should do *anything* to help the poor. The rest believe the poor should instead help themselves.

Even those who think the government should take action to reduce poverty are not sure which steps the government might take. As Table 1.1 reveals, the preferred steps range from better child care to an increase in the minimum wage. No single action is endorsed by a majority of respondents.

TOO LITTLE GOVERNMENT ASSISTANCE?

The most radical suggestion for curing poverty is simply to have the government reslice the income pie. The government already does this by taxing higher incomes and providing welfare benefits, food stamps, subsidized housing, and other assistance for the poor. But advocates for the poor demand still more redistribution. They want to keep reslicing the pie until everyone has at least an adequate slice. These critics regard continuing poverty as a manifestation of societal failure.

As Table 1.1 confirms, not everyone shares these views. Only 12 percent of American adults want the government to give more money to the poor. Far more support exists for programs that expand economic opportunities—more jobs, more training, better schools.

OR TOO MUCH AID?

As noted above, one-third of all Americans think even those government initiatives are unnecessary. A lot of people resist more government aid because they think America's so-called poverty problem is greatly exaggerated. Relatively few Americans, they say, experience real impoverishment. The so-called poor often own their own homes and a car, and have a television, modern plumbing, and a microwave oven as well. Moreover, what they can't provide for themselves, the government will. If people need more food, they can get food stamps; if they are sick, they get free medical care (through Medicaid or Medicare), and the government provides housing at little or no cost. In other words, the government already assures every American an adequate slice of the multitrillion-dollar economic pie.

Opponents of increased government assistance for the poor go a step further. They argue not only that we have already fulfilled our obligation to the poor, but that we have perhaps provided too much help to people at the bottom of the income ladder. In a market-based economy, incomes tend to reflect how much people produce. In 2005, Terry Semel, the chief executive officer (CEO) of Yahoo, earned $230 million. That was one of the biggest slices of the economic pie that year. In that same year, 27 million households had an income of less than $25,000—comparatively small slices. Does that mean that Terry Semel's income was too high or, worse, unjust? Shouldn't we also consider how much output he contributed to the pie? As CEO of Yahoo, he brought Internet services to millions of households, a feat consumers were willing to pay for. Certainly he got a large slice of the pie, but he also made life easier or more interesting for millions of people. Shouldn't that effort be rewarded?

Market Incentives

Economists emphasize the importance of material rewards in spurring innovation and efficiency. In other words, the *promise* of a large slice encourages people to help bake a larger pie. If market participants think that the government will take a big chunk of their earnings, they may not be so willing to contribute to the size of the pie.

Government reslicing of the pie may also affect the work behavior of low-income people. Why work hard to earn rent money if the government offers free rent to people who do not work? It is at least possible that helping the poor may actually discourage them from working. If society offers a free slice of the pie to people who do not work, why should other people work hard for similarly sized slices? The provision of welfare benefits, food stamps, free medical care, and subsidized housing may destroy the *incentive* to work. The combination of higher taxes on the rich and more assistance to the poor may end up shrinking the size of the pie we are attempting to reslice.

Rational Choices

Economists not only emphasize how material incentives affect market behavior but also caution that low income may be a deliberate choice. Economists view individuals as rational beings who make informed choices. We make choices about whether to study, whether to complete school, and how much to work. In this context, a low income may reflect a person's preference for leisure over study or work. By the same token, a high income may be the product of decisions to study or work harder. In this view, government redistributions are not only inefficient (by blunting work incentives) but unfair (by violating individual preferences).

EQUITY AND EFFICIENCY

Even if one accepts the premise of consumer choice and the importance of material incentives, one does not have to accept market outcomes as completely fair or efficient.

Even if market incentives are important to our economic prosperity, must the slices received by the poor be so small, and those served to the rich so large? Would Terry Semel have worked just as hard for, say, only $20 million? That would have left a lot more pie for the hungry and homeless. In other words, couldn't we *redistribute* incomes somewhat more equally, without impairing our production of goods and services?

Other critics of the existing inequities go even further, questioning the whole relationship between income and contributions to output. The market does *not* reward people, they argue, in relationship to their ability and effort. Some people command high incomes because they have the "right connections," "inside information," or other insulation from the competitive forces of the marketplace. At the other end of the income distribution, many people are forced to accept low incomes because they are "locked out" of good jobs, schools, and neighborhoods. In other words, the market *discriminates*, giving some people better opportunities than others.

CAUSES AND CURES

These contrasting explanations of inequality are mirrored in arguments about the causes of poverty. The presence of millions of poor people in the midst of the world's richest country begs explanation. Are the poor "left out"—excluded from access to the social and economic systems that assure most Americans a comfortable living? Or are the poor simply shiftless and lazy—with no desire to contribute to society or their own personal welfare?

Here again, public opinion is sharply divided. As Figure 1.1 reveals, a plurality of Americans blame the poor themselves for their plight. Slightly fewer people blame circumstances beyond the control of the poor.

FLAWED CHARACTER

Those Americans who blame the poor themselves for poverty see the problem as one of flawed character. From this perspective, poverty is regarded as the natural result of individual defects in aspiration or ability. In colonial times, this perspective was aptly summarized by the puritanical Humane Society, which concluded that "by a just and inflexible law of Providence, misery is ordained to be the companion and punishment of vice." In more modern times, theories of sin and immorality have not fared well, and there now exists a general reluctance to ascribe to the laws of Providence the misery of the poor. Instead, we speak in terms of "motivation" or "work ethic": Poverty is thought to result from insufficient amounts of either. According to this view, modern poverty originates from flawed character, much as in puritanical times.

A theoretical foundation for the Flawed Character argument can be found in the economic concept of *human capital*. Everyone starts out with a certain set of abilities. The critical question is how much those abilities are developed and expanded via later *investments*. Going to school and doing assigned homework represent an investment of time that will increase a person's productive capabilities. A retail clerk who takes night classes in accounting expects to get better job opportunities as a result of such efforts. A software writer who spends weekends examining new program codes expects her increased knowledge to result in superior products. A father who reads books to his children every night is making an investment in his offspring's human capital. In all such cases, the investments in human capital are expected to generate a later payoff in the form of better jobs and higher incomes.

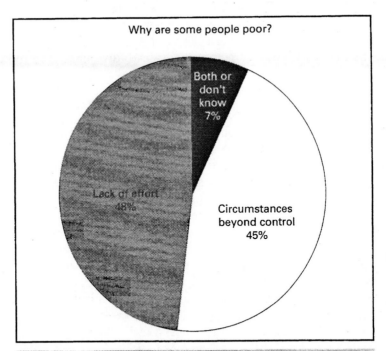

FIGURE 1.1   Blame for Poverty

Source: "National Survey on Poverty in America—Toplines/Survey," (#3118), NPR/The Henry J. Kaiser Family Foundation/Harvard University, May 2001. This information was reprinted with permission from the Henry J. Kaiser Family Foundation. The Kaiser Family Foundation, based in Menlo Park, California, is a nonprofit, private operating foundation focusing on the major health care issues facing the nation and is not associated with Kaiser Permanente or Kaiser Industries.

The human capital theory implies that people who get ahead are those individuals (and families) who make the necessary investments. By implication, those who don't make it—the poor—have only themselves to blame. They chose to watch MTV rather than do homework. They didn't want to give up evenings or weekends for special classes. Or they chose to watch television rather than read to their kids. They ended up poor because they didn't invest enough time, energy, or money in the development of their own human capital. They might even be part of a cultural underclass that disparages such investments, focusing instead on more immediate gratifications.

There are three essential links in the human capital explanation of flawed character. The first is the assumption that human capital is rewarded in the marketplace. If college graduates don't make more money than college dropouts, then investments in college don't pay. There must be consistent and tangible payoffs to human capital investment if we expect people to make such investments.

The human capital model also assumes rational *choice*. People need to know what their options are and be able to choose from among them. If they voluntarily make the wrong choices, their poverty is understandable.

Finally, the human capital interpretation of flawed character depends on the existence of pervasive opportunity. From this perspective, anyone who wants to move up the income ladder can do so by making the required effort—the human capital investment.

The Flawed Character argument applies both to jobs and schools. In the labor market, people who do not find good jobs are assumed to lack sufficient initiative or diligence. To the extent that they are less able, as measured by education, skills, or ability tests, their disadvantage is to be explained by earlier lack of motivation in school. Individuals who do not work hard in school end up failing in the job market as well. Thus, the Flawed Character perspective sees individuals as in full control of their socioeconomic status.

RESTRICTED OPPORTUNITY

An alternative explanation of poverty claims that impoverishment may result from circumstances beyond the control of the individual (see Figure 1.1). According to this argument—the Restricted Opportunity argument—the poor are poor because they do not have adequate access to good schools, jobs, and income. They are discriminated against on the basis of race, sex, or income class. As a result, they can't get the education, the jobs, or the housing they need to get ahead. Even government services are denied them. They don't get adequate police protection; they get few tax breaks; and they are denied more mainstream public services (e.g., transportation service, street repair, public facilities). In the face of these external barriers, no amount of work ethic or effort assures escape from poverty.

The Restricted Opportunity argument denies a critical premise of the Flawed Character argument. If individuals don't have an equal opportunity to acquire education, then their lack of human capital isn't so easily explained by poor choices they may have made. Likewise, if the achievements of minority workers are rewarded less in the marketplace, the incentive to invest in their human capital is diminished as well.

Restrictions on opportunity need not originate in overt discrimination. One of the most rapidly growing segments of the poverty population is single mothers and their children. The failure of absent fathers to provide financial support for their children handicaps a mother's ability to raise the children or secure employment.

A basic implication of the Restricted Opportunity argument is that improved opportunities are needed if the number of people we count as poor is to be reduced. The improved opportunities may entail improved access to quality education, better enforcement of child-support obligations, new job openings, or expanded health and child care assistance.

BIG BROTHER

There is a third view of poverty that falls between these two extremes. This view—the Big Brother argument—blames the government for destroying incentives for stable families and economic self-sufficiency. From this perspective, poor people are not *inherently* flawed. Rather, the government perverts their perspectives and behavior through high taxes, welfare benefits, racial quotas, and other public policies. These policies, though intended to help the poor, actually destroy work incentives and create what George Gilder has called a "blight of dependency."[1]

The availability of welfare benefits, for example, may discourage people from working. Long hours working at low wages may look decidedly unattractive when the government offers the option of welfare benefits for those who do not work. Decisions to get married, to have a baby, or to move to another community may also be influenced

---

[1]George Gilder, *Wealth and Poverty* (New York: Basic Books, 1981), p. 12.

by the kinds of public assistance the government offers. By *curtailing* welfare benefits and related services, the government might encourage people to make greater efforts on their own. Charles Murray suggests that the total elimination of welfare programs would ultimately change both the culture and the behavior of the poor in ways that promote financial independence.[2]

SELF-INTEREST

While examining these different views of poverty, we must be mindful of how they appeal to self-interest. The Flawed Character argument, for example, appeals directly to the psychological needs of the middle-class majority. If the poor are poor because of flawed character, then the higher incomes of the *non*poor must reflect *non*flawed character. (Otherwise, how are we to explain the superior position of the latter class?) Hence, the Flawed Character argument implies a psychological pat on the back for the nonpoor. Adam Walinsky made note of this same phenomenon when he observed that ego satisfaction requires each of us to ascribe the status of "those above us" to luck and the status of "those below us" to character and ability.[3] Thus, the Flawed Character argument not only explains poverty but justifies the position and privileges of the non-poor as well. To deny the Flawed Character argument is tantamount to questioning the whole social order.

Economic interests are also concealed in the Flawed Character argument. A basic implication of this argument is that society is already doing everything it can to help the poor. The poor have only themselves to blame for not taking advantage of the opportunities society offers. There isn't any need for more antipoverty programs or the taxes that pay for them. To the harassed taxpayer who equates higher taxes with more money for "the bums on welfare," the Flawed Character argument is economically appealing.

The Restricted Opportunity argument likewise derives support from unspoken biases. Some people are totally convinced that society is to blame for all social ills, that individuals are forever innocent and blameless. As a consequence, they are not inclined to collect or even examine evidence that might fault individuals for their own plight. This type of bias is often referred to as "bleeding heart liberalism." Often, this liberalism may be buttressed by economic interests (e.g., university researchers and public employees who benefit from expanded social programs and budgets).

The Big Brother argument also appeals to identifiable interests. The principal implication of the Big Brother view is that the government is trying too hard to take care of people's needs. By doing less, the government would foster greater private initiative and ultimately eliminate more poverty. In the process, of course, government spending and taxes would be reduced—a goal many people desire for its own sake. Also, if the government were to cut back on affirmative action and related activities, many white males and others would reap direct gains. Hence, there are political and economic interests wrapped up in the Big Brother argument that go beyond its antipoverty effectiveness.

---

[2]Charles Murray, *Losing Ground* (New York: Basic Books, 1984).

[3]Adam Walinsky, "Keeping the Poor in Their Place," *New Republic*, July 4, 1964.

Knowing our potential biases does not settle the controversy about the causes of poverty. But awareness of them may help engender just a bit more objectivity as we try to sort out the various arguments about poverty and inequality. At least we know that the deck may be stacked before the game begins.

POLICY IMPLICATIONS

Which view of poverty we ultimately embrace will have a direct bearing on the public policies we pursue. If we conclude, for example, that people are poor because they cannot find decent jobs, our antipoverty efforts are likely to focus on the creation of more and better jobs. On the other hand, if we believe that people are poor simply because they are lazy, we are likely to provide fewer jobs and services. We may instead try to change the behavior of the poor with sanctions (e.g., work *requirements* rather than incentives).

Some people reject the notion that society's antipoverty efforts should be predicated on the causes of poverty. An ethical obligation to help everyone maintain a decent standard of living may supersede concern about who is to blame for poverty. A related argument is that a minimum standard of living is necessary for the exercise of one's rights to liberty and self-determination. To assure everyone those rights, society must offer universal access to basic living standards.[4]

Even if we accept an *ethical* obligation to help the poor, we may still be concerned about the *efficiency* of our antipoverty efforts. If people cannot find decent jobs because they lack basic skills, then the provision of more and better jobs will not eliminate much poverty. If welfare mothers can't find child care, then creating more training programs won't increase their employment very much. In such cases misperceptions of the causes of poverty would result in expensive failures for antipoverty policy. Hence, it is important that our public antipoverty policies be based on informed perceptions of the nature and causes of poverty.

HISTORICAL PERSPECTIVES

Different historical phases of antipoverty activity in America illustrate this interdependence of causal perspectives and policy prescriptions. As noted earlier, poverty was viewed in colonial times as a curse on those of disreputable character. Impoverishment was seen as the companion to and punishment for vice. Accordingly, early antipoverty prescriptions focused on religious training, corporal punishment (to drive out sin), and physical expulsion. Very little was done to help the poor become more self-sufficient or even to alleviate their suffering.

It was not until the depression of the 1930s that many people seriously began to question the Flawed Character proposition that poverty resulted from sin and slovenliness. The march of unemployed and poor men—Coxey's Army—on Washington, D.C., in 1934 helped stimulate fresh perspectives on the origins of poverty. But it was not until 15 million Americans simultaneously experienced unemployment in the depths of the Great Depression that the Restricted Opportunity perspective on poverty took hold. Only when millions of otherwise responsible and industrious individuals fell abruptly

---

[4]See Lesley A. Jacobs, *Rights and Deprivation* (New York: Oxford University Press, 1993), for an elaboration of this perspective.

into joblessness and poverty did the American public begin to view poverty as being outside the control of the individual. Awareness grew that poverty might be the consequence of social and economic forces rather than of immorality and vice.

From one point of view, our experience with depressions and poverty may have been too brief. With the passage of time and the return to prosperity, poverty lost its middle-class constituency, and people became less generous toward the poor. When everyone else is prospering, poverty becomes suspect. In good times, most observers again question the ambition, motivation, ability, and the entire cultural orientation of the poor.

In 1961, President Kennedy proclaimed that "a rising tide lifts all boats." As he saw it, a rapidly expanding economy would virtually eliminate poverty and dependency. But welfare caseloads continued to increase even during the economic expansion that began in 1962. People began to wonder about the character of the poor. Middle-class concerns about flawed character were clearly reflected in the following editorial from the Tulsa, Oklahoma, *Tribune:*

> Relief is gradually becoming an honorable career in America. It is a pretty fair life, if you have neither conscience nor pride. The politicians will weep for you.
>
> The state will give a mother a bonus for her illegitimate children, and if she neglects them sufficiently she can keep enough of her AFDC [welfare] payments to keep herself and her boyfriend in wine and gin.[5]

When economic growth faltered in the mid-1970s, Americans viewed the problems of the poor in a more charitable light. President Carter emphasized the restricted opportunities facing people in poor neighborhoods and pushed for better schools, guaranteed jobs, and more training opportunities.

During the economic expansion of the 1980s, public sentiment shifted again. From 1981 to 1989 over 20 million new jobs were created and average incomes rose sharply. By the end of the expansion (1989) it appeared that nearly everyone who wanted a job had one: "Full" employment was deemed to have been achieved. In the midst of such a strong economy, how could anyone remain poor unless his or her character was flawed? President Reagan urged compulsory work programs that would prevent people from getting a "free ride" from taxpayers. In 1990, over 90 percent of Americans attributed poverty to "lack of effort" by the poor themselves.[6] The Big Brother theory of poverty also attracted more attention. A spate of new research and books suggested that public welfare programs were responsible for undermining incentives for family stability, work effort, and saving. It was not lack of opportunity but flawed character and flawed handouts that were perpetuating poverty and welfare dependence.

Another economic boom took place from 1991 to 2001. In the middle of that boom, Congress passed a set of tough welfare reforms that restricted access to the "free" welfare ride, effectively forcing millions of people off welfare. For several years, welfare rolls fell dramatically, but the number of poor people receded only slightly. By the time the economy stalled again in the 2001 recession, a lot of people were questioning the commitment of poor people to help themselves. With the national unemployment rate

---

[5]Quoted in Edgar May, *The Wasted Americans* (New York: Harper and Row, 1964), p. 7.

[6]Lawrence Bobo and Ryan Smith, "Antipoverty Policy Affirmative Action, and Radical Attitudes," in *Confronting Poverty,* eds. S. Danziger, G. Sandefur, and D. Weinberg (Cambridge, MA: Harvard University Press, 1994), Table 1.

so low for so long, why hadn't poor people moved up the economic ladder? As Figure 1.1 revealed, "lack of effort" was the favorite explanation for continuing poverty in America as the twenty-first century began.

Current American attitudes toward poverty are best described as ambivalent. Polls reveal that 70–80 percent of Americans believe that anyone who is poor can get rich by working hard.[7] So anyone who remains poor is suspect. At the same time, the disquieting suspicion that external social and economic forces are at the root of poverty continues to stir the public conscience. When unemployment rates reach crisis proportions—as in the early 1980s—this perspective gathers significant strength. Even then, however, President Reagan was careful to draw a distinction between the "truly needy" and those who could get by if they wanted to.

Against this background of uncertainty about the causes of poverty, it is not surprising that public policy is ambivalent and often ineffective. Tax laws are "reformed" to reduce inequalities one year, then revised to promote work and investment in another year. The historic welfare reforms of 1996 likewise both punished welfare dependency by imposing time limits and work requirements (the Flawed Character view) and attempted to expand opportunities for self-sufficiency with increased child care and medical assistance (the Restricted Opportunity view). Such carrot-and-stick combinations are perhaps inevitable. So long as the causes of poverty remain the subject of intense debate, we cannot expect consistent policies, much less substantial success. Even if we shared a consistent vision of the causes of poverty, conflicting goals and priorities might necessitate compromises and inconsistencies.

Before reaching any policy conclusions, however, we should at least try to sort out the various arguments. Which explanations of poverty make the most sense? To answer this central question, we will first look at the dimensions of poverty and then examine their causes. Once this foundation is set, we will be in a position to evaluate current antipoverty policies and to suggest new ones.

INEQUALITY

The poverty debate is often treated as a self-contained issue. In reality, however, it is hard to isolate discussions of poverty from broader concerns about inequality. The $230 million that Yahoo's chairman made in 2005 looks like an awful lot of money, even from a middle-class perspective. Indeed, income differences between the truly rich and the middle class dwarf distinctions between the middle class and the poor. Can we really identify the causes of poverty without examining the sources of such inequality?

DIFFERING EXPLANATIONS

The various theories offered to explain poverty can be tested in the broader context of inequality. The same forces that consign one person to poverty may push someone else to a low but not a poor position in the distribution of income. Human capital theory, for example, suggests that everyone's income reflects individual choices about investments in education and training. Accordingly, the Flawed Character argument may explain not only distinctions between rich and poor but also much smaller gradations in income.

---

[7]Robert Blendon and John Benson, "How Americans Viewed Their Lives in 2005," *Challenge* (May–June 2006), Table 16.

Restricted Opportunity perspectives may also be relevant. Differences in opportunity (e.g., "Old Boy" networks, affluent school districts) may be as instrumental in creating class divisions as in explaining pockets of poverty.

The Big Brother argument is also germane to broader inequality concerns: Government taxes, expenditures, and regulations rarely affect everyone equally. The hand of government may push some people up the income ladder while pushing others down. "Corporate welfare" in the form of tax breaks and subsidies increases the incomes of the rich. So do limits on payroll taxes and capital gains taxes. Mortgage-interest deductions are a critical benefit for middle-class families. Income transfers help some low-income families more than others. Public decisions about where to build schools, subways, and highways also have significant effects on income.

Public opinion recognizes these multiple influences on inequality. A majority of Americans attributes the success of the rich to "strong effort" alone (see Figure 1.2). Only a third of the population credits external circumstances (e.g., luck, good connections, race, gender) for the attainment of high incomes. In other words, Flawed Character is viewed as more important than Restricted Opportunity in explaining not only poverty but the broader distribution of income as well.

Public attitudes toward inequality, like those concerning poverty, also tend to mirror cyclical changes in the economy. When the economy is booming, individual incomes tend to rise. People have confidence in the future and many harbor hopes of "striking it rich." There is little resentment of those who have already acquired wealth and little political pressure to reslice the economic pie.

FIGURE 1.2 Credit for Being Rich

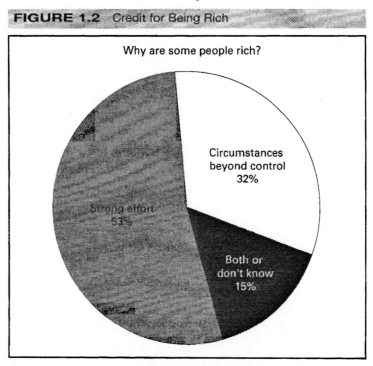

Source: Adapted from the Gallup Organization, "Social Audit" opinion poll, 1999.

When the economy slumps, however, perceptions change. People who lose their jobs or have wages cut suddenly feel cheated by the system. The conviction spreads that rich people have rigged the market to assure that only they can succeed. This sentiment rose to the surface again in 2001–2002, when a wave of dot-com, telecommunications, and energy company bankruptcies destroyed the financial status of many hard-working, middle-class families. The political pressure to reslice the economic pie increases at such times.

EQUITY VERSUS EFFICIENCY

Equity and efficiency are also key issues in the inequality debate. The opportunity to strike it rich can serve as a tremendous incentive to seek out new and better ways of producing goods and services. Why else would people give up weekends and evenings to write new software programs or design new apparel? Or give up current job opportunities in order to attend graduate school? Or explore for new deposits of oil or gold? The essence of the Horatio Alger ethos is that the market will provide handsome rewards to those who try a little harder (or get lucky). Even if inequalities spur efficiency in production, however, they may be so large that they violate our notions of equity.

DIMENSIONS OF WELL-BEING

Most debates about inequality and poverty focus on income, that is, how much money some people receive compared to others. But money isn't our only measure of well-being; we get satisfaction from both tangible and intangible things. In fact, the often quoted maxim that "money can't buy happiness" implies a weak correlation between the distribution of income and the distribution of well-being. Research by Robert Lane, a political scientist, seems to confirm that maxim. After examining the relationship of economic status to self-reported levels of satisfaction, he concluded that the maxim has merit: Income and happiness are not well correlated. The things that bring daily happiness to people—friendship, family, work—are largely unrelated to income.[8] Accordingly, income inequalities may tell us little or nothing about differences in well-being. Perhaps we focus on them simply because they are so visible.

Professor Lane did make an exception for poor people. For people at the lowest rungs of the income ladder, Lane observed that additional money did increase the level of happiness. This suggests that money can buy happiness, at least for those in poverty. Even at the low end of the income distribution, however, Charles Murray, a conservative sociologist, reminds us not to confuse poverty with unhappiness.[9]

INCOME VERSUS WEALTH

Even if we confine ourselves to tangible indices of well-being, we should not regard income as the only barometer of economic well-being. At a minimum, we have to distinguish between *income* and *wealth*.

---

[8]Robert E. Lane, "Does Money Buy Happiness?" *The Public Interest, 113* (Fall 1993), pp. 56–65. Similar conclusions are drawn in Daniel Kahneman et al., "Would You Be Happier if You Were Richer? A Focusing Illusion," *Science* (June 2006), pp. 1908–1910. See also Kahneman and Alan Krueger, "Developments in the Measurement of Subjective Well-Being," *Journal of Economic Perspectives* (Winter 2006), pp. 3–24; and Rafael DiTella and Robert MacCulloch, "Some Uses of Happiness Data in Economics," *ibid.,* pp. 25–46.

[9]Charles Murray, "What's So Bad About Being Poor?" *National Review,* October 28, 1988, p. 36.

Income refers to the amount of money receipts a person collects in a year. Most income comes in the form of a paycheck. In addition to wages and salaries, households also get income in the form of dividends and interest, rent, and capital gains from the sale of property. Much of the income Terry Semel received in 2005, for example, came from capital gains on the sale of stock options that Yahoo had given him; only a fraction of his $230 million income was paid in salary. Although retired people do not receive paychecks, they may get monthly pension checks, as well as interest payments and stock dividends.

The common characteristic of all forms of income is that they represent a *flow* of receipts received during some period of time. This contrasts with wealth, which represents a *stock* of value. The value of accumulated possessions (e.g., home, stocks and bonds, a farm or business) measures one's material wealth.

A person can be rich in one of these dimensions but poor in the other. A star athlete, for example, may command a huge salary but have little accumulated wealth. By contrast, a farmer may own thousands of valuable acres but earn little income in a particular year.

The distinction between income and wealth raises some preliminary questions about notions of inequality and poverty. Two individuals with identical incomes may have vastly different asset portfolios. Should we be worried about people who have low incomes but great wealth? This question is particularly relevant to many retired persons who have relatively modest incomes from pension benefits, dividends, and interest but own homes, savings accounts, stocks, bonds, and retirement funds. Because assets can be converted into income by selling them, people with assets have some discretion in determining how much income they receive in any year. The possession of wealth also provides economic security and creditworthiness that may compensate for income.

TRANSITORY VERSUS PERMANENT INCOME

The ability to convert wealth into income also raises a question about the time frame used to assess inequalities. A farmer who has a bad harvest may receive little income in one year. The farmer may still possess valuable land, however, and have a reasonable expectation of a much better harvest next year. In this case, the farmer's low income in a single year is not representative of his or her economic status. To assess the true economic circumstances, we might want to consider not only the farmer's wealth, but also his or her average income over a period of years.

A graduate student in law or medicine raises similar problems for characterizations of inequality. The typical graduate student subsists on a budget that resembles poverty standards. Yet students have the expectation of earning exceptionally high incomes after graduation. When assessing the degree of inequality, should we consider only the income received while in graduate school or take a longer view of economic status? If we were to take a longer view, we would recognize that graduate students are acquiring human capital that, like physical capital, can be converted into future income.

Incomes fluctuate from year to year for many reasons. When the economy stumbles into a recession, millions of workers experience brief periods of unemployment that reduce their incomes below normal. So long as the spell of unemployment is brief, the temporary decline in income may have no lasting consequences. While unfortunate, such transitory declines in income may be of little consequence for the longer-term economic welfare of an individual. In fact, short-run *expenditure* patterns may change very little when income declines. Stocks of consumer goods, accumulated savings, other wealth, and credit provide shock absorbers against transitory income changes. As a result, expenditure patterns tend to be more equal than annual incomes.[10] The distinction between expenditure levels and income levels is particularly striking when poor families are compared to nonpoor families. Nonpoor families have average incomes that are six times those of poor families, yet their expenditures are only three times larger than those of the poor.[11] Accordingly, the distinction between transitory incomes and more permanent measures of economic status should be considered in characterizations of either inequality or poverty.

LIFE-CYCLE DYNAMICS

When viewed over a period of time, individual incomes also exhibit a pattern of change associated with age. When young people first enter the labor market, their wages are usually quite low and their hours erratic. As they gain education and experience (human capital), their wages increase. Indeed, incomes tend to rise substantially during the first 20 years or so of labor-market participation. As a result, middle-aged workers typically have much higher incomes than younger workers. Wage growth tends to slow in later years, and often declines as older workers reduce their work activity.

These life-cycle patterns create substantial inequality across age groups. Workers in their peak earning years will tend to cluster at the top of the income distribution, while younger and older workers will gravitate to the lower rungs of the income ladder. Accordingly, much observed inequality may be no more than a reflection of typical age-earnings cycles. Should such life-cycle inequality merit the same concern as the inequality among individuals of similar age? Do we want to reduce inequalities across age cohorts? At a minimum, life-cycle dynamics add an important dimension to interpretations of observed inequality.

PUBLIC PROVISIONS

Even when perceptions of inequality are adjusted for wealth holdings, transitory fluctuations, or life-cycle dynamics, they may still fail to capture the full dimensions of economic status. Income and wealth provide access to goods and services sold in the marketplace. Lots of goods and services are provided by the public sector, however. Public schools, libraries, parks, and roadways are available to everyone without explicit payment. Accordingly, private income and wealth do not completely determine how many goods and services one consumes.

The provision of public goods and services complicates perceptions of inequality in at least two ways. International comparisons of inequality are distorted by the varying public provisions in different countries. A nation that offers universal health services,

---

[10]Dirk Krueger and Fabrizio Perri, "Does Income Inequality Lead to Consumption Inequality?" (Cambridge, MA: National Bureau of Economic Research, 2002); also Susan E. Mayer and Christopher Jencks, "Recent Trends in Economic Inequality in the United States: Income versus Expenditures versus Material Well-Being," in *Poverty and Prosperity in the U.S.A. in the Late Twentieth Century,* eds. D. Papadimitriou and E. Wolff (New York: St. Martin's Press; 1993), pp. 121–203; also Daniel T. Slesnick, "Gaining Ground: Poverty in the Postwar United States," *Journal of Political Economy* (February 1993), pp. 1–38.

[11]Maya Federman et al., "What Does It Mean to Be Poor in America?" *Monthly Labor Review* (May 1996), pp. 3–17.

day care, or college scholarships has less economic inequality than another country with fewer such provisions but an identical distribution of market incomes.

Perceptions of *changes* in inequality or poverty are also affected by the public provision of goods and services. As the welfare state has expanded in size and scope, people have become less dependent on market incomes. Medicare, for example, tends to mitigate income inequality among people over the age of 65. Forty years ago, the availability of health care for aged persons was more conditioned on income and wealth. Money still matters but much less so since the federal government established subsidized health care for the aged. As a result, even an unchanged distribution of income over time might conceal a trend toward greater equality of living standards.

SOCIAL EQUALITY

A full measure of inequality would take into account not only the *material* dimensions of life but its *social* dimensions as well. As Mickey Kaus has emphasized, *money* inequality is more palatable if *social* equality is preserved. Social equality implies that people share access to public amenities and responsibilities regardless of economic status. Access to justice, to police protection, to voting polls and civic liberties must be unconditioned by income or wealth. Similarly, everyone must have an equal likelihood of serving on juries or fulfilling other civic responsibilities.

Social equality also implies the absence of class stratification. People from all income classes should be able to interact, not only in schools and courthouses, but in the entire spectrum of social and civic activities. Where such access and equality prevail, money inequality has less social significance.

Kaus laments that a reduction in social equality has made money inequality less bearable. The end of the military draft, for example, not only eliminated a mechanism of social class mixing but also made military service income conditioned. Young people from low-income backgrounds are more likely to volunteer for military service, while "rich kids" pursue college and civilian careers. Cutbacks in funding for public schools, parks, and other public amenities also have made income and wealth more important determinants of economic welfare. Even the observance of public holidays on Mondays and Fridays has torn the threads of social equality. Midweek holidays tend to foster local community celebrations, whereas three-day weekends encourage out-of-town travel and class separation. Kaus proposes that we reverse these trends, thereby making money inequality less important.

DISCRIMINATION

The concept of social (in)equality also raises the issue of discrimination. Polls reveal that minority members feel they get less than a fair deal, when compared to white persons with similar money incomes. Their money incomes don't buy the same access to housing, schools, jobs, or justice. Money helps but doesn't fully overcome racial barriers. As a consequence, social inequalities persist even when income inequalities are eliminated.

Discrimination not only drives a wedge between social equality and income equality but also prevents the attainment of income equality in the first place. When discrimination bars access to better schools and jobs, it reduces the chances for moving up the income ladder. Although many minority households reach the top rungs of the income ladder, a disproportionate number of black, Hispanic, and other minority households are detained on the lower rungs.

POVERTY: DRAWING A LINE

How far down are the lower rungs of the economic ladder? Aside from broader concerns about inequality, nations everywhere also worry specifically about the lowest rungs of the ladder—the ones on which "poor" people reside. Being "poor" is seen as a more serious calamity than merely being unequal. Poverty implies not just "less" but also "not enough."

Although concern for the poor is nearly universal, there is no real consensus on who exactly is "poor." Lots of people feel poor even though they may possess substantial income and wealth. Just not being able to buy everything one desires, or having less income than one's neighbor, can make one feel poor. These sociopsychological perspectives do not provide us with a very useful definition of poverty, however. When we speak of poverty, we envision families who don't have enough income to provide minimally acceptable standards of food, shelter, and clothing.

But where are these people in the income distribution? If we want to know how many people are poor in our society, we have to be willing to draw a line that separates the poor from the nonpoor. Without such a line, we will not know whom to help or be able to determine how successful such help is in reducing poverty.

Any attempt at drawing a poverty line will have to confront all of the inequality issues outlined previously. The distinction between transitory and permanent incomes, life-cycle dynamics, changing family composition, the public provision of goods and services—all are relevant phenomena to measures of poverty.

In the next three chapters, the concepts of inequality and poverty will be examined more closely, first in the context of the U.S. economy (Chapters 2 and 3), then in the global economy (Chapter 4). After that, we will assess in detail the various explanations people offer for the inequality and poverty we observe in the United States. The final section of the book looks at an array of policy options for overcoming these social problems.

Summary

Inequality and poverty are subjects that generate impassioned debates. The debates begin with truly basic questions about the *dimensions* of inequality and poverty. What degree of inequality is too much? How low a level of income implies poverty? Is income the only criterion for measuring poverty and inequality, or are other dimensions of inequality more important?

The debate over *causes* of poverty and inequality is even more intense. Does flawed character relegate people to poverty? Or do restricted opportunities prevent poor people from moving up the distribution of income? And what role does the government play? Do government programs facilitate income mobility or does Big Brother create barriers and disincentives that keep people in poverty?

Inequality is a complex notion that is not adequately reflected in a single dimension. Money incomes, for example, are an incomplete index of well-being, as they do not represent wealth, access to publicly provided services, or maybe even happiness.

The significance of any given level of income also depends on how representative it is of longer-term economic status.

Discrimination plays a dual role in inequality dynamics. Unequal access to the levers of economic success generates some income and wealth inequalities. Discrimination also prevents individuals from enjoying the full social measure of whatever economic status they attain.

Poverty refers to those individuals at the bottom of the income distribution who don't have enough income to satisfy basic needs. The definition of basic needs is conditional, however, on societal perceptions of both absolute and relative deprivation.

Further Reading

Blendan, Robert, and John Benson, "How Americans Viewed Their Lives in 2005," *Challenge* (May–June 2006), pp. 48–67.

Cox, W. Michael, and Richard Alm, *Myths of Rich and Poor: Why We're Better Off Than We Think.* New York: Basic Books, 1999.

Egendorf, Laura K., *Poverty: Opposing Viewpoints.* San Diego, CA: Greenhaven Press, 1999.

Friedman, Milton, "Reducing Poverty, Not Inequality," *The Public Interest* (Fall 1999), pp. 33–41.

Hunt, Matthew O., "Religion, Race/Ethnicity, and Beliefs About Wealth and Poverty,"

Social Science Quarterly (September 2004), pp. 827–853.

Katz, Michael B., *The Undeserving Poor.* New York: Pantheon, 1989.

Kaus, Mickey, *The End of Equality.* New York: Basic Books, 1992.

Ladd, Everett C., and Karlyn H. Bowman, *Attitudes Toward Economic Inequality.* Washington, DC: American Enterprise Institute, 1998.

Lardner, James, and David A. Smith, eds., *Inequality Matters.* New York: Free Press, 2005.

Web Links

Children's Defense Fund. Issue briefs and studies on poverty:
http://www.childrensdefense.org

EPN News. Directory of new research and policy papers from think tanks and advocacy groups:
http://www.movingideas.org

Gallup Organization. Periodic opinion polls on attitudes about poverty and discrimination:
www.galluppoll.com

Institute for Research on Poverty. Periodic studies on poverty-related topics:
http://www.ssc.wisc.edu/irp

Joint Center for Poverty Research. Periodic studies on poverty-related topics:
http://www.jcpr.org

CHAPTER 2
INEQUALITY
☙

The Declaration of Independence boldly proclaims that all men are created equal. But we know that's not true. Individuals are stamped with unique genetic codes. Some start out with great athletic or intellectual potential; others start out with much less innate talent. And people are born into wildly different material circumstances. Some babies start out with silver spoons; others start out with no spoons at all.

Later in life, fortune also smiles unequally on individuals. Although a handful of people may win the lottery, others may lose their homes or businesses to natural disasters. Being lucky is often more important than being good. Being a white man helps, too; women weren't even included in the Declaration (and couldn't vote until 1920), and signers of the Declaration owned black slaves.

With all these genetic, environmental, institutional, and random forces shaping individual lives, no one can seriously expect to see equality in the real world—certainly not equality of status, achievements, or possessions. The Founding Fathers only meant to assert that all people are to be treated equally (fairly) under the law. They never imagined nor sought an equality of status for all individuals.

America is demonstrably not a land of equal status. Some families live in million-dollar mansions, whereas others seek shelter in abandoned cars. Some families spend more money on a single gourmet dinner than others earn all month. Inequality—often striking—is pervasive in the United States. Even nations such as China, which continues to espouse equalitarian goals, exhibit substantial inequalities.

This chapter describes the degree of inequality in the United States. As we'll see, understanding the broader phenomenon of inequality is an important foundation for assessing the narrower issue of *poverty*. In this chapter, we examine how inequality is measured and how inequality patterns have changed. We also look at some of the problems in interpreting the meaning of statistics on inequality. We start, however, with a more basic question: Why is inequality such a critical issue?

WHY INEQUALITY MATTERS

Many people regard *inequality* as a synonym for *unfair*. In their mind, a society that distributes large slices to some people and crumbs to others is morally corrupt. Such egalitarians believe everyone should share equally in the fruits of a just society. In the communist utopia envisioned by Karl Marx and others, each member of society would contribute to communal output according to ability and share in that output as needed.

Less extreme visions of a just society relax the inequality standard. Incomes don't have to be *exactly* equal; some inequality is acceptable. However, the inequalities can't be "too great." Clearly, this standard requires a subjective judgment of how much inequality is "acceptable."

COSTS OF INEQUALITY

Other critics of inequality emphasize the social consequences of inequality. Too much inequality may foster resentment and breed crime. Hence society has a collective interest in limiting the gap between the haves and the have-nots. A society steeped in inequalities may suffer from excessive crime rates or end up allocating too much of its scarce resources to property protection, criminal justice, and confinement.

Inequalities of income may also foster more troubling inequities. Rich people who can afford talented lawyers may get a different brand of justice than might the poor, thereby violating the Founding Fathers' core notion of equality. If money buys access to better neighborhoods and schools, then unequal educational opportunity also becomes a counterpart to unequal incomes. This solidifies class divisions and perpetuates them across generations.

Last but certainly not least, income inequalities may skew the distribution of political power. If "one dollar, one vote" replaces "one person, one vote," the legitimacy of democracy is threatened. In the extreme, a moneyed class may so dominate the political system (through candidate selection, campaign finance, political lobbying, etc.) that it perpetuates its privileges with officials and laws that serve its narrow interests. Karl Marx was convinced that such capitalistic domination of the political system is what doomed the working-class proletariat to virtual serfdom.[1]

Inequalities of income need not spawn all these other inequities. In principle at least, the links between income and other dimensions of social participation could be broken. Public funding of schools, compensatory education, preschool programs (e.g., Head Start), and affirmative action are all designed to weaken the link between income status and educational opportunity. Likewise, campaign-finance reforms are typically designed to lessen the influence of moneyed special interests on the political process. But these strategies focus on the *consequences* of inequality, not the *existence* of inequality. Were income inequalities eliminated, such compensatory interventions wouldn't be necessary.

BENEFITS OF INEQUALITY

Before seeking to eliminate income inequalities, however, we should at least consider the potential virtues of inequality. Some people would emphasize the *equity* of inequalities, especially those stemming from personal effort or risk. The Little Red Hen of the children's story had no qualms about keeping all of the pie for herself. After all, no one else on the farm had offered to help her grow the wheat, grind the flour, knead the dough, and make the pie. She felt it was only fair that she alone enjoy the fruits of her labor. In real life, isn't it just as fair that the individual who works harder, studies longer, or takes greater risks ends up with more income than those who make lesser efforts? From this perspective, egalitarianism is not synonymous with equity.

Economists also emphasize that inequalities can be a powerful motivation for working, studying, or investing. Imagine for the moment that there were no grades

---

[1]This argument resurfaces in Kevin Phillips, *Wealth and Democracy: A Political History of the American Rich* (New York: Broadway Books, 2002).

assigned in the courses you take. The only record kept was whether you complete the course. Would that affect the amount of effort you put into the course? Experience shows that grades are not simply a reward for performance, but also a powerful incentive for keeping up with reading assignments, homework, and exams.

Inequalities create the same kind of material incentive in labor markets. After working a 40-hour week, very few workers are excited about the prospect of working additional hours. Yet, when employers offer overtime wage premiums (typically, 50 percent over base pay) employees often clamor for the extra work.

Inequalities are also the by-product of incentives for saving and investing. Why deny yourself any current consumption by saving some of your income? Why not spend every dime you make? In part, people limit their consumption and save some fraction of their current income so as to increase *future* income and consumption. People go into business for the same reason—hoping that their investments of time and money will increase their future income. Without such a prospect—without a chance to get ahead—few people would choose to save or invest. When they do, however, the entire society benefits from greater output. In other words, the inequality-based incentives are a prod for producing an ever-larger pie from which everyone gets a slice (however unequal that slice may be).

The focus on the size of the *collective* pie is important. From a dynamic perspective, the distribution of incomes is not a zero-sum game. If someone acquires a larger slice by working harder, saving more diligently, or investing more wisely, no one else's slice is necessarily smaller: The entire pie is *larger*. This is the allure of economic *growth*—enlarging the *total* quantity of goods and services produced. That way some people can get richer without anyone getting poorer.

EQUITY VERSUS EFFICIENCY

The link between incentives and economic growth suggests a certain trade-off between equity and efficiency. The promise of material riches may spur some people to produce more and better products—enhancing our economic *efficiency*. The payoff to those efforts, however, will enlarge income inequalities, thereby raising *equity* concerns. This trade-off suggests that nations must try to achieve a delicate balance between conflicting goals. Society benefits from the economic growth encouraged by material incentives, but incentive-based distributions may foster resentments, social tensions, and political discords.[2]

One last consideration in assessing the degree of inequality is the perceived level of fairness in slicing the pie. Lottery winners who take home multimillion-dollar prizes are rarely resented. Sure, all of us losers are jealous. But few among us hold a grudge. Why not? Because we perceive a state-run lottery to be fair. Opinion polls likewise reveal that few Americans begrudge millionaires their wealth. Most nonrich believe the rich earned what they got. When the sources of wealth become suspect, however, respect quickly turns into resentment.[3]

---

[2]Communist nations attempted to substitute nonmaterial rewards (e.g., public honors) and patriotic exhortation for material rewards as work incentives, but these failed to elicit the desired responses. "Creeping materialism" proved to be a more potent stimulant for economic growth.

[3]For an array of public-opinion surveys on inequality see Everett Carll Ladd and Karlyn H. Bowman, *Attitudes Toward Economic Inequality* (Washington, DC: American Enterprise Institute, 1998).

INEQUALITY OF WHAT?

When we speak of inequality, most people immediately think in terms of income or wealth. But these aren't the only relevant dimensions of social status. Nor are the concepts of income and wealth themselves as precise as one might assume. Before embarking on a description of inequalities, we have to clarify what we are looking for.

INCOME CONCEPTS

The term *income* refers to the *flow* of economic compensation received in a given time period. Most income comes in the form of paychecks, interest payments, dividends, and rent. This flow of receipts is distinguished from *wealth*, which is the stock of assets one owns. Although income and wealth are often correlated, they don't necessarily go hand in hand. A rock singer or professional athlete may have an exceptionally high income, but little accumulated wealth. By contrast, a retired CEO may have vast wealth holdings (e.g., homes, cars, yachts, artwork, and stocks and bonds) but relatively modest income. As a result, two people with identical incomes may be in very different economic circumstances.

We also have to recognize that income takes many forms. Two people might both have a $50,000 per year job. But one job might offer substantial fringe benefits (e.g., pension plan, health insurance, sick leave, company car), while the other offers few such benefits. In that case, the equality of *salaries* would disguise an inequality in total compensation. With fringe benefits now comprising in excess of 25 percent of total compensation, such distinctions are important.

Consider capital gains. Capital gains arise when a stock or other asset is sold for a price higher than it was bought. The gain is counted as *income* in the year the sale occurs. Hence, a person's income in any year depends in part on the timing of asset sales. Two people with otherwise identical incomes and assets may register different incomes in a year because of differing sales decisions. Upon sale, a *realized* capital gain transforms wealth into income, while the *unrealized* capital gain remains as wealth, not income. Accordingly, differences in observed income may exaggerate differences in economic circumstances.

The existence of wealth, fringe benefits, and unrealized capital gains implies that "income" won't always be reflected in the size of the pie slice a person receives. In other words, *consumption* patterns (the distribution of slices) may depart significantly from the distribution of *incomes*.

The gap between consumption and income may be particularly large for low-income people. Low-income people get a lot of income in-kind rather than in cash. Food stamps are an example. The federal government doles out over $30 billion of food stamps each year. These coupons allow poor people to buy more food (a larger slice of pie) than their *cash* incomes would permit. Low-income households may also get free health care (Medicaid), subsidized rents, and school lunches. Researchers have observed that such in-kind income helps poor people consume *twice* as much output as their cash incomes alone would purchase.[4]

---

[4]Susan E. Mayer and Christopher Jencks, "Recent Trends in Economic Inequality in the United States: Income Versus Expenditures Versus Material Well-Being," in *Poverty and Prosperity in the U.S.A. in the Late Twentieth Century,* eds. D. Papadimitriou and E. Wolff (New York: St. Martin's Press, 1993). Credit cards and savings also reduce consumption inequalities; see Dirk Krueger and Fabrizio Perri, "Does Income Inequality Lead to Consumption Inequality?" *Journal of Economic Studies* (January 2006), pp. 163–193.

The tax system also creates a divergence between income and consumption patterns. Tax laws make a critical distinction between "taxable" income and "gross" income. Some forms of income (fringe benefits, unrealized capital gains, tax-free interest) aren't counted at all by the Internal Revenue Service. Then a maze of deductions, exemptions, and credits substantially reduces both taxable income and tax liabilities. As a consequence, two people with identical gross incomes can end up with very different levels of taxable income—and consumption. Because most data on income come from tax returns, these tax-induced distortions can significantly affect the observed distribution of incomes.

UNIT OF OBSERVATION

We run into another conceptual problem with the unit of observation. Whose slices are we concerned about? Is our primary concern with the income received by *individuals*? Or is the *family* a more appropriate unit of observation? Surely, the economic circumstances of a toddler are not reflected in his or her own income; it's the *family's* income that counts. Yet families come in all shapes and sizes. Does equality imply that all families have the same income? Or should differences in size, structure, and age be taken into account when assessing income inequalities across families?[5] *Whose* equality do we really care about?

A common unit of observation is the *household*. A *household* is defined as one or more persons living under the same roof and sharing kitchen facilities. A *family,* by contrast, refers to people related by blood or marriage. Of the roughly 115 million households in the United States, only 78 million contain families. Over 30 million people live alone, in a one-person household. Because U.S. Census Bureau data are collected from households, observed patterns of income may not reflect individual or interfamily patterns of well-being and consumption.[6]

TREND DISTORTIONS

All of these complications become more pressing when *trends* in inequality are sought. People want to know how the degree of inequality has changed over time. But the size and composition of households and families have changed as well. A generation ago, nine out of ten families contained a married couple. Today, fewer than eight out of ten families include a married couple. Families are also substantially smaller. Figure 2.1 illustrates how such demographic shifts can affect the observed distribution of income. In year 1, two identical families have identical incomes, thereby generating perfect equality. By year 2, however, family A has dissolved, creating a third household. In year 2, husband A is still working the same job, but single mom A has gone to work as well. As a consequence, the size of the

---

[5]The significance of both in-kind benefits and household size for inequality assessments is explored in Daniel Radner, "Noncash Income, Equivalence Scales, and the Measurement of Economic Well-Being," *Review of Income and Wealth, 43* (March 1997), pp. 71–88.

[6]The sensitivity of income rankings to the unit of observation is demonstrated in Congressional Budget Office, *Effective Federal Tax Rates, 1979–1997* (Washington, DC: Government Printing Office, October 2001), pp. 30–36.

FIGURE 2.1 Demographic Effects on Inequality

collective pie has grown (to $140,000 from $100,000). As a result of the extra income, no one has an evidently smaller slice than they had before. But the *average household* slice has shrunk (from $50,000 to $46,667) and income inequality has surfaced. Clearly, though, this *statistical* reduction in average incomes and equality is not very informative.

If in year 3, husband A remarries and son A goes off to college and lives in an apartment, observed income trends become even less meaningful. Those changes in living arrangements cause average income and equality to decline further. Whereas every household had a $50,000 income in year 1, in year 3 household incomes range from $15,000 to $80,000. Yet no one is demonstrably worse off.

Similar distortions in income trends arise when the composition of incomes changes. A generation ago, in-kind transfer programs such as food stamps, Medicaid, and subsidized housing were relatively small. Since then, they have mushroomed, widening the gap between income and consumption patterns. The relatively fast growth of fringe benefits has had similarly distorting effects on the observed distribution of income.[7]

International comparisons of income suffer from these same distortions. Among industrialized nations there are substantial differences in the provision of public services and in-kind transfers. Tax rules also vary tremendously, as do demographic patterns. In less developed nations, a large share of income is still produced and consumed outside of formal markets (e.g., home-grown food; barter). Moreover, survey methods

---

[7]See Brooks Pierce, "Compensation Inequality," *Quarterly Journal of Economics* (November 2001), pp. 1493–1525; also Gregory Acs and C. Eugene Steuerle, *Trends in the Distribution of Non-Wage Benefits and Total Compensation* (Washington, DC: Urban Institute, 1993).

are much less precise.[8] Accordingly, available data can offer only rough international comparisons of income equality.

ALTERNATIVE YARDSTICKS

Despite the many difficulties in defining income and its distribution, people want to measure the distribution and track changes therein. To this end, several related yardsticks are commonly employed.

BETWEEN-GROUP AVERAGES

One of the most common measures of inequality is the difference in incomes between distinct groups. Figure 2.2 shows, for example, differences in median incomes across race and ethnic groups. The median income of white families substantially exceeds that of minority families. Although these racial gaps have diminished somewhat over time, they are still huge.

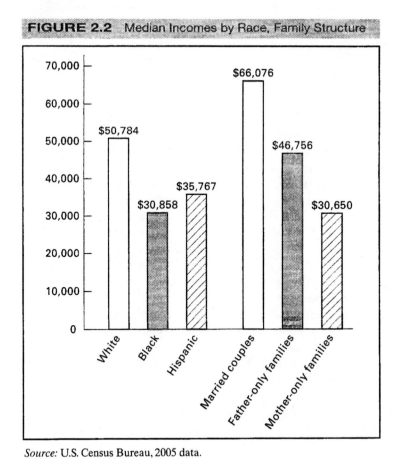

FIGURE 2.2   Median Incomes by Race, Family Structure

Source: U.S. Census Bureau, 2005 data.

---

[8]Nonincome data imply different income distributions than available income data, as demonstrated in I. S. Saltz, "Income Distribution in the Third World: Its Estimation via Proxy Data," *American Journal of Economics and Sociology, 54*:1 (1999), pp. 15–31.

Also shown in Figure 2.2 are the income differences across family structures. Married-couple families have by far the highest incomes. Families headed by a single-parent male have only two-thirds as much income, while female-headed families have less than half as much income.

These between-group averages are often the primary focus of inequality concerns. In later chapters we will explore some of the reasons why such inequalities arise and persist. Before doing so, however, we will examine broader measures of inequality—measures that go beyond simple between-group differences.

INCOME SHARES

To develop broader measures of the distribution of income, the population must first be arrayed in order of relative income. The *size distribution of income* refers to the rank ordering of individuals (or families or households) by the size of their incomes. This rank-ordered distribution enables us to discern who has the highest incomes and who has the lowest.

Typically, the size distribution is categorized into various subclasses, again based on relative incomes. The most common categorization entails the identification of *quintiles,* that is, subgroups containing one-fifth of the population. This enables one to distinguish the highest quintile (that fifth of the population with the highest incomes) from the successively lower quintiles.

Most people use much less precise references to income ranks. "Rich" people, for example, are unquestionably in the highest quintile. But not everyone in the top 20 percent is necessarily rich. As Table 2.1 reveals, a household needed only $91,705, of income in 2005 to make it into the highest quintile. That threshold is significantly below what most Americans perceive as rich. Accordingly, we may want to delve further into quintiles, identifying the top 10 percent (decile), top 5 percent (ventile), or the top 1 percent. The same kind of disaggregation occurs within the bottom quintile, where an effort is made to distinguish "poor" people from the larger group of low-income recipients in that bottom quintile.

Table 2.1 shows not only the income thresholds that define each quintile, but also the share of aggregate (total) income reserved by each quintile. Any household with at least $91,705 of income in 2005 was in the highest quintile. Together, these households received 50.4 percent of all the income generated in that year. In other words, the highest quintile got half of the pie.

Slices of the pie get progressively smaller as we move into lower quintiles. The bottom quintile got an income share of only 3.4 percent, a tiny sliver of the pie. Without question, the U.S. distribution of income is highly unequal.

TABLE 2.1 Income Shares, by Quintile

Quintile	*Income Range*	*Income Share*
Highest	$91,705 and over	50.4%
Fourth	$57,660–91,705	23.0%
Third	$36,000–57,660	14.6%
Second	$19,178–36,000	8.6%
Lowest	below $19,178	3.4%

Source: U.S. Census Bureau, 2005 data.

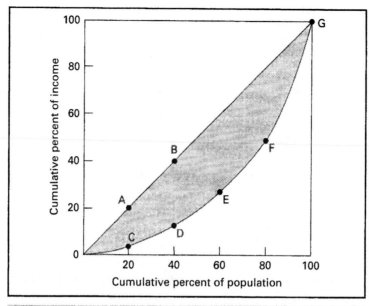

FIGURE 2.3 The Lorenz Curve

Source: U.S. Census Bureau; 2005 data.

THE LORENZ CURVE

A popular method for illustrating the size distribution of income is the Lorenz curve. The Lorenz curve graphically illustrates the relationship between population shares and income shares.

Suppose again that the population is arrayed in order of relative income. Starting with the lowest incomes, the Lorenz curve depicts the *cumulative* share of total income received by *cumulative* percentages of the population.

Were incomes *equally* distributed, then 20 percent of the population would receive exactly 20 percent of all income. This egalitarian outcome is illustrated by point A in Figure 2.3. In that egalitarian society, 40 percent of the population would get 40 percent of total income (point B), and so on. Accordingly, the size distribution of income would be along the diagonal in Figure 2.3 if all slices of the pie were equal.

We already know from Table 2.1 that U.S. incomes aren't distributed so equally. In fact, the bottom quintile gets only 3.4 percent of total income, as illustrated by point C. The cumulative share of income received by the lowest 40 percent of the population is only 12.0 (point D). By plotting the rest of the income-share data we end up with the actual Lorenz curve in Figure 2.3. As is evident, the Lorenz curve lies well below the diagonal, visually confirming a high degree of income inequality among U.S. households.

The Lorenz curve not only provides a visual summary of the size distribution of income, but also provides a convenient mechanism for illustrating changes in that distribution. The closer the Lorenz curve is to the diagonal, the more equal is the distribution. Hence, by comparing Lorenz curves for different years, one can see whether inequality is increasing or decreasing.[9]

---

[9]For detailed analysis of this and other distributional measures see Anthony Atkinson and F. Bourguignon, eds., *Handbook of Income Distribution* (Amsterdam: North Holland, 1999).

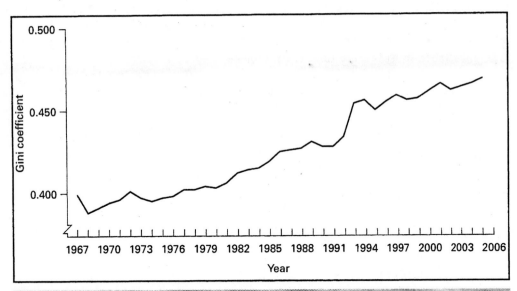

FIGURE 2.4   The Gini Coefficient for U.S. Households, 1967–2005

Source: U.S. Census Bureau.

GINI COEFFICIENT

A single statistic is often used to summarize the information arrayed along the Lorenz curve. Developed in 1912 by an Italian mathematician, the Gini coefficient measures how far the Lorenz curve departs from the diagonal of equality. It is measured as the area between the diagonal and the Lorenz curve (shaded area in Figure 2.3), divided by the area of the triangle formed by the diagonal. This Gini ratio gets smaller as the Lorenz curve moves closer to the diagonal and attains a value of zero when absolute equality is achieved. Accordingly, the Gini coefficient varies between 0 (perfect equality) and 1 (complete inequality, wherein one household gets all the income).[10] The Gini coefficient for the U.S. distribution of income in 2005 (Table 2.1) was 0.469.

The Gini coefficient provides a remarkably simple mechanism for tracking and measuring changes in inequality. Figure 2.4 shows how the Gini coefficient has changed among U.S. households since 1967. With few exceptions, the Gini coefficient has increased every year. By comparing the 1967 Gini (0.399) with the 2005 Gini (0.469), it appears that income inequality has worsened by 17 percent.

NORMATIVE VERSUS OBJECTIVE OBSERVATIONS

In principle, some value for the Gini coefficient represents the optimal level of inequality. As we observed earlier, that optimal value is not zero. Complete equality (Gini = 0) is neither inherently fair nor consistent with efficiency goals. Hence, some

---

[10]The mathematical formula for the Gini coefficient is

$$\text{Gini} = \frac{1}{2n^2 \bar{y}} \sum_{i=1}^{n} \sum_{j=1}^{n} (y_i - y_j)$$

where y equals the income of the ith and jth individuals and n is the number of individuals.

nonzero Gini value must be optimal. But where is that elusive optimal Gini? People who decry existing inequalities as "too large" evidently peg the optimal Gini closer to zero than its current value (0.xxx). All such normative judgments about the degree of inequality, however, are inherently subjective—and greatly influenced by one's position in the income distribution.

Without making a normative judgment about how much inequality is acceptable, we can still compare and contrast income distributions across time and space. This at least enables us to distinguish which distributions are "more equal" or "less equal," an objective observation. As Figure 2.4 documented, the U.S. income distribution among households has become less equal over the last three decades. Tracking changes in the Gini coefficient also allows us to assess how government tax and transfer policies alter the distribution of income. A tax cut that increases the Gini coefficient clearly favors the "rich." If economic growth lowers the Gini coefficient, then growth is undeniably a mechanism of progressive (pro-poor) redistribution.

INCOME MOBILITY

No one has an objective measure for ascertaining the optimal degree of inequality. As noted earlier, the inequality that some people regard as excessive others may regard as perfectly acceptable. One of the criteria often used to judge the degree of inequality is the perceived fairness in how that inequality was generated. As we observed earlier, lottery winners aren't held in contempt, but envied. As long as the lottery itself is fair, everyone accepts the enormous inequality between winners and losers. At least every ticket holder has an *equal chance* of becoming a winner.

STRATIFICATION VERSUS EQUALITY

The same kind of normative considerations are relevant to income inequality. Income disparities are less onerous if everyone has a plausible chance of "hitting it big." Equality of *opportunity,* not equality of *status,* is the principle that commands near-universal allegiance. Opinion polls reveal that many more Americans *believe* they will one day get rich than will ever actually do so.[11] They have faith in the *system*—the mechanisms that distribute individual incomes. This faith makes it easier to accept glaring inequalities.

Were people not able to move across class (quintile) boundaries, existing inequalities would be much less tolerable. Class *stratification* refers to a situation in which people are trapped in a particular income rank: They can't move from "rags to riches," as Horatio Alger did. Instead, social, economic, and institutional barriers obstruct interclass movements, keeping everyone "in their place." In such a stratified society, low-income people have no real hope of becoming rich, no matter how hard they study, work, save, or invest. Such complete class stratification destroys the incentive arguments for inequality, thereby undermining its politico-economic justification.

---

[11]Robert Blendon and John Benson, "How Americans Viewed Their Lives in 2005," *Challenge* (May–June 2006), Table 16.

SOURCES OF MOBILITY

If equal opportunity is the litmus test for the acceptability of status inequality, then the extent of interclass mobility is critical to normative judgments about inequality patterns. In fact, interclass mobility is extensive, for a variety of reasons.

Age-Related Mobility

A prime source of income mobility is the life cycle itself. Young people entering the labor market typically start out with low wages and short hours. With time, however, they not only age, but gain education, experience, and labor-market networks. This increased *human capital* generates ever-rising wages. In the process, an individual moves up the income distribution.

As an individual approaches retirement, work hours often diminish and income begins to decline. Upon retirement (labor-market exit), income declines even more abruptly, pushing retirees down the income distribution. This life-cycle pattern generates substantial intergenerational mobility across income classes.

Changes in Family Structure

Changes in family structure also cause a lot of income mobility. Marriages typically bring two income earners together, eliminating one household and enlarging the income of the residual one. Divorces have the opposite effects. Childbirth also causes many women to leave the labor market temporarily, thereby abruptly reducing family income. These kinds of demographic changes cause substantial intragenerational income mobility.[12]

Immigration

Another important source of both intra- and intergenerational mobility is immigration. Well over 1 million immigrants enter the United States each year. The new immigrants tend to be younger, less educated, and less skilled than the average U.S. worker. Hence, they tend to enter the income distribution at its lowest ranks.

The influx of immigrants into the lowest ranks of the income distribution has two important effects on measured inequality. First, it pushes nonimmigrants up into higher quintiles, even those whose own incomes don't change. In other words, observed mobility increases due to crowding into the lowest income ranks.

The second effect of immigration on income mobility comes from the process of assimilation. Many, if not most, immigrants are drawn to the United States by the prospect of striking it rich. They may often *start* out working at low-wage jobs, but they, like native-born Americans, aspire to move up the economic ladder. As they do, the rate of income mobility increases.

Labor-Market Changes

In addition to the demographic forces of aging, family dynamics, and immigration, changes in the labor market also foster income mobility. Short-run instability in the broader economy reshuffles the distribution of income. A recession throws thousands of workers out of jobs and shrinks the paychecks of millions more. The impacted workers slide down the income distribution. When the economy recovers, jobs are plentiful,

---

[12]Mary C. Daly and Robert G. Valletta document how changes in family structure increased income inequality in the 1970s and 1980s; see "Inequality and Poverty in the United States: The Effects of Rising Dispersion of Men's Earnings and Changing Family Behaviour," *Economica* (February 2006), pp. 75–98.

paychecks grow, and many workers leapfrog up the income distribution. Because the impact of a recession varies across regions, industries, and employers, such cyclical forces generate a lot of income mobility.

Even in stable macroeconomic circumstances, a lot of income mobility is generated by labor-market forces. Consumer demands are continually changing, altering the employment and profit prospects of specific industries and firms. Changes in technology also alter the product mix and labor requirements. In the process, some workers move ahead more quickly while others lag behind; more income mobility results.

Financial Markets Volatility

The financial markets also reshuffle income shares. In the late 1990s, the stock market bestowed multimillion-dollar prizes on dot-com entrepreneurs and investors. Clerical workers at some companies became overnight millionaires. When the dot-com bubble burst in 2000–2001, this income mobility reversed course; the people who went from rags to riches on stock-market gains returned to rags when the value of their stocks plummeted.

MOBILITY PATTERNS

All of these and other forces keep relative income positions in constant flux. As a result, the people who are on the lowest rungs of the income ladder in one year aren't necessarily still on the lowest rungs in a later year. In every year there will be a lowest rung, of course. But so long as individuals can move to higher rungs (being replaced by immigrants, labor-market entrants, splintered families, retirees, and the unlucky), the distribution of incomes takes on the character of a lottery.

In reality, the reshuffling of income positions isn't so random nor so frequent. However, there is a lot more income mobility than most people expect. There is enough mobility in the U.S. income distribution to characterize the process as akin to the game of musical chairs. People move around the chairs until the music stops, then find themselves with a comfortable chair, an uncomfortable one, or none at all. It is this kind of income mobility that gives credence to the Horatio Alger story and a distinctive character to the U.S. socioeconomic structure.

THE MOBILITY MATRIX

In principle, income mobility is easy to measure. To do so, we must once again rank everyone according to relative income in a given year. Then we do the same thing in another year, and observe how many people change relative position. Such observations could be summarized in a transition matrix like that of Figure 2.5. On the vertical axis are the rank positions for one year; rank positions for a later year are arrayed horizontally. In this case, the distribution is divided into 20 equally sized ventiles. Each individual then fits into one cell of the matrix, based on his or her income ranks in those two years.

In a completely stratified society, everyone would be arrayed along the diagonal in Figure 2.5. That is to say, a person in rank X in year 1 would be at that same rank in year 2. All the matrix cells off the diagonal would be empty. By contrast, if relative income positions were randomly reassigned each year, then individuals would be scattered evenly across the entire matrix. In that event, every cell would contain the same number of people. That outcome would reflect *complete* equality of opportunity—a situation

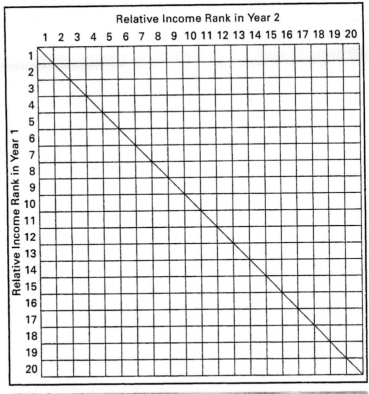

FIGURE 2.5 Mobility Matrix

wherein one year's accomplishments (e.g., occupation, grades, investments) had *no* effect on another year's status.

Although the mechanisms of measuring income mobility are straightforward, evidence of actual mobility patterns is scarce. This is because such evidence must be gathered by observing the *same* individuals over a period of time. Such *longitudinal* studies are complex and expensive. Most surveys are *cross-sectional* rather than longitudinal. They take a snapshot of a random sample of the distribution in one year, then a snapshot of another sample the next year. The odds of an individual being surveyed in repeated years are minuscule. Hence, mobility data must be gleamed from explicitly longitudinal surveys or from data archives that track individual histories.

EARNINGS MOBILITY

One source of longitudinal data is the U.S. Social Security Administration. Virtually all employees are required to pay Social Security (FICA) taxes. For employees, the taxes are deducted automatically by the employer. Self-employed persons make tax payments directly. All of these payments are recorded on an individual basis, thereby creating a wage history for later computation of Social Security retirement benefits.

The Social Security Administration's earnings histories were used to complete one of the first studies of earnings mobility. Mobility among all workers was tracked; then mobility among workers of approximately the same age (five-year age cohorts) was tracked. The latter *intra*cohort observations are most interesting because they exclude the intergenerational mobility due to life-cycle patterns. The same-age (intracohort) comparisons are akin to a high school reunion, where attendees discover who's (still) doing well and who's not.

The intracohort earnings mobility of male workers was measured over a 14-year period, beginning in 1957. In effect, a transition matrix like Figure 2.5 was developed, with everyone assigned to a relative income rank (ventile) in the first (1957) and last (1971) years. Relatively few workers remained in the same relative income position during that period. As Table 2.2 shows, only 29 percent of male workers were in the same relative earnings rank fourteen years later; 71 percent had experienced earnings mobility. Hence, status mobility is the norm; stratification is the exception.

Table 2.2 also reveals that people move considerable distances up and down the earnings distribution in a short time period. The mean move was 4.22 ventiles, that is, a move of over one-fifth the distance along the distribution.

Although earnings mobility is pervasive, it is not as common at the ends of the income distribution. Over 40 percent of the workers who are at the top of the distribution

TABLE 2.2 Earnings Mobility

Ventile Rank in 1957	Percent in Same Rank, 1971	Mean Absolute Rank Change (in ventiles)
1	48	4.12
2	42	4.51
3	31	4.75
4	28	4.56
5	27	4.45
6	25	4.34
7	25	4.27
8	24	3.93
9	24	3.92
10	24	3.82
11	23	4.05
12	24	3.98
13	25	4.13
14	26	4.08
15	26	4.31
16	30	4.04
17	33	4.01
18	35	4.26
19	—	—
20	—	—
Average	29	4.22

Note: An earnings threshold excluded workers in the lowest two ventiles, most of whom worked only part-time.

Source: Bradley R. Schiller, "Relative Earnings Mobility in the United States," *American Economic Review,* 67:5 (December 1977), pp. 926–941.

in the early year are still there in the later year. Workers at the bottom of the distribution are also a bit less likely to move. But even at the top and bottom of the distribution, mobility is more common than immobility. A later study confirmed that such mobility was at least as prevalent in the 1980s, and common among women and minority workers as well.[13]

INCOME MOBILITY

Earnings are the largest but not the sole component of income. Other components of income (e.g., profits, capital gains) may in fact be even more variable, thus making *income* mobility greater than *earnings* mobility. However, income mobility is more difficult to measure and assess. Income records (e.g., tax returns) typically focus on *families,* not individual workers. Furthermore, no government agency has a mandate to track specific family incomes over time. Even if such a historical profile were sought, it would be hard to interpret. As we observed earlier (Figure 2.1), changes in family configurations can have a major impact on measured inequality. Longitudinal observations would have to keep track of all the subfamilies that develop, then create some way of categorizing their diverse experiences.[14] By contrast, *earnings* histories are tied to individual workers, making longitudinal observations easier to measure and interpret.

Despite these difficulties, some longitudinal surveys have been successfully undertaken. In general, they document substantial mobility over relatively short periods of time (two to five years).[15] An IRS study was particularly revealing about the fluidity of America's richest households. The IRS identified the 400 tax filers with the most income in any given year. What they observed is that less than 1 out of 4 of these filers showed up more than once in a nine-year period and only 1 out of 8 appeared in the top 400 more than twice. In other words, the cast of super-rich households is always changing.[16]

Over a lifetime, income mobility is even more substantial. One study showed that 80 percent of all Americans will experience at least one year of poverty, one year of

---

[13]Bradley R. Schiller, "Relative Earnings Redux: Youth Mobility in the 1980's," *Review of Income and Wealth, 40*:4 (December 1994), pp. 441–456. Unemployment insurance records suggest exceptional upward mobility for low-wage workers according to Fredrik Anderson, Harry Holzer, and Julia Lane, *Moving up or Moving On: Who Advances in the Low-Wage Labor Market* (New York: Russell Sage, 2005).

[14]Some of the problems in using tax returns to estimate family income mobility are discussed in Dunbar and Groff, "Determination of Income Mobility Using Tax Return Data," *Public Finance Review, 28*:6 (November 2000), pp. 511–539.

[15]One of the classic studies of family income mobility is Greg Duncan et al., *Years of Poverty, Years of Plenty* (Ann Arbor, MI: Institute for Social Research, 1984). See also Peter Gottschalk and Sheldon Danziger, "Family Income Mobility—How Much Is There and Has It Changed?" in *The Inequality Paradox: Growth of Income Disparity,* eds. J. Auerbach and R. Belous (Washington, DC: National Policy Association, 1998); also Peter Gottschalk, "Inequality in Income, Growth and Mobility: The Basic Facts," *Journal of Economic Perspective, 11* (1997), pp. 21–40. Suggestions that intragenerational household mobility may have slowed in the 1980s are found in Katherine Bradbury and Jane Katz, "Women's Labor Market Involvement and Family Income Mobility When Marriages End," *New England Economic Review, 4* (2002), pp. 41–74.

[16]See Michael Parisi and Michael Studler, "The 400 Individual Income Tax Returns Reporting the Highest Adjusted Gross Incomes Each year, 1992–2000," *Statistics of Income Bulletin* (Spring 2003), pp. 7–9.

affluence, or both situations during their lifetime; only one out of five individuals will experience neither.[17]

Intergenerational mobility appears to be just as pervasive. That is to say, the *children* of the rich have no permanent hold on the highest rungs of the income ladder. Nor are the children of the poor forever enmeshed in a "poverty trap." People *do* move up and down the income ladder over generations, as well as within generations. Mobility isn't universal, but is still more the rule than the exception.[18]

SOCIAL INEQUALITY

The studies on mobility shed important new light on inequality statistics. As suggested earlier, the principle of equal opportunity commands more universal acceptance than the principle of equal income. Consequently, the more mobility there is among income ranks, the less deleterious is any given degree of inequality. Even *increasing* (cross-sectional) inequality might be accepted if it were accompanied by increasing mobility.

Mickey Kaus emphasizes that even extensive income mobility isn't synonymous with increased *social* equality. When the military draft was universal, for example, both poor and rich had to confront the possibility of military service. The draft not only helped equalize social responsibilities, but also forced a lot of interclass interaction. An all-volunteer army, by contrast, tends to draw recruits from lower-income classes and reinforces class separation. Kaus also laments the celebration of holidays on Fridays and Mondays. Midweek holidays are more prone to promoting civic and neighborhood celebrations, whereas three-day weekends encourage out-of-town travel and greater class isolation.[19]

Summary

Inequality is an issue that evokes great social concern. Many people worry that inequality is not only inherently unjust, but that it also spawns social resentment, political isolation, and crime. On the other hand, inequalities also act as an economic incentive to study, work, save, and invest harder. The optimal degree of inequality entails a subjective balancing of these equity and efficiency concerns.

At best, incomes gauge only a portion of social status. Wealth, political power, and social access are also important, and not always correlated with current income. Income itself is also difficult to measure, especially when fringe benefits, in-kind transfers, profits, capital gains, and other receipts are available.

Inequality in the United States also increased over the last 30 years. To some extent, that increased inequality of cash incomes has been offset by the tremendous growth of in-kind transfers.

---

[17]Mark Rank and Thomas Hirschl, "Rags or Riches? Estimating the Probabilities of Poverty and Affluence Across the Adult American Life Span," *Social Science Quarterly* (December 2001), pp. 651–669.

[18]For a discussion of intergenerational mobility see the symposium on this topic in *Journal of Economic Perspectives* (Summer 2002), pp. 3–66. Also see Samuel Bowles, Herbert Gintis, and Mulissa Groves, eds., *Unequal Chances: Family Background and Economic Success* (Princeton, NJ: Princeton University Press, 2005).

[19]Mickey Kaus, *The End of Equality* (New York: Basic Books, 1992).

Income inequality need not imply class stratification. People in fact move from one income rank to another. Such income mobility makes income inequality more socially acceptable.

Further Readings

Bowles, Samuel, Herbert Gintis, and Melissa Groves, eds., *Unequal Chances: Family Background and Economic Success.* Princeton, NJ: Princeton University Press, 2005.

Dunbar, Amy, and James E. Groff, "Determination of Income Mobility Using Tax Return Data," *Public Finance Review, 28*:6 (November 2000), pp. 511–539.

Kaus, Mickey, *The End of Equality.* New York: Basic Books, 1992.

Ladd, Everett C., and Karlyn H. Bowman, *Attitudes Toward Economic Inequality.* Washington, DC: American Enterprise Institute, 1998.

Litchfield, Julie A., "Inequality: Methods and Tools." Washington, DC: www.worldbank.org/poverty/inequal/index.htm, March 1999.

McMurrer, D., and I. Sawhill, *Getting Ahead: Economic and Social Mobility in America.* Washington, DC: Urban Institute, 1998.

Piketty, Thomas, and Emannuel Saez, "Income Inequality in the United States, 1913–1998." Cambridge, MA: National Bureau of

Economic Research, Working Paper No. 8467, September 2001.

Slesnick, Daniel, *Consumption and Social Welfare: Living Standards and their Distribution in the United States.* New York: Cambridge University Press, 2001.

Solon, Gary, "Mobility Within and Between Generations," in *The Causes and Consequences of Increasing Inequality,* ed. Finis Welch. Chicago: University of Chicago Press, 2001.

Stonecash, Jeffrey, "Inequality and the American Public," (Syracuse University, Maxwell School, January 2007)

U.S. Census Bureau, *Money Income in the United States.* Washington, DC: Government Printing Office, annual.

Wolff, Edward N. and Ajit Zacharias, "Household Wealth and the Measurement of Economic Well-Being in the United States." New York: Levy Economics Institute, May 2006.

Web Links

American Enterprise Institute. Summaries of research and conferences on inequality and related topics: www.aei.org

Federal Reserve. Data on household wealth and income from Survey of Consumer Finances: www.federalreserve.gov

Pew Research Center surveys on U.S. perceptions of inequality: www.people-press.org/surveyreports

U.S. Census Bureau. Detailed tabulations on incomes of households, families, and individuals: www.census.gov/hhes/www/income

CHAPTER 3
COUNTING THE POOR
⚶

As the previous chapter documented, defining, measuring, and interpreting inequality are not simple tasks. Identifying who is "poor" in the broader distribution of income is no easier. Conceptual and measurement efforts are bedeviled by different forms of income, varying household sizes and needs, and a lack of consensus about what standard of living defines the boundary between "poor" and "nonpoor." As a consequence, defining *poverty* and counting the "poor" are highly controversial endeavors. They are nevertheless essential steps in the process of policy development. A nation can't embark on a War on Poverty if it can't identify the enemy. And progress in reducing poverty can't be assessed without some yardstick for measuring the extent of poverty. In this chapter, we examine alternative concepts of poverty, identify the official poverty definition, and then decide who is poor by that definition.

POVERTY: DRAWING A LINE

As we observed in Chapter 2, the distribution of income is a continuum, stretching from the lowest-income individual to the individual with the highest income. In general, the frequency distribution of income has the shape of a disfigured bell, with a mass of people around the middle of the distribution and increasingly fewer people at the extremes ("tails") of the distribution. The "bell curve" in Figure 3.1 illustrates the income distribution for U.S. families.

Studies of inequality typically partition the income distribution into rank-ordered categories, each containing an equal number of individuals (or other household unit). In Chapter 2, for example, we partitioned the distribution into quintiles, deciles, and ventiles of equal size, then observed their differing income shares.

Now the challenge is to identify who is "poor" in these partitions. Surely the poor reside in the lowest income ranks, but where exactly should the line separating the poor from the nonpoor be drawn? Is everyone in the lowest ventile poor? The lowest decile? The lowest quintile?

Two distinct approaches are used for identifying poor people in the broader distribution of income. The first approach seeks an *absolute* standard of deprivation, while the second relies on *relative* standards of adequacy.

THE ABSOLUTE APPROACH

The absolute approach to defining poverty begins with the concept of minimum subsistence, that is, some bundle of goods and services that is regarded as essential to the physical well-being of a family unit. Those who do not possess the economic resources to obtain these goods and services are considered poor. In the most severe conception of the absolute approach, this bundle of economic goods and services consists of the

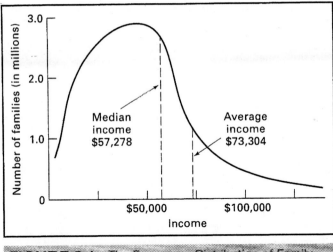

FIGURE 3.1   The Frequency Distribution of Family Incomes

Source: Approximated from U.S. Bureau of the Census (2005 data).

minimum caloric intake essential to human existence, and perhaps some form of shelter. The World Bank says people can cover these primitive needs with only $1 per day. Hence, it classifies people around the world as "poor" only if their income is less than $1 a day. (Global poverty is discussed in Chapter 4.)

People in industrialized communities tend to have more generous notions of "minimum" needs. This, of course, is the fundamental problem with the absolute definition of poverty. Once the bare-bones, life-sustaining minimum caloric diet has been exceeded, there is no agreement as to how many additional frills can be included in the definitional bundle of minimum goods and services. In the 1930s, no one felt particularly poor if he or she did not possess electric lights. Yet, today, a family without electricity will most likely be considered poor. So we include a provision for electricity in our minimum poverty-defining budget. But consensus is far more difficult to achieve on a television, much less on a DVD, a CD player, a car, or a six-pack of beer. How many of these items will we include in a poor family's budget? Our answer will determine where to draw the poverty line.

A British survey conducted in the 1980s asked people to identify items that were absolutely necessary for subsistence. The list included not just a "damp-free home" and "three meals a day for children" but also a much longer list that included a television, a car, a VCR, and a pack of cigarettes every other day.[1] People who did not have three or more items on this list were deemed to be poor.

In principle, a list of absolute necessities should change very little over time. The concept of minimum needs should also have universal applicability. In reality, neither condition is fulfilled with absolute standards. People's perceptions of what is absolutely necessary for subsistence is conditioned by the array of goods and services available and prevailing living conditions in their own society. Notice in Figure 3.2 how American perceptions of how much money is needed to "just get by," "to live in reasonable

---

[1]J. Mack and S. Lansley, *Breadline Britain, 1990s* (New York: HarperCollins, 1991).

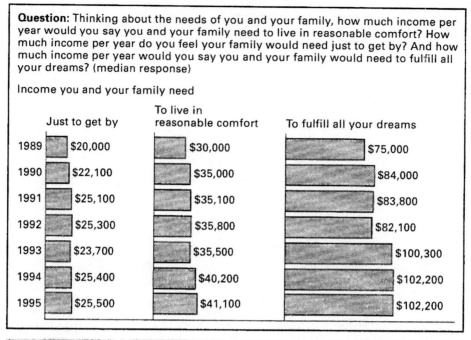

Question: Thinking about the needs of you and your family, how much income per year would you say you and your family need to live in reasonable comfort? How much income per year do you feel your family would need just to get by? And how much income per year would you say you and your family would need to fulfill all your dreams? (median response)

Income you and your family need

	Just to get by	To live in reasonable comfort	To fulfill all your dreams
1989	$20,000	$30,000	$75,000
1990	$22,100	$35,000	$84,000
1991	$25,100	$35,100	$83,800
1992	$25,300	$35,800	$82,100
1993	$23,700	$35,500	$100,300
1994	$25,400	$40,200	$102,200
1995	$25,500	$41,100	$102,200

FIGURE 3.2   Increased Expectations

Source: Roper Starch Worldwide.

comfort," and to "fulfill all your dreams" has changed over time. Notice also how much more money the average American family says it needs to "just get by" than the World Bank says is "minimally necessary."

These diverse perceptions of the minimal needs raise the question of who should draw the absolute poverty line. Should experts in nutrition and physiology define subsistence standards? Or should a cross section of society be consulted, as in the public-opinion surveys? Faced with all these complexities, many observers have suggested an alternative approach to defining poverty, one that depends on relative standards.

THE RELATIVE APPROACH

As a practical matter, the yardstick used to measure absolute poverty is not really so absolute. Inevitably, it incorporates subjective views about what is minimally necessary for survival—either in physiological or social terms. As an alternative approach, some people prefer a relative definition of poverty. The relative approach is simply more explicit about this subjectivity. In essence, it states that a person is poor when his or her income is significantly less than the average income of the population. For example, we might say that a person or family with less than one-half of the average income is poor. By defining poverty in these terms, we not only avoid the need to define absolute needs but also put more emphasis on the (in)equality of incomes. This broader perspective underscores the relationship between our views of poverty and our perspectives on the fairness of the entire distribution of incomes.

As attractive as the relative approach might appear, it doesn't resolve our core measurement problem. There are just as many relative measures of poverty as there

TABLE 3.1	Cumulative Family Income Distribution, 2006 and 1935–1936 (in 2006 dollars)					

Percentage of Families with Income Less Than:

	$4,000	$8,000	$11,000	$15,000	$18,000	$30,000
2006	2.2	3.6	6.2	9.0	11.7	24.3
1935–1936	8.8	21.5	32.8	45.5	54.3	66.3

Source: U.S. Bureau of the Census (author extrapolations).

are absolute ones. Perhaps the most extreme version of relative measures is one that defines poverty as the low end of the income distribution: For example, anyone in the lowest fifth (or tenth, or third) of the distribution is regarded as poor. From this perspective, poverty will persist as long as inequality does.

Table 3.1 illustrates the basic distinction between absolute and relative definitions of poverty in another way. The table compares the income distributions in 2006 and 1935–1936, with incomes in both categories expressed in 2006 dollar values. Note, for example, that 2.2 percent of all American families earned less than $4,000 in 2006, 3.6 percent less than $8,000, and so forth. Only 25 percent of American families earned more than $75,000. Note also that incomes were much lower in the 1935–1936 period, even after adjusting for inflation (expressing amounts in 2006 dollar values). In the middle of the Depression, 1 out of 11 families earned less than $4,000, and 1 out of 5 survived with less than $8,000 per year.

Suppose we wanted to compare the number of Americans who were poor in 2006 with the number who were poor in 1936. Franklin Roosevelt spoke of one-third of the nation as being "ill-housed, ill-clad, ill-nourished." Apparently he regarded an income of about $11,000 as a threshold of poverty (see Table 3.1). By Roosevelt's definition, only 6.2 percent of the American population was poor in 2006. From a historical perspective, then, we could conclude that the incidence of poverty in the United States had declined markedly over a period of 70 years.

But what would we conclude about the course of poverty between 1936 and 2006 if we had instead applied the relative concept of poverty to the comparison? If we consistently regard the lowest third of the American income distribution as poor, then by definition we would find that 33.3 percent of the population was poor in 1936 and continued to be so in 2006.

This example illustrates the basic weaknesses of the relative measure of poverty. First, it perpetuates poverty in a statistical sense if some fixed proportion of the population is always regarded as poor. Poverty will always exist if the lowest fifth of the income distribution is regarded as poor. Second, a relative measure of poverty alone says nothing about the quality of life for the people at the bottom of the income distribution. Yet we want to know not only how many people are in poverty but also how desperate their situation is. In a similar vein, we may want to know how much money poor families need to reach an acceptable standard of living.

THE FUCHS POINT

An improved measure of relative poverty, developed by Stanford economist Victor Fuchs, meets at least the first objection to relative definitions. By his definition, those with incomes less than *half* of the national median are poor. In 2005, for example, the median family income was just over $57,000. Thus, according to the "Fuchs point," families with less than $28,500 (half of the median) should have been considered poor. The advantage of the Fuchs point over simpler relative definitions is that it distinguishes the elimination of poverty from the elimination of inequality. The simpler relative definition precludes the elimination of poverty until complete equality of incomes is attained. The Fuchs point, by contrast, creates the possibility of eliminating poverty by merely *reducing* inequality, that is, narrowing but not wholly eliminating income differences.

There is nothing sacred, of course, about the use of one-half the median as a relative standard of poverty. We could just as easily have chosen to define poverty in relative terms as one-fourth, one-third, or three-sixteenths of the median income. There is as much subjectivity involved in defining the Fuchs point as there is in defining absolute minimum standards of poverty. In reality, one's choice of a *relative* standard is likely to be influenced by the *absolute* standard of living implied, just as the choice of an absolute standard is likely to be affected by the degree of inequality and the general standards of living we observe.

WHOSE STANDARD?

Professor Morton Paglin of Portland State University raised another troubling issue.[2] With whom, he asks, should we compare our incomes? A young family with children has different needs and income sources than an older couple living in retirement. Should both households be treated equally when computing the median income? Or should relative incomes be measured only in comparison with families of similar size and age? In the former case, older couples and single-parent households will be most likely to appear poor. By the latter standard, however, more equal proportions of each population subgroup would be classified as poor.

In view of the conflicting measures of poverty, it is tempting to abandon the search for a poverty line. But this response is neither necessary nor appropriate. We need a definition of poverty in order to identify the people we desire to help. We also need some standard for assessing our success in helping them. The search for a poverty line is analogous to the search for highway speed limits. No one really believes that all speeds in excess of 55 miles per hour are somehow dangerous and all speeds less than 55 miles an hour are somehow safe; the realities of highway driving are much more complex. Yet, we use 55 miles per hour as a convenient gauge of highway safety in urban areas. The same is true of our poverty line. On the continuum of misery and human happiness, we cannot pretend that there is some point below which people are unhappy or poor and above which people are content. But, like highway speed limits, we do need a cutoff point—the poverty line.

In searching for the poverty line, we cannot conclude that one approach to defining poverty is inherently better than another. Instead, we will simply note that the contrast between relative and absolute measures of poverty highlights a basic policy issue. Is our primary policy concern the misery of those who command low incomes, or are we concerned with the unequal distribution of incomes? Though income distribution and poverty are intrinsically related, they can be approached separately.

---

[2]Morton Paglin, "The Measurement and Trend of Inequality: A Basic Revision," *American Economic Review* (September 1975).

THE OFFICIAL POVERTY LINE

The official government measure of poverty uses the absolute approach to defining poverty. This has required the government to identify the minimum amount of money required to sustain a family. For 2005, the government decided that a family of four needed a minimum of $19,971 to purchase basic essentials. But before we look at who is poor according to this definition, or what conditions give rise to such poverty, we should first take a closer look at how that figure was obtained. One of the problems with not being poor is that it is difficult to comprehend just what it means to be poor. A short review of our current definition of poverty should help increase that comprehension.

THE CONCEPT OF MINIMUM NEEDS

As we noted earlier, the establishment of an absolute poverty line requires some notion of what bundle of goods and services is "minimally adequate." Such a bundle will presumably include minimum food, clothing, shelter, and fuel requirements, as determined by appropriate experts. To this list of basic minimums we may choose to include means of transportation, some recreation, and whatever additional goods and services we deem appropriate, if not absolutely essential. The sum total of our efforts, assuming consensus can be achieved, is a shopping list of what we consider to be essential goods and services. Those persons who cannot obtain all the items on our list will be considered poor, those who can as not poor.

Suppose for the moment that nutritionists, physiologists, and other assorted scientific experts could actually detail the minimum subsistence requirements we have outlined. Such a list might be like the one in Table 3.2. Note that each functional requirement is expressed in its generic measure. To this list of social and biological minimums we might add additional food, clothing, or entertainment, depending on our sense of generosity. In this way we could construct a complete specification of what we deem to be the minimum acceptable (or poverty) standard of living.

But consider carefully the list we have compiled. To begin with, how are we to translate 2,471 calories into more familiar staples, such as yogurt, bananas, and pizza? As anyone who has ever dieted well knows, there is an infinite number of ways in which a person can consume the requisite number of calories. Or consider the clothing requirement. The specification "4 pounds" tells us nothing at all about the appropriate type of clothing or even whether we should shop at Saks Fifth Avenue or at a Salvation Army store. Similar problems arise with every item on our list.

As if this vagueness were not a serious enough problem, let us return to the generic specifications. Though there is some conceptual foundation for speaking of minimum food, shelter, clothing, or fuel requirements, there is no firm basis for specifying what

TABLE 3.2 Hypothetical Minimum Needs	
Category	*Amount*
Minimum food requirements	2,471 calories per day
Minimum fuel requirements	37 kilowatt-hours per week
Minimum shelter requirements	180 square feet per day
Minimum clothing requirements	4 pounds per month
Minimum transportation requirements	7 miles per week

these minimums are. People do survive on varying amounts of calories; the warming and protective value of clothing cannot be adequately gauged in pounds; and the need for shelter varies enormously. Consequently, any claim to scientific precision, even in the generic specifications of a poverty standard, is pretentious and misplaced.

Although the specification of a poverty standard is an imprecise endeavor, it is not necessarily useless. If we could identify a list of goods and services that most people regard as minimum needs, we would have a consensual basis for measuring poverty. That would greatly facilitate discussions of how much poverty exists and what policy options to pursue.

MONETARY MEASURES

The achievement of consensus on an absolute poverty standard is facilitated by translating generic standards into dollars. In a market economy the ability of an individual to obtain needed goods and services is determined by his or her purchasing power. Accordingly, we can simplify our poverty standard by expressing that measure not in terms of a list of necessary goods and services but instead in terms of the purchasing power required to obtain those same goods and services. The necessary conversion requires that we price all the goods and services on our list, then add up their prices to determine the amount of money involved. That total is our gauge of poverty, for it represents command over the goods and services we have specified.

Not only is such a summary measure convenient, but it also facilitates the compromise that produced the standard itself. Suppose, for example, that Mr. Blixen believes that 1,437 calories and 1.57 pounds of clothing are the absolute daily minimum needs of one person. You, on the other hand, contend that 2,113 calories and 0.86 pound of clothing are necessary. Given your respective resolutions, you and Mr. Blixen are unlikely to reach a compromise on the generic specifications of minimum needs. However, what if current market prices indicate that your "needs" require $8.37 to fulfill, while Mr. Blixen's budget is $8.35 per day. In monetary terms, it is obvious that you are not far away from a potential compromise and that agreement on the generic components of a minimum budget might be postponed indefinitely.

Although we need the food, shelter, and other items on our shopping list daily, it is not necessary to have the right amount of cash every day. Shopping each day for the minimum requirements of shelter, fuel, clothing, and food would be extraordinarily inconvenient, if not downright impossible. Our real interest lies in ascertaining that a person has an adequate *flow* of cash so that he or she can acquire the basic necessities as the need arises. Hence, the poverty standard can be expressed in terms of the amount of income needed during some period of time to purchase basic necessities. Whether an individual then elects to shop monthly, weekly, or daily is immaterial.

The best single indicator of a person's purchasing power over a period of time is income. But here, too, there are complications. As we saw in Chapter 2, income is not the sole determinant of purchasing power. Where credit is available, goods and services can, in effect, be borrowed. No current income is necessary, just a promise to make repayment when time and circumstances permit (or when the creditors demand).

A similar situation holds true with assets. Here again, a person may acquire goods and services without an income. Older persons who own their own homes, for example, don't need income to pay the rent; they enjoy "rent-free" living in the houses they purchased earlier. Likewise, farmers don't need much cash income to put food on the table. Other consumers have different assets (for example, shares of corporate stock) that they can sell.[3] You can put just about anything on the auction block at eBay and other auction sites. Or people can take jewelry, watches, or other possessions to a pawnshop and borrow some cash.

Finally, many people obtain goods and services directly without payment of cash or even a promise to pay (credit). The government has assumed an increasing responsibility for providing basic goods and services to people directly, especially if they have insufficient income or assets. Food stamps, for example, allow one to "buy" groceries with coupons ("stamps") rather than money. Food-stamp recipients, therefore, need less cash income to achieve any particular minimum standard. Likewise, families that live in public housing or receive free medical care enjoy a standard of living higher than their money income suggests. Money incomes have become a less reliable index of living standards, especially at the low end of the income distribution.[4]

HARDSHIP INDICES

An alternative approach to identifying impoverishment is to specify the essentials of everyday life that people *don't* have. Inadequate nutrition, overcrowded housing, utility interruptions, lack of access to telephones or transportation, and unmet medical needs all represent socioeconomic hardships. By identifying the prevalence of such hardships, one could conceivably distinguish who was poor and who was not without knowing their money incomes. However, such "hardship" indices require more detailed information than is typically available. By piecing together information from several sources, one study found relatively little hardship in households the government counts as "poor."[5] Furthermore, even some observed "hardships" (e.g., no health insurance) may reflect consumption choices rather than inadequate income.

Because hardship indices are difficult to construct, money incomes remain the most convenient index of a family's living standard, and it is the yardstick the government uses for measuring poverty. We'll now examine the official U.S. poverty index, then discuss some of its limitations.

---

[3]Robert Haveman and Edward Wolff document changes in the level of "asset poverty" in "Who Are the Asset Poor? Levels, Trends, and Composition, 1983–1998" (Madison, WI: Institute for Research on Poverty, 2001).

[4]In-kind income is not limited to poor families; Middle-class families benefit from subsidized public schools, job-related fringe benefits, special tax advantages, and an array of other noncash ("in-kind") forms of income. If all in-kind benefits were added up—not just those the poor receive—the poor might actually appear relatively worse off than their money incomes imply.

[5]Robert Rector, Kirk Johnson, and Sarah Youssef, "The Extent of Material Hardship and Poverty in the United States," *Review of Social Economy* (September 1999), pp. 351–387. For more discussion of hardship indices, see Sondra Beverly, "Measures of Material Hardship: Rationale and Recommendations," *Journal of Poverty* 5:1(2001), pp. 23–41. See also Susan Mayer and Christopher Jencks, "Poverty and the Distribution of Material Hardship," *Journal of Human Resources* (Winter 1989), pp. 88–113; Mary E. Corcoran, Colleen M. Heflin, and Kristine Siefert, "Food, Insufficiency and Material Hardship in Post-TANF Welfare Families," *Ohio State Law Journal*, 60 (1999), pp. 1395–1422.

POVERTY THRESHOLDS

We are now in a position to identify what may be called a poverty line. We have established the process by which an absolute poverty line may be formulated; all that remains is to apply the process. Charles Booth, an English sociologist, used the same process to establish one of the first poverty lines in 1890. Booth identified the goods and services necessary to maintain a family in what he called a "state of chronic want." He then priced those commodities and concluded that a weekly income of approximately 24 shillings or less was necessary to achieve the condition he described. At about the same time, American economists estimated that from $400 to $600 per year was necessary to attain this condition in the United States.

Since Booth's time our standards of living have grown enormously. The number of proposed poverty lines has grown also, each varying with the circumstances of the time and the perspectives of the architect. While it is not necessary to review the history of those poverty lines, each of which had significance in its own time, it is instructive to examine two of the most influential formulations.[6]

THE CEA LINE

In 1963, the President's Council of Economic Advisers (CEA) officially sanctioned a poverty line of $3,000 per annum for a typical American family. The CEA's line was rooted in the concept of absolute poverty. At the heart of its concept was the notion of minimally adequate food intake. The CEA asked the U.S. Department of Agriculture to identify the minimum nutritional requirements of a typical American family. Then they worked out a menu and priced its ingredients in the supermarket. The Agriculture Department concluded that three minimally adequate meals a day would cost the typical family of two adults and two children exactly $2.736 a day.

The Department of Agriculture's estimates established a dollar threshold for the nutrition content of an absolute standard of poverty. But what about other minimum needs? The CEA adopted a pragmatic approach to their estimation. They simply looked at how much people *spent* on food and nonfood items. Consumer studies indicated that low-income families spent approximately two-thirds of their incomes on nonfood items. Using this observation as a benchmark, the CEA then multiplied their basic food budget by three to determine how much *total* income a poor family needed. The results of their calculation are depicted in Table 3.3. The CEA then rounded off the total budget estimate to the $3,000 figure. Using this measure, the CEA decided that there were 33.4 million poverty-stricken persons in America in 1963.

TABLE 3.3 The CEA Poverty Budget, 1963

Food budget	$2.736 per day × 365 days =	$ 998.64
Nonfood budget	2 × food budget	= 1,997.28
Total budget		$2,995.92

---

[6]A historical review of attempts to define poverty is provided by Gordon M. Fisher, *From Hunter to Orshansky: An Overview of (unofficial) Poverty Lines in the United States from 1904 to 1965* (Washington, DC: U.S. Department of Health and Human Services. Office of Assistant Secretary for Planning and Evaluation, October 1993).

Michael Harrington once warned us "not to allow statistical quibbling to obscure the huge, enormous, and intolerable fact of poverty in America."[7] This is a warning we must take seriously, especially when millions of families may be involved. Accordingly, we would do well to overlook some of the imperfections in the CEA's estimation procedures and concentrate on the mass of poverty they identified. Whether the true size of the poverty population in 1963 was then 33 million, 33.5 million, or even 35.23 million would not seem to be of much consequence.

Family Size

But one glaring error in the CEA's estimation procedure doomed it to obsolescence. To appreciate the nature of the CEA's error, let us look at three families from the 1963 income distribution.

The husband in family 1 is 37 years old and supports six children and a pregnant wife on his income of $3,200 a year.

Family 2 consists of a soon-to-be-retired couple, both in their mid-sixties. The wife does not work and the husband's earnings amount to $2,800 per year. They own their home, having made the final mortgage payment last Christmas.

Family 3 consists of a struggling graduate student, his working wife, and their three-month-old child. They both work at the college carry-out store in their spare time. Their combined earnings, including overtime and tips, amount to $2,400 a year.

How did these three families place in the CEA's census of poor Americans? Family 1, consisting of eight and one-half persons, was officially classified as nonpoor. Families 2 and 3 were counted as poor, as their incomes were under the $3,000 limit. Does this make sense? Family 1 was clearly desperate, but family 2 was living a quiet and perhaps comfortable life. Our graduate-student family was not exactly affluent, but they were not desperate on $200 a month in 1963.

The source of the CEA's error should be obvious at this point. The CEA calculated a poverty budget for a typical family of two adults and two children. But not all families consist of four persons, nor do all four-person families have consistently typical needs. Clearly, the CEA's definition of a poverty line had to be adjusted for varying family size. The possibility that families of the same size might have different needs due to age, location, or family structure also had to be considered.

THE SSA INDEX

These basic refinements of the CEA's poverty line were undertaken by Mollie Orshansky of the Social Security Administration (SSA). She first adjusted for family size. This was not simple division. Rather, Ms. Orshansky had to compute "equivalency scales" that translated a four-person poverty budget into thresholds for households of other sizes. A family of four enjoys some economies of scale; they use a single kitchen, share bathrooms, and all live under one roof. If there were only two people in the house, the cost of rent and heat wouldn't decline that much. And even the food budget might not decline by 50 percent. So Ms. Orshansky had to figure out what an equivalent poverty budget really was for households of one, two, three, four, or more persons.[8]

---

[7]Michael Harrington, *The Other America* (New York: Macmillan, 1962), p. 10.

[8]For illustrations of how alternative equivalency scales affect measured poverty see Dale W. Jorgenson, "Did We Lose the War on Poverty?" and Robert K. Triest, "Has Poverty Gotten Worse?" both in *Journal of Economic Perspectives* (Winter 1998).

She also took into account how many adults were in the household and whether they lived on a farm or in the city. Using these variables, she identified 124 family types and meticulously calculated an appropriate poverty budget for each one.

For the "typical" family of four the SSA poverty budget and the CEA's own budget were very similar. The SSA adjustments, however, counted many more large families and fewer smaller families as poor due to different family needs. Our earlier examples illustrate the difference. Ms. Orshansky found that family 3, the struggling graduate student and his wife and child, needed only $2,275 for a minimum budget. Hence, they were not counted as poor under the SSA index. Family 2, the soon-to-be-retired couple, required a minimum of only $1,855 and was living quite comfortably on their income. Family 1, however, with eight persons, needed at least $5,100 per year to meet essential needs and was classified as poor by the SSA index.

THE OFFICIAL POVERTY INDEX

Despite the considerable sophistication of the 1963 SSA poverty index, no one claimed it was perfect. It was recognized that as prices and living standards continued to rise, the SSA poverty lines would require repeated upward adjustments.

Inflation Adjustments

The official poverty index now in use has been revised to account for the rising prices of goods and services but not for steadily increasing standards of living. According to Ms. Orshansky's earlier calculations, an average family of two adults and two children required a minimum of $3,130 in 1963. In 2001, after 38 years of inflation, that index stood at $18,104. We are saying that it cost $18,104 in 2001 to buy those goods and services that cost $3,130 in 1963. The increased dollar amount of the official definition does not imply in any way an increased standard of living for the poor. It adjusts only for rising prices. Because consumer prices more than quintupled between 1963 and 2001, the dollar value of the poverty line had to be increased by a like percentage if the bundle of minimum needs were to be affordable by a poor family. Even since 2001, the poverty threshold has crept up with general inflation. Notice in Table 3.4 how the 2005 poverty standard for a family of four ($19,971) is higher than the 2001 standard ($18,104). The increased poverty threshold reflects four more years of inflation. If we

TABLE 3.4 Poverty Thresholds

Size of Family	Poverty Standard	
	2001	2005
One member	$ 9,039	$ 9,973
Two members	11,569	12,755
Three members	14,128	15,577
Four members	18,104	19,971
Five members	21,405	23,613
Six members	24,195	26,683
Seven members	27,517	30,249
Eight members	30,629	33,610

Source: U.S. Census Bureau.

wanted to increase the standard of living of those whom we define as poor—and not many affluent persons are so inclined—then we would have to raise the index by more than the inflation adjustment.

Declining Relative Standard

A poverty line that adjusts only for changing prices leaves the absolute standard of living of the poor unchanged. But the income and living standards of the rest of the population continue to advance as the American economy grows. Hence, poverty lines adjusted only for inflation imply a growing disparity between the status of the poor and that of the rest of the population. Like any absolute poverty line, the official poverty thresholds imply increasing *relative* poverty over time.

Despite the limitations of current poverty line adjustments, we will adhere to official standards. Accordingly, a 2005 income of less than $19,971 will qualify a family of four for inclusion in our head count of the poor. The application of this standard to other family sizes is summarized in Table 3.4.

Enumeration of the persons below either the 1963 or the updated poverty line is a simple and straightforward task. Unfortunately, the clinical nature of the statistical operation tends to impress the observer very little with the real impoverishment that the numbers represent. Consequently, it is worthwhile to dwell for a few moments on the standard of living that the official poverty budget implies.

The austerity of the poverty budget was well described by B. Seebohm Rowntree, an English sociologist, in 1901. The essence of his description is still valid today.

> A family, living upon the scale allowed for in this estimate, must never spend a penny on railway fare or omnibus. They must never go into the country unless they can walk. They must never purchase a half-penny newspaper or spend a penny to buy a ticket for a popular concert. They must write no letters to absent children. They must never contribute anything to their church or chapel, or give any help to a neighbor that costs them money. They cannot save, nor can they join sick or Trade Union, because they cannot pay the necessary subscription. The children must have no pocket money for dolls, marbles or sweets. The father must smoke no tobacco and drink no beer. The mother must never buy any pretty cloths for herself or for her children, the character of the family wardrobe as for the family diet being governed by the regulation, "nothing must be bought but that what is absolutely necessary for the maintenance of physical health, and what is bought must be of the plainest and most economical description."[9]

That Mr. Rowntree's description of poverty living remains appropriate can be seen by looking more closely at the poverty budget for 2005 (Table 3.4). A budget of $19,971 per year may sound generous. It allows only $4.56 per person for food each day, however. That is $4.56 for breakfast, lunch, dinner, and any snacks—an amount less than the price of a single meal at McDonald's. This means that the homemaker must plan, buy, and prepare a nutritious meal for a family of four for less than six dollars. When even hamburger costs around three dollars a pound, it is pretty clear that this poverty family is not eating either very well or very much. And if they have aspirations to eat

---

[9]B. Seebohm Rowntree, *Poverty: A Study of Town Life* (London: Longmans, Green, 1901).

out on occasion, their only hope is to save money by eating lots of hot dogs and spaghetti at home.

Hard Choices

You may respond that this is a gross exaggeration of how the poor live. You may even know of a poor person who eats steak. And in a sense you are right. We have described how a poor family would act if they spent only their food allowance on food. In fact, poor families do not follow these carefully budgeted allowances. They tend to forgo other items and spend some of their nonfood allowance money on better and more palatable meals—maybe even an occasional beer. And it is this process that comes closest to describing what it means to be poor. Every day a poor person or family must choose between an adequate diet of the most economic sort and some other necessity because there is never enough money to have both. Consequently, some of the poor eat steak and walk around with holes in their shoes.[10]

It is interesting to contrast what is officially regarded as a poverty income to what Americans generally believe is required to make ends meet. Opinion polls periodically ask a cross section of Americans: "What is the smallest amount of money a family of four (husband, wife, and two children) needs each year to get along in this community?" In 1996, the median answer was $30,000 (see Figure 3.2). Price rises since that time have moved the threshold closer to $40,000. Historically, the public's view of minimum needs is always well above official poverty thresholds.[11] Quite clearly, most Americans do not believe that the official poverty standard is enough, that is, that families really could get by for long on the government's definition of minimum needs. It is nevertheless true that poor families must find a way to cope. Indeed, most poor families command even less income than the official standard. For these families, even having the opportunity to choose between steak and new shoes would seem like affluence.

If the prospect of existing for a short time on a poverty budget or less is not disquieting enough, consider the prospect of subsisting at that level into the indefinite future. A poor family must not only adjust to a subsistence budget but must also be prepared to remain at that standard of living. That is why a more affluent person cannot adequately grasp the significance of poverty by adopting a subsistence budget for a brief time. The affluent person knows that such an experiment can and will be terminated shortly. The poor person possesses no such luxury. As reported by Robert Hunter on a similar experiment by the Russian novelist Tolstoy, "poverty is not the lack of things; it is the fear and the dread of want. That fear Tolstoy could not know."[12]

---

[10]Descriptions of how people cope with poverty-level budgets are provided in Mark Rank, *Living on the Edge* (New York: Columbia University Press, 1994); Carol Walker, *Managing Poverty: The Limits of Social Assistance* (London: Routledge, 1993); Jonathan Freedman, *From Cradle to Grave: The Human Face of Poverty in America* (New York: Atheneum, 1993); and Frank Munger, ed., *Laboring Below the Line* (New York: Russell Sage, 2002).

[11]See Denton R. Vaughan, "Exploring the Use of the Public's Views to Set Income Poverty Thresholds and Adjust Them over Time," *Social Security Bulletin* (Summer 1993), pp. 22–46. For a longer-run view of budget standards, see David Johnson, John M. Rogers, and Lucilla Tan, "A Century of Family Budgets in the United States," *Monthly Labor Review* (May 2001), pp. 28–45.

[12]Conversation quoted in Robert Hunter, *Poverty* (New York: Macmillan, 1904), p. 1. This same emphasis on psychological insecurity is expressed by poor people around the world; see World Bank, *World Development Report 2000/2001* (Washington, DC: World Bank, 2001), Chapter 1.

For children growing up in poor families, the insecurities and deprivations of inadequate income can constrain their development in both physical and psychological ways. They have less access to health care, nutrition, education, and stability.[13] Poverty then becomes much more than a *budgeting* problem; it becomes a determinant of life chances.

Cultural Context

Let us then be clear about what the official poverty index implies. The line we have drawn separating the poor from the nonpoor does not indicate what is enough—it only expresses a common and contemporary view of what is too little. As Hunter observed in 1904, "to live up to the standard . . . means no more than to have a sanitary dwelling and sufficient food and clothing to keep the body in working order."[14] But what is regarded as sufficient has changed dramatically since Hunter's time. The official U.S. poverty line embodies contemporary American living standards. Robert Rector of the Heritage Foundation points out that today's poverty thresholds allow a lifestyle equal to what the *average* American family had in the 1950s. And most people in developing nations around the world live on *far* less than U.S. poverty budgets. Indeed, even *homeless* people in America have incomes far in excess of world poverty standards.[15] So our official conception of poverty is inherently culture-bound, no matter how scientifically its "absolute" foundation was developed. All we can say with certainty is that those who fall below the line are unquestionably poor by contemporary American standards, even though they might appear well-off by historical or international standards. Moreover, many of those who have incomes above our standard cannot be regarded as rich or even as moderately well-off. While we will concentrate our discussion on those persons we have defined as poor, it is important to remember that there are a great many more people whose standard of living is only marginally higher than that of the poor (the "near poor").

THE NUMBER OF POOR PEOPLE

With the official poverty index, the task of counting the number of poor people is straightforward. The U.S. Bureau of the Census does a household survey every March. In that survey they ask people how much income they received in the previous year. By comparing the reported income with the poverty index, the Census Bureau determines who is poor and who is not.

When the Census Bureau first counted the number of poor people in 1963, it concluded that 36 million Americans—one out of every five people in the United States—were poor. The widespread poverty convinced Presidents Kennedy and Johnson to start a "war on poverty." As Michael Harrington observed at the time, the number of poor Americans was simply unconscionable.

---

[13]For a discussion of poverty-related disparities in children's well-being, see Guy Stevens, "Welfare Reform and the Well-Being of America's Children," *Challenge* (January–February 2002), pp. 6–46.

[14]Hunter, op. cit., p. 7.

[15]For details on the homeless population, see U.S. Department of Housing and Urban Development, *Homeless Programs and the People They Serve* (Washington, DC: Government Printing Office, 1999).

THE OFFICIAL POVERTY COUNT

Figure 3.3 updates the poverty count. The top half of the figure shows the number of persons counted as poor each year. The poverty population shrank from 36 million in 1963, when the War on Poverty began, to a low of 23 million in 1973. After that, the number of poor people started increasing again. By 1993, the poverty population was at a new high (39.3 million). Poverty then started receding again, dropping to 31.6 million

FIGURE 3.3 The Official Poverty Count

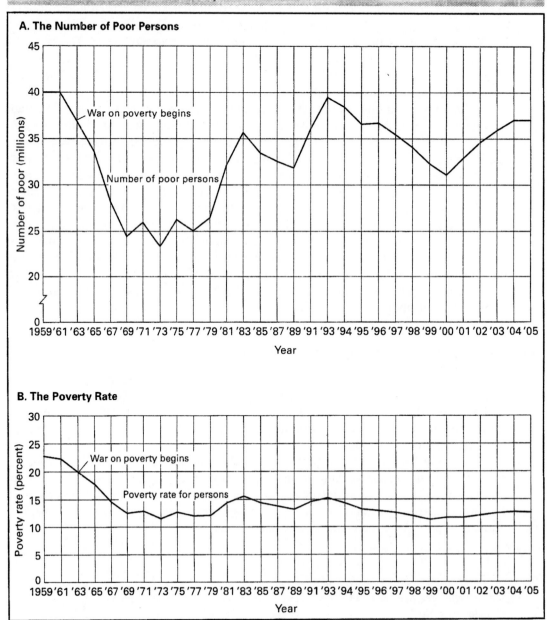

A. The Number of Poor Persons

B. The Poverty Rate

Source: U.S. Bureau of the Census.

in 2000. After that, the trend reversed again, with the poverty population increasing by 7 million people between 2000 and 2005.

THE POVERTY RATE

The increase in the size of the poverty population is hard to fathom, particularly in view of the growth of the American economy since 1963. Before examining that anomaly more closely, however, it will be helpful to put the raw numbers into context. Since 1963, the general U.S. population has increased by nearly 120 million persons. In view of this growth, changes in the *number* of poor persons are more appropriately gauged in percentage terms. The lower half of Figure 3.3 does this by illustrating the official poverty *rate*. In 1963, the poverty rate was just under 20 percent. The poverty rate fell to a low of 11.1 percent in 1973, then started rising again. Despite the growth in the poverty population from 1973 to 1993, however, the official poverty *rate* in 1993 (15.1%) was significantly below that of 1963 (19.5%). Even the growth of the poverty population after 2000 left the 2005 poverty rate far below the 1963 level. Hence, the *relative* decline in poverty paints a far more meaningful picture than the increase in the *absolute* size of the poverty population during those years.

HOW POOR?

The poverty count tells us how many people fall below the official poverty index but not *how far* below it they are. This is a critical issue. If most poor people were only a few dollars short of the poverty line, the poverty problem would be much less serious. If people have fallen far below the poverty line, however, it may take much more effort to pull them up.

The Poverty Gap

The aggregate poverty gap refers to the total amount of the income shortfall experienced by poor people. In 2005, the poverty gap amounted to $120 billion. Although huge in absolute terms, the aggregate poverty gap amounts to less than 1 percent of total U.S. income.

The aggregate poverty gap implies that the average poor person has an annual income that is roughly $3,200 below the official poverty threshold. There is great variation, however, in the size of that income deficit. The per capita income deficit is much larger for single-parent families headed by women ($2,600 per person) than for two-parent families ($2,000). It is larger still ($5,400) for the 10 million poor individuals who don't live with their families.[16]

MEASUREMENT PROBLEMS

Although both the size of the poverty population and the poverty rate have fallen sharply over the last forty years, one out of eight Americans is still officially counted as poor. Worse yet, the dimensions of the poverty gap imply that most of these people are *very* poor.

---

[16]For a measure of poverty that reflects the distribution of income deficits, see John L. Rodgers and Joan R. Rodgers, "Measuring the Intensity of Poverty among Subpopulations," *Journal of Human Resources* (Spring 1991), pp. 338–361. For historical trends, see Mark Littman, "Poverty in the 1980s: Are the Poor Getting Poorer?" *Monthly Labor Review* (June 1989), pp. 13–18.

Are so many Americans really so bad off? Many people question the validity of the pictures in Figure 3.3. They say the official poverty count is distorted by several flaws in the government's official measuring rod.

TOO LOW A STANDARD?

Liberal critics of the official poverty census say the government's count of the poor is too *low*. They emphasize that the basic poverty standard hasn't been updated in real (inflation-adjusted) terms since 1963. They see two problems with this. First, the absolute poverty line has fallen sharply in relative terms. In 1963, the four-person poverty line was 50 percent of the median family income. By 2005, it had fallen to 34 percent. So the poor had fallen yet further behind American living standards.

Liberals argue that it is not simply an issue of *relative* deprivation, but changing *absolute* needs as well. When poverty thresholds were developed in 1963, women were more likely to be married, at-home moms. Today, a lot of poor people live in single-parent homes. As a consequence, more families need child care and work expenses, neither of which was explicitly in the government's 1963 poverty standards. If allowance for these expenses were made in the official poverty lines, the poverty population would increase by 5 million people.[17]

Liberals also object to the continuing use of the 1963 "food multiplier." Recall that the official poverty line was based on a minimum food budget and the observation that people spent one-third of their income on food. Today, American households allocate less than one-fifth of their budgets to food purchases. Were the same methods used to construct poverty lines today, the food-cost multiplier would be five, not three. With that higher multiple, the 2005 four-person poverty threshold would be closer to $30,000 than to $20,000 and a lot more people would be regarded as poor.

Popular opinion on what constitutes an adequate income appears to reflect these concerns about the adequacy of the official poverty standard. In 1963, the prevailing view of the level of income that was adequate to "get along" was close to the official poverty line. Today, however, the public's view of minimum needs exceeds the official poverty line by a wide margin (see Figure 3.2).[18]

TOO HIGH A STANDARD?

Conservatives scoff at the notion that the government undercounts the poor. The reverse is true, they say. The official poverty count does not take all income into account and ignores completely a household's assets. The Census Bureau also relies on personal survey responses that may conceal some income. As a result, the official numbers vastly exaggerate the number of poor people and understate the achievements of the war on poverty. As far back as 1973, Professor Martin Anderson of Stanford's Hoover

---

[17]See Jared Bernstein and Arloc Sherman, "Poor Measurement" (Washington, DC: Employment Policy Institute, Issue Paper, March 2006). Specific budgets and poverty rates for single-parent families are estimated in Trudi J. Renwick and Barbara R. Bergmann, "A Budget-Based Definition of Poverty," *Journal of Human Resources* (Winter 1993), pp. 1–24. See also U. S. Census Bureau, *Experimental Poverty Measures: 1990–1997* (Washington, DC: Government Printing Office, 1999).

[18]An historical comparison of official and popular poverty standards is provided in Denton R. Vaughan, "Exploring the Use of the Public's Views to Set Income Poverty Thresholds and Adjust Them over Time," *Social Security Bulletin* (Summer 1993), pp. 22–46. Alternative measures of income inadequacy are discussed in Garth Mangum, Andrew Sum, and Neeta Fogg, "Poverty Ain't What It Used to Be," *Challenge* (March–April 2000), pp. 97–130.

Institution asserted, "The war on poverty has been won, except for perhaps a few mopping up operations."[19] According to his reading of the data, there were only a few million people still poor in America ten years after the official poverty counts began. Robert Rector of the Heritage Foundation echoes that appraisal today, claiming that the extent of poverty is only a small fraction of the government's official count.

IN-KIND INCOME

The major deficiency of official poverty statistics is that they count only a family's *cash* income. Yet all families receive some "in-kind" income. Most low-income families, for example, receive food stamps, Medicaid, Medicare, or subsidized housing. Instead of giving poor families the cash needed to buy groceries, health care, or housing, the government provides these goods directly. As a result, low-income families don't need as much cash income to maintain a given standard of living; in-kind transfers substitute for cash income.

The in-kind income offered to low-income families can be substantial. A family of four can get food stamps worth nearly $3,000 a year and housing subsidies of similar size. Medicaid can eliminate another major cash expense. Hence, a family with $19,000 of *cash* income might actually have a *total* income far above the official poverty line ($19,971 in 2005). However, the Census Bureau ignores the in-kind income and includes such a family in its poverty count. In FY 2005, the federal government paid out a total of $33 billion in food stamps, $182 billion in Medicaid benefits, and $38 billion in housing subsidies. Hence, the value of just these three in-kind programs was two times larger than the (cash) poverty gap ($120 billion) in official poverty statistics.

How much poverty is eliminated by these in-kind transfers depends on how they are distributed. Figure 3.4 indicates how serious the neglect of in-kind income might be. Nearly 60 percent of the female-headed families officially classified as poor on the basis of their cash income get food stamps. Thirty percent of these same families get housing assistance, and over two-thirds use Medicaid to pay doctor bills. The value of these in-kind

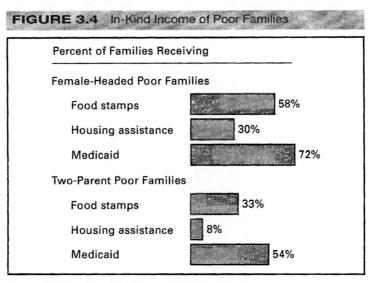

FIGURE 3.4 In-Kind Income of Poor Families

Percent of Families Receiving

Female-Headed Poor Families

Food stamps — 58%

Housing assistance — 30%

Medicaid — 72%

Two-Parent Poor Families

Food stamps — 33%

Housing assistance — 8%

Medicaid — 54%

Source: U.S. Bureau of the Census (2005 data).

---

[19]Martin Anderson, *Welfare* (Stanford, CA: Hoover Institution Press, 1975), p. 37.

TABLE 3.5 Alternative Poverty Counts

Income Counted	Number of Poor Persons	Poverty Rate
1. Market income (no taxes or transfers)	56.4 million	19.4%
2. Money income (including cash transfers)	36.6 million	12.6%
3. Disposable income (including noncash transfers, taxes, rental value of own home)	30.2 million	10.4%

Source: U.S. Census Bureau, "The Effects of Government Taxes and Transfers on Income and Poverty," February 2006.

benefits raises the living standard of these families nearly 50 percent above the level of their cash income. Two-parent poor families get a similar boost from in-kind benefits.

The poverty count would clearly be quite different if both cash and in-kind incomes were taken into account. Table 3.5 illustrates how great a difference a fuller accounting of real income might make. We start with "Market" incomes, which counts all income from market activities and excludes all government taxes and transfers. Absent government redistributions, more than 19 percent of the U.S. population would be poor.

The second line in Table 3.5 shows how much government cash transfers reduce poverty. Largely because of Social Security benefits, the "Money" income rate of poverty drops to 12.6 percent. This is the official poverty rate.

The third line in Table 3.5 incorporates *non*cash government transfers (food stamps, housing subsidies) and taxes (including the earned income tax credit that *pays* poor people who work). As a result of these additional transfers, over 6 million people officially counted as poor in 2004 would have been classified as nonpoor with a more complete accounting of their income.[20] This would have dropped the poverty rate down to 10.4 percent.

The neglect of in-kind transfers in official poverty counts distorts not only the size of the true poverty population but also trends in poverty rates. The major in-kind transfer programs were first created in the mid-1960s. By 1968, in-kind benefits accounted for 55 percent of welfare transfers. They continued to grow enormously in scope and benefits throughout the 1970s. By 2001, in-kind transfers accounted for 75 percent of all welfare benefits. Accordingly, the distortion in the poverty count originating from in-kind benefits has grown over time.[21] This growing distortion has given an upward bias to the trend in poverty rates (Figure 3.3B).

Valuation Problems
Although it is evident that the official poverty counts are exaggerated by the neglect of in-kind transfers, the corrected estimates are subject to criticism as well. Not all in-kind transfers represent an improved standard of living. The amount of medical assistance a person receives, for example, depends on how sick one is. Accordingly, it isn't appropriate

---

[20]The effects of an array of in-kind and tax benefits on the size and composition of the poverty population are detailed in John Iceland et al., "Are Children Worse Off? Evaluating Well-Being Using a New (and Improved) Measure of Poverty," *Journal of Human Resources* (Spring 2001).

[21]The availability of in-kind transfers, savings, and owner-occupied housing help explain why consumption-based measures of poverty indicate more poverty reduction than income-based measures; see D. T. Slesnick, "Gaining Ground: Poverty in the Postwar United States," *Journal of Political Economy* (February 1993), pp. 1–38.

to regard a person as nonpoor just because he or she receives a lot of in-kind medical assistance (Medicaid or Medicare).[22]

There is also a problem in assigning dollar values to in-kind benefits. Is a dollar's worth of food stamps really the equivalent of a dollar bill? Food stamps aren't accepted everywhere and can only be used to purchase food. There's also a stigma attached to using food stamps. Hence, a dollar bill is more highly valued than a dollar's worth of food stamps. If food stamps are to be counted as income, they should be discounted to reflect their lesser worth.

The same kind of problem affects housing subsidies. The government may spend $800 a month on a public housing apartment. The tenant might be able to find better housing, however, if provided with only $700 in cash. What is the in-kind assistance worth: $800 or $700? These kinds of valuation problems limit the Census Bureau's ability to include in-kind transfers in its official poverty count.

UNDERREPORTING

The official poverty count is also distorted by underreporting of income. The tendency of survey respondents to underreport their incomes has been documented repeatedly. People may fail to disclose all their income because some of it comes from illegal sources; because they fear higher taxes or welfare reductions; or because they simply forget infrequent payments (e.g., casual labor, child support, dividends, and interest).[23] According to a 1992 University of Michigan study, $2,000 of income per person goes unreported in the United States. Poor people may be particularly prone to underreporting. According to some estimates, poor families *spend* more than *twice* as much income as they report *receiving*. Moreover, the gap between expenditures and reported income continues to widen.[24] To the extent that poor people engage in such underreporting, their poverty is substantially exaggerated in official accounts.[25]

---

[22]Taking explicit account of medical expenses significantly alters the level and composition of poverty; see Kathleen Short and Thesia Garner, "Experimental Poverty Measures: Medical Expenses," *Monthly Labor Review 125*:8 (August 2002), pp. 3–13; and Gary Burtless and Sarah Siegel, "Medical Spending, Health Insurance, and Measurement of American Poverty" (Madison, WI: Institute for Research on Poverty, 2001).

[23]The concealment of child support among low-income mothers is documented in Kathryn Edin and Laura Lein, *Making Ends Meet: How Single Mothers Survive Welfare and Low-Wage Work* (New York: Russell Sage, 1997).

[24]Bruce Meyer and James Sullivan, "Measuring the Well-Being of the Poor Using Income and Consumption," *Journal of Human Resources 38* (2003), pp. 1180–1220; also Susan E. Mayer and Christopher Jencks, "Recent Trends in Economic Inequality in the United States: Income versus Expenditures versus Material Well-Being," in *Poverty and Prosperity in the U.S.A. in the Late Twentieth Century,* eds. Dimitri B. Papadimitriou and Edward N. Wolff (New York: St. Martin's Press, 1993), pp. 132–136. A more general exploration of survey measurement error is contained in John Bound, Charles Brown, Greg J. Duncan, and Willard Rodgers, "Evidence on the Validity of Cross-Sectional and Longitudinal Labor Market Data," *Journal of Labor Economics* (July 1994), pp. 345–368.

[25]For data on actual expenditures and assets of poor and nonpoor families, see Rector et al., "The Extent of Material Hardships," op. cit., and Maya Federman et al., "What Does It Mean to Be Poor in America?" *Monthly Labor Review* (May 1996), pp. 3–17. For illustrations of how measured poverty rates and trends change when consumption-based (rather than income-based) yardsticks are used, see Thesia Garner and Kathleen Short, "Economic Well-Being Based on Income, Consumer Expenditures, and Personal Assessments of Minimum Needs," (U.S. Bureau of Labor Statistics, Working Paper 381, March 2005); Dale W. Jorgenson, "Did We Lose the War on Poverty?" and Robert K. Triest, "Has Poverty Gotten Worse?" both in *Journal of Economic Perspectives* (Winter 1998).

TABLE 3.6 Ownership of Consumer Goods

Item Owned	All Households (percent)	Poor Households (percent)
Home	65.0	45.9
Car or truck	85.7	72.8
Two or more vehicles	61.9	30.2
Refrigerator	99.2	98.4
Clothes washer	80.0	64.7
Clothes dryer	77.1	55.6
Telephone	93.7	86.8
Air conditioning	75.4	76.6
Dish washer	58.1	33.9
Garbage disposal	47.0	29.3
Microwave oven	93.2	75.2
Color television	98.2	97.5
Two or more color TVs	66.9	55.3
Stereo equipment	72.5	50.6
Personal computer	59.3	24.6

Source: Robert Rector, and Kirk Johnson, "Understanding Poverty in America" (Washington, DC: Heritage Foundation, January 2004), also U.S. Census Bureau, *Supplemental Measures of Material Well-Being.* December 2005.

Consumer Assets

Further evidence on the gap between reported income and spending levels is found in the array of consumer goods "poor" households own. As Table 3.6 shows, over 45 percent of poor households own their home. Nearly 73 percent own at least one car or truck, 30 percent own at least *two* vehicles. Although there are notable differences between poor and nonpoor households in the ownership of consumer goods, it is also evident that officially designated poverty isn't synonymous with material deprivation.

INCOME MOBILITY

A third criticism of the official poverty count is that its time horizon is too short. Consider these two possibilities. The first family enjoys a middle-class lifestyle throughout the year. But the family head was laid off from work for three months due to a back injury and yearly income fell by 25 percent. The temporary loss of a paycheck lowered the family's current income below the poverty threshold for the year. By drawing on savings and credit, however, the family was able to maintain its middle-class lifestyle. After the injury healed, the family's income recovered as well.

Should this family be counted as poor? The 25 percent drop in income was clearly a temporary setback. The same kinds of transitory earnings losses occur when plants close, people move, or the economy falters. These transitory events cause some family incomes to dip below the poverty standard. If income recovers quickly, though, there is likely to be little change in living standards. Consumption levels may be maintained by using accumulated savings or by borrowing. Even if living standards do drop briefly, the exposure to poverty may be very limited. Should the census of poverty be restricted to those who are poor *throughout* the year or should it include everyone who experiences even a temporary episode of poverty? The official Census survey counts everyone with low *annual* income and, therefore, includes many families whose permanent income and lifestyle exceed poverty standards. In reality, three out of five families that fall into poverty in one year are out of poverty in the following year.[26] As we observed in Chapter 2, this kind of *income mobility*—year-to-year variations in income—is common among poor and nonpoor families alike.

In fact, longitudinal studies reveal that persistent poverty is rare among U.S. households. University of Michigan Professor Rebecca Blank studied the income mobility of U.S. households over a 13-year period (1979–1991). She discovered that one out of three households experienced poverty in at least one year. But only one out of 20 families was poor in at least ten years, and only one out of 60 was poor in all 13 years.[27] A similar observation was made for the years 1996—1999. During that four-year period, a lot of people *experienced* poverty, as the "episodic" rates in Figure 3.5 reveal. But "chronic" poverty was rare: only about 2 percent of the U.S. population was continuously poor during that period. Hence, *permanent* poverty is far less frequent than *transitory* poverty.

THE UNCOUNTED POOR

Although in-kind benefits, underreporting, and income mobility all imply that the official poverty count is too high, there are other reasons for thinking it might be too low. The most obvious reason is that the Census Bureau doesn't count everyone. The Census surveys are directed at *households* and so fail to identify or include people without a fixed address. This means that the entire *homeless* population is excluded from annual surveys.[28] Hence, some of the lowest-income individuals are left out of the poverty count.

Because the homeless aren't counted in household surveys, no one knows how many of them there are. Estimates range from several hundred thousand to as many as 3 million. Christopher Jencks estimates that the homeless population peaked at around 400,000 in 1988.[29] Virtually all of these homeless individuals are destitute and thus properly should be included in a full count of the poor. Adding them wouldn't change the official poverty count (37 million) substantially, however.

---

[26]Peter Gottschalk, Sara McLanahan, and Gary Sandefur, "The Dynamics and Intergenerational Transmission of Poverty and Welfare Participation," in *Confronting Poverty,* eds. S. Danziger, G. Sandefur, and D. Weinberg (Cambridge, MA: Harvard University Press, 1994). As Ann Stevens points out, however, many families that leave poverty in one year *return* in a later year. Hence, *cumulative* poverty rates exceed *continuing* poverty rates. See Ann Huff Stevens, "Climbing Out of Poverty, Falling Back In," *Journal of Human Resources* (Summer 1999), pp. 557–588. A technique for isolating persistent poverty is proposed in Joan R. Rodgers and John L. Rodgers, "Chronic Poverty in the United States," *Journal of Human Resources* (Winter 1993), pp. 25–54.

[27]Rebecca Blank, *It Takes a Nation: A New Agenda for Fighting Poverty* (Princeton, NJ: Princeton University Press, 1997).

[28]An exception is that portion of the homeless population residing in permanent shelters.

[29]For a comprehensive profile of the homeless population, see U.S. Department of Housing and Urban Development, *Homeless Programs,* op. cit. For other descriptions of the homeless population, see Brendan O'Flaherty, *The Economics of Homelessness* (Cambridge, MA: Harvard University Press, 1996); Christopher Jencks, *The Homeless* (Cambridge, MA: Harvard University Press, 1994); Martha Burt, *Over the Edge: The Growth of Homelessness in the 1980s* (Washington, DC: Urban Institute, 1992); U.S. Conference of Mayors, *A Status Report on Hunger and Homelessness in America's Cities* (Washington, DC: U.S. Conference of Mayors, annual); and Ralph Nunez, *The New Poverty: Homeless Families in America* (New York: Plenum Publishing, 1996).

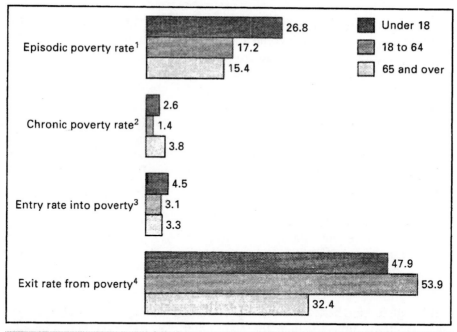

FIGURE 3.5   Permanent vs. Temporary Poverty

[1]Episodic poverty rate is the percent of people who were poor in 2 or more consecutive months in a given time period.

[2]Chronic poverty rate is the percent of people who were poor every month during 1996 to 1999.

[3]Entry rate into poverty is the percent who were not poor in 1996 but were in a subsequent year, using an annual poverty measure.

[4]Exit rate from poverty is the percent of people who were poor in 1996 but not in a subsequent year, using an annual poverty measure.

Note: The reference population for these data is the civilian noninstitutionalized population.

Source: U.S. Census Bureau, *65+ in the United States* (Washington, DC: Government Printing Office, December 2005), Figure 4-15.

The official poverty count excludes not only the homeless but also poor individuals who reside in institutions. An aged person who resides in a public hospital or nursing home is not in the Census survey. The household surveys also exclude prison inmates. Because poor people have higher rates of morbidity and incarceration, the omission of institutionalized persons from the Census survey may understate both the *number* of poor people and the poverty *rate*.[30]

Another group that Census surveys miss are those poor people who live with relatives. An aged person without adequate resources of his or her own may be compelled to live with relatives. If the living arrangement is dictated more by economic necessity than by familial affection, the element of free choice is compromised. Furthermore, the unwanted relative may not share equally in the household's income or wealth, as Census Bureau statistics would imply. In this case, the aged resident of the household may be living in disguised poverty.

---

[30]As much as one-third of the population over age 85—nearly 1 million individuals—lives in an institution; see Daniel B. Radner, "Economic Well-Being of the Old Old," *Social Security Bulletin* (Spring 1993), p. 4.

Professor Paul Leigh of San Jose State University has emphasized another downward bias in Census procedures. The Census Bureau surveys only *living* persons. This eminently practical approach would not seem to affect poverty statistics. Professor Leigh points out, however, that poor people tend to die at younger ages than nonpoor people.[31] Hence, the observed poverty *rate* is biased downward at older ages.

LATENT POVERTY

Besides failing to count many people who are manifestly poor, the Census Bureau also ignores those who are kept out of poverty only by government assistance. Remember that the official poverty count is based on the ratio of cash income to family needs, without regard to the source of the income. For many families, the most important sources of income are income transfers such as Social Security benefits, welfare checks, and unemployment benefits. Without these income transfers, people now counted as nonpoor would be classified as poor. As Table 3.5 documented, pure "market" incomes would leave 56.4 million Americans in poverty. Twenty million of these people escape poverty only with the help of government *cash* transfers (Social Security, unemployment benefits, etc.) and another 6 million stay above poverty thresholds with the help of government *non*cash transfers (food stamps, housing subsidies, etc.) Because these individuals are so dependent on income transfers rather than market incomes, they might also be included in a more complete enumeration of deprivation. Charles Murray has called these transfer-dependent individuals the *latent* poor; they would be poor in the absence of government help.[32]

ASSET POVERTY

It is also important to look at the wealth people hold. As Table 3.6 documented, income-poor households do own cars, TVs, appliances, and even homes. These assets clearly contribute to their living standards. But what if their *income* flow were disrupted? How long could poor and near-poor families survive if the income flow ceased (e.g., due to illness, disability, divorce, natural disaster). To get by without current income, people have to convert assets into cash. Used TVs and refrigerators don't count for much in that case, but savings accounts, stocks, and other investments do.

Caner and Wolff define "asset poverty" as having assets less in value than three months of a poverty income.[33] In other words, a household is "asset poor" if it can't cash in enough assets to cover a three-month shortfall in poverty-level income. These are families who are already in poverty or at great risk of falling into poverty in adverse conditions.

Asset poverty rates are *double* those of income poverty and higher still if only non-home assets are counted. Hence, the poverty-vulnerable population is much larger than the official (income) poverty population.

---

[31]J. Paul Leigh, "Distribution of Lifetime Income Allowing for Varying Mortality Rates among Women, Men, Blacks and Whites," *Journal of Economic Issues* (December 1992), pp. 1191–1220. See also Orazio P. Attanasio and Hillary Hoynes, "Differential Mortality and Wealth Accumulation," *Journal of Human Resources* (Winter 2000), pp. 1–29.

[32]For the antipoverty impact of specific in-kind transfers, see John Iceland and Josh Kim. "Poverty among Working Families," *Social Science Quarterly* (June 2001), pp. 253–267.

[33]Asena Canes and Edward Wolff, *Asset Poverty in the United States* (New York: Levy Economics Institute, 2004).

THE CALL FOR REVISION

It is evident that the official poverty lines do not command universal acceptance. On the contrary, both liberals and conservatives are dissatisfied with official standards and urge major changes. To address these concerns, the National Academy of Sciences undertook a comprehensive review of the official poverty thresholds. After two and a half years of study, the Academy panel concluded in late 1994 that major changes were needed in the official poverty standards and offered a variety of recommendations for that revision. Most notable were the need to include in-kind transfers and allow for child care expenses. Five years later, the U.S. Census Bureau issued a report showing how the level and distribution of measured poverty is affected by diverse changes in the official yardstick. As expected, many changes demanded by conservatives decreased measured poverty rates, while changes demanded by liberals increased measured poverty. The Census Bureau also demonstrated, however, that measured *trends* in poverty in the 1990s were little affected by the choice of yardstick.[34]

CHARACTERISTICS OF THE POOR

While the debate over the official poverty line continues, the need for statistics on the poverty population persists. Our ability and even our willingness to develop antipoverty policies are dependent on some sense of who the poor are and their numbers. Although poverty profiles are dependent on the poverty standards employed, we need a common starting point for empirical analysis. The official poverty index provides that foundation. It has the advantages not only of familiarity but also accessibility, since virtually all government data on poverty are based on the official index.

In some countries, poverty is so pervasive that profiles of the poor are largely unnecessary. In the United States, however, poverty is an affliction of a minority of the population. Accordingly, middle-class people may have relatively little contact with the poor. As a consequence, perceptions of who is poor are likely to rely on chance observations and unfounded stereotypes. This is an inadequate basis for public policy.

To formulate intelligent policies to combat poverty, we need to know not only how many persons are poor but also whether they are young or old, infirm or employed, and whether they live in Abbeville, Louisiana, or Littleton, Colorado.

A complete statistical profile of the poor would demand considerable effort and patience. In addition, such an array of statistics might smother any meaning the numbers might possess. Therefore, we will examine the composition of the poverty population only as it relates to three major characteristics: age and family status; geography and residence; and labor force status. We will observe also the racial makeup within each category.

AGE AND FAMILY STATUS

Table 3.7 provides a brief profile of the poverty population. Notice in particular the striking differences between the number of people and poverty rates among demographic subgroups. For example, there are a great many more poor whites (16 million)

---

[34]For a fuller discussion, see U.S. Bureau of the Census, *Experimental Poverty Measures: 1990–1997* (Washington, DC: Government Printing Office, June 1999), and Kathleen Short and John Iceland, "Who Is Better Off Than We Thought? Evaluating Poverty with a Different Measure," *American Economic Review* (May 2000). Each year, the Census Bureau now publishes both official and experimental poverty statistics.

TABLE 3.7 The Poverty Population, 2005

Group	U.S. Population	Poor	Poverty Rate (percent)
All persons	293,135,000	36,950,000	12.6
Race			
White	195,553,000	16,227,000	8.3
Black	36,802,000	9,168,000	24.9
Hispanic	43,020,000	9,368,000	21.8
Asian	12,580,000	1,402,000	11.1
Family type*			
Two-parent	113,890,000	8,424,000	7.4
Single-parent			
Male	7,916,000	1,435,000	18.1
Female	30,893,000	11,750,000	38.0
Age			
Over 65	35,505,000	3,605,000	10.1
Under 18	73,285,000	12,896,000	17.5
Nativity			
Native born	256,860,000	31,030,000	12.1
Naturalized citizen	13,856,000	1,441,000	10.4
Not a citizen	21,710,000	4,429,000	20.4

*People in families with children under 18.

Source: U.S. Bureau of the Census.

than poor blacks (9 million). But the poverty *rate* among blacks (24.9 percent) is three times higher than among whites (8.3 percent). The same kinds of differences in poverty numbers and rates are evident for Hispanics. Accordingly, we may say that blacks and Hispanics face a far greater likelihood of being poor, although they still comprise a minority of the poor. Persons of Asian extraction have a poverty rate (11.1 percent) much closer to that of whites.

Single Parents

Another striking disparity in poverty rates exists between two-parent and single-parent families. The incidence of poverty in single-parent families is far higher than in two-parent families. The incidence of poverty is particularly high (38 percent) in families where the single parent is female.

Since the 1970s, the number of female-headed households in the United States has increased greatly. This growth in the number of female-headed families, together with the high poverty rate of such families, led to an increasing feminization of poverty. In 1963 only one out of four poor people lived in female-headed households. Today, one out of three poor people reside in female-headed families.

Age

Table 3.7 also indicates that poverty is far more prevalent among the young than the old. While one out of ten older persons lives in poverty, one out of six children is so impoverished. Children alone comprise almost 35 percent of all poor persons in the United States. We might well reflect on how equitable such a distribution of poverty is and what kind of preparation for adulthood an impoverished childhood provides. Will poor children become poor adults? If so, we may confidently predict that poverty has a great future in this country.

Immigrants

Table 3.7 also shows that recent immigrants experience twice as much poverty as native-born Americans. The individuals classified in Table 3.7 as "not a citizen" are mostly recent immigrants who have not yet applied for or been granted U.S. citizenship. For the most part they are likely to be legal (documented) immigrants, since illegal immigrants are rarely counted in Census surveys. Those immigrants who have been in the United States long enough to gain citizenship actually have a *lower* poverty rate than native-born Americans.[35]

GEOGRAPHY AND RESIDENCE

In an increasingly urban nation, it is not surprising to find a high proportion of poor families in metropolitan areas.[36] Seventy-five percent of the poor population lives in metropolitan areas, most of them in the central city. In general, the residential distribution of poor families resembles the residential distribution of all families. However, there does exist a tendency for the poor to be overrepresented in large central cities and in rural areas and underrepresented in suburban communities.

The racial distribution of poverty among metropolitan and nonmetropolitan areas is very similar; that is, poor whites are just as likely as poor blacks to reside in metropolitan locations. However, a marked racial difference is apparent within metropolitan areas. While poor whites are likely to be found in either central cities or suburban communities, poor blacks and Hispanics are much more concentrated in the cities. It is important to note, though, that the high number of poor minorities in central cities is a result of the greater degree of urbanization among the minority populations rather than a higher likelihood of poverty in the cities. Indeed, black or Hispanic people in a rural area are more likely to be poor than their counterparts in an urban metropolis.

Nonmetropolitan areas include smaller cities, rural communities, and farms. While nearly one-fourth of all the poor live in such localities, very few poor persons actually live on farms. Farm poverty is a serious problem in the sense that the incidence of poverty among black and Hispanic farmers is very high (34 percent for blacks and 47 percent for Hispanics). Because the entire U.S. farming population is relatively small, however, poor farmers constitute only 2 percent of all the poor. Here again we must distinguish between the incidence of poverty among a particular group and the prevalence of that group within the entire poverty population.

Because the economic resources and social conditions of different regions in the United States vary tremendously, it is important to know the geographic location of the poor. Slower economic growth or less opportunity in a region is likely to create a regional concentration of poor families and require special programs. Were the poor all concentrated in Appalachia, for example, targeted antipoverty policies would be appropriate.

---

[35]Jeff Chapman and Jared Bernstein, "Immigration and Poverty: How Are They Linked?" *Monthly Labor Review* (April 2003). For a comparative analysis of the characteristics and work patterns of immigrant women, see George Vernez, *Immigrant Women in the U.S. Labor Force* (Lanham, MD: Lexington Books, 1999); see also the symposium on "Immigrants and Refugees" in *Social Science Quarterly* (June 1997).

[36]The term *metropolitan* essentially refers to cities of at least 50,000 and their surrounding communities.

TABLE 3.8 Regional Distribution of the Poor

Region	Number of Poor Persons (thousands)	Poverty Rate (percent)			
		Total	White	Black	Hispanic
Northeast	6,103	11.3	5.3	22.3	20.9
Midwest	7,419	11.4	6.0	29.4	19.6
South	14,854	14.0	6.8	22.8	20.9
West	8,523	12.6	5.4	21.6	20.5

Source: U.S. Bureau of the Census (2005 data).

It is apparent from Table 3.8 that the South contains the largest number of poor persons.[37] Less than a third of the total U.S. population lives in the South, but over 40 percent of the poor reside there. This excess of poverty results not only from a high concentration of minority households in the South but also from the fact that the South is simply poorer and less urban than any other region.[38] A southern resident, regardless of race, is more likely to be poor than his or her northern counterpart. In both the North and the South a black or Hispanic person is two to three times as likely to be poor as a white person.

LABOR FORCE STATUS

The geographic and family characteristics of the poor are important considerations in the formulation of antipoverty policies. Their primary value, however, is to identify the potential of the poor to participate in national employment and income-generating patterns. In a market economy the relationship of individuals or their families to the labor market is the prime determinant of their income. Furthermore, society's willingness to provide for the poor is materially affected by whether the poor are thought to work—or at least to seek work. Accordingly, the last characteristic we observe is the labor force status of the poor.

To be "in the labor force" signifies that a person is either employed or actively seeking employment (unemployed). Also included in this category are persons who are temporarily not working because of illness, bad weather, vacation, or a labor–management dispute. All these people are regarded as idle only momentarily, with visible prospects of returning to work. Their regular work may be full-time or part-time (less than 35 hours per week), and it must be monetarily compensated. Volunteer work is regarded as activity outside the labor force.

Being "out of the labor force" means essentially that a person does not fall into one of the foregoing categories. These persons are keeping house; attending school; unable to work because of age or disability; or, if otherwise able to work, are not actively seeking employment. The inactivity of the last group may result from a desire for leisure or the fact that employment prospects are too dim to merit job hunting.

[37]The Census Bureau includes the following states in its definition of the South: Alabama, Arkansas, Delaware, District of Columbia, Florida, Georgia, Kentucky, Louisiana, Mississippi, Maryland, North Carolina, Oklahoma, South Carolina, Tennessee, Texas, Virginia, West Virginia.

[38]The official poverty index ignores regional differences in the cost of living. Since costs are lower in the South, measured poverty may be exaggerated. See National Academy of Sciences, *Measuring Poverty: A New Approach* (Washington, DC: National Academy Press, 1994).

TABLE 3.9 Work Experience of Family Head

Families	Percent Who Worked During the Year	
	Poor	Nonpoor
Two-parent families		
White	46	85
Black	43	85
Hispanic	61	84
Female-headed families		
White	56	90
Black	52	89
Hispanic	51	86

Source: U.S. Bureau of the Census. (2005 data for family heads under age 65.)

It is widely believed that the poor are essentially a lazy lot. While we examine this contention in considerable detail in later chapters, Table 3.9 provides a preliminary perspective on the employment behavior of the poor. This table indicates what percentage of poor family heads worked at some time during the year.

The right column of the table confirms that working is what keeps most families out of poverty. Virtually all nonpoor householders (family heads) work at least part of the year. This is as true for single-parent families as for two-parent families, and for all ethnic/race groups. Simply put, virtually every nonpoor family has at least one working member.

Work experience is decidedly less common in poor families: Only 1 out of 2 poor family heads works at all during the year. Differences among poor families (e.g., by race or family type) are small, especially in comparison to differences across poor/ nonpoor families.

Table 3.9 raises two core questions about the relationship between work and poverty, namely: (1) Why are *any* people who work poor? (2) Why don't poor families work more? We'll explore these questions in later chapters.

SIMILARITIES AND DIFFERENCES

The statistical profiles of the preceding sections are not intended to dull one's senses nor to obscure the many problems of the poor. Rather, they are offered as a backdrop to the analytical discussions that follow in later chapters. If any general impressions are possible, we might say that the statistical profiles of the poor are not markedly different from those of the rest of the population. For the most part, the poor population is a little younger, more southern, more often black or Hispanic, and less attached to the labor force than is the rest of society. Nevertheless, the poor, like the larger society, consist primarily of whites, of younger families with children, of urban dwellers, and of labor force participants. There do exist important distinguishing demographic characteristics, but they must not be allowed to conceal the basic similarities between the poor and nonpoor populations.

The demographic characteristics we have reviewed here by no means provide a complete description of the poor. Among the more obvious omissions in our profile are education, family size, and health. These characteristics are discussed in later chapters, where a more complete examination of the traits previously described is also found.

But our profiles are incomplete in other important ways. We deal in this book almost exclusively with measurable, or at least observable, phenomena. Thus, we may report how old, white, or employed the poor are, or whether they live in cities or suburbs. What we are unable to do is relate how oppressed, politically isolated, or hostile the poor may be. In *The Other America*, Michael Harrington argued that today's poor are "more isolated and politically powerless than ever before." Those characteristics are difficult to measure. Moreover, no matter how completely we describe the *characteristics* of the poor, we cannot fully assess *causation* in this way. Knowing that the poor work less than the nonpoor, for example, doesn't inform us whether Flawed Character, Restricted Opportunity, or Big Brother caused the difference in work behavior. The critical questions of causality are pursued in subsequent chapters.

Summary

Incomes are distributed so unevenly that the top quintile (fifth) of all families has ten times as much income as the lowest quintile. Poverty is not officially defined in relative terms, however; an absolute standard of minimum needs is used. According to that standard, 37 million Americans are classified as poor.

The official poverty count is exaggerated by the neglect of in-kind income transfers (e.g., food stamps) and underreporting of income. The poverty statistics also include many people who experience only brief income losses and otherwise enjoy higher standards of living. A high degree of income mobility results in very few households being persistently poor.

There are also downward biases in the official poverty count. The homeless population, people in institutions, and people living together out of economic necessity are not counted. In addition, there are millions of latent poor people who are kept out of poverty only by government assistance. Finally, if the poverty index itself were updated to today's living standards and family circumstances, many more individuals would be counted as poor.

The official poverty population is a bit younger than a cross section of America and includes higher proportions of minority and single-parent families. Poor families also have substantially less work experience than the nonpoor.

Further Reading

Canes, Asena and Edward N. Wolff, *Asset Poverty in the United States.* New York: Levy Economics Institute, 2004.

Danziger, Sheldon, and Robert Haveman, eds., *Understanding Poverty: Progress and Prospects.* Cambridge, MA: Harvard University Press, 2001.

Eberstadt, Nicholas, "Mismeasure of Poverty," *Policy Review* (August-September 2006).

Fisher, G. M., "The Development and History of the Poverty Thresholds," *Social Security Bulletin* (Winter 1992), pp. 3–14.

Iceland, John and Josh Kim, "Poverty among Working Families: New Insights from an Improved Poverty Measure," *Social Science Quarterly* (June 2001), pp. 253–267.

Mangum, Garth, Andrew Sum, and Neeta Fogg, "Poverty Ain't What It Used to Be," *Challenge* (March–April 2000), pp. 97–130.

Meyer, Bruce D. and James X. Sullivan, "Three-Decades of Consumption and Income Poverty," University of Michigan, National Poverty Center Working Paper pp. 6–35, September 2006.

National Academy of Sciences, *Measuring Poverty: A New Approach*. Washington, DC: National Academy Press, 1995.

Roleff, Tamara, ed., *Inner-City Poverty*. Farmington Hills, MI: Greenhaven Press, 2003.

U.S. Bureau of the Census, *Experimental Poverty Measures, 1990–1997*. Washington, DC: U.S. Government Printing Office, 1999.

——, *Poverty in the United States,* Series P60. Washington, DC: U.S. Government Printing Office, annual.

Web Links

U.S. Bureau of Labor Statistics and U.S. Bureau of the Census. Annual data on income and poverty:
http://www.ferret.bls.census.gov/macro

U.S. Bureau of the Census. (1) Annual data on the size and characteristics of the poverty population:
http://www.census.gov/hhes/www/poverty.html

(2) Annual data on household incomes:
http://www.census.gov/hhes/www/income.html

(3) Experimental poverty measures:
http://www.census.gov/hhes/www/povmeas.html

U.S. Conference of Mayors. Annual Survey of homeless population:
www.usmayors.org

CHAPTER 4
GLOBAL POVERTY AND INEQUALITY

~

However we might define "poverty" in the United States, most of the world's inhabitants would still envy America's "poor" population. Over half the world's population has an income below America's official poverty standard. They can't even begin to fathom how rich Americans are—or why "poverty" is still a front-page issue in the United States. All they see (usually via television in a retail store) is that Americans have far more goods and services than global poor households can even imagine. Even the poorest Americans seem to have roofs over their heads, plenty to eat, indoor toilets, safe water, a car, and access to schools, hospitals, and entertainment. How could anyone with so much, they wonder, consider themselves "poor"?

This chapter takes an international detour to survey global poverty. What does it mean to be "poor" in the rest of the world? How much inequality exists in other nations? What hope do global poor households have for escaping poverty?

GLOBAL POVERTY THRESHOLDS

The *average* per capita income outside of the "high income" developed nations is roughly $5,000 per year. So defining global poverty in the context of U.S. standards would classify most people in the developing world as poor. Yet, there are great differences between the haves and have-nots even in nations that are generally "low income." Those at the bottom of the income ladder are often struggling for basic sustenance, while those at the top enjoy an array of goods and services—sometimes even a swath of luxury.

NATIONAL POVERTY LINES

Like the United States, other nations often develop their own poverty thresholds. These indices, like the official U.S. poverty line, reflect national judgments about what constitutes minimum acceptable living standards. As you might expect, perspectives on poverty thresholds are strongly influenced by prevailing income levels. Just as the United States sets a relatively high threshold for "poverty," poor nations like Burundi, Ethiopia, Paraguay, and Bangladesh set the "minimum" standard of living so low that relatively few people are counted as "poor." Many nations don't even bother to construct poverty measures.

In nearly all cases, the national poverty lines are based on the "cost of basic needs" approach. As was the case in the development of the official U.S. poverty line, analysts seek to determine the cost of acquiring a minimally acceptable diet. They then look to see what percentage of their budget people spend on food and derive an implied budget.

We have already seen how difficult it is to identify a minimally acceptable diet in a single nation. The concept becomes even more elusive in an international context. In the poorest countries a diet of starchy staples, a few beans, and maybe a few vegetables might seem minimally adequate. In richer countries, people will expect more variety, higher quality, and more produce in a minimally adequate diet. Here again, scientific judgments about minimal caloric intake don't suffice; cultural norms play a critical role in defining national poverty thresholds.

WORLD BANK THRESHOLDS

Because national poverty lines are so diverse and culture-bound, the World Bank decided to establish a uniform standard for assessing global poverty. And they set the bar amazingly low. In fact, the World Bank regularly uses two thresholds, namely, $1 per day for "extreme" poverty and a higher $2 per day standard for less severe poverty.

The World Bank thresholds are incomprehensively low by U.S. standards. How much could you buy for $1 a day? A little rice, maybe, and perhaps some milk? Certainly not a Big Mac. And part of that dollar has to go for rent. Clearly, this isn't going to work. Doubling the World Bank standard to $2 per day doesn't reach a whole lot further.

The World Bank, of course, wasn't defining "poverty" in the context of American affluence. They were instead trying to define a rock-bottom threshold of absolute poverty—a threshold of physical deprivation that everyone would acknowledge as the barest "minimum"—a condition of "unacceptable deprivation."

The World Bank relied on the nation-specific poverty lines to set this global standard. The official poverty lines in the world's twelve poorest countries were remarkably similar. So the World Bank computed an *average* threshold from these twelve national indices, using 1985 prices. This led them to select $370 per year as the "upper" poverty line and $275 as the "lower" poverty line. The upper line was so close to $365 that it became known as the "dollar-a-day" standard for "extreme" global poverty.[1]

INFLATION

The World Bank lines were established in the context of 1985 prices and translated into local currencies.[2] Like the U.S. poverty lines, the World Bank's global poverty lines are adjusted each year for inflation. They are also recalculated on occasion (e.g., in 1993) to reflect changing consumption patterns. In today's dollars, the "$1" standard of 1985 is actually about $1.50 per day in U.S. currency. That works out to $2,190 per year for a family of four—about a tenth of the official U.S. poverty threshold. In nations with higher inflation rates, the *nominal* value of the global poverty line has risen even faster, even though its *real* value has remained constant.[3] Nevertheless, the World Bank standard is still referred to as the "dollar-a-day" index of extreme poverty.

---

[1]See World Bank, *1990 World Development Report* (New York: Oxford University Press, 1990) for more detail.

[2]The World Bank uses "purchasing power parity" rather than market exchange rates to make this translation. Purchasing power parity focuses on the amount of national currency needed to buy basic goods and services in two different countries.

[3]For a methodological critique of the World Bank's poverty standard, see Thomas W. Pogge and Sanajy G. Reddy, "How Not to Count the Poor," *Economic and Political Weekly* (June 2006; also at www. socialanalysis.org).

GLOBAL POVERTY COUNTS

To compute the size of the global poverty population, the World Bank analyzes household surveys. Representative samples in more than 100 nations provide the data needed for the annual poverty count. Well over a million households have been surveyed, generating representative profiles for roughly 95 percent of the world's population.

Based on these surveys, *the World Bank classifies over a* billion *people as being in "extreme" poverty (<$1/day) and nearly 3 billion people as being in "severe" poverty (<$2/day).*

Table 4.1 shows where concentrations of extreme poverty are the greatest. Concentrations of extreme poverty are alarmingly high in dozens of smaller, less developed nations like Mali, Zambia, and Sierra Leone, where average incomes are also quite low. However, the greatest *number* of extremely poor people reside in the world's largest countries. China and India alone contain a third of the world's population and over half of the world's extreme poverty. In all these nations the extremely poor populations are overwhelmingly rural (70 percent) and engaged in subsistence agriculture.

Table 4.2 reveals that the distribution of "severe" poverty (<$2/day) is similar. The incidence of this higher poverty threshold is, of course, much greater. In three of

TABLE 4.1 Geography of Extreme Poverty

Country	Percent of Population in Extreme Poverty (<$1/day)	Number of People in Extreme Poverty (millions)
Zambia	76%	7
Mali	72%	9
Nigeria	71%	98
Madagascar	61%	10
Haiti	54%	10
Bangladesh	36%	50
India	35%	378
Bolivia	23%	2
China	17%	221
WORLD	21%	1,080

TABLE 4.2 Population in Poverty (<$2/day)		
Country	*Percent*	*Number (millions)*
Zambia	94	11
Nigeria	92	129
Mali	91	11
Burundi	88	6
Niger	86	10
Madagascar	85	14
Central African Republic	84	3
Rwanda	84	7
Haiti	83	7
Bangladesh	83	117
Nicaragua	80	4
India	80	864
Ethiopia	78	55
China	47	611
WORLD	**54**	**2,700**

Source: Adapted from the WORLD BANK DEVELOPMENT REPORT by WORLD BANK. Copyright 2006 by WORLD BANK. Reproduced with permission of WORLD BANK in the format Textbook via Copyright Clearance Center.

the nations depicted in Table 4.2 more than 90 percent of the population is in poverty. In another nine nations, the incidence of poverty exceeds 80 percent. By contrast, only 13 percent of the U.S. population falls below the official *American* poverty threshold and virtually no American household has an income below the *global* poverty threshold.

SOCIAL INDICATORS

The levels of poverty depicted in Tables 4.1 and 4.2 imply levels of physical and social deprivation few Americans can comprehend. Living on less than a dollar or two a day means always being hungry, malnourished, ill-clothed, dirty, and unhealthy. The problems associated with such deprivation begin at birth. In low-income countries only a third of all births are attended by a skilled health practitioner. If something goes awry, both the mother and the baby are at fatal risk. Nearly all of the children in global poverty are in a state of chronic malnutrition. At least one out of ten children in low-income nations will die before reaching age 5. In the poorest sectors of the population infant and child mortality rates are often two to three times higher than that. Children often remain unimmunized against preventable diseases. And AIDS is rampant among both children and adults in the poorest nations. All of these factors contribute to frighteningly low life expectancies. Whereas life expectancies at birth are 75–80 years in developed nations like the U.S., Europe, and Japan, life expectancy is only 40–50 years among the global poor.

Fewer than one out of two children from extremely poor households are likely to stay in school past the eighth grade. Women and minority ethnic and religious groups are often wholly excluded from educational opportunities. As a consequence, great stocks of human capital remain undeveloped: In low-income nations only one out of two women and only two out of three men are literate.

INEQUALITY

Not everyone in low-income countries lives in such deprived circumstances. Poor nations are not *uniformly* poor. On the contrary, an economic elite exists in even the poorest nations, enjoying lifestyles and privileges that even the American middle class might envy. Income *inequality* is in fact often greatest in the very poorest nations.

GINI COEFFICIENTS

We have used the Gini coefficient before (Chapter 2) to depict the degree of inequality in U.S. incomes and changes therein. Recall that the Gini ranges from 0 (complete equality) to 1.0 (extreme inequality). For the United States, the Gini was 0.469 in 2005.

As Table 4.3 reveals, inequalities were far greater in some of the world's poorest nations. In the tiny African nation of Namibia (made famous by the birth of Angelina Jolie and Brad Pitt's daughter in 2006), the Gini index is far higher (0.743) than in the United States (0.469), and the top echelon of Namibian society gets nearly two-thirds of all income generated in that nation (vs. less than one-third in the United States). Maternal and infant death rates in Namibia are among the world's highest, HIV is rampant, and life expectancy is a shockingly low 41 years. With two-thirds of that nation's income, however, the top-ranked Namibian households live quite comfortably.

INCOME SHARES

As Table 4.3 documents, the degree of inequality is also high in other poor countries. The richest *tenth* of the population typically gets 40–50 percent of all the income in the poorest nations. This *income* inequality translates into substantial social, educational, health, and political inequalities. In effect, a slew of "inequality traps" keeps the global poor households destitute and disenfranchised.

TABLE 4.3 Measures of Within-Nation Inequality

Country	Gini Index	Percent of Income Going to Top Decile
Namibia	.743	64.5
Lesotho	.632	48.3
Botswana	.630	56.6
Sierra Leone	.629	43.6
Central African Republic	.613	47.7
Swaziland	.609	50.2
Brazil	.580	45.8
Guatemala	.551	43.4
United States	.469	29.9
China	.447	33.1
India	.325	28.5

Source: WORLD DEVELOPMENT INDICATORS 2005 by WORLD BANK. Copyright 2005 by WORLD BANK. Reproduced with permission of WORLD BANK in the format Textbook via Copyright Clearance Center.

In its 2006 *World Development Report*, the World Bank synthesized the implications of all this within- and between-nation inequality for the life prospects of children:

> Consider two South African children born on the same day in 2000. Nthabiseng is black, born to a poor family in a rural area in the Eastern Cape province, about 700 kilometers from Cape Town. Her mother had no formal schooling. Pieter is white, born to a wealthy family in Cape Town. His mother completed a college education at the nearby prestigious Stellenbosch University.
>
> On the day of their birth, Nthabiseng and Pieter could hardly be held responsible for their family circumstances: their race, their parents' income and education, their urban or rural location, or indeed their sex. Yet statistics suggest that those predetermined background variables will make a major difference for the lives they lead. Nthabiseng has a 7.2 percent chance of dying in the first year of her life, more than twice Pieter's 3 percent. Pieter can look forward to 68 years of life, Nthabiseng to 50. Pieter can expect to complete 12 years of formal schooling, Nthabiseng less than 1 year. Nthabiseng is likely to be considerably poorer than Pieter throughout her life. Growing up, she is less likely to have access to clean water and sanitation, or to good schools. So the opportunity these two children face to reach their full human potential are vastly different from the outset, through no fault of their own.
>
> Such disparities in opportunity translate into different abilities to contribute to South Africa's development. Nthabiseng's health at birth may have been poorer, owing to the poorer nutrition of her mother during her pregnancy. By virtue of their gender socialization, their geographic location, and their access to schools, Pieter is much more likely to acquire an education that will enable him to put his innate talents to full use. Even if at age 25, and despite the odds, Nthabiseng manages to come up with a great business idea (such as an innovation to increase agricultural production), she would find it much harder to persuade a bank to lend her money at a reasonable interest rate. Pieter, having a similarly bright idea (say, on how to design an improved version of promising software), would likely find it easier to obtain credit, with both a college diploma and quite possibly some collateral. With the transition to democracy in South Africa, Nthabiseng is able to vote and thus indirectly shape the policy of her government, something denied to blacks under apartheid. But the legacy of apartheid's unequal opportunities and political power will remain for some time to come. It is a long road from such a (fundamental) political change to changes in economic and social conditions.
>
> As striking as the differences in life chances are between Pieter and Nthabiseng in South Africa, they are dwarfed by the disparities between average South Africans and citizens of more developed countries. Consider the cards dealt to Sven—born on the same day to an average Swedish household. His chances of dying in the first year of life are very small (0.3 percent) and he can expect to live to the age of 80, 12 years longer than Pieter, and 30 years more than Nthabiseng. He is likely to complete 11.4 years of schooling—5 years more than the average South African. These differences in the quantity of schooling are compounded by differences in quality: in the eighth grade, Sven can expect to attain a score of 500 on an internationally comparable

math test, while the average South African student will get a score of only 264—more than two standard deviations below the Organisation for Economic Cooperation and Development (OECD) median. Nthabiseng most likely will never reach that grade and so will not take the test.

These differences in life chances across nationality, race, gender, and social groups will strike many readers as fundamentally unfair. They are also likely to lead to wasted human potential and thus to missed development opportunities.

UNEQUAL WEALTH

Differences in wealth also create significant "inequality traps." In fact, wealth inequalities are typically more severe than income inequalities. In the United States, for example, the top quintile of income households gets roughly 50 percent of all income but owns more than 65 percent of all wealth. In poorer nations, wealth disparities are larger still.

LAND OWNERSHIP

Because most low-income countries still have large agricultural sectors, land ownership is a central component of wealth. Not surprisingly, this form of wealth is concentrated in very few hands. Where statistics are available, the Gini coefficients for land ownership inequality are often substantially higher than Ginis for household incomes. In Bangladesh, for example, the land Gini is 0.62, twice as high as the income Gini (0.31). In Paraguay, the land Gini is 0.93, suggesting that a very few families own nearly all the land.

STOCK MARKET WEALTH

Data on the ownership of corporate stock depict similarly high levels of wealth concentration. In Indonesia, the richest *ten families* own nearly 60 percent of all stock market capital in the nation. Figure 4.1 shows that comparable levels of stock market inequality exist in several other nations. In Japan, the richest ten families own only 2.4 percent of stock market wealth; in the United States, the concentration ratio is even less.

STATUS MOBILITY

As we observed in Chapter 2, there are two distinct ways of assessing inequalities. First there is the simple question of status differentials at a point in time. This question is answered by adding up the incomes and wealth of individual households, then observing how those receipts are distributed, that is, who is at the top of the heap and who is at the bottom.

The second question takes a longer view of inequality. It asks whether people stay on specific rungs of the economic ladder—or instead move up and down the rungs over time. If people are *stuck* on specific rungs, then point-in-time inequalities represent permanent status differentials. If, instead, people move up and down the ladder over time, then point-in-time inequalities exaggerate permanent status disparities.

INEQUITY VERSUS INEQUALITY

The phenomenon of status mobility draws attention to the distinction between *inequity* and *inequality*. As we described in Chapter 2, unequal outcomes are common in sports,

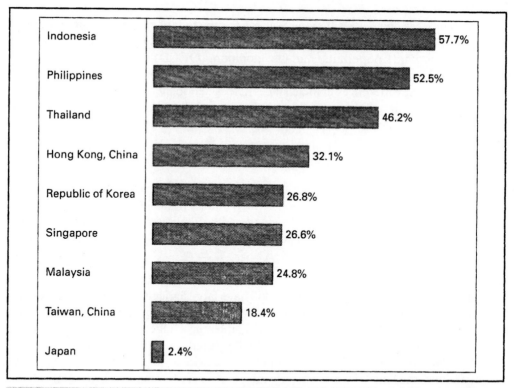

FIGURE 4.1 Market Capitalization Controlled by the Top 10 Families

Source: Reprinted from the *Journal of Financial Economics*, *58*, Claessens, Stijn, Simeon Djankou and Larry Lang, "The Separation of Ownership and Control in East Asian Corporations," pp. 81–112, Copyright (2006), with permission from Elsevier.

entertainment, gambling, education, investments, and careers. Unequal outcomes are not inherently "unfair," however. What matters is how fair the contests are. Does everyone have a chance to win? Or are the outcomes rigged in favor of certain individuals or groups? If the same people win every time, there is reason to suspect the game is rigged. On the other hand, if the profiles of winners and losers change frequently, the contest is perceived as fair.

With respect to economic status, the critical question is thus *mobility*. If people can move up and down the income and wealth ladders, then point-in-time inequalities aren't necessarily unfair. In fact, unequal outcomes may spur education aspirations, work effort, investment, and entrepreneurship, making society better off. By contrast, *immobility*—when the rich stay rich and the poor stay poor—implies a rigged game that is inequitable.

As we observed in Chapter 2, there are millions of rags-to-riches stories in the United States. Only a minority of households remain poor over extended time periods. A combination of economic, family, and personal circumstances keeps people moving up and down the economic ladder—justifying the rubric "land of opportunity."

There are no comparable data to assess the extent of status mobility in the poorest nations of the world. But there is a lot of anecdotal evidence to suggest that global inequalities are often rooted in inequities. In India, a rigid caste system still defines differential opportunities for millions of rich and poor villagers. Studies in Brazil, South

Africa, Perú, and Ecuador document the barriers that block access to health care, education, and jobs for children of poor families. Hence, inequalities in poor nations are not only more severe than in developed nations but also tend to be more permanent, and thus inequitable.

INEQUITY AND DEVELOPMENT

The "inequality traps" that impede upward mobility hurt not only individual families but national economic growth as well. In its 2006 *World Development Report,* the World Bank focused on the links between inequality and economic development. Without access to land ownership or credit, poor rural families can't become efficient farmers. Without access to schools, health care, or reliable transportation, urban poor families can't work efficiently. Without access to credit markets, poor entrepreneurs can't put their ideas to work. The accumulation of these barriers to opportunity—these inequality traps—impedes national economic growth and development. With such large concentrations of poor people, these traps constitute a substantial barrier to economic growth. As the World Bank concluded, "equity is complementary . . . to the pursuit of long-term prosperity."

POLICY STRATEGIES

THE MILLENNIUM GOAL

Global poverty is so extensive that no policy approach offers a quick or even substantial solution. Even the World Bank doesn't see an end to global poverty. The United Nations, in fact, set a much more modest goal back in 2000. They set a "Millennium Goal" of cutting the incidence of global poverty in half by 2015 (from 30 percent in 1990 to 15 percent in 2015). Since then, the incidence of global poverty has shrunk significantly (to 24 percent), but general population growth has kept the absolute size of the global poverty population fairly constant. How, then, can we expect faster progress?

REDISTRIBUTION

Many people have long suggested that the quickest route to eliminating global poverty is simply to *redistribute* incomes and assets, both within and across countries. The potential for redistribution is often exaggerated, however, and its risks underestimated.

Take another look at those nations with the highest concentrations of extreme poverty. Mali is second on the list in Table 4.1, with an incredible 72 percent of its population in extreme poverty. Yet 10 percent of the population lives fairly well, taking in 40 percent of that nation's income. So what would happen if we somehow forced Mali's richest households to share that wealth? Sure, Mali's poorest households would be better off. But the gains wouldn't be spectacular: The *average* income in Mali is only $360 at official exchange rates and less than $1,000 even at purchasing-power equivalents. Nigeria, Haiti, Zambia, and Madagascar—all near the top of Table 4.1—also have such low *average* incomes that outright redistribution doesn't hold great hope for income gains by the poor.

Then there's the downside to direct redistribution. How is the income pie going to be resliced? Will the incomes or assets of the rich be confiscated? How will underlying jobs, stocks, land, and businesses be distributed to the poor? How will *total* output (and income) be affected by the redistribution? If savings are confiscated, people will no longer want to save and invest. If large, efficient farms are divided up into small parcels, who will manage them? If the government expropriates factories, mills, farms, or businesses, who will run them? If the *rewards* to saving, investment, entrepreneurship, and management are expropriated, who will undertake these economic activities?

This is not to suggest that *no* redistribution of income or assets is appropriate. More progressive taxes and land reforms can in fact reduce inequalities and poverty. But the potential of direct within-nation redistribution is often exaggerated. Historically, nations have often been forced to reverse land, tax, and property reforms that have slowed economic growth and reduced average incomes.

FOREIGN AID

Redistribution *across* national borders might help. After all, the United States and other industrialized nations are so rich that they could make a real dent in global poverty if they wanted to. Currently, developed nations give poorer nations roughly $80 billion a year in "official development assistance." That's a lot of money. But even if it were distributed exclusively to globally poor households it would only amount to less than $35 per year per person.

Developed nations have set a goal of delivering more aid. The Millennium Goal is to raise foreign aid levels to 0.7 percent of donor-country GDP. That may not sound too ambitious, but it's a much larger flow than at present. As Table 4.4 reveals, few "rich" nations now come close to this goal. Although the United States is by far the world's largest aid donor, its aid equals only 0.16 percent of U.S. total output. For all developed nations, the aid ratio averages around 0.25 percent—just over a third of the U.N. goal.

Given the history of foreign aid, the U.N. goal is unlikely to be met anytime soon. But what if it were? What if foreign aid *tripled*? Would that cure global poverty? No. Tripling foreign aid would generate only $100 a year for each of the nearly 3 billion people now in global poverty. Even that figure is optimistic, because it assumes all aid

TABLE 4.4 Foreign Aid		
Country	*Total Aid ($ millions)*	*Percent of Donor Total Income*
Australia	1,465	0.25
Canada	2,537	0.26
Denmark	2,025	0.83
France	8,475	0.42
Japan	8,859	0.19
Italy	2,484	0.15
Norway	2,200	0.87
United Kingdom	7,836	0.36
United States	18,999	0.16
22 Nation Total	$78,569	0.25

Source: WORLD BANK DEVELOPMENT REPORT by WORLD BANK. Copyright 2006 by WORLD BANK. Reproduced with permission of WORLD BANK in the format Textbook via Copyright Clearance Center.

is distributed to the poor—in a form (e.g., food, clothes, medicine) that directly addresses their basic needs.[4]

ECONOMIC GROWTH

Economic growth offers far more promise for reducing global poverty. The faster an economy grows, the faster the reduction in poverty. The 61 nations classified as "low income" by the World Bank have a combined output of nearly $1.5 trillion. "Lower middle income" nations like China, Brazil, Egypt, and Sri Lanka produce another $4 trillion or so of annual output. Hence, every 1.0 percentage of growth increases total income in these nations by roughly $55 billion. According to the World Bank, if these nations could grow their economies by just 3.8 percent a year (an extra $200 billion of output in the first year and increasing thereafter), global poverty would be cut in half by 2015.

China has demonstrated just how effective economic growth can be in reducing poverty. Since 1990, China has been the world's fastest-growing economy, with GDP growth rates routinely in the 8–10 percent range. This sensational growth has not only raised *average* incomes, but also has dramatically reduced the incidence of poverty. In fact, *the observed success in reducing global poverty from 30 percent in 1990 to 24 percent in 2006 is almost entirely due to the decline in Chinese poverty.* By contrast, slow economic growth in Africa, Latin America, and South Asia has *increased* their respective poverty populations.

Because roughly 70 percent of the extreme global poor live in rural areas, agricultural productivity is a critical factor in economic growth. Productivity gains in agriculture not only raise farm incomes but also free more people to move into expanding urban areas.

INSTITUTIONAL REFORM

Although economic growth is undeniably the best hope for reducing global poverty, GDP growth alone will not assure success. As economies grow, more of the benefits of that growth must be channeled to the poor. A substantial amount of redistribution occurs "naturally" as new jobs are created, unemployment declines, and productivity advances. The migration of rural populations into expanding urban centers also accelerates income growth for the poorest households.

The government can further accelerate both growth and equality by reducing the "inequality traps" that keep the global poor from full participation in an expanding economy. Rural development, investments in farm technology, transportation systems that facilitate migration to expanding urban areas, improved health and educational services, and low-income housing projects all help poor households benefit from a growing economy. Although governments in developing economies have relatively few resources to spend, directing more of that spending to the dismantling of inequality traps can have a high payoff.

Basic institutional reforms can also foster both GDP growth and greater equality. All too often, bureaucratic obstacles make it too expensive, too slow, and too risky to

---

[4]The importance of selectivity, not mere quantity in foreign aid, is emphasized in William Easterly, "Can Foreign Aid Buy Growth?" *Journal of Economic Perspectives* (Spring 2003), pp. 23–48.

start a business or expand a farm. There may be too little protection for property rights or enforcement of commercial contracts. Such institutional roadblocks may prevent low-income households from escaping their poverty traps. China and India have demonstrated how even limited deregulation can spur business growth and reduce poverty at the same time.[5] While "old" development theory focused on the labor, capital, and technological resources needed for economic growth, "new" development theory emphasizes the role of these institutional features in promoting growth.

Summary

Global poverty is very different from U.S. domestic poverty. First, global poverty thresholds represent rock-bottom subsistence; the "dollar-a-day" World Bank standard for extreme poverty is only a tenth of the official U.S. poverty standard. Second, global poverty is pervasive in low-income nations. While less than 13 percent of U.S. households are considered "poor" by U.S. standards (and virtually none by global standards), 30–70 percent of the population is extremely poor (<$1/day) in most low-income nations. Inequalities of income and wealth are also more pronounced in low-income nations.

The United Nations has set a goal of cutting global poverty rates in half by 2015. Only China has made substantial progress toward this goal. To reduce extreme poverty, low-income nations have to pursue faster GDP growth (at least 3.8 percent annually) and give greater priority to eliminating the structural, cultural, and legal "inequality traps" that both impede upward mobility for the poor and inhibit economic development.

Further Reading

Banerjee, Abhijit and Esther Duflo, "The Economic Lives of the Poor," *Journal of Economic Perspectives* (Winter 2007), pp. 141–167.

Besley, Timothy, and Robin Burgess, "Halving Global Poverty," *Journal of Economic Perspectives* (Summer 2003), pp. 3–22.

Miles, Mase A., ed., *The Road to Prosperity* (Washington, DC: Heritage Books, 2004).

Smeeding, Timothy, "Poor People in Rich Nations: The United States in Comparative Perspective," *Journal of Economic Perspectives* (Winter 2006), pp. 69–90.

World Bank, *World Development Report and World Development Indicators*, Washington, DC, annual.

Web Links

Luxembourg Income Study. Cross-national data on low-income populations in developed nations:
http://www.lisproject.org

World Bank. Current statistics on world poverty are available at:
http://iresearch.worldbank.org/PovcalNet/jsp/index.jsp

[5]Every year the Heritage Foundation publishes an *Index of Economic Freedom* that identifies key institutional features of an economy and shows how they correlate with economic growth.

CHAPTER 5

LABOR FORCE PARTICIPATION

The most obvious reason people are poor is that they don't earn enough income. Indeed, the most salient difference between poor households and nonpoor households is their attachment to the labor market: Over 90 percent of nonpoor families earn some income in the labor market. By contrast, only 60 percent of poor families earn any income. Not working—or not working enough—is a compelling explanation for poverty.

Unfortunately, the strong correlation between work and income raises as many questions as it answers. Do poor people *choose* not to work? Do they prefer idleness and even impoverishment to the rigors of the workplace? Or are there simply not enough good jobs to go around? In other words, what *causes* the low level of labor force participation by the poor? Is Flawed Character to blame? Or do Restricted Opportunities prevent poor people from fulfilling their employment and income ambitions? What role does the government play in determining the number or types of jobs available and who gets them? Does Big Brother prevent some people from getting jobs by setting minimum-wage levels, imposing expensive workplace safety requirements, or imposing high taxes?

In this chapter we examine in greater detail the workforce behavior of the poor. Our objective is to determine how often they work, as well as how often they *look* for work. In the next chapter we examine the *wages* and *hours* of the working poor and explore some of the reasons for their low incomes.

INCOME SOURCES

The attachment of the poor to the labor market can be measured in many ways. The most direct way is simply to ask how many poor households receive *any* income from wages and salaries. This at least tells us whether *anyone* in the household worked at *any time* during the year. An even more telling figure is the percentage of *total* household income derived from wages and salaries. This figure tells us the extent to which poor people depend on labor-market income as opposed to other income sources.

Two-parent households have a much better opportunity to participate in the labor market. Although many single-parent households do work, their labor force participation remains much below that of two-parent households. Because of this gap, we will examine two-parent and single-parent female-headed families separately. In both cases, the emphasis is on the *differences* in income sources of poor and nonpoor families. We confine our attention to families with children (under 18)—a category that encompasses about two-thirds of the poverty population.

TABLE 5.1 Income Sources of Two-Parent Families*

	Percent of Families Receiving Income	
Income Source	*Poor*	*Nonpoor*
Earnings	63.7	97.3
Interest, dividends	12.3	64.3
Pensions	2.2	5.0
Social Security	10.2	6.5
Welfare		
Cash benefits	24.8	6.5
Food stamps	36.1	2.4
Housing assistance	12.5	2.1

*Families with children (2005 data).

Source: U.S. Bureau of the Census.

TWO-PARENT FAMILIES

Table 5.1 summarizes the sources of income for two-parent families with children under age 18. The most striking observation is the overwhelming incidence of earnings. Virtually all (97.3 percent) nonpoor two-parent families earn some wages. Although two-parent poor families are less likely to have wage and salary income, their incidence of earnings is also substantial (63.7 percent).

There are huge differences between poor and nonpoor families in the receipt of *non*labor income. The largest difference occurs with interest and dividends: Only 12 percent of poor families get any interest or dividends, as compared with over 64 percent of all nonpoor families. This gap in dividend and interest income is easily explained by the greater assets of nonpoor families. The median American family owns net assets of roughly $93,000. Those assets held in the form of bonds and savings accounts generate interest income, while stock holdings pay dividends. Since poor people own relatively few assets, they are less likely to receive interest or dividend income. Note, however, that one-fifth of all poor families receive at least *some* nonlabor income from these sources.

Few two-parent families with children receive any income from Social Security or private pensions. This is simply a reflection of their relatively young age. As we will observe in Chapter 7, older Americans depend heavily on Social Security and pension benefits.

Also shown in Table 5.1 is the receipt of cash and in-kind welfare. Not surprisingly, poor families are likely to get welfare benefits; nonpoor families are not. The most common source of welfare income for two-parent families is food stamps, which a third of these poor families get. Even some nonpoor families get food stamps, cash benefits, and housing assistance. These nonpoor families are typically "near poor," with incomes just a bit above the official poverty threshold. Some may be a bit higher up the income ladder but have slipped briefly into poverty at some time during the year.

IMPORTANCE OF SOURCES

Figure 5.1 looks at the sources of income from a different perspective. Rather than looking at how many families receive *any* income from each source (Table 5.1), this figure indicates *how much* income each source provides. The question of "how much" is

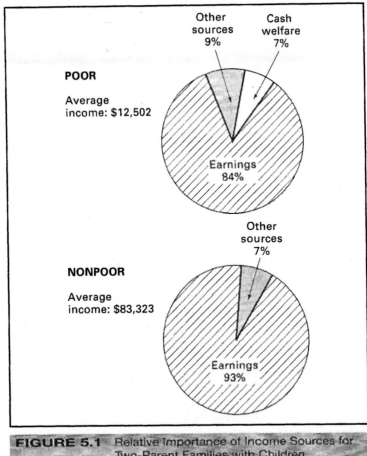

POOR

Average
income: $12,502

Other
sources
9%

Cash
welfare
7%

Earnings
84%

NONPOOR

Average
income: $83,323

Other
sources
7%

Earnings
93%

FIGURE 5.1 Relative Importance of Income Sources for
Two-Parent Families with Children

Source: U.S. Bureau of the Census (2000 data for cash incomes only).

answered in two ways. The first answer indicates the *percentage* of total family income
coming from each source, that is, the extent to which families depend on various
sources of income flows. The second dimension of Figure 5.1 reveals the dollar amount
of income from each source.

Notice first in Figure 5.1 the huge gap between the average *cash* incomes of poor
families ($12,502) and nonpoor families ($83,323). As we observed in Chapters 2 and 3,
that gap would be smaller if in-kind benefits like food stamps and housing assistance
were counted. Even with that adjustment, however, the absolute gap between poor and
nonpoor families would be huge.

Figure 5.1 underscores an important difference in the *relative* importance of various income sources. Income from working (wages, salaries, and self-employment)
accounts for only 84 percent of total income for poor two-parent families but over 93
percent for nonpoor families. Cash welfare provides only a small (7 percent) share of
the income of poor families, while Social Security and unemployment insurance
provide more income. The contrasts in Table 5.1 and Figure 5.1 are striking. These
statistics tell us that the huge income gap between poor and nonpoor two-parent families is almost completely explained by differences in labor-market earnings. Nonpoor

TABLE 5.2 Income Sources of Female-Headed
Families with Children

Income Source	Percent of Families Receiving Income	
	Poor	Nonpoor
Earnings	66.3	95.3
Interest, dividends	10.8	44.7
Pensions	2.1	5.6
Social Security	9.2	13.9
Welfare		
Cash benefits	37.4	9.3
Food stamps	58.5	12.2
Housing assistance	32.6	8.2

Source: U.S. Bureau of the Census (2000 data).

two-parent families are more likely to work (Table 5.1) and to earn more income when they do (Figure 5.1). The problem, then, is that poor families don't work enough, or are paid too little. Nothing else comes close to explaining their relative income status.

FEMALE-HEADED FAMILIES

Female-headed poor families have entirely different patterns of income than two-parent poor families. In general, the female-headed families have far less earned income and rely heavily on various forms of welfare. Yet, even among female-headed families there are vivid contrasts in labor force activity between the poor and nonpoor.

Table 5.2 depicts the percent of female-headed families receiving various income flows. Most noteworthy is the universal presence of earnings from work for *nonpoor* female-headed families. By contrast, only two out of three *poor* female-headed families get *any* income from working. Clearly, most female-headed families stay out of poverty by working; those without earnings are apt to be poor.

One-third of all poor female-headed families receive cash welfare benefits. Food stamps (59 percent) and housing assistance (33 percent) are also common for this poverty subgroup. Only about one out of ten nonpoor female-headed families receives any form of welfare.

The significance of earnings in distinguishing the poor from the nonpoor is strikingly apparent again in Figure 5.2. Over 80 percent of the income of nonpoor female heads comes from their own work effort. By contrast, poor women in identical household situations earn only half of their family's total cash income.

Welfare benefits are clearly the economic mainstay of poor female-headed families. They get a fourth of their cash income from welfare checks. Were the value of food stamps, housing assistance, and Medicaid taken into account, their dependence on the welfare system would be even more evident.

Child-support payments also augment the income of both poor and nonpoor female-headed families. Nonpoor mothers are much more likely (48 percent) to receive child support than poor mothers (29 percent). In either case, however, the child-support payments are relatively small. The problems and potential of child support are discussed more fully in Chapter 8.

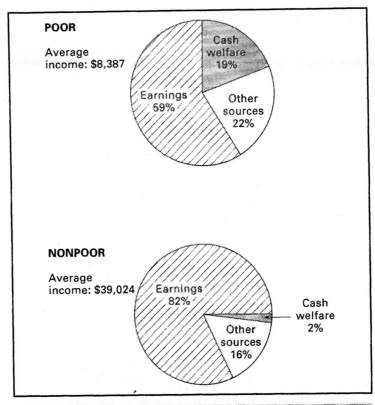

POOR

Average income: $8,387

Cash welfare 19%

Earnings 59%

Other sources 22%

NONPOOR

Average income: $39,024

Earnings 82%

Cash welfare 2%

Other sources 16%

FIGURE 5.2 Relative Importance of Income Sources for Female-Headed Families with Children

Source: U.S. Bureau of the Census (2000 data).

LABOR FORCE STATUS

The foregoing figures and tables highlight the importance of earned income as the primary determinant of poverty status. Good earnings keep families out of poverty; a lack of wages causes families to be poor. This simple observation is as valid for single-parent families as it is for more traditional two-parent families. Although single-parent families earn much less income than two-parent families—and women less than men— what keeps both single mothers and two-parent families out of poverty is work.

Although the outcomes of the labor market are clear, the mechanisms that produce these outcomes are less evident. Why do poor families have such low earnings? Do they work less? Are they paid less?

PARTICIPATION AND POVERTY

A convenient way to start answering these questions is by classifying people according to their labor force status. The labor force includes not only all people who are working for pay, but also people who are actively looking for jobs. Hence, both employed persons and unemployed persons are counted as labor force participants. Nonparticipants are people who are neither working for pay nor actively seeking paid employment.

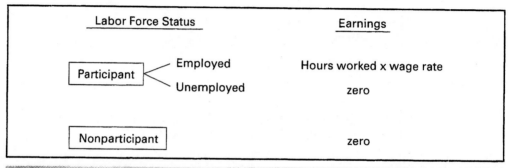

FIGURE 5.3 Labor Force Status and Earnings

Figure 5.3 provides an overview of the relationship between labor force participation and earnings from employment. People who don't participate in the labor market (the nonparticipants) have zero earnings. Only participants have a shot at paychecks. But participants must also be able to find jobs (employed), decent wages, and work enough hours to stay out of poverty.

Figure 5.4 suggests how important labor force participation is in determining poverty status. For each family type, the poverty rate is shown both for families whose head participates in the labor market during the year and for families headed by nonparticipants. In nearly every case, the poverty rate more than *quadruples* if the household head is a nonparticipant.

FIGURE 5.4 Poverty Rate, by Labor Force Status of Household Head

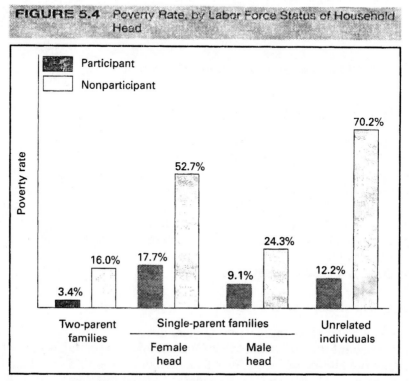

Source: U.S. Bureau of Labor Statistics (1998 data).

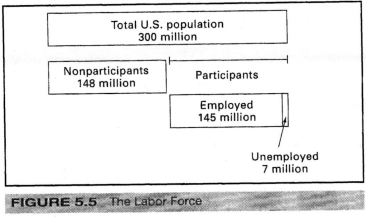

FIGURE 5.5 The Labor Force

Source: U.S. Bureau of Labor Statistics (2006 data).

The extent of participation in the U.S. labor market is illustrated in Figure 5.5. In 2006 the total U.S. population numbered roughly 300 million. Only half of the population participated in the labor market, however. Of these, 145 million were employed and another 7 million were actively searching for jobs.

THE NONPARTICIPANTS

People who don't participate in the labor market obviously run the risk of poverty. But the link between poverty and participation is not that simple. Most nonparticipants live in families where someone else works. Almost half of the nonparticipants are children under the age of 16. Few people expect them to work. In fact, child-labor laws in the United States forbid them to work in most cases. Their income depends on the labor force status of their parents, not their own participation. (In poor nations the earnings of young children are often critical to a family's survival.)

Another 32 million individuals are retired. Until recently, many older people were forced to quit working by mandatory retirement provisions. After such rules were struck down, however, older people still had an incentive to quit working. Social Security and private pensions offer significant income in retirement, giving older individuals an opportunity to enjoy more leisure without enduring poverty. Many older Americans also retire for health reasons or because they confront discrimination in job opportunities.

Nine million of the labor force nonparticipants are full-time students over age 16. Like children and retirees, they must largely depend on their families or savings for income support. Another 10 million individuals are either institutionalized, sick, or disabled.[1]

Clearly, most nonparticipants are out of the labor force because they are too young, too old, in school, institutionalized, or disabled. However, not all nonparticipants fall into one of these five groups. Two additional groups of nonparticipants are important.

---

[1]Disabilities are themselves not completely objective. Donald Parsons has shown that labor force withdrawal of prime-age males is related to the availability of disability benefit payments. See Donald O. Parsons, "The Decline in Male Labor Force Participation," *Journal of Political Economy* (February 1980). For an alternative view, see John Bound, "The Health and Earnings of Rejected Disability Insurance Applicants," *American Economic Review* (June 1989), pp. 482–503.

One group consists of the 20 million women who describe themselves as homemakers. The other are the individuals who offer other reasons for nonparticipation.

The 20 million women who are classified as homemakers include the nearly 1.3 million nonworking single mothers whose families are in poverty. They also include another 2 million married women whose families could move above the poverty threshold if they worked outside the home. This is not to say that all women—much less all mothers of young children—should work. The point is instead that there is an element of individual *choice* here. Over 70 percent of women with preschool children work regardless of whether they are married or single. Hence, the presence of children can't be viewed as an insurmountable barrier to labor force participation. Most mothers in fact choose to work or at least decide that they need the extra income that comes from market employment.

At-home single moms often cite lack of child care as an impediment to their labor force participation. They also note that the wages they'd earn would barely cover child care expenses and the loss of welfare benefits. In other words, they stress the Restricted Opportunities unique to single moms. Critics respond, however, by pointing to subsidized child care programs and the work behavior of nonpoor single moms.

Labor force nonparticipation is much less common among adult men. Yet, in many cases, such nonparticipation is even more difficult to explain. Why do these men fail to participate in the labor force? Is it because they prefer idleness and impoverishment, or because they are physically unable to work or locate a job? A U.S. Department of Labor study suggested that a good many such persons were "dreamers and drifters who were able to adjust both financially and psychologically to nonworker status." No data were available, however, to support that allegation. More recent studies have shown that very few men with family responsibilities desire to "dream and drift" rather than work. Many have not looked for jobs because they are convinced that no employment opportunities are currently available for them. Here again, however, causation is not cut-and-dried. People may *choose* not to try very hard before concluding that there aren't any jobs available. People counted as nonparticipants may also be involved in illegal or other "underground" (unreported) activities that bring in enough income to allow them to shun mainstream jobs.

Status Mobility

The phenomenon of nonparticipation is not a permanent state. Labor force status changes over time along with marital, child-rearing, and economic conditions. Indeed, a salient characteristic of the poor is their extraordinarily high rate of mobility between different labor force statuses. The poor are constantly moving in and out of the labor force and from employment to unemployment. A poor person out of the labor force one week may well be working or looking for a job the next week.[2]

To note that nonparticipation is likely to be a temporary condition is not tantamount to denying its causal importance for poverty. The observed status mobility simply reformulates the basic question of causality. The question is not simply why don't poor people participate in the labor market, but why don't they participate *more often*. In that context, both continual and sporadic nonparticipation emerge as salient causes of poverty. In later chapters we examine the causes of this nonparticipation in more detail.

---

[2]The fluidity of labor market status is explored in Steven J. Davis, R. Jason Faberman, and John Haltiwanger, "The Flaw Approach to Labor Markets," *Journal of Economic Perspectives* (Summer 2006), pp. 3–26; also see Brett Theodos and Robert Bednarzik, "Earnings Mobility and Low-wage Workers in the United States," *Monthly Labor Review* (July 2006), pp. 34–47.

UNEMPLOYMENT

Labor force participation is not a guaranteed ticket out of poverty. Figure 5.4 shows that participants are much less likely than nonparticipants to be poor. Nevertheless, millions of people who do participate in the job market remain poor. One reason for this is unemployment. People participate in labor markets by either working for pay *or* actively seeking a job (see Figure 5.3). Those who aren't working but who are actively looking for a job are counted as unemployed.

Just because someone is looking for work doesn't mean he or she is poor. In 2006, for example, nearly 7 million people were unemployed at any time. An even larger number — over 15 million — experienced at least a brief spell of unemployment at some time during the year.[3] Millions of these job searchers, however, were students seeking summer jobs or graduates looking for their first permanent job. Many were middle-class women returning to the labor force after their kids entered school or left home. In such circumstances, unemployment may not be accompanied by economic hardship, much less poverty. Even mainstream workers who are involuntarily laid off or displaced from their jobs are likely to stay out of poverty if other family members work or if they find new jobs quickly. Unemployment may still cause financial and emotional pain in such cases, but it doesn't necessarily cause poverty. All told, less than one-fifth of the families who experience unemployment have incomes below the poverty standard.

The *duration* of unemployment is an important determinant of its poverty consequences. Forty percent of the people who experience unemployment stay unemployed less than five weeks. Less than one out of five unemployed persons remains jobless for as long as six months. Only these long-term unemployed individuals are likely to suffer substantial economic losses from joblessness.[4]

Although unemployment does not necessarily lead to poverty, it is apparent that joblessness afflicts many poor families. As Table 5.3 indicates, 17.6 percent of all families

TABLE 5.3 Poverty Rates Among Labor Force Participants by Family Type and Unemployment Experience

	Poverty Rate (Percent) of Households with at Least One Labor Force Participant and	
	With No Member Unemployed During Year	*With at Least One Member Unemployed During Year*
All families	6.1	17.6
Two-parent families	4.4	11.4
Single-parent families		
Male-headed	5.8	21.7
Female-headed	17.0	44.1
Persons living alone	9.3	35.3

Source: Paul O. Flaim, "Unemployment in 1982: The Cost to Workers and Their Families," *Monthly Labor Review* (February 1984). Bureau of Labor Statistics.

---

[3]The U.S. Bureau of Labor Statistics documents the high degree of employee Turnover in its Job Openings and Labor Turnover surveys.

[4]The relationship between unemployment and economic hardship is also discussed by the National Commission on Employment and Unemployment Statistics in *Counting the Labor Force* (Washington, DC: U.S. Government Printing Office, 1979).

TABLE 5.4 Methods Used by Families to Meet Living Expenses, by Duration of Unemployment (percent distribution)

Method	Duration of Unemployment	
	5 to 26 Weeks	*27 Weeks or More*
Used savings	49.1	39.9
Borrowed money	23.7	18.8
Moved to cheaper housing	8.8	12.0
Received help from friends	18.0	22.5
Received welfare or private charity	14.7	31.9

Sum of percents is more than 100 because many families resorted to more than one method.

Source: Adapted from Stanley Lebergott, ed., *Men Without Work* (Englewood Cliffs, NJ: Prentice-Hall, 1964), p. 144. See also Table 4 in Congressional Budget Office, *Family Income of Unemployment Insurance Recipients.* March 2004.

experiencing unemployment are poor. This amounts to nearly half of all poor families. Hence, we may conclude that one-half of all poor families experience at least some direct income loss as a result of unemployment. The most vulnerable families are those headed by women; the poverty rate soars to 44.1 percent when the female head experiences unemployment.

THE PROCESS OF ECONOMIC DETERIORATION

Just how unemployment leads to poverty is evident when the relationship is viewed over time. Whereas a few days or a week of unemployment will not significantly diminish a family's income, several weeks of joblessness will begin to undermine a family's economic foundations. Accordingly, we expect to see more and more people slip into poverty as the duration of unemployment status lengthens. This process is confirmed by Table 5.4, which portrays the various methods families use to meet expenses as the duration of unemployment increases.[5]

Government-provided unemployment insurance ("UI") benefits help cushion the income loss that accompanies unemployment. However, not all unemployed workers get UI benefits and those who do don't get them indefinitely. To get any benefits, a worker must have a history of employment and have been laid off (not fired for cause or voluntarily quit). Even then, benefits are only about a third of prior wages and typically available for a maximum of 26 weeks (Congress often extends their availability to 39 weeks in national recessions).[6] When benefit eligibility ends, economic distress increases.

A Congressional Budget Office (CBO) study revealed in stark terms how the risk of poverty rises with the duration of involuntary unemployment. Here is the pattern of rising poverty CBO observed in 2001–02.

- 7 percent of all UI recipients were in poor families prior to receiving unemployment insurance benefits.

---

[5]For a closer look at the experiences of people unemployed for an extended period of time, see Walter Corson and Mark Dynarski, *A Study of Unemployment Insurance Recipients and Exhaustees* (Princeton, NJ: Mathematica, 1990); and U.S. Congress, Committee on Ways and Means, *1994 Green Book,* Section 7 and Appendix F.

[6]The unemployment insurance program is examined more closely in Chapter 14.

- 23 percent were poor while receiving UI benefits.
- 36 percent of those who remained jobless when their UI benefits ran out were in poverty.[7]

In Table 5.4, the income sources of short-term and long-term unemployed families are compared. It can be seen, for example, that among the short-term (up to 26 weeks!) unemployed, 49 percent of the families have savings from which to draw in order to meet their everyday living expenses. As the duration of unemployment surpasses 27 weeks, however, the number of families with savings or available credit declines. As unemployment continues and families become more desperate, they begin to sell their homes, seek aid from friends, and, most striking of all, fall back on public or private charity.

SUBEMPLOYMENT

Although it is clear that unemployment constitutes a direct and increasingly serious threat to a family's economic welfare, we have not yet completely described the dimensions of that threat. So far, we have considered only the immediate income loss to those families who suffer unemployment. There are indirect effects as well, however.

DISCOURAGED WORKERS

When unemployment rates are high in a particular area, job seekers are apt to become increasingly frustrated in their efforts to secure employment. Jobs are scarce and available to only a select few. Faced with one employment rejection after another, job seekers are likely to give up the search. This erosion of confidence was expressed by a young man who described his search for a job as follows:

> I'll tell you, man, I go to Catholic Charities, to the youth center, down by the employment people—a couple of weeks ago I try to buy a job—I talk to social worker . . . you go from place to place, you know, and you get tired. I guess you get bored. Guys say no work, no nuthin', and then you say, "to hell with it. Let the job come to me."[8]

Not surprisingly, this young man is called a *discouraged worker*. Because he no longer seeks work actively, he is not counted as among the unemployed; he belongs to the ranks of the nonparticipants previously discussed. Yet it is clear that the two categories are not wholly separable. The extent and likely duration of unemployment in an area has a significant effect on the size of the nonparticipating population. Accordingly, many discouraged workers must be counted among the casualties of unemployment.

No one knows the exact number of discouraged workers among the poor. We do know, though, that a household head cannot maintain both a discouraged status and a family for long. The family must eat, and the head of the household will be compelled to locate some work, any work, just to keep body and soul together.

---

[7]Congressional Budget Office, *Family Income of Unemployment Insurance Recipients* (March 2004). See also Walter Corson, Kasen Needels, and Walter Nicholson, *Emergency Unemployment Compensation: The 1990s Experience* (Princeton, NJ: Mathematica Policy Research: January 1999).

[8]Quoted in Edgar May, *The Wasted Americans* (New York: Harper and Row, 1964), p. 60.

Discouragement is not limited to household heads. In families with both a mother and a father present, high rates of unemployment are most likely to affect the mother's labor force participation. Where unemployment is prevalent, a wife's chances for employment are likely to be even smaller than her husband's. Hence, the family may decide that her job search is fruitless and that her productivity will be highest in the home. Unfortunately, in withdrawing from the labor force—giving up the search for paid employment—the wife markedly increases the family's chances of becoming poor. Working spouses are one of the surest escape routes from poverty.

Considerable statistical attention has been directed recently toward the phenomenon of discouraged workers. As a result, the U.S. Department of Labor estimated that in 2005—a year of low unemployment—there were 436,000 persons at any time who wanted a job but were not currently looking for work because they felt their search would be in vain. A much larger number of people were out of the labor force for this reason at some time during the year.

OTHER MARGINALLY ATTACHED WORKERS

In addition to the discouraged workers there are many more nonparticipants who say they want a job but aren't currently looking. Like discouraged workers, they looked for a job at some time in the previous year, but haven't looked within the last month. Unlike discouraged workers, these nonparticipants cite *personal* rather than *job-market* reasons for not actively seeking a job. Typically, these nonparticipants say that child care responsibilities, transportation problems, ill health, or school attendance keep them from job searching. But they *want* a job and say they would accept it if one became available.[9] High unemployment rates reduce the chances of that happening.

UNDEREMPLOYMENT

Another indirect hardship resulting from unemployment concerns the type and amount of work people undertake when jobs are scarce. As noted, the head of a low-income family, facing a dismal labor market, may have to accept whatever employment or wages are available. The work may not fully utilize his or her time or talents and is likely to be menial. But the person accepts the work as a temporary measure while waiting for better employment opportunities to emerge. A person who is in this situation is *underemployed*. That is, the person is at work (hence not unemployed) but not working to capacity. Commonly, the underemployed work full-time at menial jobs or part-time at any job, while seeking more or better employment. In 2005, the U.S. Department of Labor estimated that 1.3 million people were involuntarily employed on a part-time basis. Most of these workers had seen their hours cut because of slack work; the rest had not been able to find full-time jobs. Millions more were underemployed because the full-time jobs they had located paid wages below their usual experience. All of these manifestations of underemployment worsen markedly when the national economy slips into a recession.

---

[9]For a discussion of the distinction between "marginally attached" and "discouraged" workers, see Monica Castillo, "Persons Outside the Labor Force Who Want a Job," *Monthly Labor Review* (July 1998), pp. 34–42.

SUBEMPLOYMENT

The phenomena of unemployment, discouragement, marginal attachment, and under-employment combine to form the concept of *subemployment*. Taken as a whole, the distressing impact of subemployment on a family's finances is reasonably clear. Very few families have enough economic resources to maintain themselves in the face of these forces for long. What is not so obvious is that the social foundation of the family, as well as its economic foundation, may suffer from the impact of these phenomena. Can we expect the parent(s) in a low-income family to gain self-respect or familial admiration when employment prospects and income diminish? Do we anticipate a Charles Dickens kind of increased solidarity as the family begins to sink into impoverishment?

It is more reasonable to expect intrafamily tensions to mount along with economic distress. In fact, studies show that both divorce and child abuse increase when fathers are out of work.[10] According to one study, children of unemployed fathers are three times as likely to be abused than are children of employed fathers.[11] These kinds of effects are difficult to measure but are potentially of greater social significance than lost wages alone.[12]

POVERTY IMPLICATIONS

As the list of direct and indirect consequences of unemployment grows, the crushing burden of nonemployment on the economic status of the poor becomes apparent. Table 5.5 offers a summary assessment. The top panel (A) contrasts the work experience

TABLE 5.5 Work Experience of Adults Living in Families

	Poor	Nonpoor
A. All persons aged 18–64	20,450,000	163,895,000
Didn't work at all	56%	16%
Worked year-round, full-time	14%	61%
Worked less than year-round, full-time	30%	23%
B. Mothers in single-parent families with children	2,902,000	4,378,000
Didn't work at all	37%	7%
Worked year-round, full-time	21%	83%
Worked less than year-round, full-time	42%	10%
C. Fathers in two-parent families with children	1,340,000	24,051,000
Didn't work at all	21%	53%
Worked year-round, full-time	54%	90%
Worked less than year-round, full-time	25%	5%

Source: U.S. Bureau of the Census (2005 data).

---

[10]Scott South, Katherine Trent, and Yang Shen; Changing Partners: Toward a Macrostructural Opportunity Theory of Marital Dissolution; *Journal of Marriage and Family*, 63:3 (2001), pp. 743–754.

[11]This and other studies are reported in U.S. Congress, House Committee on Education and Labor, "Hearings on the Impact of Unemployment on Children and Families," January 31, 1983.

[12]We should also note that an involuntary change in status from employed to unemployed may have serious and long-term effects on a person's self-perception and social behavior. See Mary Merva and Richard Fowle, *The Effects of Diminished Economic Opportunities on Social Stress, Heart Attacks and Crime* (Washington, DC: Economic Policy Institute, 1992).

of all adults in poor and nonpoor families. Less than half of all poor adults work at all, whereas nearly 85 percent of nonpoor adults do so. If only household heads are considered (panels B and C), similar gaps in work experience are apparent. Among single mothers (panel B), 93 percent of the nonpoor but only 63 percent of the poor have *any* work experience during the year. The gap is particularly striking for full-time, year-round work, a status occupied by 83 percent of *non*poor single mothers but only 21 percent of poor single mothers. Panel C displays similar disparities in work experience for fathers in two-parent families.

The message of Table 5.5 is clear: Millions of American families and unrelated individuals are in poverty because they don't work, or they don't work enough. If all poor families participated in the labor market at the same rate as nonpoor families and were equally likely to find jobs in the market, the poverty population would be a small fraction of its present size.[13]

THE QUESTION OF CAUSATION

The tremendous significance of subemployment for the extent and depth of poverty is apparent. However, we have not really resolved the question of *causation*. The evidence we have reviewed only confirms that subemployment is a major correlate of poverty; it does not tell us *why* so many poor people work so little.

DO THE POOR REALLY TRY?

When we seek to explain why so much subemployment exists among the poor, we may fall back on our earlier distinction among the Flawed Character, Restricted Opportunity, and Big Brother perspectives. On the one hand, the poor may not be serious or persistent enough in their job search activity. They may be unrealistic in their employment demands or simply too lazy to go out and secure available work. On the other hand, the subemployment of the poor may result from no fault of their own; perhaps there simply aren't enough decent jobs available. A third possible explanation might take into account the work disincentives imposed by government programs, especially the implied loss of unemployment or welfare benefits.

Not Enough Jobs?

Liberal analysts emphasize the restricted opportunities that poor people confront. David Ellwood, for example, sees in Table 5.5 (panel B) that most poor mothers and fathers do work at least part of the year. Ellwood argues that this work effort—even though often only part-time or part-year—suggests that the poor are willing to work. He notes that the actual employment rates of these families rise and fall with the strength of the general economy. Finally, he observes that the reasons poor adults give for not working more appear legitimate. As Table 5.6 shows, most poor adults who don't work at all during the year blame their joblessness on illness, disability, or on homemaking responsibilities. Poor adults who participate in the labor market only part

---

[13]Current spells of joblessness may also lower *future* employment and income prospects; see Ronald D'Amico and Nan L. Maxwell, "The Impact of Post-School Joblessness on Male Black-White Wage Differentials," *Industrial Relations* (Spring 1994), pp. 184–205.

TABLE 5.6 Reasons for Nonparticipation Given by Poor Adults

	Work Experience During Year	
Reason for Nonparticipation	*None*	*Some*
A. All adults (ages 18–64)		
Ill or disabled	35%	17%
Retired	11%	1%
Home or family reasons	30%	29%
School or other	19%	44%
Could not find work	5%	9%
B. Mothers in single-parent families with children		
Ill or disabled	31%	16%
Retired	2%	0
Home or family reasons	55%	54%
School or other	9%	24%
Could not find work	3%	6%
C. Fathers in two-parent families with children		
Ill or disabled	44%	29%
Retired	13%	1%
Home or family reasons	16%	7%
School or other	20%	42%
Could not find work	7%	21%

Source: U.S. Bureau of the Census (2000 data).

of the year give similar explanations. This leads Ellwood to conclude that circumstances rather than attitudes keep poor people from working more.[14]

Not Enough Effort?

Conservative critics question both the accuracy and legitimacy of these explanations. They note that it is easier—and more socially acceptable—to blame one's joblessness on a lack of job vacancies than to admit to a preference for staying at home. In their view, explanations for not working given by the poor should be treated with a grain of salt. A Census study tracked discouraged workers and other marginally attached workers from one year to the next. Over half of these workers were still out of the labor force the following year. Those who said they were discouraged by labor-market conditions in the first year were no more likely than other marginally attached workers (for personal reasons) to be in the labor market in the following year. This seemed to cast doubt on their stated desire to work.[15]

Finally, conservatives are struck by how few nonworking poor adults even claim that a shortage of job opportunities kept them from working. Fewer than one out of ten poor parents who spend time outside the labor force say they "couldn't find work" (Table 5.6). The other reasons given for not working entail elements of individual choice, for example, how urgent child care needs are or how ill one is.

---

[14]For further details, see David T. Ellwood, *Divide and Conquer* (New York: Ford Foundation, 1987).

[15]Monica Costello, "Persons Outside."

Nathan Glazer is among those critics who sense a certain irresponsibility on the part of the poor. He perceives that at "the heart of the crisis is a massive change in values which makes various kinds of work that used to support families undesirable to large numbers of potential workers today."[16] In other words, the jobs are there but the poor simply refuse to take them. Glazer offers no evidence to support his Flawed Character allegation. However, a later attempt by a second observer in New York City yielded the following evidence:

> No one who rides the subways can fail to see the numerous ads for electrician's helper (about $7,000 per year), subway patrolmen (around $8,000 per year), Office Temporaries, and Kelly Girls. The New York Telephone Company urges people to join them and be trained by them. No one who walks down Madison, Lexington, or Third Avenue will miss the signs for Help. No one who has had the misfortune of staying in a hospital recently, or even visiting one, is untroubled by the shortage of auxiliary and service personnel. . . . and any one who rides taxis with any frequency is aware of the number of taxis in the garage despite the industry's efforts to recruit additional drivers. . . . One of the fascinating statistics about New York City is that fewer persons were employed in domestic service in 1968 than in 1960. This is surely not the result of diminished demand but of a refusal to accept such employment.[17]

Despite this catalogue of apparent opportunities, there seems to be little evidence to support the notion that the poor are turning down abundant job offers. At the time Bernstein related her impressions there were about 5,000 standing job openings for unskilled workers in New York City. Confronting these vacancies were 139,000 unemployed individuals and over 200,000 heads-of-household receiving public assistance. With so many potential job seekers, the number of available jobs for the poor is hardly significant. Even if a poor person desires to secure a dead-end job, his or her chances to do so hardly seem encouraging; opportunities may be too restricted.

Another study in Washington, D.C., compared the job vacancies advertised in the local Sunday paper (the *Washington Post*) with the number and characteristics of the poor people in the metropolitan area. At the time of the study, 36,400 people were officially counted as unemployed, and 28,000 adults were receiving welfare payments. Yet, 3,028 job vacancies were listed in the paper, suggesting that many of the jobless could have found work if they really wanted to. Closer examination of the ads revealed a very different story, however. Most of the jobs required educational attainments or experience that poor people simply do not have. In all, only 354 of the job vacancies (12 percent) were jobs that poor people might get. Phone calls to the employers listing these jobs confirmed that nearly all of the job vacancies were filled, usually in a day or two.[18]

---

[16]Nathan Glazer, "Beyond Income Maintenance," *The Public Interest* (Summer 1969), p. 120.

[17]Blanche Bernstein, "Welfare in New York City," *City Almanac* (February 1970), p. 6. Political scientist Lawrence Mead also sees a "culture of defeat" that causes marginal labor force attachment; see his "The Twilight of Liberal Welfare Reform," *The Public Interest* (Spring 2000), pp. 22–34.

[18]Bradley R. Schiller, "Want Ads and Jobs for the Poor," *Manpower* (U.S. Department of Labor, January 1974).

Despite evidence to the contrary, the conviction that the poor are shunning job vacancies persists. This conviction is particularly strong regarding welfare mothers, whose families account for an increasing proportion of the poverty population. Not only is their reported search for employment regarded with skepticism, but their claim of overriding child care responsibility is also questioned. Single mothers not in poverty have the same child care responsibilities but somehow manage to work. In addition, critics wonder whether the daily example of a nonworking household head might not set undesired expectations and standards for the children of single mothers.[19] Conservatives also stress the role of government welfare programs in discouraging poor women from working.[20] They argue that Big Brother's minimum-wage requirements, workplace-safety regulations, unemployment benefits, and affirmative-action policies drive a wedge between poor people and jobs.[21]

MACROECONOMIC FORCES

Although there is ample scope for arguments about the efforts of the poor to work, no one denies completely the importance of macroeconomic forces. The U.S. economy is subject to periodic bouts of sluggishness—years in which the volume of output declines. In those years workers have a hard time holding onto jobs and people looking for work discover that job vacancies are scarce. In other years the economy is strong and both output and employment increase. This pattern of ups and downs in the business cycle is the central concern of *macroeconomics*.

Policy makers seek to create the conditions that will assure jobs for all individuals who seek them. But our historical record is testimony to the failure of macroeconomics to assure *full employment* at all times. The worst failure was the Great Depression of the 1930s. Total output declined so much in the early 1930s that as many as one out of every four labor force participants was unable to find work. There was no argument about what caused the sudden and widespread poverty—jobs had simply vanished.

In more recent times the U.S. economy has not suffered from such a deep and prolonged period of macroeconomic failure. But there have been 13 recessions since World War II—two of them in the early 1980s, another in 1990–1991, and a brief one in 2001. The recession of 1981–1982 pushed the national unemployment rate to 10.8 percent, the highest level since the 1930s. These macroeconomic downturns diminished employment opportunities and increased the number of people in poverty.

The Hiring Queue

To visualize the potential impact of fluctuating labor-market demand on unemployment and poverty rates, imagine that all potential workers could be ranked on the basis of their employability. That is, suppose that we could somehow assign everyone a relative position based on the amount of human capital they bring to the labor market. The most productive workers will be at the front of the line, the least productive at the back.

---

[19]Kevin R. Hopkins, *Welfare Dependency: Behavior, Culture, and Public Policy* (Alexandria, VA: Hudson Institute, 1987), esp. Chapter 7.

[20]Charles Murray, *Losing Ground: American Social Policy, 1950–1980* (New York: Basic Books, 1984).

[21]Richard K. Veder and Lowell E. Galloway, *Out of Work: Unemployment and Government in Twentieth-Century America*, 2d. ed. (New York: New York University Press, 1998).

It seems reasonable to assume that employers will seek to hire the most productive workers first, and thus will start filling job vacancies from the front of the line. In many cases, of course, an employer will not be able to determine exactly who is the more productive job applicant. But an employer will try to approximate that distinction, perhaps with the aid of aptitude tests, school records, even racial and sexual prejudices. All we need to note at this point is that employers will start making their selections at the front of the line and proceed toward the back.

The question that concerns us now is how far back in the line employers will go; that is, how many jobs will be available. Clearly, an individual's chances of getting a job depend not only on his or her position in line (supply characteristics), but also on how many workers employers decide to hire (demand characteristics). What we want to emphasize here is that deficiencies in demand can overwhelm supply characteristics, leaving otherwise qualified people among the ranks of the unemployed and poor.

Cyclical Unemployment

The potential of demand fluctuations to overwhelm forces on the supply side of the picture is perhaps most apparent when we compare labor-market conditions at different points in time. Consider the years 1989 and 1992, for example. The average unemployment rate in 1989 was 5.3 percent. That relatively low rate of unemployment left 6.5 million people out of work and searching for jobs. In 1992, by contrast, the unemployment rate was 7.4 percent and 9.4 million people were out on the streets at one time. Can anyone reasonably argue that the increased unemployment was due to deteriorating supply characteristics? Had our labor force grown less educated, less experienced, less motivated, less intelligent, or generally less able? Surely not. In fact, we would expect that the supply characteristics of the labor force improve with the passage of time. Seen in this context, fluctuations in the *demand* for labor emerge as a primary cause of unemployment and, by implication, the level of poverty.

The relationship between fluctuations in demand and the extent of unemployment is illustrated in Figure 5.6. Note that we have arrayed all labor force participants according to their skills (human capital), with the most skilled at the top. As we suggested earlier, the distinction between those who are employed and those who are unemployed depends not on any absolute level of skill development, but on just how far down the line employers choose to go. In 1992 employers stopped far short of where they went in 1989, leaving millions of previously employable (and employed) workers on the jobless side of the line. Hence, we may conclude that the additional unemployment represented by the shaded area in the figure was due to a deficiency of demand in 1992. The same kind of displacement occurred in 2001–2003.

Although deficiencies of demand clearly emerge as a major cause of unemployment and poverty, we cannot attribute all unemployment to demand forces. Instead, economists distinguish between four types of unemployment: frictional, seasonal, cyclical, and structural. *Frictional* unemployment arises when people move from one job to another with only a slight interval of time in between. People who are frictionally unemployed normally have visible job prospects and are simply in geographic or occupational transition. Likewise, people who are *seasonally* unemployed often face the

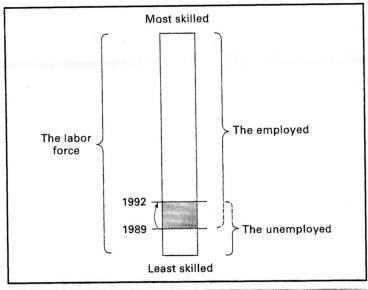

FIGURE 5.6 The Impact of Cyclical Unemployment (Deficient Demand)

sure prospect of renewed employment as the weather or season changes. This is not to say that their unemployment is not serious; we merely distinguish its sources from other types of unemployment.

Cyclical unemployment is markedly different from the first two types of unemployment. Cyclical unemployment exists when there is less demand for labor in the economy than there is labor willingly available. In this situation, neither a change in the weather nor a change of residence is likely to create employment for the jobless. For this reason the jobless have no certain prospect of later employment. Instead, they must wait for an expansion of the demand for labor. This is the kind of unemployment depicted in Figure 5.6.

Structural Unemployment

Structural unemployment is, in many respects, similar to cyclical unemployment. Here, however, the shortage of demand appears to be confined to only a few occupations or areas. While most people seem able to locate jobs, there may be a large number of pipe fitters, coal miners, or flight engineers seeking employment. There may be a large number of people out of work in the Texas Panhandle or downtown Detroit but relatively few in other areas of the country. Thus, it appears that localized or structural deficiencies in demand are more at fault than general demand shortages. The *dislocated worker* has become a popular symbol of such unemployment. Changing technology, trade patterns, and consumer demands have eliminated thousands of jobs in the steel, auto, and textile industries. The dot-com implosion of 2000–2002 likewise displaced thousands of highly specialized workers. As a result, many experienced workers were forced to seek new jobs in other industries, occupations, or locations. In principle, this kind of structural unemployment looks less damaging than cyclical unemployment, since an occupational or geographical move appears to hold promise of improved employment opportunities.

The purely structural character of structural unemployment can, however, be easily exaggerated. Can we maintain that the jobless situation of steelworkers and flight engineers is impervious to the state of demand in other occupations or areas? While it is reasonable to expect some hesitancy in moving across geographical or occupational boundaries, the speed and extent of such moves are conditioned by macroemployment opportunities. When good jobs exist in plentiful supply elsewhere, the structural character of structural unemployment is bound to erode. People will move and change occupations as alternative prospects merit. Even in Appalachia, an area often presumed to exist in economic isolation, unemployment rates follow national patterns. Accordingly, the apparent dimensions of structural unemployment are shaped in part by the state of aggregate demand and are subject to the social decisions that we have mentioned. As Paul Samuelson has noted, "the alleged hard core of the structurally unemployed is in fact a core made of ice and not of iron. The core of ice can be melted over a period of time by adequate effective demand, or it can be solidified from inadequate overall demand."[22]

This was certainly the case in the 1990s. After the recession of 1990–1991, the U.S. economy embarked on the longest peacetime expansion in history. Over 20 million new jobs were created, and the national unemployment rate fell from a high of 7.8 percent to 4.0 percent in January 2000. Job opportunities increased at all skill levels and in all regions, making it relatively easy for structurally displaced workers to find new jobs.[23] In the process, the national poverty rate fell to a generational low (11.3 percent). The subsequent economic slowdown of 2001–2002 reversed those trends.

POVERTY IMPACT OF CYCLICAL UNEMPLOYMENT

The strong macroeconomic expansion of the late 1990s permitted many poor people to work their way out of poverty. This outcome was consistent with a well-established link between cyclical unemployment and poverty rates.

Figure 5.7 illustrates the strength of the link between unemployment and poverty. The national unemployment rate (left scale) and the aggregate poverty rate (right scale) are shown for each year. They obviously follow similar patterns: When unemployment increases, poverty rates start increasing as well. Likewise, declining poverty rates follow close on the heels of declining unemployment rates. According to a study by Rebecca Blank and Alan Blinder, sluggish macroeconomic conditions

---

[22]Paul A. Samuelson, *Economics,* 8th ed. (New York: McGraw-Hill, 1967), p. 802.

[23]Ryan T. Helwig, "Worker Displacement in a Strong Labor Market," *Monthly Labor Review* (June 2001), pp. 13–28. See also Michael J. Handel, *Walker Skills and Job Requirements* (Washington, DC: Economic Policy Institute, 2003. A more pessimistic appraisal is offered by John Schmitt, "The Rise in Job Displacement, 1991–2004," *Challenge* (November 2004), pp. 46–67.

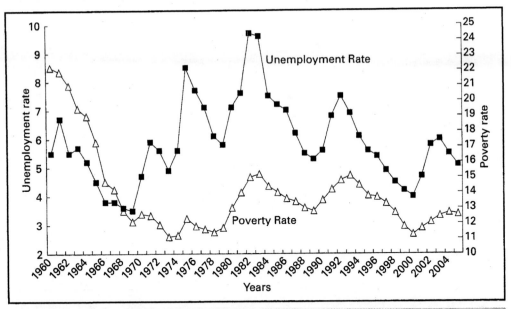

FIGURE 5.7 Unemployment and Poverty Rates for All Persons, 1960–2005

alone raised the national poverty rate by 4.5 percentage points in the 10 years from 1973 to 1983.[24]

The link between business cycles and poverty isn't equally strong for all demographic groups. Poverty among two-parent families is very responsive to changes in unemployment. Single mothers with children, however, don't move in and out of poverty quite so cyclically. This is evident in Figure 5.8.

In the period from 1982 to 1989, for example, the economy grew very sharply, but the number of single women (and their children) in poverty barely budged. As a result, the poverty *rate* declined for female-headed families much less than for two-parent families. This is consistent with our earlier observation that nearly half of these women report that they are not even looking for work.[25] In the 1990s a combination of a strong economy and work-oriented welfare reforms made a bigger dent in both poverty and welfare caseloads.[26]

[24]Rebecca M. Blank and Alan S. Blinder, "Macroeconomics, Income Distribution, and Poverty," in *Fighting Poverty*, eds. Sheldon H. Danziger and Daniel H. Weinberg (Cambridge, MA: Harvard University Press, 1986), p. 207.

[25]Among female family heads there is substantial variation in labor force participation—and thus poverty responsiveness to cyclical unemployment—by race and education. See Irene Browne, "Explaining the Black-White Gap in Labor Force Participation among Women Heading Households," *American Sociological Review* (April 1997), pp. 236–252. For an analysis of more recent trends, see Hilary Hoynes, Marianne Page, and Ann Stevens "Poverty in America: Trends and Explanations," *Journal of Economic Perspectives* (Winter 2006). pp. 47–68.

[26]Council of Economic Advisers, *Explaining the Decline in Welfare Receipt*, 1993–1996 (Washington, DC: White House, May 1997).

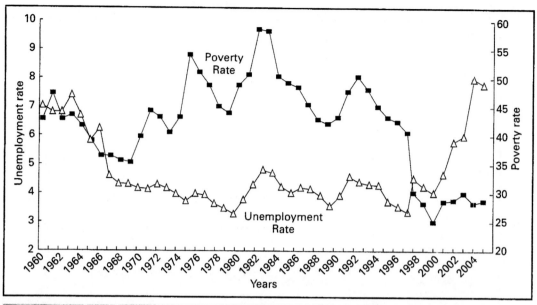

FIGURE 5.8 Unemployment and Poverty Rates for Female-Headed Families, 1960–2005

Summary

Labor earnings are by far the most important source of income for American families. The *receipt* of earnings also creates one of the sharpest distinctions between poor and nonpoor families.

The earnings gap between poor and nonpoor families is largely explained by differences in labor force participation. Whether in two-parent or single-parent (female-headed) families, poor householders are much less likely to participate in the labor market. The disparity is particularly striking for female-headed households; less than half of single mothers who are poor are active in the job market. By contrast, almost all *nonpoor* mothers either work or actively seek employment.

Poor families rely heavily on income transfers. Food stamps, cash welfare benefits, and housing subsidies provide one-fourth of the total income of two-parent poor families. For female-headed poor families such welfare benefits account for more than half of total income. Many single mothers receive child support and alimony as well, but the amount of such income is small.

Labor force participants are assured neither a job nor high income. Many participants remain unemployed, that is, unable to find work. Others are working part-time, part-year, or at skill levels below their capability. Many of these underemployed participants are poor. Finally, we note that the frustrations associated with unsuccessful job search may so discourage job seekers that they cease looking for work. The combination of these forces—subemployment—keeps millions of people in poverty.

The core controversy about poverty focuses on the causes of subemployment. Liberals emphasize the lack of available jobs and other barriers (e.g., child care) that preclude poor people from working more. Conservatives point out that there are always some jobs available and that nonpoor families in similar circumstances do manage to work. The most heated debates focus on poor families headed by single (never married, separated, or divorced) mothers.

However willing or unwilling poor people might be to work, the number of job opportunities is constrained by macroeconomic forces. Strong economic expansion creates more jobs and income; business downturns increase unemployment and poverty. The cyclical component of poverty is particularly important for two-parent families, but less significant for female-headed families.

Further Reading

Blank, Rebecca M., "Why Were Poverty Rates So High in the 1980s?" in *Poverty and Prosperity in the U.S.A. in the Late Twentieth Century*, eds. Dimitri B. Papadimitriou and Edward N. Wolff. New York: St. Martin's Press, 1993, pp. 21–55.

Freeman, Richard B., "The Rising Tide Lifts . . .?" in *Understanding Poverty*, eds. S. Danziger and R. Haveman. Cambridge, MA: Harvard University Press, 2001.

Hoynes, Hilary, M. Page, and A. Stevens, "Poverty in America: Trends and Explanations; *Journal of Economic Perspectives* (Winter 2006). pp. 47–68.

Meade, Lawrence M., *The New Politics of Poverty: The Nonworking Poor in America.* New York: Basic Books, 1992.

Newman, Katherine S., *Declining Fortunes: The Withering of the American Dream.* New York: Basic Books, 1993.

Riemer, David R., *The Prisoners of Welfare.* New York: Praeger, 1988; esp. Chapters 2–5.

Schiller, Bradley R., "Who Are the Working Poor?" *The Public Interest* (Spring 1994), pp. 61–71.

U.S. Bureau of Labor Statistics, *A Profile of the Working Poor.* Washington, DC: U.S. Government Printing Office, annual.

Wilson, William J., *When Work Disappears.* New York: Knopf, 1996.

Web Links

Federal Reserve Board of Governors. Data on wealth holdings from Survey of Consumer Finances: www.federalreserve.gov/pubs/oss/oss2/scfindex.html

U.S. Bureau of Labor Statistics. Monthly data on employment, unemployment, as well as historical series on discouraged workers and other nonparticipants: http://stats.bls.gov

CHAPTER 6
THE WORKING POOR
℘

If nonemployment is a major cause of poverty, we should be able to eliminate most poverty by providing everyone with a job. According to this reasoning, employment is a sure route to economic security. This route, however, is not so certain. We know, for example, that many poor people whom we think of as unemployed do work a great deal. In fact, a salient characteristic of the subemployed poor is that they are repeatedly engaged in part-time or part-year work. Hence, we can reject the naive assumption that employment automatically lifts a person out of poverty.

As we observed earlier in Figure 5.3, economic security depends not just on *whether* one works but also on *how much* one works and what *wage rate* one is paid. By and large, economic security is reserved for those individuals and their families who work full-time throughout the year. In this chapter, we examine this expectation in greater detail. In so doing, we focus on those individuals who fail to meet our expectations — the *working* poor.

WORK EXPERIENCE AND POVERTY

The expectation that increased employment improves one's chances of escaping poverty is fully supported by available data. As Figure 6.1 shows, the more one works, the lower the poverty rate.

WEEKS OF WORK AND HOURS

The amount of time a person works is typically measured in two distinct ways: (1) the number of employed weeks in a year, and (2) the number of employed hours per week. In principle, these two measures could be combined so that people could be classified on the basis of how many hours they work during the year. Census survey procedures preclude such simple multiplication, however. The Census survey asks how many hours a person "usually" works when employed. Since an individual may depart frequently from his or her "usual" hours, the implied annual hours of work are likely to be in error. As a result, annual hours of work can only be approximated. In any case, there is some interest in the separate measures of employment activity because they distinguish year-round workers from people who work sporadically.

Figure 6.1 clearly shows that poverty rates fall when householders work more weeks in the year. Among household heads who typically work full-time (35 hours per week), those who are employed less than half the year have a one out of four chance of being poor. By contrast, household heads who work full-time all year round have a one in 30 chance of being poor. The same relationship between the duration of employment and poverty is true for part-time workers, as Figure 6.1 also indicates.

FIGURE 6.1 Poverty and Work Experience

Source: U.S. Bureau of the Census (2005 data).

THE WORKING POOR

The relationships depicted in Figure 6.1 are likely to instill the comfortable feeling that there are few full-time, year-round workers among the poor. But this impression is dispelled quickly when the numbers are examined more closely. Because year-round workers in the economy vastly outnumber part-year workers, the incidence rates do not adequately reflect the work experience of the poor. Once again, absolute numbers and proportions convey very different impressions.

Table 6.1 and Figure 6.2 summarize the work experiences of the poor in absolute numbers. As noted in Chapter 5, only half of all poor household heads have any work experience during the year. What is new about Table 6.1 and Figure 6.2 is the *amount* of work experience by those poor people who do participate in the labor market.

TABLE 6.1 Work Experience of the Poor

	Number of Poor Household Heads	
Work Experience During Year	**Part-Time**	**Full-Time**
Worked		
1–26 weeks	834,000	987,000
27–49 weeks	477,000	611,000
50–52 weeks	813,000	1,788,000
Subtotal	2,124,000	3,386,000
Did not work	5,956,000	
Total, poor household heads	11,465,000	

Source: U.S. Bureau of the Census (2005 data for household heads aged 16–65).

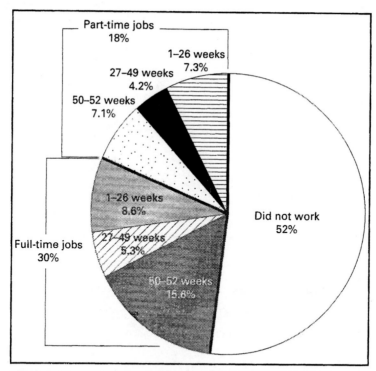

FIGURE 6.2 Work Experience of the Poor (2005 data for household heads aged 16–65).

Among those who work, the largest subgroup is clearly the 1.8 million adults who work year-round (50–52 weeks) and full-time. Another 813,000 other adults in poverty appear to work year-round at part-time jobs.

While Figure 6.1 seems consistent with the notion that hard work pays off, Figure 6.2 appears to contradict that same expectation. Although the pie chart reinforces the observation half of the adult poverty population doesn't work, it also reveals a sizable minority that *do* work—often year-round (50–52 weeks) and full-time (at least 35 hours per week). The presence of so many workers among the poor is a blatant contradiction of the accepted wisdom that "to get ahead, get a job." Apparently, everyone can't get ahead by working. This kind of observation has spawned calls for more education and training, higher minimum wages, more tax incentives, and more political participation by the poor.[1]

HOW MUCH WORK?

The increased attention given to the working poor has sparked some measurement questions. The most obvious question is who should be included in this new category. The U.S. Department of Labor defines the *working poor* as all "persons who have devoted 27 weeks or more to working or looking for work and who lived in families

---

[1]See, for example, Lucy Gorham and Bennett Harrison, *Working Below the Poverty Line* (Washington, DC: Aspen Institute, 1990); and Frank Munger, ed., *Laboring Below the Line* (New York: Russell Sage, 2002).

with incomes below the official poverty threshold." That is a broad definition, however, since it encompasses all individuals who *participate* in the labor market at least six months of the year, rather than just those who actually *work*.

Another definition includes among the working poor all workers whose annualized earnings are too low to lift a family of four out of poverty.[2] There are two problems with this definition. Earnings are annualized by extrapolating actual earnings into a full-time, year-round equivalent. Part-time jobs seldom offer the same pay or conditions as full-time jobs, however. Furthermore, the decision to work only part-time or part-year may entail individual choices (e.g., attending school, raising a family) that preclude better job opportunities.

Even if this second notion of working poor is restricted to full-time, year-round workers, its validity is questionable. This second definition presumes that every full-time worker must be able to support a family of four. Most low-wage workers are not even household heads, much less responsible for four-person families. They are more likely to be spouses, teen-aged children, or unrelated individuals.[3]

In view of these considerations, the definition of the working poor should focus on the key dimensions of *work* (not just labor force participation) and poverty (income in relation to actual family size). Were year-round, full-time employment used as the index of working, then just 1.8 million household heads would be counted as working poor according to Figure 6.2. That would account for less than one out of eight poor household heads.

MORE MEASUREMENT PROBLEMS

Conceptually, the designation of those poor adults who work year-round, full-time as the "working poor" is unambiguous. Identifying these individuals is not so easy, however.

As noted earlier, the Census Bureau does not measure actual hours worked in a year. The Census survey instead asks how many hours an individual "usually" worked when employed. A person might usually work full-time but experience occasional "short weeks" as well. In reality, one out of ten individuals classified as a year-round, full-time worker was actually employed part-time at least six weeks of the year.[4] Accordingly, the official Census data in Figure 6.2 exaggerate the number of working poor.

The Census count of the working poor is also exaggerated by the incomplete accounting of income. The annual Census survey inquires about regular wages but neglects tips, commissions, and bonuses. These irregular forms of compensation may be particularly important for workers with low hourly pay (e.g., salespeople and food servers).

Finally, the concept of the working poor is often thought to apply to people who work for low wages. However, the official statistics on working poverty do not distinguish paid workers from individuals who are self-employed. Closer examination of Census data reveals that of the 5.6 million individuals identified as workers in Figure 6.2, roughly 400,000 are *self-employed*. Although these self-employed individuals may have had similarly low incomes in a given year, their circumstances are not the same as the

---

[2]Gorham and Harrison, *Working Below the Poverty Line,* are among those who use this definition.

[3]U.S. Bureau of the Census, *Workers with Low Earnings: 1964 to 1990,* Series P-60, no. 178 (revised May 1994). See also John Formby, John Bishop, and Hoseong Kim, *The Economic Well-Being of Low-Income Working Families* (Washington, DC: Employment Policies Institute, March 2002).

[4]Ralph E. Smith and Bruce Vavrichek, "The Minimum Wage: Its Relation to Incomes and Poverty," *Monthly Labor Review* (June 1987), p. 29.

working poor who are paid by the hour. Self-employed persons may own farms or business assets of considerable value. They also have deductions and tax credits that leave them with little *taxable* income. In 2005, for example, nearly 80,000 *poor* self-employed individuals reported *negative* incomes. Self-employed persons also have some discretion in calculating their incomes and are prone to underreporting it. This does not mean that all self-employed persons are well-off, but rather that the perceived poverty of the self-employed working poor is exaggerated.

These measurement issues substantially change the portrait of the working poor painted by official Census data. Clearly, the number of year-round, full-time workers with incomes below the poverty index is much lower than Figure 6.2 suggests. That still leaves a lot of hard-working poor, but they constitute a small portion of the poverty population.

THE SIGNIFICANCE OF SECONDARY WORKERS

So far, we have examined the extent of poverty among *individuals* of varying work experience. Most individuals live in *families,* however, and families may supply more than one worker to the labor market. In fact, in two out of three married-couple families at least two people work for pay during the year. Accordingly, a family's participation in the labor market should be gauged not solely by the work activity of the house-holder (household head) but also by the work experience of other family members (secondary workers).

Secondary workers are in fact often decisive in keeping a family out of poverty. As Figure 6.3 illustrates, poverty rates fall dramatically when a second worker contributes

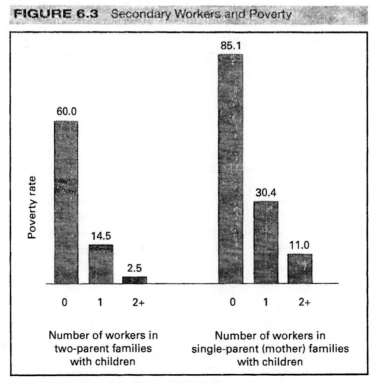

FIGURE 6.3 Secondary Workers and Poverty

Source: U.S. Bureau of the Census (2005 data).

to family income. A secondary worker in two-parent families drives the poverty rate down to 2.5 percent. In female-headed, single-parent families the poverty rate declines from 30 percent to 11 percent when a second worker appears. Clearly, the presence of a secondary worker is a decisive determinant of poverty status.

The presence of a secondary worker also distinguishes poor families from nonpoor families. Seventy percent of *non*poor families have the equivalent of at least 1.5 full-time workers on the job all year round. Among the poor, only two out of ten families have at least that many full-time workers.[5]

Such statistics suggest that the difference between poverty and a more comfortable living standard for the typical family may depend on the paychecks of secondary workers. Indeed, Professor Sar Levitan figured that 50 to 70 percent *more* two-earner families would be in poverty without the earnings of a secondary worker.[6] As it is, over 800,000 families who *are* in poverty have at least two members in the workforce. More than 100,000 families remain poor despite the presence of two *full-time* workers. A broader concept of the working poor might well encompass the combined employment activity of an entire family. If this were done, working poverty would appear more widespread than earlier suggested.

SEARCHING FOR EXPLANATIONS

Ambiguities about the nature and number of "working poor" cloud poverty perceptions, making policy decisions less certain. Two observations seem appropriate, however. First, there are far fewer working poor households than commonly thought. Second, *any* working poverty demands more explanation. How can people who work remain in poverty? Doesn't this paradox violate the very principles that make up our capitalist ideology? If we cannot guarantee economic security to those individuals who contribute their maximum work effort, what sort of admonitions or incentives can be directed to those who work less?

Setting aside the conceptual and statistical problems of identifying the working poor, we may proceed to potential explanations for the overlap between work and poverty. Two general explanations for the status of the hard-working poor come to mind.

The most obvious suggestion is that their wages are unusually low. At poverty wages, very few people can work hard enough or long enough to attain economic security. But low wages are not the only possible explanation for the plight of the working poor. Poverty refers to the relationship between a family's income and its needs. Thus, it might also be the case that the poor simply have above-average needs, due to either larger families or special expenses, for example, medical bills. In this situation, even average wages might leave the family financially destitute. The distinction between income and needs is vital for policy concerns. The one situation implies the need for labor-market intervention of some kind, while the second implies the need to address *non*market phenomena, such as family planning or health insurance.

---

[5]U.S. Congress, Committee on Ways and Means, *1992 Green Book* (Washington, DC: U.S. Government Printing Office, 1992), pp. 1280–1281. For more detail on recent employment activity by married mothers, see Howard V. Hayghe and Suzanne M. Blanchi, "Married Mothers' Work Patterns: The Job-Family Compromise," *Monthly Labor Review* (June 1994), pp. 24–30.

[6]Sar Levitan, "Part-Timers: Living on Half-Rations," *Challenge* (May–June 1988); see also Jennifer M. Gardner and Diane E. Herz, "Working and Poor in 1992," *Monthly Labor Review* (December 1992), pp. 20–28.

MINIMUM-WAGE JOBS

The federal minimum wage is an obvious candidate for explaining the coexistence of work and poverty. Congress first set the minimum wage at 25 cents per hour in 1938 (Fair Labor Standards Act). Since that time the wage floor has been increased numerous times (see Table 6.2) and reached $5.15 in 1997. Accordingly, a person who worked year-round, full-time (roughly 2,000 hours) in 2005 at the minimum wage would have earned only $10,300. That was barely enough income to keep one individual out of poverty, much less a family (see Table 3.4).

In 1981, a minimum-wage job was more effective in helping people out of poverty. In 1981, the minimum wage was only $3.35 an hour. But prices were much lower, too. Accordingly, the income from a year-round, minimum-wage job could have almost kept a three-person family out of poverty. Between 1981 and 1990, however, the federal minimum wage was not increased, even though prices of goods and services kept rising. As the *real* (inflation-adjusted) value of the minimum wage declined, it became more difficult for the working poor to escape poverty. Increases in the federal minimum wage in 1996–1997 helped restore its real value. After 1997, however, the real value of the minimum wage resumed its decline, as Figure 6.4 confirms. At the end of 2006 the nominal wage of $5.15 was worth only $2.09 in inflation-adjusted dollars. In 2007, Congress began to restore some of the lost real value, raising the minimum to $7.25 over a period of two years.

COVERAGE

Compounding the problem of a declining real minimum wage is the lack of complete coverage in federal law. Contrary to popular opinion, the federal minimum wage law doesn't apply to all jobs. Generally, the law applies only to businesses with at least $500,000 in annual revenue. Hence, most small businesses are excluded. Also excluded

TABLE 6.2 Minimum-Wage History

Date	Minimum Wage	Date	Minimum Wage
October 1938	$0.25	January 1979	$2.90
October 1939	0.30	January 1980	3.10
October 1945	0.40	January 1981	3.35
January 1950	0.75	April 1990	3.80
March 1956	1.00	April 1991	4.25
September 1961	1.15	October 1996	4.75
September 1963	1.25	September 1997	5.15
February 1967	1.40	May 2007	5.85
February 1968	1.60	January 2008	6.55
May 1974	2.00	September 2008	7.25
January 1975	2.10		
January 1976	2.30		
January 1978	2.65		

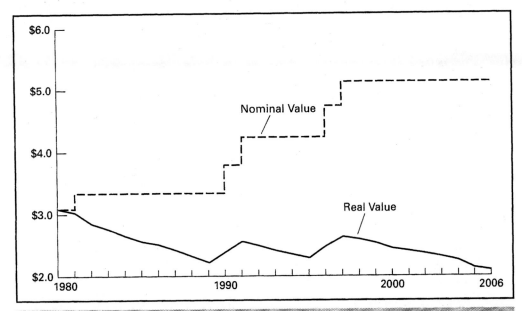

FIGURE 6.4 Nominal versus Real Value of Federal Minimum Wage

Note: Real value in 1980 dollars (adjusted by CPI).

Source: Economic Report of the President, 2006 (Washington, DC: Government Printing Office, 2006).

are many seasonal, charitable and educational employers. All told, as many as 30 percent of all workers aren't covered by the federal minimum wage.[7]

Individual states plug some of the holes in the federal law with their own minimum-wage statutes. Many states have also raised their own minimum-wage households above the federal level. However, the patchwork of state laws still leaves millions of workers uncovered or with a below-poverty-wage threshold.[8]

Although the coverage gaps and declining real value of the minimum wage contribute to working poverty, they are not as complete an explanation as first appears. As Table 6.3 shows, most of the people who hold minimum-wage jobs are *not* poor. They are more likely to be teenagers or other secondary workers from families with above-poverty incomes, working part-time in the leisure and hospitality (restaurants, hotels) industries. Only one out of four minimum-wage workers lives in a poor family. Or, to look at the relationship from a different perspective, we observe that less than one out of ten poor families contains a minimum-wage worker. Moreover, the earnings from that minimum-wage worker account for less than 10 percent of the family's cash income.[9]

---

[7]For more details on coverage, see Bradley R. Schiller, "Below Minimum-Wage Workers: Implications for Minimum-Wage Models," *Quarterly Review of Economics and Finance* (Summer 1994).

[8]For a discussion of state coverage, see Bradley R. Schiller, "State Minimum-Wage Laws: Coverage and Impact on Youth," *Journal of Labor Research* (Fall 1994). For the impact of state minimum wage thresholds on welfare caseloads, see Marianne Page, Joanne Soetz, and Jane Miller, "Does the Minimum Wage Affect Welfare Caseloads?" Joint Center for Poverty Research (September 1999).

[9]John Formby, John Bishop, and Hoseong Kim, *The Economic Well-Being of Low-Income Working Families* (Washington, DC: Employment Policies Institute, March 2002), Tables 1.3 and 1.4.

TABLE 6.3 Characteristics of Minimum-Wage Workers

Age		Gender	
16–19	26%	Male	34%
20–24	27%	Female	66%
25 and over	47%	**Marital Status**	
Race		Never married	64%
White	71%	Currently married	22%
Black	11%	Other	14%
Hispanic	15%	**Education**	
Asian	3%	Not high school graduate	30%
Poverty Status		High school graduate	29%
Poor	24%	Some college	34%
Nonpoor	76%	College graduate	7%
Work Experience		**Region**	
Full-time	40%	South	43%
Part-time	60%	North/West	57%
Industry			
Leisure and hospitality	64%		
Retail trade	9%		

Source: U.S. Bureau of Labor Statistics, "Characteristics of Minimum Wage Workers: 2005" (May 2006); poverty status extracted from John Formby, John Bishop, and Hoseong Kim, *The Economic Well-Being of Low-Income Families* (Washington, D.C.: Employment Policies Institute, March 2002). Table includes workers paid at or below 2005 federal minimum of $5.15 per hour.

It is also important to recognize that workers don't *stay* in minimum-wage jobs. By and large, minimum-wage jobs are simply stepping-stones for workers who are moving on to better-paying employment. Brad Pitt started out as a minimum-wage worker and went on to make millions of dollars as an actor. Not all minimum-wage workers make out so well. But minimum-wage jobs give labor-market entrants the opportunity to acquire experience, job information, and the employment references that are critical for career advancement. Accordingly, many individuals who are now working for minimum wages and in poverty may be earning higher wages and out of poverty quickly.[10]

Were the minimum wage increased, relatively few poor people would be lifted out of poverty.[11] There is also a risk that a higher minimum wage might reduce job opportunities for new labor-market entrants. If that were the case, some people

---

[10]See Bradley R. Schiller, "Moving Up: The Training and Wage Gains of Minimum-Wage Entrants," *Social Science Quarterly* (Summer 1994), pp. 622–636.

[11]Most of the benefit of a higher minimum wage would go to families that depend on it the least; see David Neumark, Mark Schweitzer, and William Wascher, "The Effects of Minimum Wages on the Distribution of Family Incomes," *Journal of Human Resources* (Fall 2005), pp. 867–894; Michael W. Horrigan and Ronald B. Mincy, "The Minimum Wage and Earnings and Income Inequalities," in *Uneven Tides: Rising Inequality in America,* eds. Sheldon Danziger and Peter Gottschalk (New York: Russell Sage, 1993), pp. 251–275. See also David Neumark and William Wascher, "Do Minimum Wages Fight Poverty?" (Cambridge, MA: National Bureau of Economic Research, 1997); Laura Connolly and Lewis M. Segal, "Minimum Wage Legislation and the Working Pool" (Oregon State University Mimeo, 1997); and Pade, Soetz, Miller, op. cit.

would be worse off and poverty might spread. Although the exact dimensions of such *disemployment* are hotly debated, the risk of job losses is universally recognized.[12]

LOW WAGES

Even though the federal minimum wage may not play a major role in explaining working poverty, wage rates are still relevant. The issue, however, is *low* wages, not necessarily the *minimum* wage set by Congress. The hourly wage needed to escape poverty via the route of year-round, full-time employment started at $10 in 2006 for a family of four and ratchets upward with increasing family size. Many people prefer to focus on these higher wage levels, rather than the federal minimum. The wage rate needed to generate enough earnings to reach the four-person poverty line is often referred to as the "living wage." Clearly, there is a substantial gap between the federal minimum wage and the living wage. Any household head earning wages in that gap is likely to be among the working poor.[13]

Table 6.4 provides some evidence on the actual earnings of individuals who head poverty families. Those who worked year-round, full-time (the prototypical "working poor") are distinguished from those who worked less than that or not at all. If it is assumed that "year-round, full-time" work entails at least 1,820 hours of work per year, a minimum-wage worker would have earned close to $10,000 in 2005. According to Table 6.4, seven out of ten working-poor heads of households earned wages in excess of that threshold. But only 7 percent of these year-round, full-time workers earned enough to keep a four-person family out of poverty, that is, at least $20,000 a year. The median wage of the working poor was around $6 per hour.

The working poor are not the only workers paid low wages. Table 6.5 shows the distribution of wages for all workers paid on an hourly basis.[14] Over 1.4 million workers were paid less than the minimum wage in 2005. Nearly 26 million workers were paid less than the $10 an hour needed to keep a four-person family out of poverty.

---

[12]David Neumark, Mark Schweitzer, and William Wascher, "Minimum Wage Effects Throughout the Wage Distribution," *Journal of Human Resources* (Spring 2004), pp. 425–450; Tessence Yuen, "The Effect of Minimum Wages on Youth Employment in Canada," *Journal of Human Resources* (Summer 2003), pp. 647–672. Oren Levin-Waldman emphasizes that the risk of job loss is small when the real value of the minimum wage declines, as in 1997–2002; see his "The Minimum Wage Can Be Raised," *Challenge* (March–April 2000), pp. 86–96; for an early review of empirical studies, see Charles Brown, Curtis Gilroy, and Andrew Kohen, "The Effect of the Minimum Wage on Employment and Unemployment," *Journal of Economic Literature* (June 1982), pp. 487–528; for updates, see Allison J. Wellington, "Effects of the Minimum Wage on the Employment Status of Youths," *Journal of Human Resources* (Winter 1991), pp. 27–46; Janet Currie and Bruce C. Fallick, "The Minimum Wage and the Employment of Youth," *Journal of Human Resources* (Spring 1996), pp. 404–428; and David Neumark and William Wascher, "State-Level Estimates of Minimum-Wage Effects," *Journal of Human Resources* (Winter 2002), pp. 35–62.

The nature and impacts of *state* minimum-wage laws are examined in Bradley R. Schiller, "State Minimum-Wage Laws: Youth Coverage and Impact," *Journal of Labor Research* (Fall 1994), pp. 317–329; David Neumark and William Wascher, "Employment Effects of Minimum and Subminimum Wages: Panel Data on State Minimum-Wage Laws," *Industrial and Labor Relations Review* (October 1992), pp. 55–81; David Card, "Do Minimum Wages Reduce Employment? A Case Study of California, 1987–89," *Industrial and Labor Relations Review* (October 1992), pp. 38–54.

[13]Local living wage ordinances typically affect relatively few jobs but do raise wages; see David Neumark and Scott Adams, "Do Living Wage Ordinances Reduce Urban Poverty?" *Journal of Human Resources* (Summer 2003), pp. 490–521.

[14]Recall that the Census Bureau tends to underestimate wage rates by overestimating hours worked and omitting tips, commissions, and bonuses.

TABLE 6.4 Annual Earnings of Household Heads of Poor Families

Earnings	Worked During Year	
	Full-Time Year-Round	*Less Than Full-Time*
Less than $2,000	13.4%	20.2%
$2,000–$3,999	4.2	18.9
$4,000–$5,999	5.2	17.5
$6,000–$7,999	7.2	14.9
$8,000–$9,999	10.8	10.8
$10,000–$11,999	15.7	10.0
$12,000–$13,999	11.0	4.0
$14,000–$15,999	13.7	2.2
$16,000–$19,999	11.4	0.9
Over $20,000	7.4	0.4
	100.0	100.0
Number who worked	1,801,000	3,806,000
Number without earnings	8,722,000	

Source: U.S. Bureau of the Census (2005 data).

What keeps most of these low-wage workers out of poverty is the absence of family responsibilities or the work efforts of other family members. Among women earning less than this living wage, half have no children and another 37 percent have only one or two children. Hence, relatively few families remain in poverty because of low wages.[15]

TABLE 6.5 Hourly Wage Rates by Age, 2005

Hourly Wage	Number of Workers (in Thousands)			
	Age 16–19	*Age 20–24*	*Age 25+*	*Total*
Under $5.00	196	347	541	1,090
$5–5.99	791	403	819	2,013
$6–6.99	1,441	1,072	2,317	3,530
$7–7.99	1,254	1,668	3,681	6,603
$8–8.99	809	1,754	4,829	7,392
$9–9.99	364	1,227	4,383	5,974
$10 or more	673	4,375	42,666	47,714
Median wage	$7.05	$8.91	$12.48	$11.19
Mean wage	$7.40	$9.58	$14.64	$13.38

Table includes only those workers normally paid on an hourly basis (U.S. total = 74.3 million).
Source: U.S. Bureau of Labor Statistics.

---

[15]See Formby, op. cit.; also Marlene Kim, "Women Paid Low Wages: Who They Are and Where They Work," *Monthly Labor Review* (September 2000), pp. 26–30. For more information on workers who continue to work at or near the federal minimum wage, see William Carrington and Bruce Fallick, "Do Some Workers Have Minimum Wage Careers?" *Monthly Labor Review* (May 2001), pp. 17–27.

TABLE 6.6 Escape Routes from Low-Income Earnings
(percent distributions)

Number of low-earning households	17.03 million
In poverty	36%
Not in poverty	64%
Escape routes from poverty	
Small family size	43.5%
Other workers in family	27.1%
Nonearnings income	13.1%
Welfare benefits	11.6%
Combinations of above	4.3%

Notes: Households include only those "expected to work," i.e., heads under age 65, nondisabled, not in school, and not sole parent of child under six. Low earnings are defined as wages below $204 per week, the amount needed in 1984 to reach the poverty threshold for a family of four.

Source: Adapted from Sheldon Danziger and Peter Gottschalk, "Work, Poverty, and the Working Poor: A Multifaceted Problem," *Monthly Labor Review* (September 1986), p. 19.

Danziger and Gottschalk looked specifically at household heads, rather than all workers. They discovered that one-fourth of all household heads who are neither aged, disabled, nor single parents of preschool children earn less than the average poverty threshold. Surprisingly, two-thirds of these low earners were able to escape poverty. Table 6.6 shows how they escaped. Smaller family size was the most frequent explanation for escaping poverty, followed by the presence of an additional worker in the family.

The low-wage workers who escaped poverty in Table 6.6 may not stay out of poverty long. Although nonpoor, these families are not far removed from poverty. A downturn in the economy, illness, or a new birth can push these low-earning households back into poverty quickly. This is, in fact, a frequent sequence.[16] In view of the fact that over 6 *million* year-round, full-time workers were still earning less than $20,000 per year in 2005, the potential for sudden surges in poverty is apparent. In the best of circumstances, they are referred to as the near-poor. In less favorable times these workers and their families become part of the poverty population.

POOR JOBS

If there is any moral to be gleaned from the foregoing figures, perhaps it is this: A poor janitor who works hard stands a very good chance of becoming a hard-working poor janitor. Low wages can be a barrier to escaping poverty. They can also deter people

---

[16]See Duncan Greg et al., *Years of Poverty, Years of Plenty* (Ann Arbor, MI: Institute for Social Research, 1984): also Peter Gottschalk, Sara McLanahan, and Gary D. Sandefur, "The Dynamics and Intergenerational Transmission of Poverty," in *Confronting Poverty*, eds. S. Danziger, G. Sandefur, and D. Weinberg (Cambridge, MA: Harvard University Press, 1994), pp. 85–108. Transitions in and out of jobs and poverty look even more frequent when viewed in monthly (versus annual) periods; see Kathleen Mullan Harris, "Work and Welfare among Single Mothers in Poverty," *American Journal of Sociology* (September 1993), pp. 317–352.

from taking jobs that are available. Elliot Liebow summarized the dismal prospects of many low-wage workers in this way:

> ... the man does not have any reasonable expectation that, however bad it is, his job will lead to better things. Menial jobs are not, by and large, the starting point of a track system which leads to even better jobs for those who are able and willing to do them. The busboy or dishwasher in a restaurant is not on a job track which, if negotiated skillfully, leads to chef or manager of the restaurant. The busboy or dishwasher who works hard becomes, simply, a hard-working busboy or dishwasher. Neither hard work nor perseverance can conceivably carry the janitor to a sit-down job in the office building he cleans up.[17]

Not all the poor, of course, are janitors. Most middle-class persons, in fact, probably think of janitors as low-income workers, but not poor. More likely to come to mind—if we admit the poor work at all—are office cleaners, dishwashers, day laborers, low-skill production workers, plus a small army of aged farmers and migrant farm workers. Once again, however, the preconception departs considerably from the reality of everyday poverty. The working poor are likely to be found in all broad occupational categories. Table 6.7 depicts the actual occupational distribution of those individuals officially classified as "working poor." While it is true that one out of six farmers and farm workers are poor, these two occupations account for less than 2 percent of the jobs held by the poor; many more poor people work as craft or production workers. Even white-collar jobs do not guarantee financial security, as more than 1.2 million people depicted in the table testify.

It is just as easy to overstate the occupational status of the poor as it is to understate it. The occupational profile of Table 6.7 includes very broad employment categories and may lead to erroneous impressions. While there are 250,000 poor managerial and financial workers, there are very few poor bank managers or tax professionals, among them.

TABLE 6.7 Occupations of Poor Heads of Household

Occupation	Number of Persons
Managerial, business financial	250,000
Clerical workers	478,000
Sales workers	688,000
Cleaning, maintenance	457,000
Personal care	392,000
Health care	295,000
Food service	576,000
Construction, mining	419,000
Operators, production	491,000
Transportation	347,000
Farming, fishing, forestry	77,000
Other	1,136,000
Total	5,609,000

Source: U.S. Bureau of the Census (2005 data).

---

[17]Elliot Liebow, *Tally's Corner: A Study of Negro Streetcorner Men* (Boston: Little, Brown, 1967), p. 63.

Similarly, in other occupational categories, the poor tend to hold the least desirable, most marginal kinds of jobs. They are dishwashers, loggers, food processors, porters, tailors, office cleaners, and laundry workers. Accordingly, while it is true that the working poor are distributed throughout the labor market and in all industries, they will always be found in the lowest-ranking, least noticeable jobs. They constitute what might be called a phantom labor force. John Schwartz calls them the "forgotten Americans": As they continue working hard for poverty wages, the problems of other poor people (e.g., displaced workers, teenage mothers) capture the public's attention.

WHY WAGES ARE SO LOW

While poverty and employment might seem incompatible, there is no shortage of available explanations for the low wages of the working poor. The poor are undereducated, inexperienced, underskilled, geographically handicapped, and trained in the wrong occupations. They also have to compete with a flood of immigrants who are willing to work for low wages.

Abundant evidence exists to support each of these explanations. We must also recognize, however, that these explanations focus almost exclusively on the *supply* side of the labor market. They tell us what qualities an individual brings to the labor market but don't really explain why the worker is paid so little for them. To understand the process by which wages are determined, we must also ask what the *demand* side of the labor market looks like.

In the most general terms, we say that a worker's wages are determined by the contribution he or she makes to output, that is, by his or her marginal product. But what is it that makes the output of a pipe fitter less valuable than the output of an advertising executive? What differentiates the incomes of these two people is not the physical output that each produces, but rather the value that society attaches to their products. If society suddenly became disenchanted with the wares of advertising executives and found increased value in fitted pipes, the incomes of pipe fitters would exceed those of advertising executives, regardless of their respective physical outputs. By the same reasoning, if society were to attach more value to the kinds of output that the poor can and do produce, we could expect the incomes of the working poor to rise.

The notion that the extent and structure of demand are significant determinants of the wages of the poor does not constitute a revolution in economic thinking. Economists have long taken credit for the discovery that prices, and thus wages, are determined by the interaction of supply and demand. In antipoverty discussions, however, the impact of the demand side of the market on the economic position of the poor is easily neglected. Doing so ignores tremendous potential for eliminating poverty.

During the 1940s, there was a tendency for wage rates and incomes at the bottom of the occupational ladder to rise faster than those at the top. This was due to an upsurge in demand for unskilled, semiskilled, and operative kinds of labor needed for war production. The structure of demand since the 1940s, however, has primarily benefited workers with higher education and more technical expertise. This trend has been particularly strong since 1979.[18] Accordingly, we find the unskilled, semiskilled, and

---

[18]See the symposium on wage inequality in the *Journal of Economic Perspectives* (Spring 1997). For international comparisons, see Peter Gottschalk and Timothy M. Smeeding, "Cross National Comparisons of Earnings and Income Inequality," *Journal of Economic Literature* (June 1997), pp. 633–687.

operative workers heavily represented among the poor. The distribution of wages and incomes is partly a reflection of collective social decisions regarding the merits of particular kinds of output. Sociopolitical decisions to expand the educational system, to develop missile systems, to build an information highway, to explore space, and to expand international trade have all had a profound impact on the structure of demand for labor. Had we decided instead to dredge more rivers, to build more houses, or to clean up our cities, the extent and nature of poverty might now be markedly different. Without attempting to predict those changes here, we may at least take note of the fact that the poor suffer from both inadequate human capital investment (the supply side) as from the pattern of labor utilization (the demand side). By the same token, the working poor could benefit from more education and training, as well as an expansion and reconfiguration of labor demand. In later chapters we will examine policies that affect both the supply and demand for workers from low-income backgrounds.

Summary

Labor force participation is a necessary but not sufficient prerequisite for escaping poverty. Millions of people live in poor families despite extensive labor force activity by family members.

Problems in defining and measuring the "working poor" complicate analysis of this phenomenon. The purest measure of working poverty focuses on individuals who live in poverty despite working year-round at a full-time job. These full-time workers are only a small fraction of the poverty population. Nevertheless, their plight is incompatible with the notion that work is a sure route out of poverty.

While it is true that the federal minimum wage is not high enough to keep a family out of poverty, most minimum-wage workers are not poor. They are more likely to be teenagers or secondary workers from middle-class families. The broader phenomenon of low (not necessarily minimum) wages is a better explanation for working poverty.

The structure of wages reflects both supply characteristics of workers and the pattern of demand for labor. The low end of the wage structure does not itself necessitate poverty, as millions of low-wage but nonpoor workers attest. However, low wages in combination with greater family needs do leave millions of individuals in poverty and others near poor. To reduce the ranks of the working poor requires changes in both labor supply (e.g., education and training) and labor demand (a strong economy and restructured demand).

Further Reading

Andersson, Frank, Harry Holzer, and Julia Lane, *Moving Up or Moving On: Who Advances in the Low-Wage Labor Market.* New York: Russell Sage, 2005.

Blank, Roberta, Sheldon Danziger, and Robert Schooni, *Working and Poor.* New York: Russell Sage, 2006.

Burkhauser, Richard and Joseph Sabia, "The Effectiveness of Minimum-Wage Increases in Reducing Poverty: Past, Present, and Future," *Contemporary Economic Policy* (April 2007), pp. 262–281.

Egendorf, Laura, ed., *Poverty: Opposing Viewpoints.* San Diego, CA: Greenhaven Press, 1999, Chapter 3.

Formby, John, John Bishop, and Hoseong Kim, *The Economic Well-Being of Low-Income Working Families.* Washington, DC: Employment Policies Institute, March 2002.

Mishel, Lawrence, Jared Bernstein, and Sylvia Allegretto, *The State of Working America, 2006/2007*. Washington, DC: Economic Policy Institute, 2006.

Munger, Frank, ed., *Laboring Below the Line.* New York: Russell Sage, 2002.

Neumark, David, and William Wascher, "Minimum Wages and Employment: A Review of Evidence from the New Minimum Wage Research." Cambridge, MA: National Bureau of Economic Research, 2006.

Schiller, Bradley R., "Who Are the Working Poor?" *The Public Interest* (Spring 1994), pp. 61–71.

Schwarz, John E., *Illusions of Opportunity*. New York: Norton, 1997.

Schwartz, John E., and Thomas J. Volgy, *The Forgotten Americans*. New York: Norton, 1992.

Theodos, Breft, and Robert Bednarzik, "Earnings, Mobility and Low-Wage Workers in the United States," *Monthly Labor Review* (Summer 2006), pp. 34–47.

U.S. Bureau of Labor Statistics, *A Profile of the Working Poor*. Washington, DC: U.S. Government Printing Office, annual.

Web Links

National Bureau of Economic Research. Research studies relating to employment, earnings, and wage rates: www.nber.org

U.S. Bureau of Labor Statistics. Annual report on characteristics of the working poor: http://bls.gov

U.S. Department of Labor. Minimum wage legislation, history, effects, and research studies: www.dol.gov/dol

University of Michigan, Research from the National Poverty Center: www.npc.umkh.edu.

APPENDIX 1

☙

DOES PROSPERITY TRICKLE DOWN?

This and the previous chapter have documented the labor-market problems of poor people. Poor people don't participate enough in the labor market. When they do, a combination of unemployment and low wages keeps them in poverty.

While the poverty population has remained at a high level since 1980, the U.S. economy has grown substantially. This has led many people to question whether and how Main Street's prosperity is shared with the poor. Do the poor benefit from general economic growth or do they live in an isolated subeconomy?

THE TRICKLE-DOWN PERSPECTIVE

The *trickle-down theory* asserts that people at the bottom of the economic hierarchy benefit from any increased prosperity at higher income levels.[19] If this is true, then public policy need not focus on the poor but can instead pursue more general growth and income strategies.

The reasoning behind the trickle-down theory is straightforward. Suppose that the federal government decides to build a shuttle capable of taxiing busloads of scientists and tourists back and forth to the moon. Such an undertaking would require the expenditure of tens of billions of dollars and the employment of highly skilled labor and capital equipment. The question is whether and how the poor would benefit from this excursion into space.

It is possible, of course, that some of the poor would be employed directly in the moon shuttle program, say, as grounds sweepers, gate attendants, or other low-skilled jobs. But the potential for such direct job creation is apt to be small. A far likelier source of jobs is the multiplier effects that will take place once the program gets under way. The aerospace workers will want to spend their increased incomes, and in so doing will add to the demand for more conventional goods and services, such as houses, hot dogs, beer, gardeners, and maids. As the production of these goods and services expands, more jobs and incomes will be created, thereby increasing the chances that some needy souls from the ranks of the poor will obtain better jobs and wages. Such multiplier effects will continue to reverberate through the economy as the income spent by the aerospace workers is passed from hand to hand.

Although multiplier effects provide the best hope of jobs and income for the poor, there are other ways in which the poor might benefit from the moon shuttle program. The people who obtain jobs directly in the moon shuttle program will probably vacate positions that offered lower wages or benefits, jobs that then are available to others, including the poor. Such substitution effects may continue all the way down the occupational ladder, ultimately resulting in job vacancies for the poor. In addition, employers faced with a sudden shortage of labor will have an economic incentive to train the poor and unskilled, thereby further enlarging the size of the trickle.

An increase in government spending may also put upward pressure on wages. As the demand for workers outstrips supply, all wages—including those of the working poor—will creep upward. Hence, there are three distinct avenues by which prosperity may trickle down to the working poor.

---

[19]The expression *trickle down* was coined by W. H. Locke Anderson in "Trickling Down: The Relationship between Economic Growth and the Extent of Poverty among American Families," *Quarterly Journal of Economics* (November 1964) and has earlier origins in William Jennings Bryan's 1896 "Cross of Gold" speech in which he declared, "There are those who believe that, if you will only legislate to make the well-to-do prosperous, their prosperity will leak through on those below."

THE DUAL LABOR MARKET PERSPECTIVE

Although the trickle-down hypothesis seems plausible enough, not everyone shares the expectations it generates. In particular, it is argued that the poor do not really participate in the mainstream economy and are excluded from the jobs and income that a moon shuttle program would create. In effect, it is argued, the poor participate in a separate and distinct labor market, a *secondary labor market*, which is distinguished from the mainstream or *primary labor market*.[20] From the perspective of the dual labor-market hypothesis, an expansion of demand that occurs in the primary market such as in a moon shuttle program will not benefit workers in the secondary market. A variety of barriers allegedly exclude the poor from the primary labor market, in effect creating the secondary market. Outright discrimination against minority groups or the poor, for example, would exclude the poor from the trickle. So, too, would recruiting practices that emphasized skill, experience, and stable work histories, prerequi-sites that the poor job seeker can rarely satisfy. Institutional barriers like strong labor unions could have the same effect, especially if unions opted to maximize the earnings of their current members rather than to expand employment and union membership.

It is unlikely, of course, that these barriers would be so great as to exclude all poor job seekers from the benefits created by a moon shuttle program (or any other form of demand expansion). It is much more reasonable to expect that some additional jobs and income will in fact trickle down, thereby reducing the number of people we count as poor. This expectation still appears valid.[21] However, recent changes in the structure of labor markets may have slowed the trickle. What the dual labor market hypothesis tells us is that the really critical issue is *how much* actually trickles down. And it also suggests that public policy can be used to increase the size of that trickle by reducing the barriers that separate the poor from the jobs and incomes an expanding economy creates.

---

[20]Peter Doerringer and Michael Piore popularized these concepts in "Unemployment and the Dual Labor Market," *The Public Interest* (Winter 1975). Also see Glen G. Cain, "The Challenge of Segmented Labor Market Theories to Orthodox Theory: A Survey," *Journal of Economic Literature* (December 1976).

[21]For case studies of trickle down, see Paul Osterman, "Gains from Growth? The Impact of Full Employment of Poverty in Boston," and Richard B. Freeman, "Employment and Earning of Disadvantaged Young Men in a Labor Shortage Economy," both in *The Urban Underclass*, eds. C. Jencks and P. Peterson (Washington, DC: Urban Institute, 1991).

For more aggregated results, see Richard B. Freeman, "The Rising Tide Lifts . . .?" in *Understanding Poverty*, eds. S. Danziger and R. Haveman (Cambridge, MA: Harvard University Press, 2001); Rebecca Blank and David Card, "Poverty, Income Distribution, and Growth: Are They Still Connected?" *Brookings Papers on Economic Activity* (1993:2).

CHAPTER 7
AGE AND HEALTH

∽

Lack of employment is the principal cause of poverty for able-bodied adults of working age. But what about people who are past traditional working ages and people with illness or disabilities that preclude employment? What special problems do they have? Why are some older individuals poor while others live comfortably? How completely does illness or disability explain the poverty of people with such problems? These are the questions pursued in this chapter.

AGE

We observed in Chapter 3 that more than 3.6 million individuals over age 65 were officially counted as poor in 2005. We also noted that the official poverty count omits institutionalized persons and older individuals who live with nonpoor relatives because they cannot afford to maintain households of their own. Accordingly, the official count understates the number of older individuals with incomes below the poverty index. Yet even the official count suggests that one out of ten Americans in poverty is over the age of 65.

DECLINING POVERTY RATE

Although a sizable fraction of the poverty population, the aged actually have a lesser probability of being poor. While popular images of poverty often feature older people, persons over age 65 are less likely to be poor than are younger adults. Older individuals are also much less likely to be poor than are children.

The lower incidence of poverty among the aged is a relatively new phenomenon. When the war on poverty began in the mid-1960s, poverty rates among the aged were triple those of younger adults and far above those of children. As Figure 7.1 illustrates, that disparity has been reversed. The incidence of poverty among the aged has declined dramatically, while poverty rates for younger groups have crept upward.

The dramatic decline in poverty among the aged is cause for celebration. Despite these favorable trends, however, poverty among the aged remains a serious concern. As people age they become more vulnerable to changing health, economic conditions, and public policy. Most of the decline in aged poverty since the mid-1960s is due to rising income transfers like Social Security. Medicare and Medicaid have also increased the uncounted but real income of the aged. Without these financial props, poverty among the aged would be far more common. We might wonder, therefore, why so many older people *would* be poor without such public support.

We have to recognize also that poverty among the aged tends to be more permanent. As we observed in Chapter 3, there is a lot of movement in and out of poverty

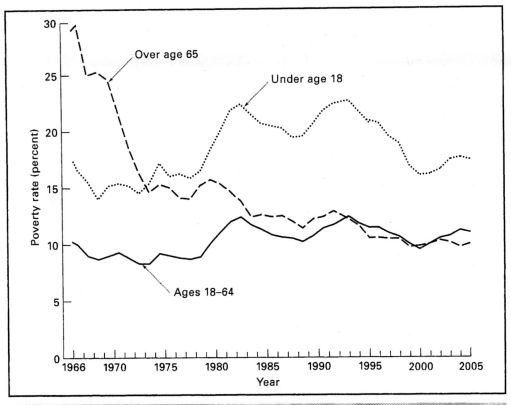

FIGURE 7.1 Poverty Rates by Age, 1966–2005

Source: U.S. Bureau of the Census.

each year. For older persons, however, poverty exit rates are much lower. As a consequence, older people who fall into poverty are likely to *stay* poor.[1]

We should also note that the economic problems of the aged will become increasingly important as the number of people living past the age of 65 continues to grow. Since 1900, the number of people living until age 65 has increased dramatically. In addition, the life expectancy of people at age 65 has also increased. Life expectancy for people reaching 65 was about 11 years in 1900; now it is more like 18 years. Hence, there are far more aged people today and they are living longer. This is partly reflected in the overall increase in life expectancies. In 1900, life expectancy at birth was 49 years; today it is over 76 years.

This increase in the size of the older population is continuing. In fact, the post–World War II "baby boom" will become a "seniors' boom" in the next two decades. (The baby boomers were born during the period 1946–1960. They start reaching age 65 in 2011.) In the process, the number of aged persons will jump from 35 million in 2000 to 61 million in the year 2025. By then, nearly one-fifth of the total U.S. population will be over age 65. Continuing discoveries in medical science may expand the aged population

---

[1]Ke Bin Wu, "Poverty Experience of Older Persons" (Washington, DC: AARP Public Policy Institute, March 2003).

FIGURE 7.2 Poverty Rates by Age

Source: U.S. Bureau of the Census (2005 data).

still further. Just to hold the line on the *number* of aged poor, we will have to cut their poverty *rate* almost in half.

These considerations led Michael Harrington to observe that "the poverty of old age in America is rooted in a biological revolution."[2] We must take care, however, not to attribute to biology the economic ills of the aged. Changing fertility patterns and medical advances are responsible only for the fact that so many more people live to old age. They do not explain why so many of these people live in poverty.

DIVERSITY AMONG THE AGED

Before looking closer at the economic situation of the aged, it is important to recognize the diversity among the aged. Young people tend to regard all people over 65 as "old." But people in their sixties often feel quite youthful and look at their *parents* or similarly aged individuals when asked about the "old people." With so many Americans living long past age 65, it has become increasingly necessary to distinguish the *old old* from those who are merely *old.* Traditionally, age 65 has been the threshold for defining *old,* while ages 75, 80, or even 85 have been used to identify the *old old.*

The distinction between the old and the old old is not simply a matter of age. The old old tend to have more health problems and to live alone. As a consequence they are also more likely to be poor. As Figure 7.2 illustrates, poverty rates rise as older people age. The poverty rate for people over age 80 is 25 percent higher than the rate for people aged 65–69. The young old often still work, are generally healthy, and typically live with a spouse. Because men die at earlier ages than women, the old old are predominantly widows: Three out of four poor individuals over age 85 are women.

These demographic changes that occur past age 65 are summarized in Table 7.1, which distinguishes the *old old* (over age 85) from the *young old* (ages 65–84). The largest subgroup of people over age 85 are widows living alone (shown as "nonmarried" Table 7.1). For people aged 65–84, married couples comprise the largest group. Whereas only 12 percent of the married couples aged 65–84 are poor, one out of five

---

[2]Michael Harrington, *The Other America* (New York: Macmillan, 1962), p. 102.

TABLE 7.1 Age, Sex, and Marital Status of Individuals over Age 65

Characteristic of Person	Age of Person	
	85 or Older	65–84
Total (percent)	100	100
Female	**66**	**57**
Married	8	26
Nonmarried	58	31
Living alone	38	21
Living with family	20	10
Male	**34**	**43**
Married	19	32
Nonmarried	14	12
Living alone	10	8
Living with family	4	4
Number of persons (in millions)	3.5	30.7

Source: U.S. Census Bureau (2003 data).

widows over age 85 is poor. What makes the latter statistic particularly frightening is that the fastest growing subgroup among the aged are the widows over 85.

Racial patterns also change at older ages. As is true for younger people, poverty rates among the old are much higher for blacks (23 percent) and Hispanics (20 percent) than whites (9 percent). However, whites far outnumber minorities among the aged poor, accounting for 8 out of 10 of the old old poor. In part, this discrepancy reflects the fact that low-income blacks and Hispanics die at earlier ages than whites (Anglos).[3]

SOURCES OF ECONOMIC SUPPORT

To explain so much poverty among the aged, we need to examine their actual and potential sources of income. These include earnings, returns on capital (e.g., interest and dividends), and income transfers.

Earnings

The most obvious constraint on the incomes of the aged is the fact that so few older individuals remain in the labor force. Only about one out of six older persons participates in the labor market at all. Moreover, participation and actual employment decline rapidly with increasing age. The poor among the aged are even less likely to work; in 2005 only 5 percent of the aged poor had any work experience. Full-time, year-round work was even rarer: Only one out of 100 aged poor worked that much. This low level of employment is a major constraint on their economic status.

---

[3]Race differences in mortality and morbidity rates are discussed in J. Paul Leigh, "Distribution of Lifetime Income Allowing for Varying Mortality Rates, Among Women, Men, Blacks, and Whites," *Journal of Economic Issues* (December 1992), pp. 1191–1220; Gregory Pappas et al., "The Increasing Disparity in Mortality between Socioeconomic Groups in the United States, 1960 and 1986," *New England Journal of Medicine* (July 1993), pp. 103–109; and Orazio Attanasio and Hillary Hoynes, "Differential Mortality and Wealth Accumulation," *Journal of Human Resources* (Winter 2000), pp. 1–29.

Low labor force participation among the aged reflects a continuing trend in American society. At the beginning of the twentieth century, more than two-thirds of all men over the age of 65 were in the labor force; today, only one out of five older men works. The reasons for this decline in labor force participation are many, but surely they do not include the increased physical requirements of labor or diminished health status of the aged: Jobs aren't as physically demanding today as they were a generation or more ago and people's health has improved. Hence, the cause of declining labor force participation lies elsewhere. An increased desire for leisure, an abatement of the economic necessity to work, and a reduced demand for the skills of the aged are more likely explanations for the decline in labor force participation.

There is evidence that many older workers are involuntarily removed from the labor force because of forced retirement and prolonged unemployment. If older workers are laid off for any reason (for example, plant shutdowns, production slowdowns, or forced retirement), they face little chance of finding another job. They often have developed highly specialized skills in a declining occupation. Moreover, because of their advanced age, other employers see little benefit in retraining them or redirecting their skills. Other employers also anticipate the increased costs of higher disability rates and imminent retirement. Simple economics weigh against the older job seeker. Because employment prospects are so unpromising, the older job seeker is likely to drop out of the labor force earlier than desired, eliminating a prospective income source.[4] Of those older persons already retired, over one-third report they were forced out of their jobs. Nearly half of those older persons in poverty report forced retirements.[5]

Assets

There are alternatives to employment income, of course. Some of the most common substitutes are income from savings, assets, and various retirement plans. The income flow from such assets can help reduce the impact of lost employment income. Indeed, the availability of alternative sources of income could actually encourage retirement, with no implied loss of individual welfare. The question is: Are the aged adequately provided with nonemployment retirement income?

A potentially important source of income for the aged is the savings they accumulated during their working years. Unfortunately, such savings are typically inadequate. Because the aged live longer and retire earlier today, they must accumulate greater savings than they once did. The unfortunate but simple economic fact is that the longer one lives, the greater are the chances of destitution. A person's employment capabilities and opportunities disappear at the same time that savings are depleted. Today's aged must command considerable assets and savings if they are to experience a comfortable retirement.

In reality, most Americans save relatively little during their working years. As a result, their wealth in the "golden years" is typically modest. The *median* household wealth of persons over age 65 is around $160,000. That in itself is not a large number,

---

[4]The influence of age on postdisplacement labor force status is discussed in Congressional Budget Office, *Displaced Workers: Trends in the 1980s and Implications for the Future* (Washington, DC: U.S. Government Printing Office, 1993). For an update, see Steven Hipple, "Worker Displacement in the Mid-1990's," *Monthly Labor Review* (July 1999), pp. 15–32.

[5]U.S. Bureau of the Census, *65+ in the United States: 2005* (Washington, DC.: Government Printing Office, 2005), Table, 4-5; also National Council on Aging, *The Myth and Reality of Aging in America* (Washington, DC: National Council on Aging, 1977), p. 87. Poor health appears to be the major cause of *early* retirement (ages 51–59).

TABLE 7.2   Income Sources of Aged Households

	Percent of Households Receiving Income	
Income Source	Poor	Nonpoor
Earnings	9.1	38.2
Interest, dividends	25.2	62.8
Alimony	0.6	1.0
Pensions	7.5	47.1
Social Insurance		
Social Security	77.9	91.7
Unemployment, disability, or veterans benefits	3.8	9.2
Welfare		
Cash welfare benefits	1.4	0.4
Food stamps	17.1	2.0
Housing assistance	15.9	3.9

Note: The term *household* refers here to individuals living alone or multiperson households in which any member is 65 or over:

Source: U.S. Social Security Administration and House Ways and Means Committee (2002 data).

particularly in view of the long life expectancies of people at age 65. To make matters worse, most of that wealth is held in the form of home equity, which cannot easily be converted to cash unless the house is sold or mortgaged. *Financial* assets like stocks and bonds, which are more readily convertible to cash, account for less than a fifth of all assets held by the aged.[6]

The *median* wealth of aged households doesn't do much for older individuals on the lower rungs of the economic ladder. There is a high correlation between wealth and income. In fact, the value of accumulated wealth rises disproportionately with income. Older people in the highest *income* quintile have 11 times more *wealth* than those in the lowest quintile.[7] Low-income persons *approaching* retirement age (ages 55–64) have median nonhousing wealth of less than $2,000. These people certainly won't be able to live off their wealth in their "golden" years.[8]

Income Sources
Table 7.2 and Figure 7.3 illustrate the consequences of these low savings accumulations. Notice in Table 7.2 that 63 percent of the aged nonpoor receive dividends and interests, while only 25 percent of the aged poor get any income from stocks, savings accounts, and bonds. Moreover, the amount of such income is pitifully small, averaging less than

[6]For details on wealth holdings, see U.S. Census Bureau, 65+., op. cit., Table 4-10, also Ana M. Aizcorbe, Martha Starr-McCluer, and Kevin B. Moore, "Recent Changes in U.S. Family Finances: Results from the 1998 and 2001 Survey of Consumer Finances," *Federal Reserve Bulletin* (January 2003), pp. 1–32.

[7]U.S. Bureau of the Census, *65+ in the United States 2005* op. cit., Table 4-10; also see Congressional Budget Office, *Baby Boomers in Retirement: An Early Perspective* (Washington, DC: U.S. Government Printing Office, 1993).

[8]If the present value of future Social Security benefits is included in the wealth computation, newly retired persons are much less vulnerable to asset poverty; see Robert Haveman, Karen Holden, Barbara Wolfe, and Shane Sherlund, "Do Newly Retired Workers in the United States Have Sufficient Resources to Maintain Well-Being," *Economic Inquiry* (April 2006), pp. 249–264.

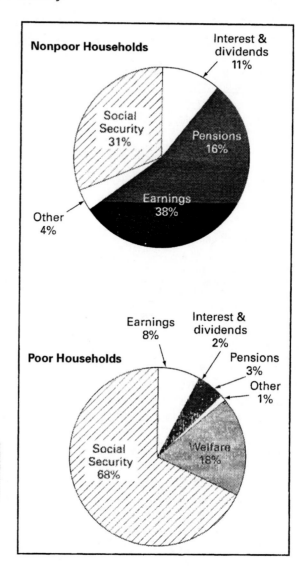

FIGURE 7.3 Relative Income Sources of Poor and Nonpoor Aged Households

Source: U.S. House of Representatives, Committee on Ways and Means, *2004 Green Book,* Table A-10.

$200 a year for poor households. By contrast, aged nonpoor households get over $4,000 a year—nearly a sixth of their income—in dividends and interest. If the poor had comparable portfolios of accumulated stocks, bonds, and savings, they would not be poor.

NEW POVERTY OR CONTINUING POVERTY?

Two more questions arise with regard to the savings of the aged: First, did the aged poor ever possess enough resources to save for old age? And second, did they save what resources they had? The distinction is important for policy purposes because many observers still believe it is necessary to distinguish the deserving poor from the undeserving poor, even among the aged. From this perspective, an impoverished older individual may simply be suffering the consequences of an earlier Flawed Character, one that chose to make merry while the sun was shining rather than save for a rainy day.

Squandered Income?

There is no evidence that the aged poor enjoyed especially lascivious or spendthrift lives. A University of Michigan study suggests that the aged poor had never earned enough income to provide for a comfortable living either before or after retirement. A congressional review of poverty among older women concluded that:

> Many have been poor or low income for a large part of their lives. If they spent time in the labor force, it was at low-paying and often intermittent jobs; many were married to someone who was a low-wage worker. The low-income and poor elderly did not, in their younger years, have the kind of work and income history that would permit accumulation of savings, pensions, and large Social Security benefits. A recent study on the causes of poverty among widows found that these women were likely to have had husbands whose health was poor, with the concomitant problems of lower earnings, less savings (or perhaps depleted savings), early labor force withdrawal due to health factors and early death. About half of poor widows had been poor before widowhood, and half became poor upon widowhood either through lack of accrual of retirement income or because of medical or death expenses.[9]

One observer of these statistics concluded that "the misery of their old age is simply the conclusion to a life of misery. They are the ones who have grown up, lived, and will die under conditions of poverty."[10] Many, probably most, of the aged poor were always in or on the margin of poverty.

Some individuals do experience impoverishment for the first time, however, as they grow old. Just as few people think about dying, few ever plan to grow old and retire. Only a small number of people make adequate provisions for old age in spite of statistical evidence showing the diminished income during retirement. People's essential optimism is revealed in consumer surveys such as one disclosing that families who have not had as much as $500 in the bank during the last five years confidently anticipate a comfortable retirement. Confidence fades with age, however; among younger families, only 9 percent foresee hard times after retirement; among middle-aged families, 16 percent sense trouble ahead. But when they reach old age, at least 20 percent of these individuals end up in poverty at some point.[11] Projections for *future* poverty of today's workers are, therefore, discouraging.[12]

Pensions

Aside from their own savings, aged persons may draw income either from private pension plans or Social Security. In fact, a 1981 poll sponsored by the President's Commission on Pension Policy disclosed that most workers expect Social Security and private pensions to provide most of their retirement income. Unfortunately, pension

---

[9]Congressional Research Service, *Retirement Income for an Aging Population* (Washington, DC: U.S. Government Printing Office, 1987), p. 45.

[10]Harrington, *The Other America*, p. 105.

[11]The substantial discrepancy between actual saving rates and those required to support postretirement living standards is illustrated in James A. Schulz and Guy Carrin, "The Role of Savings and Pension Systems in Maintaining Living Standards in Retirement," *Journal of Human Resources* (Summer 1972).

[12]The Employee Benefits Research Institute's annual Retirement Confidence Survey describes the saving behavior and retirement expectations of workers of varying ages (see http://ebri.org/surveys/rcs/).

plans are often great disillusionments. Many workers confidently subscribe to company pension plans only to find that they have no pension rights upon retirement. If a worker is laid off or disabled before working enough years with the same firm, he or she may not be eligible for any pension payments.

Many workers fail to acquire pension rights because they work for companies without pension plans (most small firms), or because they don't work long enough for a company with pensions. At present, less than 50 percent of all aged people receive private pensions. Moreover, these pensions are generally reserved for the *nonpoor* aged, that is, for those with higher *pre*retirement earnings and savings. Less than 8 percent of all aged poor households receive a private pension, and those pension benefits account for only 3 percent of their total income (see Table 7.2 and Figure 7.3). Furthermore, even those receiving private pension benefits are often disappointed to learn that private pensions are typically not adjusted for inflation. As a result, the real value of private pensions diminishes with age.

Social Security

Social Security payments reach far more of the aged—92 percent at present—and constitute the single most important source of income for the elderly. Social Security benefits account for one-third of the total income of aged nonpoor families and a whopping two-thirds of the income of the aged poor. Moreover, Social Security retirement benefits are adjusted for inflation, thereby retaining their real value. Nevertheless, Social Security benefits alone do not assure an adequate income. Because the amount of monthly benefits depends in large part on the amount of prior earnings, individuals who are poor while working are likely to be poor after retirement as well.

Families

Another source of potential support for the aged may be found in their own families. The extended family unit has in the past represented the most dependable source of social and economic security for many people. However, industrialization and urbanization have tended to disintegrate the extended family, leaving each core family unit to fend for itself. Despite the material and social benefits this development yields for others, it deprives the aged of a source of support, immediate companionship, and in many cases a roof over their heads. Today, less than a third of the aged live with relatives, and of those who do not, less than 3 percent receive any income support from their offspring. Accordingly, relatives rarely constitute a source of economic security for the aged and cannot be expected to provide an escape from poverty.

Even when the aged are supported by their families, such support may be regarded as a mixed blessing. Many aged people live with relatives simply because they cannot afford to live by themselves. Moreover, they may not be counted as poor because the income of the household in which they live exceeds poverty standards. Yet, these older people are truly dependent if their living arrangements are dictated solely by economic necessity. The basic issue is not whether the aged live with their relatives or not, but whether the aged command enough economic resources to make a free choice of their own.

Welfare

Table 7.2 and Figure 7.3 show how the aged poor have come to depend on welfare for basic support. Over one out of three aged poor individuals receives cash welfare benefits, food stamps, or a housing subsidy. Taken together, this welfare assistance accounts for one-fifth of their total income. Clearly, the aged poor would be much poorer without welfare—and destitute without Social Security.

RISING HEALTH COSTS

The serious decline in the sources and amounts of income that the aged command creates enough momentum to impoverish a high proportion of these individuals. But dwindling incomes are not their only burden; the aged also confront large, and often rising, expenses. The interaction of these two forces is a virtual guarantee that a still higher proportion of the aged will experience material want before they die.

Everyone realizes that the aged are likely to experience high rates of sickness and disability. Over half of the people over age 65 have arthritis. Aged individuals also have a high incidence of high blood pressure, hearing impairments, heart disease, cataracts, and bone deterioration. As a result of these and other ailments, only one out of six older persons rates their own health as "excellent." The elderly poor are more likely to rate their health "poor" or "fair" than "excellent" or "very good."

As people age, they not only incur more illness, but also lose the ability to perform everyday tasks. The Activities of Daily Living (ADLs) include eating, bathing, dressing, toileting, and simply getting in and out of a bed or a chair. As people age, they need more and more assistance with these activities. As Figure 7.4 shows, the old old are particularly dependent on ADL assistance.

FIGURE 7.4 Functional Disability of the Aged

Percent of persons needing assistance with Activities of Daily Living (ADLs)

Source: U.S. Bureau of the Census, *65+ in the United States: 2005* (Washington, DC: U.S. Government Printing Office, 2005).

The declining health and functional capacity of older persons not only increases their physical dependence on others, but also adds to their financial burden. The average out-of pocket health bill per year for a person 65 or older is over $3,000, including the expenses of insurance premiums and co-payments for hospital care, physician's services, and drugs. This is a bill many aged persons cannot afford to pay.

Even these average expenses understate the burden of illness for those most sick. Hospitalization expenditures, for example, are incurred by only a portion of the poor, and these individuals pay all the costs, not just the "average" cost. Furthermore, those who have endured impoverishment and hard labor the longest are most likely to be sick and least able to afford the costs of sickness. As Table 7.3 shows, disease and other disabling health conditions are far more prevalent among the aged poor than among the nonpoor. And these figures understate the disadvantage of the poor, as they exclude people who don't live until age 65 (disproportionately the poor). This suggests that illness in old age represents yet another burden for the poor. Even individuals who manage to fend off poverty during their working years may succumb to financial impoverishment when illness strikes.

Medicare and Medicaid have done a great deal to reduce the threat of impoverishment among the aged due to illness. By providing subsidized medical insurance (Medicare) and the purchasing power required to buy needed medical services (Medicaid), the government has greatly diminished a major financial burden of the aged. Even though Medicare alone spends roughly $10,000 per year on each elderly person, the financial protection provided by Medicare and Medicaid is not complete. Like most private health insurance plans, Medicare does not pay all medical costs and there are limits on the type and extent of coverage. As a consequence, the elderly still spend 11 percent of their incomes on health care, more than triple the percentage spent by nonelderly households. According to estimates of the Urban Institute,

TABLE 7.3 Poverty and Health Conditions

Condition	Percent of Population	
	Aged Poor	**Aged Nonpoor**
Heart disease	38.3	32.3
Stroke	10.9	7.5
Emphysema	7.1	4.2
Asthma	11.7	7.8
Sinusitis	17.5	14.3
Cancer	14.7	20.1
Diabetes	20.5	12.3
Ulcers	17.1	14.2
Arthritic symptoms	46.5	35.4
Hearing troubles	40.6	42.9
Vision troubles	26.3	15.8

Source: U.S. House of Representatives, Ways and Means Committee, *2004 Green Book* (Washington, DC: Government Printing Office), Table B-3.

elderly individuals in poor health and without private insurance spend 44 percent of their income on health care. For low-income women over age 85 and in poor health, medical expenses absorb over 50 percent of total income.[13]

Medicaid pays a larger share of the medical expenses of aged recipients. However, an individual must be poor to receive Medicaid benefits. Typically, this means that an aged individual must exhaust most personal income and assets before becoming eligible for Medicaid assistance. Moreover, neither Medicaid nor Medicare provides preventive health care. As a consequence, all too many older poor people are burdened with both discomfort and poverty, sometimes even relegated to unsympathetic and inadequate institutions to wait idly for death.[14]

TAX BURDENS

In many areas of the country, the aged are also burdened by taxes, particularly property taxes. For most of the aged, their homes represent the only significant asset they possess and embody a lifetime of savings. But because local property taxes continue to rise along with property values, many of the aged find themselves unable to maintain their investment. Although all states offer some form of property-tax relief for older persons, tax bills can still be a significant burden on the elderly. As a result, the U.S. Senate Special Committee on Aging reports that hundreds of thousands of aged persons are driven from their homes by mounting property taxes. Still more are forced to liquidate other assets to pay their taxes. Thus, the most visible economic security of many of the aged may itself be a burden on day-to-day budgets.

Home ownership often imposes another unforeseen cost. Many of the aged purchased their homes in city centers at a time when inner city locations seemed most attractive. As the years have passed, however, inner city neighborhoods have deteriorated. Younger families have sought the freshness and space of the suburbs, while racial segregation and hostility have contributed to a general depreciation of inner city property values. As a consequence, the aged often find themselves socially and racially isolated in neighborhoods they once thought attractive. They cannot afford to move because the value of their homes has fallen, while suburban values have skyrocketed. Hence, they can only hold on until the burden of property taxes leads them to rented quarters or nursing homes.

MAKING DO

An aged person with diminishing income and mounting expenses confronts an increasing risk of poverty. For many aged individuals, their chances have simply run out; past labors and thrift are able only to postpone impoverishment in most cases. The question arises, then, as to how the aged actually manage in the face of such

---

[13]Stephanie Maxwell, Marilyn Moon, and Misha Segal, *Growth in Medicare and Out-of-Pocket Spending: Impact on Vulnerable Beneficiaries* (Washington, DC: Urban Institute, December 2000). The Medicare program is discussed in more detail in Chapter 14.

[14]*Access* to quality health care is also a problem for the aged poor, regardless of its cost; see Annette Fitzpatrick et al., "Barriers to Health Care Access Among the Elderly and Who Perceives Them," *American Journal of Public Health* (October 2004), pp. 1788–1794.

imposing circumstances. The most succinct answer came forth in hearings before a committee of the U.S. Senate:

> "How do you manage?" I asked. A lady replied, "It's hard, Pat, oh, it's hard." "Well, what do you do?" "We don't do," someone replied. "That's how we manage!"
>
> "I don't" is a most accurate description of the older adult living in retirement. I don't entertain. I don't go out with friends. I don't eat in restaurants. I don't go to movies. I don't buy new clothes. I don't ride subways and buses. I don't buy cake. I don't eat a lot. I don't take care of my health like I should. I don't, I don't, I don't.[15]

For many aged individuals, then, growing older means giving up one thing after another until there is nothing left. When that time comes, they can only wait for death; sometime before that, they are unquestionably poor.

ASSESSING CAUSATION

Poverty among the aged is not a natural product of biological development. Rather, it emerges from a diminution of income sources, a lack of accumulated resources, and frequently rising expenses. Maintaining income sources or providing financial relief from taxation and illness will prevent many aged individuals from falling into poverty. For others, however, poverty does not emerge in old age but is, instead, a continuing condition.[16] The causes of poverty for these people must be sought elsewhere and earlier. Identifying and eliminating the causes of poverty for the nonaged is a critical step in minimizing later poverty among the aged.

HEALTH

One way to assure individuals greater prosperity and security in old age is to maintain their good health in younger years. Better health contributes to economic security in two important ways: by permitting persons to earn more income and by reducing financial expenditures arising from health needs. All other things being equal, a person with good health is likely to accumulate greater financial reserves when young and to need them less when old.

HEALTH COSTS

It is not difficult to surmise the potential that poor health has for undermining a family's economic security. A sick or disabled parent not only fails to earn a full income; he or she also increases household expenses. A sick or disabled child may limit a parent's ability to work and also add to household expenses.

Figure 7.5 illustrates the income dimension of the health problem. The probability of having a low income is highly correlated with physical and mental disability. A

---

[15]Special Committee on Aging, *Economics of Aging: Toward a Full Share in Abundance,* U.S. Senate, 91st Cong., 2d session, 1970 (Washington, DC: U.S. Government Printing Office, 1970), p. 34.

[16]This is particularly true in nonmetropolitan areas: See Diane McLaughlin and Karen C. Holden, "Nonmetropolitan Elderly Women: A Portrait of Economic Vulnerability," *Journal of Applied Gerontology* (September 1993), pp. 320–334.

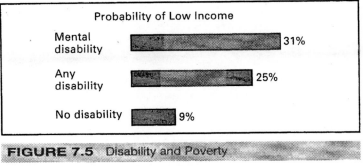

FIGURE 7.5 Disability and Poverty

Source: U.S. Bureau of the Census. 2005 Current Population Survey.

nondisabled person has only a 9 percent probability of low-income status. Any disability more than doubles the odds of low-income status. A mental disability raises the risk of poverty even further.[17]

Ill health and disability not only reduce incomes, but also increase household expenses. In 2005 Americans spent roughly $1.9 trillion on health maintenance and care. This works out to more than $6,000 per person per year. While the lion's share of these expenses fall on the aged population, even the average worker is at financial risk when illness or disability occurs.[18]

CAUSALITY

The relationship between health and income status is not simple enough, however, to permit the use of averages in ascertaining the cost of illness to the poor. Just as illness may tend to deplete a family's resources and leave it poor, so may poverty itself increase the likelihood of getting sick. Poor families suffer notoriously from chronic malnutrition and unsanitary environments, both of which nurture ill health. As a consequence, they are apt to be ill or disabled more often than the nonpoor. Poor families have higher disease and mortality rates and miss more than twice as many days of work due to illness than do the nonpoor.

Poverty and illness, then, interact in a reciprocal relationship. As shown in Figure 7.6, there is an irrefutable *correlation* between income status and health status. Households with incomes below $20,000 are seven times more likely to report "fair" or "poor" health than high-income households.[19] The critical question is again *causation*, however, not *correlation*. As Figure 7.7 illustrates, illness and poverty may exhibit a circular relationship: Illness leads to poverty and poverty leads to poor health. However, the relationship is not equally strong in both directions. We may still ask how many families or persons actually fall into poverty as a result of illness or disability, that is,

---

[17]For definitions of "severe" disability and estimated effects of disability on earnings, see Thomas W. Hale, Howard Hayghe, and John M. McNeil, "Persons with Disabilities: Labor Market Activity"; and Douglas L. Kruse, "Demographic, Income, and Health Care Characteristics," both in *Monthly Labor Review* (September 1998).

[18]The explicit recognition of medical expenses in the poverty line would significantly increase measured poverty among the aged; see Kathleen Short and Thesia Garner, "Experimental Poverty Measures: Medical Expenditures," *Monthly Labor Review 128:8* (August 2002), pp. 3–13.

[19]For a variety of specific correlates, see David Wood, "Effect of Child and Family Poverty on Child Health in the United States," *Pediatrics* (September 2003), pp. 707–711.

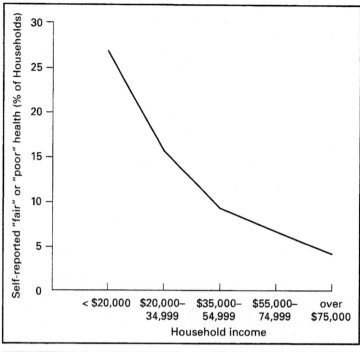

FIGURE 7.6 Income and Health

Source: National Center for Health Statistics, *Summary Health Statistics for U.S. Adults: National Health Interview Study, 2004* (Washington, DC: U.S. Department of Health and Human Services, May 2006).

ask to what extent poverty is actually *caused* by ill health.[20] Many persons were poor before they were sick, so we cannot claim that illness caused their poverty. At most, we may say that illness maintains their poverty or that it makes poverty more miserable.

It is even possible that a third factor is the common cause of both low incomes and ill health. Recent evidence suggests that low intelligence not only constrains income-earning

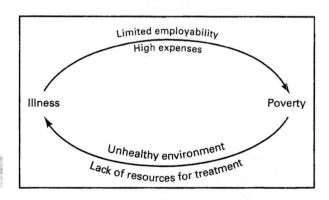

FIGURE 7.7 Illness and Poverty

[20]Some people contend that *relative* incomes (inequality), not just *absolute* deprivation, may cause psychosocial illness. However, interstate and international comparisons reveal no such link. See Jennifer Mellor and Jeffrey Milyo, "Reexamining the Ecological Association Between Income Inequality and Health," *Journal of Health Politics, Policy and Law 26* (2001), pp. 487–522; and "Income Inequality and Health Status in the United States," *Journal of Human Resources* (Summer 2002), pp. 510–539.

TABLE 7.4 Health Insurance Coverage

	Percent with Coverage	
Insurance Coverage	*Poor*	*Nonpoor*
Private insurance	23	74
Medicare	14	14
Medicaid	43	9
Military	2	4
No coverage	31	14

Source: U.S. Bureau of the Census, Current Population Survey, March 2006.

abilities, but also contributes to ill health (via shortcomings in daily self-maintenance, self-care, and accident prevention).[21]

Whatever the influence of third factors, the critical issue here still centers on the question of how many nonpoor persons sink into poverty as a result of illness or disability. The answer, of course, depends on how far above the poverty line families begin and how much illness they contract. Also important is the extent to which families are protected by insurance from the impositions of work loss and medical expenses.

A family need not be far above the poverty line to have an adequate margin against the burdens of ill health. The official poverty line for a family of four was just under $20,000 in 2005. Average out-of-pocket medical expenses for a family this size are around $3,000 per year. Hence, for the typical family, an income of over $25,000 would easily prevent slippage into poverty as a result of illness. Moreover, as we have already suggested, the incidence of illness falls as income rises, further immunizing the nonpoor against poverty.

HEALTH INSURANCE

Health insurance is another important component of economic security. In the event of severe illness or disability, health insurance can protect a family's finances from an onslaught of medical expenses. Even the more routine medical problems that can upset household budgets are typically alleviated by insurance.

The problem with health insurance is that not everyone has it. In 2005, over 50 million Americans had no health insurance. Although many of these uninsured individuals had enough income to purchase insurance, people in poverty are the most likely to be uninsured. As Table 7.4 shows, only 23 percent of the poor have private health insurance as compared to 74 percent coverage among the nonpoor. In large part, the difference in coverage is explained by the lower labor force participation of the poor. Because most private health insurance is employer-based, people without jobs are less likely to be covered. Even when health insurance is available, poor people often choose not to take it. For them, the health insurance may be viewed as a lower priority than rent, food, or other essentials.

---

[21]Linda Gottfredson, "Intelligence: Is It the Epidemiologists' Elusive 'Fundamental Cause' of Social Inequalities in Health?" *Journal of Personality and Social & Psychology 86* (2004), pp. 174–199.

The lack of private health insurance does not mean that poor people get no health care. About half of the poverty population is eligible for the government's Medicaid program, which pays hospital and doctor bills. To become eligible for Medicaid, however, a family must first deplete its own savings. In addition, many doctors and hospitals try to avoid treating Medicaid patients because of the paperwork and cost limits the program imposes.

Another option for poor people is to use emergency rooms as their basic source of health services. Emergency room services are not oriented toward *preventive* health care, however. As a result, poor people may wait too long before diagnosing or treating health problems. Emergency rooms may also refuse to treat patients without the ability to pay.[22]

Although the lack of private health insurance reduces the quality and quantity of health care received by the poor, it may not be a major cause of poverty. Health problems will push a family into poverty only if the related costs are substantial and uninsured. Even then, the poverty experience may be only temporary. Nevertheless, the economic security of families with incomes just above the poverty line is always threatened by illness or injury even if relatively few fall into poverty for those reasons.

INTERGENERATIONAL LINKS

The intergenerational links between health and poverty are more discouraging. Until now, we have considered only the impact of health on an existing family's economic status. But the illness bred by poverty may leave scars that last for generations. A child born to a poverty-stricken mother is likely to be undernourished both before and after birth.[23] Furthermore, the child is less likely to receive proper postnatal care, to be immunized against disease, or even to have his or her eyes and teeth examined. As a result, the child is likely to grow up prone to illness and poverty, and, in the most insidious of cases, be impaired by organic brain damage. A study by the U.S. Department of Health, Education, and Welfare reported that poor children

Suffer 23 percent more hearing impairment.
Do not grow as tall as other children.
Are more likely to have low hemoglobin values during their years of growth.
Suffer a higher incidence of impetigo, gastrointestinal diseases, parasitic diseases, and urinary-tract infections.
In urban areas, are more often the victims of lead-paint poisoning and insect and rodent bites.[24]

---

[22]Thirteen percent of uninsured families fail to get all the medical care they feel they need; see Paul Starr, "Health Care for the Poor: The Past Twenty Years," in *Fighting Poverty*, eds. S. Danziger and D. Weinberg (Cambridge, MA: Harvard University Press, 1986), p. 118.

[23]Ellen Meara blames the low birth weight of poor infants on their mothers' behavior, particularly smoking; see her "Why Is Health Related to Socioeconomic Status? The Case of Pregnancy and Low Birth Weight" (Cambridge, MA: National Bureau of Economic Research, April 2001).

[24]U.S. Department of Health, Education, and Welfare, Office of Child Health Affairs, *A Proposal for New Federal Leadership in Maternal and Child Health Care in the United States* (Washington, DC: U.S. Government Printing Office, 1976), pp. 9–10, 15. Similar observations are made in David Wood, "Effect of Child and Family Poverty on Child Health in the United States," *Pediatrics* (September 2003), pp. 707–711.

To what extent do these childhood health impairments affect later education, job skills, or income? No one knows for sure. However, there is a strong suspicion that poverty in one generation may result in illnesses and disabilities that become a significant cause of poverty in the next generation.[25]

MENTAL HEALTH

Mental health, as well as physical health, is an important dimension of poverty. The issue here is the same as before: Does mental disability lead downward to the slums, or does slum life accentuate tendencies toward mental illness? The former question embodies a popular "drift" hypothesis. According to this thesis, failures from all walks of life drift into the slums, creating our present poor population. The available evidence, however, once again shatters the popular myth. One of the few detailed studies undertaken on this subject traced the socioeconomic histories of schizophrenic individuals. The results were unambiguous: 91 percent of such patients were in the *same* socioeconomic class as their parents.[26] There was no evidence of substantial drift. Instead, the results suggest that poverty is more likely to lead to ill health than to result from it.[27] Further evidence of this causal direction emerged from a unique study of sudden prosperity. When a casino opening moved families out of poverty, the incidence of psychiatric disorders among affected children declined significantly.[28] The stress of poverty—the sense of losing control, of economic anxiety, of shame—is a leading cause of depression and other psychiatric disorders. When that stress is relieved, mental health improves.

Summary

Age and illness are highly visible correlates of poverty and, because of this, are often assumed to bear a causal relationship to economic impoverishment. As logical as such a conclusion is, however, there are several reasons for attaching only limited causal importance to the impact of age and illness. Many of the aged poor, for example, were always poor, so that aging itself causes little change in their economic status.

---

[25] Anne Case, D. Lubotsky, and C. Paxson, "Economic Status and Health in Childhood: The Origins of the Gradient," *American Economic Review* (December 2002), pp. 1308–1334. Poverty is shown to have a greater effect on children's health than family structure or race in L. Montgomery, J. Kiely, and G. Pappas, "The Effects of Poverty, Race, and Family Structure on U.S. Children's Health," *American Journal of Public Health* (October 1996), pp. 1401–1405. See also James P. Smith, "Healthy Bodies and Thick Wallets: The Dual Relation Between Health and Economic Status," *Journal of Economic Perspectives* (Spring 1999), pp. 145–166.

[26] The effects of socioeconomic background on IQ are discussed in Chapter 9. Also see R. J. Karp, ed., *Malnourished Children in the United States* (New York: Springer, 1993).

[27] For more discussion, see U.S. Surgeon General, *Mental Health: A Report of the Surgeon General* (Washington, DC: U.S. Government Printing Office, 1999). The unique stresses on rural poor women are discussed in Jane E. Meyers and Carman S. Gill, "Poor, Rural and Female: Under-Studied, Under-Counseled, More At-Risk," *Journal of Mental Health Counseling* (July 2004), pp. 225–242.

[28] E. Jane Costello, S Compton, G. Keeler, and A. Angold, "Relationships Between Poverty and Psychopathology," *Journal of the American Medical Association* (October 15, 2003), pp. 2023–2029. See another unique experiment in Tama Leventhal and Jeanne Brooks-Gunn, "Moving to Opportunity: An Experimental Study of Neighborhood Effects on Mental Health," *American Journal of Public Health* (September 2003), pp. 1576–1582. For a global perspective on the links between poverty and mental health, see World Health Organization, *The World Health Report 2001,* Chapter 1 (New York: United Nations, 2001).

Similarly, poor persons are more prone to illness, and illness for them represents no sudden loss of economic well-being. Even for those who are driven to poverty for the first time by age or illness, the loss of economic status is occasioned by a variety of forces, none of which is inseparable from the natural processes of aging and illness.

Even though age and illness do not explain a high proportion of poverty, there are identifiable subgroups for whom the causal link is particularly threatening. Among the aged, the most vulnerable to poverty are the old old who are at risk of exhausting their financial reserves and confront increasing health problems. Illness and disability are also especially costly for younger families without health insurance who are already perilously close to the poverty threshold.

Further Reading

AGE

Egendorf, Laura K., *An Aging Population*. San Diego, CA: Greenhaven Press, 2002.

Schace, K. W., and W. A. Achenbaum, eds., *Social Impact on Aging*. New York: Springer, 1993.

Schulz, James, *The Economics of Aging,* 7th ed. Westport, CN: Greenwood, 2001.

U.S. Bureau of the Census, *65+ in the United States*. Washington, DC: Government Printing Office, annual.

U.S. Senate, Special Committee on Aging, *Developments in Aging*. Washington, DC: U.S. Government Printing Office, annual.

U.S. Social Security Administration, *Income of the Population 55 or Older*. Washington, DC: Government Printing Office, biannual.

Wise, David A., ed., *Inquiries in the Economics of Aging*. Chicago: University of Chicago Press, 1998.

HEALTH

Currie, Janet, and B. Madrian, "Health, Health Insurance and the Labor Market," *Handbook of Labor Economics,* vol. 3, eds. O. Ashenfelter and D. Card. Amsterdam: Elsevier, 2000, pp. 3309–3415.

Hadley, Jack, "Sicker and Poorer: The Consequences of Being Uninsured," Washington, DC: Urban Institute, May 2002.

Hamilton, Erin et al., "Health Insurance and Health-Care Utilization of U.S.-Born Mexican-American Children," *Social Science Quarterly* (December 2006), pp. 1280–1294.

Montgomery, Laura E., John L. Kiely, and Gregory Pappas, "The Effects of Poverty, Race, and Family Structure on U.S. Children's Health," *American Journal of Public Health* (October 1996).

Morone, James A., and Lawrence Jacobs, eds., *Healthy, Wealthy, and Fair*. New York: Oxford University Press, 2005.

Mullahy, John, and Barbara Wolfe, "Health Policies for the Nonelderly Poor," in *Understanding Poverty,* eds. S. Danziger and R. Haveman. Cambridge, MA: Harvard University Press, 2001.

Smith, James P., "Healthy Bodies and Thick Wallets: The Dual Relation Between Health and Economic Status," *Journal of Economic Perspectives* (Spring 1999), pp. 145–166.

Wu, Stephen, "The Effects of Health Events on the Economic Status of Married Couples," *Journal of Human Resources* (Winter 2003), pp. 219–230.

Web Links

American Association of Retired Persons (AARP). Research reports on health and economic security of the aged: www.aarp.org.

Center on an Aging Society. Data and policy analysis on aging issues: www.aging-society.org

U.S. Administration on Aging. Data and policy analysis:
www.aoa.gov

U.S. Bureau of the Census. Data on demographics, income, poverty status of 65+ population
www.census.gov

U.S. House of Representatives, Committee on Ways and Means. Biennial fact book ("Green Book")

on income-transfer and health programs and target populations (including the aged)
http://waysandmeans.house.gov

U.S. Social Security Administration. Annual report on incomes of the aged.
www.socialsecurity.gov

CHAPTER 8
FAMILY SIZE AND STRUCTURE

&

There are two persistent accusations leveled against the poor. One is that the poor have too many babies; the other is that they do not maintain stable families. The implication in both cases is that the poor have flawed characters: They exhibit too little self-control and are thus responsible for much of their own plight. These accusations are examined in this chapter. As in Chapter 7, the focus of the analysis is on probable causation, highlighting the temporal relationship between poverty and family size or status. Did either large family size or family instability *precede* economic impoverishment? If so, then there may be some validity to the claim that the poor caused their own poverty by creating conditions that make it difficult or impossible to hold a job that pays an adequate income.

Although the sequence of events is important in establishing causality, it does not resolve the issue of culpability. Even in cases where family instability precedes a decline into poverty, flawed character may not be the only explanation. Restricted opportunities may have contributed to family breakup or limited the attractiveness of marriage. The welfare system (Big Brother) may also create perverse incentives for family breakup and more children.

In cases where poverty precedes family breakup or additional childbearing, the causal analysis is simpler. Here there is no reason to single out family size or status as a cause of poverty. At the most, such conditions may perpetuate or worsen poverty that already existed.

FAMILY SIZE

Children are a distinct threat to the financial security of a family. Additional children not only increase the need for more income but also limit the ability of parents to earn it. More children imply a greater demand for homemaker services, including child care, meal preparation, transportation, and other household activities. As that burden grows, it becomes more difficult to supply labor in the outside job market. If the parents choose to pay someone else to provide child care services, they may find that the net income from outside employment is too small. These considerations make paid employment increasingly difficult or financially unrewarding as family size increases. For single parents, the arithmetic of outside (paid) employment is even worse.

POVERTY RATES

The combination of increased financial need and more limited employability implies that larger families will be more prone to poverty. Figure 8.1 confirms this expectation.

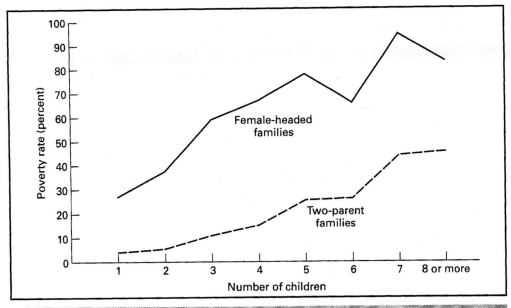

FIGURE 8.1 Poverty Rates, by Family Size

Source: U.S. Bureau of the Census (2005 data).

In both two-parent and one-parent families there is a dramatic increase in the incidence of poverty as family size increases. Among two-parent families, the poverty rate starts at 4 percent if there is only one child and jumps to 25 percent if there are five children. One-parent families have much higher poverty rates at all family sizes. Even here, however, the poverty rate triples as the number of children increases from one to five or more. Over 80 percent of female-headed families with at least five children are poor.

THE POTENTIAL IMPACT

To grasp the implications of larger family sizes among the poor, we may ask how many larger poor families would move out of poverty if they had fewer family members. For example, we know from Table 3.4 that five-member families were considered poor if their 2005 incomes were under $23,613 but the same poverty standard for a family of four was $19,971. Hence, any family of five whose income was less than $23,613 but more than $19,971 would no longer be counted as poor if it could somehow eliminate one family member. Or, to put it slightly differently, we may say that such a family would not have fallen into poverty if it had bred one less child. By counting the total number of such families, we may estimate the potential of family planning as a means for reducing poverty.

The statistical exercise required to make such an estimate is carried out on two levels. The first calculation tells how many larger poor families (of five or more persons) would move out of poverty if they had one less member. Among poor five-person families, we look for all those whose current income could support four persons; among six-person families, incomes that will support five people, and so on. Based on these calculations, we observe that 330,000 poor families, a total of nearly 2 million individuals, would no longer be counted as poor if each family had one person less.

The second calculation imposes an even stricter constraint on family size. Rather than trim all larger poor families by one person, it reduces all such families to the standard four persons. Hence, six-person families statistically lose two members, and their poverty line falls from $26,683 to $19,971. This kind of standardization creates an astounding reduction in the size of the poverty population. On these assumptions, over 500,000 families (3.3 million individuals)—nearly one-eighth of all the nonaged poor—would no longer be counted as poor.

This kind of statistical exercise leads us to the conclusion that mild restraints on family size (one person less) would reduce the nonaged poverty population by 6 percent, while severe limits on family size (maximum of four) would effect a 12 percent reduction in the number of poor. Such results underscore the potential importance of the causal link between family size and poverty. Before turning to a discussion of causality, however, we need to consider the assumptions underlying this statistical exercise.

First, our statistical exercise tacitly assumes that there is no positive relationship between family size and family income. The statistical elimination of one family member is presumed to have no effect on family income. But this is not a realistic assumption. The amount of welfare, food stamps, or other assistance a family gets depends on its size. More children, then, implies more welfare. If we were to eliminate one family member, we would also have to reduce the family's income. As a result, far fewer families would escape poverty than the foregoing arithmetic implies. Since over half of all poor families receive some form of welfare benefit, this is a serious qualification to our calculations.

Family income may also rise with family size for other reasons. The father of the family may be impelled to work overtime or at a second job as his family responsibilities expand; hence, larger families may constitute a special kind of incentive to work. Larger families may also enable other family members to work; they may have older children who can contribute directly to family income by working part-time or who enable the mother to work by assuming child-care responsibilities.[1] Hence, the statistical reduction previously carried out may diminish family income more than it reduces family needs.

Further consideration must also be given to those families and persons whom we suppose statistically to escape poverty by our calculations. Some family members are constrained by our arithmetic to disappear, and we can ignore them for the moment. Surviving family members, however, improve their economic status only marginally. Their statistical "escape" is, therefore, not very impressive. Almost all such families remain within a few hundred dollars of our poverty standards, even after they manage to leave the poverty population.

DECLINING FAMILY SIZE

The foregoing purely statistical exercise has a historical parallel. More women are electing not to have children and those who do become mothers are bearing fewer children. This downward trend in childbearing has been visible for over 30 years. In the 1960s, roughly one-third of all children were in families with at least four children. In

---

[1]The impact of household size and composition on a single mother's supply of labor is examined in Janis Barry-Figueroa and Edwin Melendez, "The Importance of Family Members in Determining the Labor Supply of Puerto Rican, Black, and White Single Mothers," *Social Science Quarterly* (December 1993), pp. 867–883. The supply behavior of married women is examined in Evelyn L. Lehrer, "Married Women's Labor Supply Behavior in the 1990's: Differences by Life-Cycle Stage," *Social Science Quarterly* (September 1999), pp. 574–590.

1990 only 15 percent of all children had so many siblings. According to estimates by Peter Gottschalk and Sheldon Danziger, this reduction in family size has had a dramatic impact on poverty, cutting the poverty rate by roughly a fifth below the trend based on the larger family sizes that prevailed in the 1960s.[2]

THE CAUSAL RELATION

Theory and historical experience both confirm the importance of family size in shaping poverty trends. These statistics do not settle the question of causation, however. There is no evidence yet that larger families now in poverty enjoyed a higher standard of living when they were smaller. It could be that more children simply lengthen a family's stay in the poverty population rather than cause it to fall from nonpoverty to poverty. Large family size thus retards the flow of people moving out of poverty and contributes over time to an expansion of the poverty population. By itself, however, it creates very little new poverty.

Against this background, we must also ponder the accumulation of evidence suggesting that the poor continue to have less access to birth control information. Public schools, especially in low-income areas, are still reluctant to provide birth control information, while public welfare authorities are, in most cases, prohibited from providing it.[3] Low-income families are also less able to afford abortions, even if they are desired. Even in quasi-public clinics, abortions cost several hundred dollars. Moreover, Congress has greatly limited the availability of Medicaid or other income transfers to pay for abortions.

Because of these constraints, poor families often end up with more children than other families, not because they want them, but because they are unable to prevent them. One study by the National Academy of Sciences indicated that over one-third of the least educated families had unwanted children, and a survey of welfare mothers in New York yielded similar findings. Even more revealing are studies that indicate the extent to which unintended births increase at lower income levels; only 22 percent of all middle-class families report unintended births, compared to a whopping 53 percent for poor families.[4] This has become an urgent concern in recent years as unmarried teenage mothers have become the fastest growing subgroup in the poverty population. This is not so much a question of family *size,* however, as a problem of family *formation.*

FAMILY STRUCTURE

The phenomenon of family formation raises one of the most contentious issues in poverty debates: the single-parent family. Single parenthood has transformed the demographic profile of America and feminized poverty. In the process it has spawned intense debates about why the traditional two-parent family has broken down and whether poverty can be eliminated in its absence.

---

[2]Peter Gottschalk and Sheldon Danziger, "Family Structure, Family Size, and Family Income," in *Uneven Tides,* eds. Danziger and Gottschalk (New York: Russell Sage, 1993), pp. 167–193.

[3]However, a universal sex-education program in New Jersey revealed that sex education alone is no panacea; see Barbara Defoe Whitehead, "The Failure of Sex Education," *Atlantic Monthly,* October 1994.

[4]Jennifer S. Barber and Amie Emens, "The Intersection among Unintended, Premarital, and Teenage Childbearing in the U.S." (Ann Arbor, MI: University of Michigan Population Studies Center, September 2006); also Lawrence Finer and Stanley Henshaw, "Disparities in Rates of Unintended Pregnancy in the United States, 1994 and 2001," *Perspectives on Social and Reproductive Health* (June 2006), pp. 90–96.

TABLE 8.1	Living Arrangements of Children	
	Percent Distribution	
Family Structure	**1960**	**2005**
Two-parent family	87.7%	67.4
One-parent family		
Mother only	8.0	23.4
Father only	1.1	4.7
Other custodian	3.2	4.5
	100%	100%

Source: U.S. Bureau of the Census.

CHANGING FAMILY PATTERNS

Recent changes in family structure have been nothing short of dramatic. In 1960, nearly nine out of ten children lived with both parents. Today, only about seven out of ten children do so. As Table 8.1 shows, the percentage of children living with only one parent has tripled. In most cases the single parent is the mother, but single fathers are also becoming more common.

Although the image of female-headed families is popularly associated with race, the upsurge in single parenthood cuts across racial boundaries. Since at least 1950, black children have been much more likely than white children to live in female-headed families. Today, over half of all black children do so. White families are following the same trend, however. The percentage of white children living in female-headed families has tripled since 1970 and is now around 18 percent. This has led Charles Murray to predict the emergence of a "white ghetto" dominated by the same fatherless families that have characterized urban black ghettos.[5]

Divorce

The spectacular growth of single-parent families reflects two distinct phenomena. The first is the increase in divorce rates. Since 1960, the divorce rate has more than doubled. This has led to a surge in "broken" families, with the mother often maintaining an independent household for many years.

Unwed Parents

The second source of growth in single parenthood has been a surge in births to unmarried women. These are not cases of family breakup but rather a failure of family formation. As Figure 8.2 illustrates, two-thirds of all black births and one-fourth of all white births are now to unmarried mothers. The problem is particularly evident among teenagers: Over 90 percent of births to black teenagers and more than half of births to white teenagers occur among unmarried mothers.

Table 8.2 illustrates how these demographic changes have altered the living arrangements of children. A generation ago very few children lived with a never-married parent. Widowed mothers were far more common than never-married mothers, both among whites and blacks. By 1996, however, never-married mothers were the most

---

[5]Charles Murray, "The Coming White Underclass," *Wall Street Journal,* October 29, 1993, p. A14.

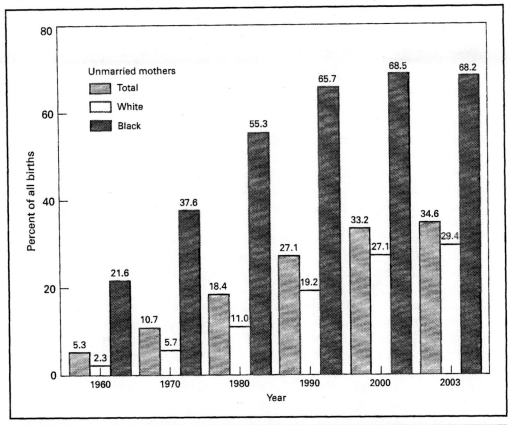

FIGURE 8.2   Percentage of Births to Unmarried Mothers, by Race for Selected Years

Source: National Center for Health Statistics and U.S. Census Bureau.

TABLE 8.2   Distribution of Children by Marital Status of Single Parents

	Percent of Children					
	White		Black		Hispanic	
Marital Status of Parent	1960	2002	1960	2002	1960	2002
Never married	1.6	30.9	9.6	63.0	19.8	46.1
Married, spouse absent (including separated)	41.1	21.0	57.2	15.7	40.6	26.8
Divorced	28.4	43.4	11.9	18.2	30.6	23.3
Widowed	29.0	4.8	21.3	2.9	8.9	3.8
Total	100.0	100.0	100.0	100.0	100.0	100.0
Number of children (in millions)	3.9	12.6	1.9	6.2	1.2	3.9

Source: U.S. Congress, Committee on Ways and Means, *2004 Green Book*, Tables G-7 to G-9.

common single parent among blacks and Hispanics and had become a substantial presence among whites as well.[6]

ECONOMIC IMPLICATIONS

The economic implications of these demographic trends are profound. A one-parent family is severely handicapped in the effort to attain economic security. The absence of one potential breadwinner is a large and obvious constraint on economic stability. Potential family income is reduced by *more than half* with the departure of one parent. Where two parents exist in the family, one parent can devote full time to labor-market activity while the other is free to combine household and labor-market activity. When only one parent resides in the family, such flexibility is diminished. The single parent is unable to devote all time to labor-market activity, at least not without paying someone else to assume household responsibilities.[7] Hence, the potential net income of a one-parent family is often closer to one-third rather than to one-half of a two-parent family's income. If women's employment opportunities in the labor market are further constricted by sexual stereotypes, their potential income will be lower still. Accordingly, one-parent families bear an extraordinarily high risk of economic impoverishment.[8]

The origin of single parenthood will also affect economic prospects. A divorced mother may have a home, a car, or other household property accumulated during her marriage. She may also be entitled to alimony or child-support payments. Even then, however, her family's income is likely to drop 40–50 percent after divorce (unless she remarries).[9] Never-married mothers fare even worse: a never-married mother will tend to have fewer assets, has no claim to alimony, and may face greater obstacles in securing child support from the father of her children.

The young age of most never-married mothers also handicaps their income potential. Teenage mothers, in particular, are likely to drop out of school. They have little or no work experience. By starting families before they accumulate human capital, they run the highest risk of living in poverty.[10]

---

[6]For longer-run trends see U.S. Bureau of the Census, *Trends in Premarital Childbearing: 1930 to 1994* (Washington, DC: Government Printing Office, 1999).

[7]Money is only one of many problems associated with getting and maintaining child care, as documented in Ajay Chaudry, *Putting Children First: How Low-Income Working Mothers Manage Child Care* (New York: Russell Sage, 2004).

[8]Single mothers also have more health problems and a greater likelihood of having disabled children, further limiting their earnings capacity; see Barbara L. Wolfe and Steven Hill, "The Health, Earnings Capacity, and Poverty of Single-Mother Families," in *Poverty and Prosperity in the U.S.A. in the Late Twentieth Century,* eds. D. Papadimitriou and E. Wolff (New York: St. Martin's Press, 1993).

[9]Marianne Page and Ann Huff Stevens, "The Economic Consequences of Absent Parents," *Journal of Human Resources* (Winter 2004), pp. 80–107.

[10]Teen childbearing reduces the mother's later wages by 13 to 23 percent according to Daniel Klepinger, Shelly Lundberg, and Robert Plotnick, "How Does Adolescent Fertility Affect the Human Capital and Wages of Young Women?" *Journal of Human Resources* (Summer 1999), pp. 421–448. See also Rebekah L. Coley and P. Lindsay Chase-Landsdale, "Adolescent Pregnancy and Parenthood: Recent Evidence and Future Directions," Joint Center for Poverty Research Working Paper, 1999. For more discussion, see David Ellwood and Mary Jo Bane, *The Impact of AFDC on Family Structure and Living Arrangements* (Cambridge, MA: Harvard University Press, 1984); Kevin Hopkins, ed., *Welfare Dependency* (Alexandria, VA: Hudson Institute, 1987), esp. Chapters 2, 4, 5, 6; and Douglas Besharov and Alison Quin, "Not All Families Are Created Equal," *The Public Interest* (Fall 1987).

TABLE 8.3 Poverty by Family Structure and Race

Family Type and Race	Number in Poverty (thousands)	Poverty Rate (percent)
White		
Two parents	2,915	3.9
Mother only	3,736	29.8
Father only	577	18.6
Black		
Two parents	1,043	10.7
Mother only	4,767	45.3
Father only	380	29.5
Hispanic		
Two parents	3,814	17.9
Mother only	2,831	44.0
Father only	375	20.3

Source: U.S. Bureau of the Census (2005 data for people in families with children).

Finally, society tends to be more sympathetic to widows and divorced mothers than to never-married mothers. Even though out-of-wedlock births have become more common, there is still a social stigma attached to them. This stigma may constrain the kinds of assistance society offers to never-married mothers.

POVERTY IMPACT

The greater economic insecurity of single-parent families is apparent in poverty statistics. Table 8.3 summarizes the consequences. Notice first that mother-only families account for the largest number of people in poverty. As a result, differences in poverty *rates* between single-parent and two-parent families are dramatic. Among whites and blacks the poverty rate for mother-only families is more than *five times* that of two-parent families. For both black and Hispanic families the poverty rate of mother-only families exceeds 40 percent.

Families headed by women are not only more likely to be poor but are also more likely to *stay* in poverty longer. Never-married mothers are particularly prone to chronic poverty and welfare dependency.[11]

Table 8.3 also confirms that the economic handicaps of single parenthood are not confined to mothers. Fathers who attempt to raise children on their own also bear higher risks of poverty. Although poverty rates of father-only families are way below those of mother-only families, they are substantially above those of two-parent households.

These varied poverty rates underscore the importance of family structure as a potential cause of poverty. Table 8.3 implies that there would be a lot less poverty in America if two-parent families were more prevalent. This proposition was put to an interesting test by Professors Peter Gottschalk and Sheldon Danziger. They asked

[11]See Mary Jo Bane and David J. Ellwood, *Welfare Realities* (Cambridge, MA: Harvard University Press, 1994), Chapter 2.

what today's poverty population would look like if family patterns had not changed so much. To answer this question, they used the poverty rates for different family types, like those depicted in Table 8.3. They then applied these to the patterns of family types that existed in 1968. The resultant computations showed how much poverty would exist today if family types had not changed since 1968.[12]

The Gottschalk-Danziger computations pointed to single parenthood as a major cause of poverty. Had the pattern of family structure not changed since 1968, the poverty rate among blacks would be a third less and among whites a fifth less.[13] Similar analyses by Robert Lerman and James Smith concluded that the surge in female-headed families completely explains the increase in childhood poverty since 1968.[14]

CAUSATION

Although the potential of family breakup (or nonformation) for impoverishment is striking, the direction of causation is once again debatable. Indeed, the surge in female headship has ignited a raging controversy about cause and effect. While some observers point their fingers at Flawed Character, others argue that family instability is a *symptom* of poverty, not an independent cause. They point to diminished economic opportunities for men, increased economic insecurity for families, and the lack of access to birth control as Restricted Opportunities that spawn single-parent families.[15]

Flawed Character

Historically, there has seldom been any reluctance to "explain" the existence of one-parent families among blacks. As late as the 1920s, allegations of "animalism," "moral putridity," and "primitive sexualism" were often advanced as explanations for the great incidence of broken families among American blacks. The latent implication was always that blacks were responsible for their own destitution because they were morally, physically, or culturally unable to stabilize family relationships. Proponents of this Flawed Character interpretation emphasize that family instability has worsened even when economic opportunities have been increasing. And they point out that instability among black families is substantially higher than among white families of similar income, education, and housing arrangements.[16]

Big Brother

Other observers place more blame on Big Brother's antifamily policies, particularly the welfare system. The nation's largest welfare program provides automatic income support for female-headed families but less certain support for intact families. This

---

[12]Gottschalk and Danziger, "Family Structure, Family Size, and Family Income."

[13]Similar results are found in Maria Cancian and Deborah Reed, "Changes in Family Structure: Implications for Poverty and Related Policy," in *Understanding Poverty*, eds. S. Danziger and R. Haveman (Cambridge, MA: Harvard University Press, 2001).

[14]Robert Lerman, "The Impact of the Changing U.S. Family Structure on Child Poverty and Income Inequality," *Economics* (May 1996), pp. 119–139; James Smith, "Children Among the Poor," *Demography* (May 1989), pp. 235–248. Similar conclusions are reached in Hilary Hoynes, Marianne Page, and Ann Huff Stevens, "Poverty in America: Trends and Explanations," *Journal of Economic Perspectives* (Winter 2006), pp. 47–68.

[15]For a forceful statement of this position, see Katha Pollitt, "Subject to Debate," *Nation*, May 30, 1994. A critique is offered in Midge Decter, "Welfare Feminism," *Commentary*, July 1994.

[16]Kevin Hopkins, "Marriage, Marital Dissolution, and Remarriage," in *Welfare Dependency*, ed. Hopkins.

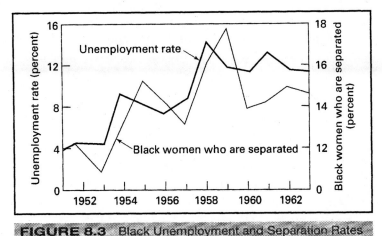

FIGURE 8.3   Black Unemployment and Separation Rates

Source: U.S. Department of Labor, *The Negro Family: The Case for National Action* (March 1965), p. 22.

gives families a perverse incentive to split up. It also enables young unwed mothers to establish households on their own rather than with their own families. The result is a "blight of dependency" that undermines family stability.[17]

Restricted Opportunity

Still another explanation for the increasing feminization of poverty emphasizes the Restricted Opportunities of *males*. This perspective was first highlighted in the mid-1960s. Daniel Moynihan, then assistant U.S. Secretary of Labor (and later a U.S. senator), focused on the relationship between unemployment rates and family structure. Looking at the trend of unemployment rates and family structures, Moynihan found that the rates of separation and divorce followed economic events very closely. Thus, the rate of separation for black women shot up shortly after the economy faltered, while it sank when the economy prospered (see Figure 8.3). Family stability was apparently the result, not the cause, of economic events. As a family faced increased unemployment and deprivation, the father's position as breadwinner became untenable; divorce, separation, or desertion often followed.

Further support for this position was found in illegitimacy statistics: In poor black neighborhoods rates of illegitimacy were more than triple those of black neighborhoods with middle-class incomes. Again it appeared that family formation itself was significantly affected by economic circumstances. Those parents with little prospect for economic security foresaw little hope for family stability; they decided not to marry.

[17]Francine Blau, Lawrence Kahn, and Jane Waldfogel, "The Impact of Welfare Benefits on Single Motherhood and Headship of Young Women," *Journal of Human Resources* (Spring 2004), pp. 382–404. For elaboration of this argument, see Charles Murray, "Does Welfare Bring More Babies?" *Public Interest* (Spring 1994), and *Losing Ground: American Social Policy, 1950–1980* (New York: Basic Books, 1984). Lowell Gallaway and Richard Wedder present a similar argument in *Poverty, Income, the Family, and Public Policy,* study for Joint Economic Committee, U.S. Congress (Washington, DC: U.S. Government Printing Office, 1986). Canadian experience suggests that welfare policy is a significant factor in the duration of single parenthood; see Pierre Lefebvre and Philip Merrigan, "The Impact of Welfare Benefits on the Conjugal Status of Single Mothers in Canada," *Journal of Human Resources* (Summer 1998), pp. 742–757.

A. Philip Randolph, long a leader in labor and civil rights movements, found evidence similar to Moynihan's in World War II experience. During the exceptionally low unemployment years of the war, rates of divorce and illegitimacy among blacks took a sharp drop. Greater economic security thus manifested itself in greater family stability.

Marriageable Men

A variant on this economic perspective has been advanced by William Darity Jr., and Samuel Myers Jr. In 1981, there were only 86 black men for every 100 black women in the age group 25 to 44. Among whites the ratio was 100 to 100. Hence, a *shortage* of black men precludes many black women from forming two-parent families.[18] William Wilson and Kathryn Neckerman have emphasized that the pool of *marriageable* men has declined even more, especially for blacks. Specifically, the ratio of *employed* black men to black women of similar age has declined sharply in the last two decades. This gives young black women very few eligible prospects.[19]

As logical as the Wilson theory might be, the evidence doesn't support it as a major explanation of family structure. Marriage rates have been declining for well-educated black men almost as fast as for poorly educated black men. Likewise, marriage rates have been declining in parallel fashion for both employed and unemployed black men. At best, the Wilson theory explains no more than 20 percent of the change in black family structure since 1960. Critics also note that there were parallel changes among white males.[20]

Persistent Poverty

Undoubtedly, social, cultural, institutional, and economic forces all influence family structure. It is difficult, however, to sort out these many forces and assign a quantitative weight to each. Nevertheless, there are ways of narrowing the range of uncertainty about whether marital instability causes poverty. The simplest way is to observe families over time. By observing whether marital instability *precedes* poverty, or vice versa, one can surmise the direction of causation.

This longitudinal approach was used by Mary Jo Bane. She discovered that a majority of poor female-headed *white* families were not poor prior to marital breakup. Among blacks, however, the ratios are reversed. Nearly two-thirds of black female-headed families were also poor prior to the split.[21]

---

[18]William Darity Jr., and Samuel L. Myers Jr., "Changes in Black Family Structure: Implications for Welfare Dependency," *American Economic Review* (May 1983); also, "Family Structure and the Marginalization of Black Men" in *The Decline in Marriage Among African Americans,* eds. M. B. Tucker and C. Mitchell-Kernan (New York: Russell Sage, 1995).

[19]William Julius Wilson and Kathryn M. Neckerman, "Poverty and Family Structure," in *Fighting Poverty,* eds. Danziger and Weinberg (Cambridge, MA: Harvard University Press, 1986). For more definitions and evidence on "marriage markets," see Michael J. Brien, "Racial Differences in Marriage and the Role of Marriage Markets," *Journal of Human Resources* (Fall 1997), pp. 741–778.

[20]See Paul Offner, "Reducing Non-Marital Births," in *Welfare Reform and Beyond,* eds. I. Sawhill et al. (Washington, DC: Brookings Institution, 2002). For other critiques of the "marriageable men" theory, see Robert G. Wood, "Marriage Rates and Marriageable Men: A Test of the Wilson Hypothesis," *Journal of Human Resources* (Winter 1995), pp. 163–193; R. Kelly Raley, "A Shortage of Marriageable Men?" *American Sociological Review, 161* (1996), pp. 973–983; and Daniel T. Lichter, Diane McLaughlin, and David Ribar, "Economic Restructuring and the Retreat from Marriage," *Social Science Research* (2002), v. 31:2, pp. 230–256.

[21]Mary Jo Bane, "Household Composition and Poverty," in *Fighting Poverty,* eds. Danziger and Weinberg.

TABLE 8.4 Single-Parent Male Families, by Income

Income Group	Percent of Families Headed by Male with No Wife Present
Under $10,000	5.6
$10,000–14,999	5.7
$15,000–24,999	7.4
$25,000–34,999	7.5
Over $35,000	4.8
All families	5.6

Source: U.S. Census Bureau (1998 data).

Other data on family and income patterns seem to confirm these observations. Table 8.4 shows the income status of families in which no wife is present. These single-parent *male* families are also disproportionately poor. Such a family structure is more likely in below-median-income circumstances (5.6–7.5 percent) than in above-median-income circumstances (4.8 percent). Similar correlations exist between income and the probability of married men living without their wives. This suggests that the men who are missing from the single-parent *female* households in poverty are likely to be poor as well. One study observed that unmarried fathers were twice as likely as married fathers to have a physical or psychological problem that interfered with their ability to find or keep a job. They were also several times more likely to abuse drugs or alcohol. More than 25 percent of unmarried fathers were out of work when their child was born.[22] In view of these realities, one cannot conclude that the failure of single moms to marry these men caused their poverty.

The impact of economic insecurity on marital instability was also noted in a seven-year study of 5,000 families. The families were first interviewed in 1967, then reinterviewed in each of the following years, until 1973. These observations, by the University of Michigan Survey Research Center, show how divorce and separation are often linked to economic status. In general, average family income turned out to be the best predictor of family stability for both whites and blacks. In addition, families that owned their own homes in 1967 or had significant savings were much more likely to be still intact in 1973. By contrast, families in which the husband was encountering employment problems in 1967 were more likely to have broken up by 1973.[23]

The relationship between family status and poverty, then, is best described as dynamic. Continued economic deprivation is likely to undermine a family's stability. At some point, the family unit is ruptured, and the female-headed family is left to fend for itself. No loss of economic status is necessarily implied by the departure of the father,

[22]Wendy Single-Ruston and Sara McLanahan, "For Richer or Poorer?" (Chicago, IL: Joint Center for Poverty Research, January 2002). See also Maureen R. Waller, *My Baby's Father; Unmarried Parents and Paternal Responsibility*. Ithaca, NY: Cornell University Press, 2002.

[23]Greg J. Duncan and James N. Morgan, eds., *Five Thousand American Families: Patterns of Economic Progress,* Vol. 4 (Ann Arbor, MI: Institute for Social Research, 1976). A parallel study of low-income and welfare families in Camden, New Jersey, found that the husband's economic performance was important for family attitudes and stability: see Samuel Klausner, "Six Years in the Lives of the Impoverished: An Examination of the WIN Thesis" (Philadelphia: Center for Research on the Acts of Man, 1978).

especially where he was unemployed and/or the female-headed unit turned to public assistance. In the University of Michigan study noted earlier, 20 percent of the families that broke up during the seven-year observation period did fall into poverty, and most of these turned to welfare. However, the average loss of income status amounted to only 6 percent of prior income status.[24] Hence, family breakup was only marginally responsible for existing poverty.

Family breakup can also have intergenerational effects, however. Children of disrupted families tend to have less subsequent schooling and a higher risk of adult poverty.[25] By observing families both before and after divorce, the causal nature of this intergenerational link has been documented.[26]

Breakups

While at any point in time a high proportion of poor families will be female-headed, family breakup cannot be identified as a major cause of poverty. Family disunity may help sustain poverty, but in most cases it appears that poverty preceded, and itself helped to cause, family dissolution.

This conclusion does not necessitate a purely economic deterministic view of family relations. Clearly, not all divorces and separations are occasioned by financial stress. Family dissolutions will continue to take place even after all families are assured of economic security. The point is that a disproportionately high percentage of family breakups occurs among the poor due to economic stress and that relatively few broken poor families were decidedly nonpoor before family dissolution occurred.

Never Marrieds

The causal sequence for never-married mothers is different. In these cases, childbirth itself may be the decisive factor in establishing another poor household. Even here, however, economic circumstances may have influenced both the decision to have a child and the decision not to marry. The Wilson thesis about a scarcity of marriageable men may be particularly relevant here, especially in view of the youthfulness of both the mother and father. The lack of visible career prospects may also convince young women that they have "nothing to lose" by having a baby.

Intriguing evidence on the "nothing-to-lose" syndrome comes from observing the *sisters* of teen mothers. While teen mothers are likely to be poor and welfare dependent, their sisters don't fare much better. Indeed, by the time they are in their mid-twenties, teen mothers and their sisters are economically indistinguishable.[27] The same conclusion was reached in a longitudinal study comparing teen moms to teens who had

---

[24]Larger income losses are reported for nonpoor families: see Duncan and Morgan, *Five Thousand American Families*, Vol. 9.

[25]See Eng Seng Loh, "Changes in Family Structure, Attained Schooling, and Adult Poverty Status," *Social Science Quarterly* (March 1996), pp. 145–158. A historical perspective on this intergenerational link is provided in Howard Bodenhorn, "Single Parenthood and Childhood Outcomes in the Mid-Nineteenth Century Urban South" (Cambridge, MA: National Bureau of Economic Research, Working Paper No. 12056, February 2006).

[26]Gary Painter and David Levine, "Family Structure and Youths' Outcomes," *Journal of Human Resources* (Summer 2000), pp. 524–549. For a less alarming view, see Keith Lang and Jay Zagorsky, "Does Growing Up with a Parent Absent Really Hurt?" *Journal of Human Resources* (Spring 2001), pp. 253–273.

[27]See Arline T. Geronimus and Sanders Korenman, "The Socioeconomic Costs of Teenage Childbearing: Evidence and Interpretation," *Demography* (May 1993), pp. 281–296; Coley and Chase-Landsdale, op. cit.

experienced miscarriages.[28] This suggests that factors other than early childbirth are the primary cause of high poverty rates.

Although economic forces have played a significant role in shaping marital patterns, they are far from a complete explanation.[29] Single parenthood has spread beyond low-income neighborhoods and across national boundaries.[30] Moreover, single parenthood has continued to spread even when economic conditions have improved. Some even fear that single parenthood has taken on a life of its own.[31] As single parenthood has spread, it has altered expectations for family life. The disruptions accompanying family dissolutions may have also contributed to higher premarital birth rates of affected children.[32]

Summary

Large families and broken families are among the most salient characteristics of the poor. Nearly 30 percent of all the poor are in families with at least five members; while 40 percent of the poor are in one-parent families, many of the latter are also from large families. Accordingly, there exists a strong presumption that family size and structure are important causes of poverty.

As is often the case, the lines of causality are not unambiguous. Poverty often precedes and even contributes to larger family size, family breakup, and premarital childbearing. By increasing stress or reducing opportunities, unfavorable economic circumstances can create demographic problems that perpetuate poverty. Available evidence suggests that most large and single-parent poor families were in or near poverty prior to a change in family size or structure. In these cases, family size and structure do more to deepen and prolong poverty than to create it.

Although family size and structure do not account for as much poverty as might be expected, they are still significant causes of poverty. This is particularly true for unwed teenagers who are producing an increasing percentage of all teenage births and are

---

[28]Hotz, V. Joseph, Seth Sanders, and Susan W. McElroy, "Teenage Childbearing and Its Life Cycle Consequences" (Cambridge, MA: National Bureau of Economic Research, October 1999). Similar results were found in Australia; see Bruce Bradbury, "The Impact of Young Motherhood on Education, Employment and Marriage" (Ann Arbor, MI: National Poverty Center, Working Paper No. 06–34, September 2006).

[29]Labor-market problems may explain no more than 20 percent of the increase in female headship, according to Robert D. Mare and Christopher Winship, "Socioeconomic Change and the Decline of Marriage for Blacks and Whites," in *The Urban Underclass,* eds. C. Jencks and P. Peterson. Also see Robert I. Lerman, "Employment Opportunities of Young Men and Family Formation," *American Economic Review* (May 1989), pp. 62–66. Derek Neal argues that increased availability of welfare benefits has been decisive for the formation of households by never-married mothers; see "The Relationship Between Marriage Market Prospects and Never-Married Motherhood," *Journal of Human Resources* (Fall 2004) pp. 938–957.

[30]Kristin A. Moore et al., *Beginning Too Soon: Adolescent Sexual Behavior, Pregnancy and Parenthood* (Washington, DC: Child Trends, Inc., June 1995); also U.S. Congress, Ways and Means Committee, *1992 Green Book,* p. 1077.

[31]Rather than fearing the spread of single parenthood, Shere Hite views it as a positive development in the evolution of adult relationships and child development; see *Women as Revolutionary Agents of Change: The Hite Report and Beyond* (Madison, WI: University of Wisconsin Press, 1994).

[32]The nature of the intergenerational link between single parenthood and second-generation premarital births is examined in Lawrence L. Wu and Brian Martinson, "Family Structure and the Risk of a Premarital Birth," *American Sociological Review* (April 1993), pp. 210–232. Also see James Q. Wilson, "On Gender," *The Public Interest* (Spring 1993), pp. 3–26, for a discussion of male childrearing in female-headed families.

most likely to become permanently poor and dependent. Nontraditional family structures also contribute to intergenerational poverty.

Further Reading

ON FAMILY SIZE

Edin, Kathryn, and Laura Lein, *Making Ends Meet: How Single Mothers Survive Welfare and Low Wage Work*. New York: Russell Sage, 1997.

Gottschalk, Peter, and Sheldon Danziger. "Family Structure, Family Size, and Family Income," in *Uneven Tides,* eds. S. Danziger and P. Gottschalk. New York: Russell Sage, 1993.

Guo, Guang, and Leah VanWey, "Sibship Size and Intellectual Development: Is the Relationship Causal?" *American Sociological Review* (April 1999), pp. 169–187.

Smith, James P., "Children Among the Poor," *Demography* (May 1989), pp. 235–248.

ON FAMILY STRUCTURE

Cancian, Maria, and Deborah Reed, "Changes in Family Structure: Implications for Poverty and Related Policy," in *Understanding Poverty,* eds. S. Danziger and R. Haveman. Cambridge, MA: Harvard University Press, 2001.

Hoffman, Saul, *By the Numbers: The Public Costs of Teen Childbearing*. Washington, DC: National Campaign to Prevent Teen Pregnancy, October 2006.

Klepinger, Daniel, Shelly Lundberg, and Robert Plotnick, "How Does Adolescent Fertility Affect the Human Capital and Wages of Young Women?" *Journal of Human Resources* (Summer 1999), pp. 421–448.

Maynard, Rebecca, ed. *Kids Having Kids*. Washington, DC: Urban Institute, 1996.

Neal, Derek, "The Economics of Family Structure," *Journal of Human Resources,* Summer 2004.

Page, Marianne, and Ann Huff Stevens, "The Economic Consequences of Absent Parents," *Journal of Human Resources,* Winter 2004, pp. 80–107.

Rector, Robert, and Kirk Johnson, "The Effects of Marriage and Maternal Education in Reducing Child Poverty" (Washington, DC: Heritage Foundation, August 2002).

South, Scott, Katherine Trent, and Yang Shen, "Changing Partners: Toward a Macrostructural-Opportunity Theory of Marital Dissolution," *Journal of Marriage and Family, 63* (2001), pp. 743–754.

Wu, Lawrence L., "Effects of Family Instability, Income, and Income Instability on the Risk of a Premarital Birth," *American Sociological Review* (April 1996), pp. 386–406.

Wu, Lawrence, and Barbara Wolfe, eds., *Out of Wedlock: Causes and Consequences of Nonmarital Fertility*. New York: Russell Sage, 2001.

Web Links

Child Trends. Data and analysis of fertility patterns
www.childtrends.org

National Vital Statistics Reports.
www.cdc.gov/nchs/Default.htm

U.S. Bureau of the Census. Marital status and living arrangements:
http://www.census.gov/population/www/socdemo/ms-la.html

U.S. Department of Health and Human Services.
(1) Annual data on teen pregnancy and births:
http://aspe.hhs.gov/hsp/teenp
(2) Research review on teen pregnancy and parenthood:
http://aspe.hhs.gov/hsp/cyp/xsteesex.htm

CHAPTER 9
THE UNDERCLASS:
CULTURE AND RACE

When Lyndon Johnson initiated the War on Poverty in the mid-1960s, there were great expectations that the combination of a growing economy and targeted assistance would eliminate poverty in America. Since then, the U.S. economy has quadrupled in size, the average household income has doubled, and the employed labor force has grown by 100 million persons. In the same 40-year period the government has spent hundreds of billions of dollars on programs to aid the poor. But poverty hasn't disappeared. As we observed in Chapter 3, the number of poor people in America today is little changed from the number in 1965. Even during the strong economic expansions of the 1980s and 1990s the poverty population shrank only modestly.

This paradox of persistent poverty in an otherwise affluent America has reignited debates about the true origins of poverty. One of the most intense debates has focused on the proposition that an *underclass* exists that is so poor and socially isolated that it does not respond to mainstream prosperity, incentives, or values. The culture of the underclass spawns single-parent households (Chapter 8), discourages labor force participation (Chapters 5 and 6), and perpetuates poverty.

There are two distinct issues bound up in the underclass debate. The first focuses on the *existence* of such an economically and socially isolated subgroup. The second one focuses on *explanations*. Do members of the underclass have only themselves to blame (Flawed Character) for their plight, or have economic obstacles (Restricted Opportunity) or perverse government incentives (Big Brother) fostered a separate and self-defeating way of life?

THE CULTURE OF POVERTY

In colonial America poverty was regarded as the manifestation of vice and sin. Because everyone except Negro slaves was thought to enjoy the opportunity to acquire economic security by his or her own labor, those who did not attain such security were deemed to be morally flawed. Poverty thus became proof of moral bankruptcy, and the poor were treated accordingly. In Pennsylvania, paupers had the shoulders of their right sleeves adorned with the letter *P* to warn unsuspecting strangers. In other jurisdictions the poor were sent packing, sometimes after a public whipping. As the puritanical Humane Society summarized the situation in 1809, ". . . by a just and inflexible law of Providence, misery is ordained to be the companion and punishment of vice."[1]

---

[1]Cited by Paul Jacobs in Jeremy Larner and Irving Howe, eds., *Poverty: Views from the Left* (New York: William Morrow, 1968), p. 40.

In more modern times the theoretical link of poverty to sin has not fared well. There now exists a general reluctance to ascribe the misery of the poor to the laws of Providence. Nevertheless, belief in the universality of economic opportunity remains firmly embedded in the American consciousness. Accordingly, we need a substitute explanation for the persistence of poverty in a land of abundance and opportunity. This, in part, explains the popularity of cultural theories of poverty. Most cultural theories of poverty assert that the poor lack sufficient desire and motivation to escape poverty. They allege that the goal of economic security is of lesser importance in the value matrix of the poor. Welfare mothers would rather have kids than jobs. Young men would rather "hustle" on street corners than accept a regular job. An overriding focus on immediate gratification discourages family planning, the pursuit of education, or the accumulation of savings. Because they are trapped by this culture, the members of the underclass don't behave in ways that would help them escape from poverty.

NORMS VERSUS TRAITS

To assess the extent to which an underclass culture perpetuates poverty, the nature of such a culture must be examined. *Culture* is not just about *behavior,* but rather the norms, values, and aspirations that underlie behavioral patterns. In other words, the key elements of a culture are not directly observable but must instead be *inferred* from observed behavior.

The potential gap between unseen norms and observable traits largely explains why the underclass controversy is so intense. Very different interpretations can easily be grafted onto commonly observed behavior. Consider the case of a welfare recipient who declines what appears to be a reasonable job offer. For many middle-class observers, such a rejection constitutes incontrovertible proof that the recipient lacks normal initiative, aspirations, and goals—clear evidence of a culture of poverty. Middle-class individuals, it is argued, would never reject an offer to improve their economic status, especially in the dire financial straits of the welfare recipient. A different set of values—flawed ones—must be shaping the welfare recipient's response.

The job rejection isn't necessarily the symptom of a flawed character, however. The rejection of employment opportunities may reflect other circumstances not readily apparent to the nonpoor observer. The job itself may be inherently unattractive and provide no economic advancement. Or the job may pose transportation or child care problems that can't be readily resolved. In that case restricted opportunities would be a better explanation of the job rejection.

The Big Brother argument may also be relevant. Welfare rules sharply limit the economic gain associated with employment. A loss of welfare benefits, as well as Medicaid, food stamps, and economic assistance, could actually *lower* a family's income when the mother leaves welfare for work.[2] Even where a job pays more than welfare, there is a distinct risk of ending up worse off. It is easy to get off welfare but time-consuming to get back on. If the job proves to be unsatisfactory or temporary, then she and her family are left without any financial support while she awaits a new job or more welfare. For fami-

---

[2]The structure of welfare benefits and incentives is discussed in Chapter 13.

lies at the margin of impoverishment and confronting largely transitory kinds of jobs, such a risk may be unwarranted. Thus, the job rejection may proceed not from different values and aspirations but from tangible behavioral constraints. Middle-class job seekers, with savings accounts and better job prospects, are not subject to these same constraints.

The culture of poverty hypothesis requires rather stringent evidence. It must be shown that the norms and aspirations—not just the behavior—of the poor are different and that these differences impede escape from poverty. It should also be shown whether and to what degree such differences would disappear under changing socio-economic circumstances.

Anthropological Studies

Oscar Lewis was one of the most forceful proponents of the culture of poverty thesis. His anthropological observations of lifestyles among the poor convinced him that the behavior patterns of the poor are different and that these differences reflect distinct values. Although his empirical research was confined largely to Mexico and Puerto Rico, he believed that these differences transcend national boundaries. He offered the following explanation for the perpetuation of poverty:

> Once [the culture of poverty] comes into existence it tends to perpetuate itself from generation to generation because of its effect on the children. By the time slum children are age six or seven they have usually absorbed the basic values and attitudes of their subculture and are not psychologically geared to take full advantage of changing conditions or increased opportunities which may occur in their lifetime.[3]

From Lewis's perspective, the poor are prolonging their own impoverishment. As evidence, he identified no less than seventy behavioral traits that distinguish the poor, including little use of banks or museums and nonparticipation in labor unions. Although he acknowledged that the poor may be aware of, or even profess, middle-class values, he regards their aberrant behavior as proof that they do not share those values.

Other sociologists and anthropologists have followed Lewis's lead. Another popular diagnosis of the poor, for example, focuses on their alleged self-indulgence. Out of Lewis's more general depiction of lower-class culture, other observers claim to perceive a pattern of nondeferred gratification: Whereas the middle-class person supposedly feels the need and desire to save, postpone, and renounce certain immediate pleasures, the poor person is alleged to experience no such motivations.[4] This alleged impulse following is presumed to be embedded in the personality dynamics of the poor individual, thus obstructing his or her self-improvement.

This pattern of self-indulgence is additionally presumed to have strong intergenerational effects. Self-indulgent parents have little interest in their children's futures, thus contributing to further poverty. As one observer has asserted:

> Where middle and upper class parents think in terms of a college education for their offspring, lower class parents' aspirations usually stop at a high school diploma, at the very best. Poor parents, with little education, are more likely to

---

[3]Oscar Lewis, *La Vida* (New York: Random House, 1966), p. xiv.

[4]Variations in time preferences by socioeconomic status are examined in J. Paul Leigh, "Accounting for Tastes: Correlates of Risk and Time Preference," *Journal of Post-Keynesian Economics* (Fall 1986), pp. 17–31.

believe in luck than in education and to be contemptuous of "book learning.". . . Indeed, among low-income families, both the low educational attainment of the head of the household and the quality of family life create a social environment that leads the poor to believe that "education is not for them."[5]

A QUESTION OF OPPORTUNITIES

Not all observers share these views of lower-class culture. On the contrary, much recent sociological discussion has focused on some of the basic weaknesses in the culture of poverty thesis. It has been pointed out, for example, that the attribution of cultural differences based on observed behavioral differences incorporates many assumptions of questionable validity. Consider again the phenomenon of deferred gratification. Do the poor act differently because of circumstances or values? To conclude that differential values cause the poor to seek more immediate gratification, the following conditions must be met:

1. The satisfaction being deferred must be equally important to the poor and nonpoor.
2. There must exist equal opportunity to defer the satisfaction.
3. The poor and nonpoor must equally suffer from deferment.
4. The probability of obtaining gratification at the end of the deferment period must be equal for both groups.

If any or all of these conditions are violated, then behavioral differences may be explained by situational differences, by differences in opportunity; no reference to alleged cultural phenomena is necessary.

Schooling

The case of educational attainment illustrates some of the foregoing conditions. The children of the poor undeniably drop out of school earlier than other children. But does this behavioral difference reflect cultural orientations? Schools in lower-income areas are notoriously ill equipped to transmit interest, enjoyment, or ability. The third and fourth conditions in our list are violated: Middle-class school experience is both more pleasant and more profitable. Furthermore, the low-income family cannot afford to support a child's education for as long as a middle-class family; thus, the second condition is also violated. Given these inequalities in opportunity, it might be equally valid to conclude that the poor value education *more* highly than the nonpoor because of the greater sacrifices they make to get as far as they do.[6]

Saving

A similar array of qualifications to the "impulse following" hypothesis is encountered when saving behavior is considered. The poor save less money less often than the nonpoor. Does this reflect a present-time orientation (as contrasted with a future-time orien-

---

[5]Oscar Ornati, *Poverty Amid Affluence* (New York: Twentieth Century Fund, 1966), p. 66. This argument has been used to explain why poor families do not undertake as much preventive health care as nonpoor families; see Peter Ferrara and Kevin Hopkins, "Health Status of the Poor," in *Welfare Dependency,* ed. Hopkins (Alexandria, VA: Hudson Institute, 1987).

[6]Some evidence for this is found in John Reynolds and Jennifer Pemberton, "Rising College Expectations Among Youth in the United States," *Journal of Human Resources* (Fall 2001), pp. 703–726.

tation)? Perhaps not. The poor have very little to save in the first place. Whatever they do manage to put aside represents a real sacrifice in terms of present consumption. Hence, there is no foundation for inferring cultural inadequacies on the basis of observed differences in saving.

The central weakness of the culture of poverty proposition is the assumption that behavioral differences between the poor and nonpoor reflect differences in goals and aspirations. In reality, the poor do not have an equal opportunity to fulfill, or even to pursue, their goals. Hence, there may be a sharp divergence between the aspirations and the behavior of the poor that does not exist among middle-class groups.

WILSON'S UNDERCLASS THEORY

Sociologist William Julius Wilson offered a different explanation for the apparent culture of poverty. Like earlier observers, he confirmed that people who lived in areas of concentrated poverty (ghettos) behave differently than do people on Main Street. He also noted that their behavior was consistent with a unique set of values that might be characterized as a culture of poverty. Rather than ascribing underclass behavior to a distinct culture, however, he emphasized its *external* causes. The restructuring of the American economy had reduced job opportunities available to inner-city residents and made high-wage jobs particularly remote. The exodus of middle-class blacks from inner-city neighborhoods had also increased the social isolation of increasingly impoverished core poverty areas. In Wilson's view, a reduction in the economic and social isolation of the underclass would alter its behavior.[7]

TESTING THE THEORY

Wilson's underclass hypothesis inspired a resurgence of research on the alleged culture of poverty. The research has pursued two distinct questions:

1. How large is the underclass?
2. What explains its unique behavior?

Size

There was a certain vagueness in Wilson's original formulation about who was a member of the underclass. Was everyone in the underclass poor? Was the underclass defined by geographic boundaries or by the socially deviant behavior of individuals? Did a person have to live in a particular neighborhood to belong to the underclass? If so, how was that neighborhood to be defined? Was everyone in that neighborhood a member of the underclass, even those who didn't exhibit deviant behavior? Was there a racial exclusiveness to the underclass, or was membership color-blind?

A dozen or so studies pursued these measurement questions and produced just as many different answers. The size of the resultant underclass was estimated as low as

---

[7]See William Julius Wilson, *The Truly Disadvantaged* (Chicago: University of Chicago Press, 1987); and his further elaboration in *When Work Disappears: The World of the New Urban Poor* (New York: Knopf, 1996). For an international view, see Godfried Engberson et al., *Cultures of Unemployment* (Boulder, CO: Westview, 1993), which describes the "fatalistic street culture" of long-term unemployed individuals in three Dutch cities.

800,000 individuals (persistently poor people who exhibit deviant behavior) to as many as 41 million (all persons living in census tracts with poverty rates of at least 20 percent).[8]

Wilson tried to facilitate more precise measurements by later stipulating that an underclass neighborhood would have a poverty concentration of at least 40 percent.[9] He even suggested that the term *ghetto poverty* might be a more accurate label than the *underclass* concept. By these standards, the underclass would include only 1 percent of the U.S. population and less than 10 percent of the poverty population.[10]

Causation

Regardless of how large or small the underclass might be, there is still the underlying question of causation. Are the deviant behaviors associated with the underclass a product of a dysfunctional culture or external forces?

Two approaches are used to disentangle cause and effect. One approach entails direct tests of cultural components like aspirations and goals. The other approach tests the *predictions* of the model by seeing how behavior changes when external circumstances change. If the underclass responds positively to improved job opportunities or housing alternatives, then the cultural explanation loses validity.

DIRECT TESTS OF ASPIRATIONS

If testimony of the poor themselves is valid, there is little reason to believe that their behavior patterns will remain the same under improved socioeconomic conditions. Welfare mothers, for example, express a strong desire to see their children attain better social and economic positions. Moreover, they perceive clearly—more so than many academic observers—the great divergence between their aspirations and their actual opportunities. One survey, for example, questioned welfare mothers about their desires and expectations for their children's employment. The responses, portrayed in Table 9.1,

TABLE 9.1 Welfare Mothers' Desires and Expectations for Eldest Child's Occupational Status (percent)

Occupation	Desire	Expectation
Professional and managerial	48	27
Clerical	22	19
Craft	8	8
Police, army	2	6
Other paid work	6	14
Homemaker	1	4
Undecided	13	23

Source: Lawrence Podell, *Families on Welfare in New York City* (New York: City University of New York Press, 1968), Tables 7-C and 7-D. Lawrence Podell, Bernard M. Baruch College. Center for the Study of Urban Problems.

---

[8]A summary of alternative definitions and size estimates is contained in Ronald B. Mincy, "The Underclass: Concept, Controversy, and Evidence," in *Confronting Poverty*, eds. S. Danziger, G. Sandefur, and D. Weinberg (Cambridge, MA: Harvard University Press, 1994), pp. 109–146.

[9]Wilson, "Public Policy Research and the Truly Disadvantaged," p. 461.

[10]Paul Jargowsky and Rebecca Yang show how the underclass has shrunk in the last two decades; see their "The 'Underclass' Revisited: A Social Problem in Decline," *Journal of Urban Affairs* (Winter 2006), pp. 55–70.

are illuminating. Seventy percent of the mothers had white-collar *aspirations* for their eldest child, yet only 46 percent had any *expectation* that their children would attain this status. (Even fewer actually do.) The lower occupational status of poor children apparently does not reflect their parents' aspirations as much as it reflects the opportunities of the poor.[11]

Other studies have come to similar conclusions regarding work orientations and other dimensions of culture. When poor families are compared to nonpoor families of the same ethnic background (for example, white, black, Hispanic), no significant cultural differences appear.[12] This conclusion also applies to welfare recipients. After reviewing available studies of work attitudes and behavior of welfare mothers, Leonard Goodwin concluded that "welfare recipients do not differ markedly from other Americans with respect to general personality characteristics or with respect to the work ethic and basic life goals."[13] A multiyear (1987–1993) survey of nearly 9,000 poor, near-poor, and nonpoor households came to the same conclusion.[14]

Other case studies have shown that teenage welfare mothers—included in almost every definition of the underclass—have mainstream aspirations for family, education, and careers. They are less certain, however, about how to attain them and less hopeful that they will.[15] Their lowered expectations could easily be a realistic response to their childrearing responsibilities rather than a source of their predicament.

The *children* in poor families also offer relevant testimony. A 1992–1993 national survey asked students in grades 6 through 12 whether they expected (1) to attend college and (2) to graduate from college. Children from poor and single-parent families had expectations resembling those of nonpoor children. Another survey revealed the chances of realizing those expectations. As Figure 9.1 reveals, poor children are much less likely than nonpoor children to achieve their educational goals. Statistics like these aren't lost on the poor: Among immigrant Mexican children, 75 percent say they "want" to complete college but only 61 percent believe that goal is "realistic."[16]

---

[11]Debrai Ray argues that the "aspirations gap"—the difference between aspirations and current status—rather than the absolute level of aspirations, should be the focus of concern; see his "Aspirations, Poverty, and Economic Change" (New York University, March 2003).

[12]See, for example, Marta Tienda and Haya Stier, "Joblessness and Shiftlessness: Labor Force Activity in Chicago's Inner City," in *The Urban Underclass,* eds. C. Jencks and P. Peterson, (Washington, DC: Brookings Institution, 1991), pp. 135–154; Barbara Coward, Joe Feagim, and J, Allen Williams Jr., "The Culture of Poverty Debate: Some Additional Data," *Social Problems* (June 1974); Chandler Davidson and Charles Faitz, "Are the Poor Different? A Comparison of Work Behavior and Attitudes Among the Urban Poor and Nonpoor," *Social Problems* (December 1974); also Roberta H. Jackson, "Some Aspirations of Lower-Class Black Mothers," *Journal of Comparative Family Studies* (Autumn 1975).

[13]Leonard Goodwin, "What Has Been Learned from the Work Incentive Program and Related Experiences: A Review of Research with Policy Implications" (Worcester, MA: Worcester Polytechnic Institute, 1977), p. 31; see also Goodwin's *Causes and Cures for Welfare* (Lexington, MA: Lexington Books, 1983).

[14]See Rachel K. Jones and Ye Luo, "The Culture of Poverty and African American Culture: An Empirical Assessment," *Sociological Perspectives, 42*:3 (1999), pp. 439–458.

[15]See Naomi B. Farber, "The Significance of Aspirations among Unmarried Adolescent Mothers," *Social Service Review* (December 1989), pp. 518–532; Elizabeth T. Oritz and Betty Z. Bassoff, "Adolescent Welfare Mothers: Lost Optimism and Lowered Expectations," *Social Casework* (September 1987), pp. 400–405.

[16]Aonghas St. Hilare, "The Social Adaptation of Children of Mexican Immigrants: Education Aspirations Beyond Junior High School," *Social Science Quarterly 83:*4 (December 2002), pp. 1026–1043.

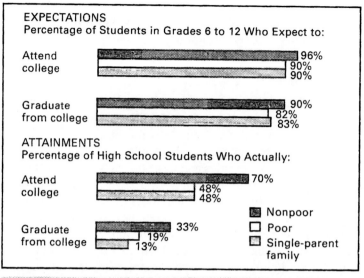

FIGURE 9.1 Expectations versus Reality

Source: Maya Federman et al., "What Does It Mean to Be Poor in America?" *Monthly Labor Review* (May 1996), Table 7. Bureau of Labor Statistics.

INDIRECT TESTS OF PREDICTED BEHAVIOR

If their aspirations and values were really as different as some observers claim, then the poor would be satisfied with their standard of living and resistant to new opportunity. Many modern cultural theorists argue, in fact, that the poor are content and unable to progress. (Similar arguments were once employed in defense of slavery.) Such views are not consistent with reality. Not only have organized groups of the poor repeatedly expressed their discontent, but the poor have demonstrated a marked ability to move out of poverty when economic opportunities have improved.

Specific tests of the underclass theory have focused on these responses of the poor to changed economic opportunities. Aggregate studies have shown that both poverty rates and welfare rolls are sensitive to economic downturns and upswings. This implies that opportunities are seized when they arise. More convincing results emerge, however, from studies that focus on specific subgroups of the underclass. One study found that young black men benefited disproportionately in terms of higher wages and lower unemployment when the local labor market tightened.[17] Another found that the probability of employment for black and Hispanic youth is correlated with the degree of spatial isolation for the neighborhood.[18] Yet another study observed that all poor persons, including single-parent families, benefit disproportionately from tight labor markets.[19]

---

[17]Richard S. Freeman, "Employment and Earnings of Disadvantaged Young Men in a Labor Shortage Economy," in *The Urban Underclass,* op. cit., eds. C. Jencks and P. Peterson, pp. 103–121.

[18]Katherine M. O'Regan and John M. Quigley, "Teenage Employment and the Spatial Isolation of Minority and Poverty Households," *Journal of Human Resources* (Summer 1996), pp. 672–702.

[19]Paul Osterman, "Gains from Growth? The Impact of Full Employment on Poverty in Boston," in *The Urban Underclass,* op. cit., pp. 122–134.

Such evidence is consistent with the notion that structural forces rather than cultural value systems are the decisive factors in shaping underclass behavioral patterns.

There is evidence for the cultural explanation as well, however. Some ethnic subgroups fare better than others in identical spatial contexts. Cuban American families, for example, fare better than Mexican American and Puerto Rican families in the same or similar neighborhoods.[20] Could part of this difference have cultural roots?

Finally, a unique experiment revealed somewhat ambiguous results about the impact of concentrated poverty. Families were randomly chosen to move out of New York public housing into less poor neighborhoods. If behavior is molded by neighborhood norms, the exiting families should manifest new behavioral patterns. In a three-year follow-up, however, researchers observed that exited families experienced much less mental stress, but adolescent behaviors were little changed.[21]

ASSESSMENT

Even the most adamant exponents of the culture of poverty thesis do not argue that *all* persons in poverty are psychodynamically attached to impoverishment. Oscar Lewis himself estimated that only 20 percent of the poor in America are culturally bound to poverty. Walter Miller, another advocate of the culture of poverty theory, does not specify what proportion of the poor are so afflicted but warns that the proportion is rising. Others, like Charles Murray and Lawrence Mead, focus on the long-term dependent, that is, those female-headed families who are poor and on welfare year after year. This group has a high degree of intergenerational welfare dependency, is least responsive to improved economic opportunity, and often becomes dependent on welfare at an early age. In that context, they survive with little self-esteem, low expectations, and minimal aspirations.

Among the 37 million people who were officially poor in 2005, there were, no doubt, some individuals with extraordinarily low aspirations. Many (for example, discouraged workers) may even have succumbed to a fatalistic attitude regarding their condition and future prospects, thus diminishing their ability to exploit new opportunities. We cannot assume, however, that this fatalism emerged from a cultural orientation or that it is totally impervious to changing circumstances. Yet the culture of poverty theory rests on these assumptions. To the extent that some of the poor do believe their chances for advancement are negligible, new opportunities will be grasped hesitantly. The more the poor experience repeated failure and disappointment, the more skeptically they will respond to new policy initiatives. This does not necessarily imply cultural dissonance; their skepticism may very well be a rational response based on prior experience.

The controversy over the nature, the size, and the origins of the so-called underclass continues. Although accumulating evidence suggests that a separate and isolated set of cultural norms may not drive underclass behavior, there is ample evidence of overlapping social and economic problems—what Kenneth Clark called a "tangle of pathologies." This suggests that the response to any particular policy initiative will be

---

[20]Nancy S. Landale and Daniel T. Lichter, "Geography and the Etiology of Poverty Among Latino Children," *Social Science Quarterly* (December 1997), pp. 874–894.

[21]Tama Levanthal and Jeanne Brooks-Gunn, "Moving to Opportunity: An Experimental Study of Neighborhood Effects on Mental Health," *American Journal of Public Health* (September 2003), pp. 1576–1582. For a broader discussion of how relocation affects behavior, see Harald Bauder, "Neighborhood Effects and Cultural Exclusion," *Urban Studies 39* (2002), pp. 85–93.

slow. Christopher Jencks asserts that it is more productive to focus on specific pathologies and opportunities, however, than to continue the search for an underlying cultural nexus that awaits a "metasolution."[22]

THE RACIAL INFERIORITY THEORY

The theory of a poverty-trapped underclass has distinct racial overtones. Indeed, Wilson's formulation of underclass dynamics stressed the spatial isolation of the black community and the declining pool of marriageable black men. Subsequent research largely focused on the experiences of urban blacks, leading some observers to conclude that the whole underclass concept was just a new way of referring to longstanding racial problems.[23] To blacks, the problems of the underclass originated in and are still aggravated by structural, institutional, and personal discrimination. To many whites, ghetto poverty is just another symptom of aberrant cultural values and inherent racial deficiencies. These divergent explanations are readily applied not only to the black community but to Hispanics as well.

In 2005 median income among black and Hispanic households was around $34,000 while among white Americans it was $51,000. As we have already seen, nearly one out of every four blacks and Hispanics is poor, compared with only one out of 12 whites. There is no question about whether a link exists between race and poverty; instead, we are concerned with the causal nature of the established link. Furthermore, in discussing the causal association between race and poverty, we need not worry about the circular relationships that attracted our attention earlier. Poverty may lead to ill health, broken families, or more children, but there is no prospect of poverty's changing people's skin color. Accordingly, both the existence of a link and the direction of causality are known: Being black or Hispanic does lead to poverty.

The causal path leading from race to poverty may be explained in two ways. Inherent racial disabilities may limit income-earning abilities. This, of course, is the racial argument that has arisen before. Another possible explanation for the established path emanates from the existence of discrimination. By this argument, minorities are more apt to be poor, not because of different physical, mental, or cultural capacities, but because they are treated differently by society. Whites have no difficulty in choosing between the alternative explanations of black status: The President's National Advisory Commission on Civil Disorders discovered that white Americans favor the racial explanation three to one. As recently as 1978, one out of two white Americans asserted that blacks have less ambition than whites. Fewer than one out of six whites saw racial discrimination as a serious problem.[24] We postpone a discussion of the discrimination argument until Chapters 11 and 12 and focus here on the racial inferiority theory.

---

[22]Christopher Jencks, "Is the American Underclass Growing?" in *The Urban Underclass*, pp. 28–100.

[23]Mickey Kaus went so far as to assert that "it is simply stupid to pretend that the culture of poverty isn't largely a black culture" in "The Work Ethic State," *The New Republic,* July 7, 1986, p. 22. Darity et al. appear to come to a similar conclusion in *The Black Underclass* (New York: Garland, 1994). Douglas Massey emphasizes racial segregation as the wellspring of the underclass in "American Apartheid: Segregation and the Making of the Underclass," *American Journal of Sociology* (September 1990), pp. 329–357. However, Hispanic communities often exhibit underclass behavior and confront similar barriers to unemployment and education.

[24]Louis Harris and Associates, *A Study of Attitudes Toward Racial and Religious Minorities and Toward Women* (New York: National Conference of Christians and Jews, 1978).

The thesis of racial inferiority is not new. Aristotle, for example, used it to explain Greek superiority over the European barbarians. Still later, the barbarians, who by then had produced Shakespeare, Kant, and Newton, used this argument to explain their superiority over the Greeks. Later still, English intellectuals were predicting that America would never achieve greatness because its colonies were heavily populated by the rejected and inferior classes of Europe.

Despite the somewhat dismal record of racial theories, they remain popular. Among the most quoted proponents of a racial explanation of black socioeconomic status in America is Dr. William Shockley. Shockley was an inventor of the transistor and a recipient of the Nobel Prize in physics. As he explained to the National Academy of Sciences in 1969: "The major deficit in Negro intellectual performance must be primarily of hereditary origin and thus relatively irremediable by practical improvements in the environment." In other words, blacks are poor because they are not smart, and they are not smart because they are black.

Shockley's position is extreme, but he is not alone in his beliefs about innate racial differences. Such beliefs are a common component of racial prejudice and linger on in the minds of many. They even acquire a certain plausibility for most white people because of the demonstrated link between genetic characteristics and achievement: Nearly everyone accepts the notion that smarter people do better and get further. Richard Herrnstein and Charles Murray documented this phenomenon in *The Bell Curve*. They showed that America is evolving into a techno-driven meritocracy in which intelligence plays an ever-larger role in distinguishing the haves from the have-nots.[25] Such a notion leads easily to the position that blacks fare poorly because they are not as smart as whites. The argument is readily extended to Puerto Ricans, Mexican Americans, American Indians, and other poor minorities.

INTELLIGENCE AND STATUS

What keeps the racial inferiority debate going (aside from ingrained prejudices) is the fact that intelligence is an unobservable dimension of an individual's genetic endowment. Although we all give nodding agreement to the notion that mental capacities, like physical capacities, are inherited, we have no direct way of weighing or measuring that inheritance. Accordingly, we depend largely on inferential reasoning to provide clues about the relationship of intelligence to economic status. Unfortunately, such reasoning often turns out to be circular. We have all heard statements like "Wow! John made a fortune in the dry cleaning business; I never realized he was so smart." From this perspective, the true test of intelligence is a person's tax return. According to this test, poverty *must* be explained by a lack of intelligence. If blacks and Hispanics tend to be poorer than whites, their plight must be explained in the same way.

Twin Studies
Fortunately, our knowledge of the relationship between intelligence and economic status does not depend exclusively on such superficial reasoning. We know, for example, that identical twins inherit identical genes, and thus identical intelligence (even if we

[25]R. Herrnstein and C. Murray, *The Bell Curve: Intelligence and Class Structure in American Life* (New York: The Free Press, 1994). A good summary is to be found in Charles Murray, *Income Inequality and IQ* (Washington, DC: American Enterprise Institute, 1998).

cannot measure that intelligence). Accordingly, if genetic endowments are important for economic status, identical twins should end up with the same status. And they tend to. A study by English sociologists determined that even when they are separated and reared in different environments, identical twins attain very similar socioeconomic statuses. Such observations confirm the significance of inherited abilities, at least for differences among *individuals*.

Genes and Environments

Demonstrating that genetic abilities are important for economic status does not deny the existence of environmental influences. In the studies of English twins, varying environments were shown to have *some* effect on achievement. Those effects would be still stronger where environmental differences were greater. The Osage Indians in America provide a dramatic illustration: Not only achievements but even measured IQ increased substantially after the tribe discovered oil!

A broader understanding of human achievement recognizes that both genetic and environmental factors influence the attainments of individuals and puts the issue of racial differences in an entirely different setting. Because black and white Americans live in distinct areas and under different conditions, racial abilities alone cannot explain disparities in economic status. To the extent that differences in racial abilities exist at all, we are led to inquire what *proportion* of observed status disparities can be attributed to them. In logical order, then, we must focus on three separate questions:

1. Do genetic differences exist between whites and blacks?
2. If so, how large are any such differences?
3. What is the relative significance of any such differences for observed socioeconomic status?

Very little interest attaches to the question of physical differences between whites and blacks, at least as far as socioeconomic status is involved. Instead, the issue of genetic differences focuses on the relative mental abilities of the two races. The first question, then, really asks whether whites are innately more intelligent than blacks.

IQ SCORES

Because we have no way of directly measuring intelligence, we cannot answer the foregoing questions directly. Instead, we must first find some independent indicator of intelligence, then test for differences among people on this basis. This is where IQ tests come in: An IQ score indicates how well an individual has performed on a standardized test relative to others of the same age. An IQ score of 100 indicates that one has performed up to average, while higher or lower scores indicate above- or below-average performance. There is a variety of such tests available, but all incorporate exercises of perceptual, verbal, arithmetical, and reasoning abilities.[26]

Since the nineteenth century there have been literally hundreds of research studies directed toward measuring the relative IQ of blacks and whites. All of them have demonstrated that blacks, on average, score lower on intelligence tests than whites. The average difference between whites and blacks amounts to 15 to 20 IQ points, indicating

---

[26]For a critical appraisal of the historical development and interpretation of IQ tests, see Stephen Jay Gould, *The Mismeasure of Man* (New York: Norton, 1983), Chapters 5 and 6.

that the typical black has an IQ of 80 to 85. These figures are now widely accepted; what is still debated is how they should be interpreted.

Basically, an IQ test measures various kinds of performance abilities, such as perception, memory, and verbal knowledge. Accordingly, it is subject to the influences of both genetic intelligence and environmental experience. A child who has never seen a giraffe or a waterfall, for example, has difficulty identifying them in an IQ examination, whatever his native intelligence may be. Minority children may also have less knowledge of testing strategies.[27] Because IQ scores incorporate both environmental and genetic experiences, there is no easy method for isolating genetic factors. All we can say with assurance is that IQ differences reflect genetic differences when administered to children who have shared very similar environmental experiences. Clearly, black and white children do not satisfy this condition.

The nature of IQ-score determinants suggests that black and white IQ scores could be brought into harmony by appropriate environmental changes. In fact, studies that have attempted to control for such differences by testing black and white children from similar backgrounds have narrowed the average IQ score difference to as little as five points. Black children adopted by white parents have also scored higher on IQ tests. Other research has demonstrated that the IQ test performances of blacks and whites move further apart the longer they are maintained in unequal situations—ghetto schools, for example.[28] Accordingly, it appears that there is nothing natural or unchangeable in any observed racial pattern of IQ scores.

Further evidence of environmental impact on IQ scores is provided by the variation in these scores for individuals and groups. We have already noted the effect of oil discoveries for the Osage Indians. Colder temperatures have also been linked to higher IQs.[29] For the country as a whole, IQ scores have been rising consistently over the last 50 years.[30] This suggests either that we are breeding selectively or that IQ scores are subject to environmental improvement (and perhaps even familiarity with testing procedures). More to our point, it has also been observed that black children moving from rural to urban areas raise their IQ scores significantly, reflecting an improved environment. Still other studies have shown that intensive teaching and supportive environments can materially improve the IQ scores of any group, even mentally retarded children. And finally, it has been demonstrated that improving the diets of poor expectant mothers results in higher IQ scores for their children.

RESOLVING THE ISSUES

The relationship between intelligence, IQ scores, and economic status is summarized in Figure 9.2. Notice that IQ scores and economic status are directly affected by intelligence. But notice also that both IQ scores and economic status are influenced by environmental

---

[27]Marybeth Walpole, et al., "The Test Is Unfair," *Urban Education* (May 2005), pp. 321–349.

[28]Mental tests in infancy appear to erase black—white differences altogether; see Roland Fryes and Steven D. Levitt, "Testing for Racial Differences in the Mental Ability of Young Children" (Cambridge, MA: National Bureau of Economic Research, Working Paper No. 12066, March 2006).

[29]Donald Templer, et al., "Temperatures, Skin Color, Per Capita Income, and IQ: An International Perspective," *Intelligence 34* (2006), pp. 121–139.

[30]The same rise in IQ scores has been observed in 14 European countries; see J. R. Flynn, "Massive IQ Gains in 14 Nations: What IQ Tests Really Measure," *Psychological Bulletin* (1987), pp. 171–191.

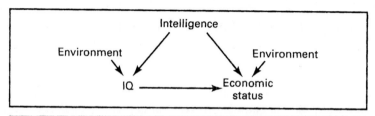

FIGURE 9.2   Intelligence, IQ, and Economic Status

factors as well. Accordingly, any demonstrated link between IQ and status may be explained by environmental forces alone. At least we may be certain that differences in IQ scores and status are less likely to reflect intelligence differences the greater are the environmental differences between the two individuals or groups in question. And this turns out to be an important qualification when comparing blacks and whites in America.

Guided by Figure 9.2 and our previous discussion, we can answer the three questions posed before. First, we must note that there is no definitive basis for concluding that genetic differences in intelligence exist between blacks and whites. This conclusion emerges from the fact that we do not really know what intelligence is and from the observation that the test scores we use to measure intelligence are themselves subject to environmental influence. We could just as easily assert that blacks are *more* intelligent than whites as the reverse. Indeed, many people argue that the entire search for an *explanation* of IQ differences is misplaced and racist. If IQ scores don't measure intelligence, then there is no white-black gap to explain.[31]

Even if there are no genetic differences in *intelligence* between blacks and whites, there are differences in *measured IQ* and these differences may be important in their own right. Measured IQ is a manifestation of cognitive ability (however acquired) that is likely to affect one's ability to succeed in the marketplace. The controlled IQ difference between blacks and whites, however, is only five to ten points. To suggest that this relatively small difference could account for an existing income disparity of over $30,000 a year would be extremely tenuous. One would then be arguing that a 5 or 10 percent difference in intelligence could account for a 50 percent disparity in income, and that status differences were not at all affected by differences in opportunities. Even if genetic differences do exist between blacks and whites, such differences are of relatively minor significance for observed socioeconomic status.[32]

OTHER COMPLICATIONS

The foregoing observations demonstrate the essential weaknesses in the racial inferiority doctrine. The evidence presented has been rather technical, but there are even simpler

---

[31]See James Cronin et al., "Race, Class, and Intelligence: A Critical Look at the IQ Controversy," *International Journal of Mental Health* (Winter 1975); also Cedric X. Clark, "The Shockley-Jensen Thesis: A Contextual Appraisal," *The Black Scholar* (July 1975).

[32]A very different view is propounded by Richard Herrnstein and Charles Murray, who argue that IQ differences are the pre-eminent determinants of inequality: see their *The Bell Curve: Intelligence and Class Structure in American Life* (New York: Free Press, 1994). See also the critiques of their argument in Claude S. Fischer et al., *Inequality by Design: Cracking the Bell Curve Myth* (Princeton, NJ: Princeton University Press, 1996).

inconsistencies that discredit racial theories of black poverty. To begin with, blacks do not fare equally well or poorly in all regions of the country. For the nation as a whole, median black family incomes are 54 percent as large as white incomes. In the Midwest, however, they were only 52 percent as large, while in the West, 63 percent. Hence, to argue that genetic disabilities account for status disparities would require one to argue that western blacks are genetically better equipped than midwestern blacks.

A similar problem arises with the rise in black status over time. In the last 30 years, black incomes have risen considerably relative to white incomes. A theory of racial determination would be compelled to explain this development on the basis of improving genetic abilities among blacks or declining genetic potential among whites.

Finally, and most damaging to the doctrine of racial superiority, is the concept of race itself. There is not, and never has been, a clear understanding of what the term *race* means, or for that matter, of how many races exist. As an English zoologist has noted, "geneticists believe anthropologists know what a race is, ethnologists assume their racial classifications are backed up by genetics, and politicians believe that their prejudices have the sanction of both genetics and anthropology."[33] In the resultant confusion, anywhere from three to 30 separate races have been identified at various times. In the American context, the term is used interchangeably to refer to religious, national, or ethnic groups. In the context of the immediate discussion, the term refers basically to skin color. Given the history of miscegenation in America, no one could conceivably argue that distinctive pure white and black genetic characteristics exist: It is estimated that over 90 percent of American blacks have some white ancestry. Hence, American blacks hardly comprise a suitable test for racial theories in inherent differences.

Interestingly enough, adherents to the racial doctrine have attempted to employ this phenomenon of miscegenation to their advantage. They argue that the success of mulattos is due to the presence of "white" genes, which improve their intellectual endowments, proving the thesis of racial superiority. The argument is also used to explain rising black status over time. The evidence presented, however, is exceedingly weak. Mulattos apparently did fare relatively better than "pure" blacks during and shortly after the slave era, but children of mixed parentage were often favored by their white father-masters. Thus, they received greater opportunity and support. Other research has shown that more successful blacks today do not differ in patterns of white ancestry. Moreover, the highest black IQ score yet reported—200—was attained by a child who had no traceable white heritage whatsoever. Hence, whatever the other virtues and liabilities of miscegenation may be, its effects on genetic abilities appear to be negligible.

Summary

Theories of poverty causation based on cultural or racial phenomena have long commanded a certain popularity. In part, they are based on prejudices of the nonpoor against the poor and, in part, on the confidence with which the nonpoor perceive economic opportunity to exist for all. Since the earliest days of colonization, it has been asserted that anyone with enough stamina and initiative could succeed in America. Accordingly, those who did not succeed have been regarded variously as immoral, culturally apart, or racially inferior.

---

[33] Anthony Smith, *The Body* (New York: Walker, 1968), p. 14.

The culture of poverty theory posits that a subculture of fatalistic aspirations, goals, and values generates deviant behavior that perpetuates poverty. The underclass concept focuses on that same self-defeating behavior that occurs in areas of concentrated poverty (ghettos) but can accommodate both cultural and structural explanations.

Because the components of culture are not directly observable, the debate over the origins of underclass behavior hinges on (1) surveys of aspirations and goals, and (2) observed responses to changed circumstances. The inferences drawn from such studies suggest that the underclass is a small fraction of the poverty population and that its behavior is shaped more by external forces than inbred cultural dissonance.

Allegations about racial disabilities suffer equally from misconception and prejudice. There is no basis for concluding that differences in intelligence exist between whites and blacks. Not only do we not yet know what intelligence is, but the instruments we assume to measure it yield ambiguous results. Moreover, even the most extreme assumptions about the meaning and reliability of observed IQ scores would still lead to the conclusion that genetic factors are of negligible significance in explaining the very large economic disparities that exist between whites and blacks.

Further Reading

ON CULTURE AND THE UNDERCLASS

Blau, David M., "The Effect of Income on Child Development," *Review of Economics and Statistics* (May 1999), pp. 261–276.

Darity, W., S. Myers, E. Carson, and W. Sabol, *The Black Underclass*. New York: Garland, 1994.

Edwards, Mark E., Robert Plotnick, and Marieka Klawitter, "Do Attitudes and Personality Characteristics Affect Socioeconomic Outcomes? The Case of Welfare Use by Young Women," *Social Science Quarterly* (December 2001), pp. 827–843.

Fauth, Rebecca, "The Impacts of Neighborhood Poverty Deconcentration Efforts on Low-Income Children's and Adolescents' Well-Being," *Children, Youth and Environments* (2004), pp. 1–55.

Jargowsky, Paul A., and Rebecca Yang, "The 'Underclass' Revisited: A Social Problem in Decline," *Journal of Urban Affairs* (Winter 2006), pp. 55–70.

Jencks, C., and P. Peterson, eds., *The Urban Underclass*. Washington, DC: Brookings Institution, 1991.

Jones, Rachel, and Ye Luo, "The Culture of Poverty and African-American Culture: An Empirical Assessment," *Sociological Perspectives* (November 1999), pp. 439–458.

Lamont, Michele, and Mario Luis Small, "How Culture Matters for Poverty." University of Michigan, National Poverty Center Working Paper 06–10, June 2006.

Lewis, Oscar, *La Vida*. New York: Random House, Inc., 1966.

Mincy, Ronald B., "The Underclass: Concept, Controversy, and Evidence," in *Confronting Poverty,* eds. S. Danziger. G. Sandefur, and D. Weinberg. Cambridge, MA: Harvard University Press, 1994.

Wilson, William Julius, *The Truly Disadvantaged*. Chicago: University of Chicago Press, 1987.

ON RACE AND IQ

Gottfredson, Linda S., ed., "Intelligence and Social Policy," *Intelligence* (Jan.–Feb. 1997).

Herrnstein, Richard, and Charles Murray, *The Bell Curve: Intelligence and Class Structure in American Life*. New York: Free Press, 1994.

Jencks, Christopher, and Meredith Phillips, eds., *The Black-White Test Score Gap*. Washington, DC: Brookings Institution, 1998.

Mortensen, Erik, and Stephanie Sanders, "The Association Between Duration of Breastfeeding and Adult Intelligence," *Journal of the American Medical Association* (May 8, 2002).

Murray, Charles, "The Inequality Taboo," *Commentary* (September 2005), pp. 13–22.

Skrentny, John D., "Inventing Race," *The Public Interest* (Winter 2002), pp. 97–113.

Turkheimer, Eric, "Socioeconomic Status Modifies Heritability of IQ in Young Children," *Psychological Science* (November 2003), pp. 623–628.

Web Links

American Enterprise Institute. Charles Murray, "The Underclass Revisited" (1999)

www.aei.org/publications/pubID.14891/pub_detail.asp

CHAPTER 10
EDUCATION AND ABILITY

ew people question the power of education and ability to propel a person up the income ladder. In fact, the observations that "to get ahead, get an education" and "you can't keep a good man down" have acquired the aura of ideological convictions. Everyone has heard of Horatio Alger, and no one doubts that doctors get rich. Conditioned by these examples, Americans react accordingly. Middle-class parents begin preparing their children for college soon after birth, and the children themselves learn to regard success as the reward for virtue, ability, and good grades in school. By the same token, those who do not succeed are regarded as less virtuous, less able, or less diligent in the pursuit of education (i.e., Flawed Characters). From this perspective, lack of ability or education emerges as an important cause of poverty. The distribution of poverty even acquires a democratic flavor, as it is also presumed that the development of abilities and education is largely a matter of individual choice (i.e., character).

The conviction that education and ability lead to material success is not easily challenged. Few persons even pause to reflect on the nature and reliability of the underlying associations. With educated people moving ahead all around them, how many individuals can take the time and effort to question the pace of events? Nevertheless, the implied importance of education for the existence of poverty demands that such an inquiry be made. Our discussion focuses on two issues: (1) whether educational achievement determines *who* is poor; and (2) whether the level of educational achievement determines *how many* people are poor. The same questions are asked of the relationship between ability and poverty.

EDUCATION AND INCOME

The conviction that more education leads to higher income finds extensive support in statistical data. The simple correlation between educational attainment and income is very strong and consistent: More years of education do lead to higher income. In 2005, for example, male high school dropouts commanded median earnings of $24,715; high school graduates had incomes of $32,498; and college graduates had median earnings of nearly $53,000 (see Table 10.1). Hence, there is an impressive foundation to the belief that education pays.

POVERTY RATES

The relationship between education and income is equally effective in separating the poor from the nonpoor. The typical nonpoor family head has at least a high school diploma, while many heads of poor families have not even *attended* high school. This disparity in educational attainment is reflected in the incidence of poverty. As Table 10.2 confirms, the

TABLE 10.1 Education and the Labor Market, Males Aged 25–64

	High School Dropouts	*High School Graduates*	*College Graduates*
Unemployment rate (percent)	5.8	4.2	2.2
Labor force participation (percent)	76.3	83.5	91.8
Full-time workers (percent)	70.4	78.7	88.4
Occupational status	Blue collar	Clerical	Professional
Median earnings	$24,715	$32,498	$52,986

Source: U.S. Department of Labor (2005 data).

likelihood of poverty declines rapidly as a person scales the educational ladder. Less than one out of 30 people who had finished college ended up in poverty in 2005, while nearly one out of four adults who failed to complete high school ended up poor.

LABOR-MARKET EFFECTS

Higher educational attainment contributes to income in several ways. It increases people's productivity (their human capital) by expanding their knowledge and skills. Prospective employers also tend to regard educational degrees as proof of commendable diligence. Diplomas, regardless of their content, are likely to provide access to more jobs. Educational institutions typically offer job placement services, providing employers and students with ready access to each other. The combination of these factors suggests that the person who stays in school longer will be treated and will perform differently in the labor market. Educational attainment affects every facet of labor-market success. A person's participation in the labor force, his or her occupation, the frequency of his or her employment, the number of hours worked, and the wage rate received are all affected by the schooling the person has achieved. In conjunction, these factors determine an individual's income.

People with little education are least likely to get and hold a job. If they do obtain jobs, they are first to be laid off by employers when production schedules change. With fewer skills and credentials, their ability to acquire other jobs will be restricted. Consequently, they are apt to be unemployed far more often and for longer periods than those with greater educational attainments. In 2005, high school dropouts experienced a 5.8 percent unemployment rate, while high school and college graduates confronted unemployment rates of 4.2 and 2.2, respectively (Table 10.1).

TABLE 10.2 Incidence of Adult Poverty, by Education

Education	*Number in Poverty*	*Incidence of Poverty (percent)*
No high school diploma	6,644,000	23.8
High school graduate (no college)	6,553,000	10.8
Some college	3,764,000	7.7
College graduate	1,940,000	3.6

Source: U.S. Bureau of the Census (2005 data for persons 25 years and older).

As was noted in Chapter 5, long and repeated spells of unemployment may induce people to leave the labor force altogether. Frustrated by lack of employment opportunities, they may give up the job search, relying instead on public or private financial assistance. Few men can, however, resign themselves to nonparticipation, in part because available social and financial supports are extremely limited. Nevertheless, the impact of educational attainment is discernible in the relevant statistics. Whereas nearly all (92 percent) male college graduates participate in the labor force, only 76 percent of male high school dropouts do so. Differences are even more striking among women: The labor force participation rate for female college graduates is nearly 75 percent versus only 30 percent for women who never got a high school diploma.

Getting and holding a job does not guarantee financial success, of course. The nature of the job one obtains, how many hours one works, and what wage one is paid are equally as important. On all these fronts, the less educated individual fares poorly. High school dropouts are disproportionately concentrated in the blue-collar occupations as unskilled laborers, operatives, service workers, and craftspeople. By contrast, high school graduates are most heavily concentrated in the lower white-collar occupations, at the clerical and sales levels, and in the higher blue-collar positions. College graduates crowd the professional and managerial classes and are virtually nonexistent in the lowest job categories.

The cumulative impact of these labor-market phenomena sharply differentiates the incomes of the lesser and greater educated. As we have already noted, the income differences amount to tens of thousands of dollars a year. Over a lifetime, this disparity becomes tremendous. During their careers, high school graduates can anticipate earning $250,000 more than high school dropouts, while college graduates will earn $800,000 more than high school graduates before retiring.[1]

INCREASING SKILL PREMIUMS

As if high school dropouts were not already sufficiently disadvantaged in the labor market, the earnings gap between better- and lesser-educated workers appears to be widening. In 1975, for example, college graduates earned 50 percent more than high school graduates. By 2005, that college premium had risen to 60 percent.

While the real earnings of college graduates were rising, the real earnings of workers without any college experience were actually falling. Hence, lower-skilled workers have not only fallen behind in a *relative* sense but in an *absolute* sense as well. In the process, their odds of falling into poverty have increased.

The increased wage premiums paid to better-educated workers reflect an increased demand for skilled labor. Technological advances, international competition, and changes in the mix of output have all fueled demand for skilled labor. At the same time, a steady flow of immigrants and low-wage goods have helped to hold down the

---

[1]Because these estimates do not account for productivity or price increase, they understate income differences: see U.S. Bureau of the Census, *The Big Payoff: Educational Attainment and Synthetic Estimates of Work-Life Earnings* (U.S. Government Printing Office, July 2002).

wages of less-skilled workers.[2] The combination of these market forces has made educational attainment an even stronger predictor of income status.

PATHS OF CAUSATION

The weight of accumulated evidence on the association between income and education reinforces the belief that inadequate education is a major cause of poverty. That the least educated will bring the least amount of human capital to the labor market and therefore receive the least income appears obvious. From this perspective, poverty can be explained by a failure to stay in school, by underinvestment in one's own human capital (by implication, Flawed Character). Before fully accepting this interpretation, however, several additional issues must be considered.

OVERLAPPING CAUSES

Figure 10.1 puts the role of education into a broader perspective. All of the evidence reviewed so far in this chapter relates to the direct link between education and income (the segment *a* in the figure). That evidence documents that education pays: Education increases an individual's *human capital* and therewith a person's income-earning potential. But not *all* of the income differences between more-educated and less-educated individuals are due to schooling per se. Education attainments themselves are an outcome of an earlier process. That outcome is itself shaped by more basic determinants, namely, individual traits and external environments (segments *b* and *c* in Figure 10.1). In this context, educational attainments are partly a reflection of more fundamental income-producing characteristics. As such, education isn't quite so powerful a force in determining who gets rich as first appears. To some extent, educational attainments simply certify who had the most talent and best circumstances to begin with. In other words, some of the individuals who got the most schooling *and* income might have gotten the most income anyway.

The link running between external environment and education also has intergenerational content. Children born into poor and minority households typically have fewer

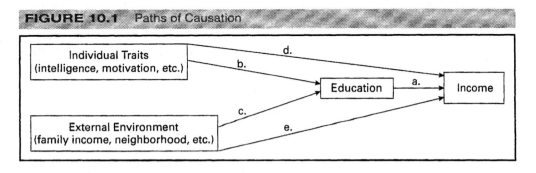

FIGURE 10.1 Paths of Causation

[2]For a description and analysis of widening wage inequalities, see the symposium in the *Journal of Economic Perspectives* (Spring 1997), pp. 21–91. Further analyses are contained in David Card and John Dinardo, "Skill-Biased Technological Change and Rising Wage Inequality: Some Problems and Puzzles," *Journal of Labor Economics* (October 2002), pp. 733–783; Gregory Acs and Sheldon Danziger, "Educational Attainment, Industrial Structure, and Male Earnings Through the 1980s," *Journal of Human Resources* (Summer 1993), pp. 618–648; C. Juhn, K. Murphy, and B. Pierce, "Wage Inequality and the Rise in Returns to Skill," *Journal of Political Economy* (January 1993), pp. 410–442.

child-development resources and inferior educational opportunities.[3] This suggests that the distribution of educational outcomes will not mirror underlying abilities. Personal preference may also a role. Education is an *investment* in *future* productivity. Going to classes, doing homework, and studying for exams entail sacrifices. To get through school, people have to sacrifice a lot of leisure time. They also sacrifice opportunities to earn current income. For people with short time horizons or high-income opportunities, finishing school may not seem worth it. College athletes who turn professional before graduation are an example. At the other end of the income distribution are high school and college dropouts who had a greater preference for current income rather than future income.[4] Hence, innate talent, economic circumstances, and personal preferences can affect not only educational attainments (segments *b* and *c* in Figure 10.1) but also segments *d* and *e*.

Figure 10.1 also depicts direct lines of causation from individual traits and environments to income. This suggests that there will be plenty of variation in incomes even among individuals with *identical* educations. Motivation, intelligence, and family connections still count, even among equally educated individuals. Likewise, even if, *on average,* better-educated individuals can earn more money, *all* persons with more schooling will not necessarily have higher incomes. No one has seriously suggested that education is the *only* determinant of income.

Income Overlaps

In fact, empirical studies that examine variations in *individual* (as opposed to *group*) wage levels find that educational attainment accounts for a very small proportion of that variation. Indeed, earnings gaps *among* people of equal education have been increasing at least as fast as gaps between individuals of different educational attainments.[5] Inherent ability, inherited wealth, geographical location, motivation, discrimination, economic conditions, and simple luck will all influence a person's income opportunities. As a result, the income distribution of college graduates overlaps that of high school dropouts. Although the *average* high school dropout earns less than the *average* college graduate, some high school dropouts earn more than college graduates. Recall also (Table 10.2) that over a million college graduates are poor.

Racial Disparities

The overlap in income distributions of individuals with different educational attainments is particularly apparent when race and sex are examined. Indeed, the labor market rewards the educational attainments of some people much more handsomely than that of others. Consider Figure 10.2, for example: Each step up the educational ladder clearly improves the incomes of black, white, and Hispanic men. Even more striking,

---

[3]Beck Taylor, Eric Dearing, and Kathleen McCartney, "Incomes and Outcomes in Early Childhood," *Journal of Human Resources* (Fall 2004), pp. 980–1007. This issue of class discrimination is explored further in Chapter 11.

[4]See Russell Rumberger, "Why Students Drop Out of School" and "What Can Be Done to Reduce School Dropouts" in Gary Orfield, ed., *Dropouts in America: Confronting the Graduation Rate Crisis*. Cambridge, MA: Harvard University Press, 2004.

[5]See Lynn A. Karoly, "The Trend in Inequality among Families, Individuals, and Workers in the United States: A Twenty Five Year Perspective," in *Uneven Tides,* eds. S. Danziger and P. Gottschalk (New York: Russell Sage, 1993); Lawrence F. Katz and Kevin Murphy, "Changes in Relative Wages, 1963–1987: Supply and Demand Factors," *Quarterly Journal of Economics* (February 1992), pp. 35–78; David Autor, Lawrence Katz, and Melissa Kearney, "Trends in Wage Inequality: Re-assessing the Revisionists" (Cambridge, MA: National Bureau of Economic Research), September 2005.

however, is the gross disparity shown on the graphs that exists between white and minority males. The average black or Hispanic *high school graduate,* for example, earns less than a white *high school dropout.* Whatever benefits education provides, they are clearly not equally accessible to all. Although lack of education is certainly an explanation for poverty, that explanation is far short of complete.

Gender Disparities

The same disparity can be observed between men and women (see Figure 10.3). Women college graduates earn only a bit more on average ($42,209) than men who complete only high school ($38,033). Moreover, the average male with one to three years of college commands an income that is higher than all groups of women, including those who have attended graduate school. Again, the rewards for educational achievement, while perhaps large, are not evenly distributed.

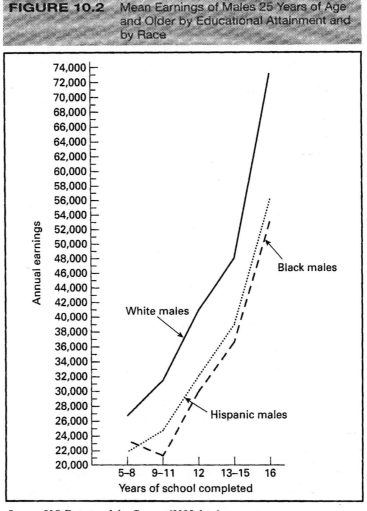

FIGURE 10.2 Mean Earnings of Males 25 Years of Age and Older by Educational Attainment and by Race

Source: U.S. Bureau of the Census (2005 data).

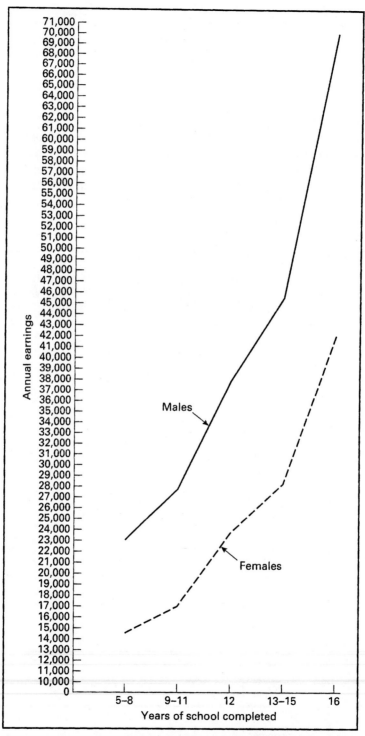

FIGURE 10.3 Mean Earnings by Educational Attainment, by Sex

Source: U.S. Bureau of the Census (2005 data for persons age 25 and older).

Explanations for the income disparities that exist between races and sexes are not difficult to find. Some of these are discussed more thoroughly in Chapters 11 and 12. For present purposes, we confine ourselves to the observation that more education does not guarantee a higher income nor even a sure escape from poverty. Keeping some poor persons in school longer may not effectively raise their incomes. Even in situations where racial or sexual discrimination is not present, the link between education and income is far from perfect.

EDUCATION AS A SORTING DEVICE

The full significance of education for the distribution and extent of poverty can be understood only in the framework of the entire labor market. As we have seen, the simple correlation between *average* incomes and *average* educational attainments may exaggerate the importance of education. The rate of return on educational (human capital) investments is unquestionably substantial. The enhanced productivity created by added schooling does give people a leg up in the labor market. In that *relative* sense, education definitely pays. In an absolute sense, however, the link between education and *aggregate* poverty isn't so clear.

A certain quantity of job vacancies and prospective employees exists in any labor market. When the number of vacancies falls far short of the number of job seekers, the economy is in a depressed state, and unemployment rates are high. This implies that employers will be able to choose among many applicants in filling any job vacancy. How will employers proceed? That is, on what basis should they or will they make their selection?

The Hiring Queue

In Chapter 5, we suggested that employers will tend to select new employees on the basis of their human capital, their potential contribution to output. In some cases, the process of selection is comparatively simple. If the job is highly technical, identifying the most competent applicants on the basis of tests or prior accomplishments may be easy.

But differences in human capital are not always large or easily observed. As a consequence, employers often depend on some guesswork. In these cases—probably the majority—employers typically rely on just a few selection criteria, educational attainment being one of the most important. The employer has sound reasons for separating the more educated from the less educated in the application process. First, it is assumed that more schooling results in greater ability. Perseverance in school also signals a certain disposition to achievement. An employer may even feel that school graduates "deserve" better opportunities. Last, but not least, employers may view an educational degree as a cheap, easy, and fairly reliable mechanism for sorting out job applicants. Why spend time and money interviewing school dropouts if school graduates are available?

"Sheepskin" Effects

These considerations transform graduation certificates into admissions tickets for job interviews. Those without the requisite ticket (e.g., college diploma) may never get interviewed for jobs they otherwise could perform.[6] In times of high unemployment,

---

[6]The "sheepskin" effects associated with educational degrees are examined in D. Belman and J. S. Heywood, "Sheepskin Effects in the Return to Education: An Examination of Women and Minorities," *Review of Economics and Statistics* (November 1991), pp. 720–724; see also David Jaeger and Marianne Page, "Degrees Matter: New Evidence on Sheepskin Effects in the Returns to Education" (Ann Arbor, MI: University of Michigan Population Studies Center, April 1994).

this "sheepskin" effect can generate some inexplicable job barriers. During the 1971 recession, for example, this help-wanted ad appeared in the Austin, Texas, *American:*

> **TOPLESS DANCERS.** Must have two years college. Prefer English major, languages or humanities.[7]

From the standpoint of this employer, all prospective dancers are in competition for available jobs, and educational attainments separate the finalists from the rejects. Other employers are likely to react similarly when jobs are scarce. For example, even though a high school dropout could easily perform the responsibilities of a sales clerk, he or she is not given the opportunity if high school graduates are also available. As a consequence, the dropout remains unemployed and poor.

The implications of this selection process for the relationship of education to poverty are profound. The distribution of education will have a significant impact on the distribution of poverty. As a rule, those with the least education will end up in poverty. This will be especially true among otherwise similar labor-market, racial, and gender groups. But what about the extent of poverty? Will education have a similar influence in determining how many persons are poor? Consider again the case of the high school dropout seeking the job of sales clerk. A high school diploma would undoubtedly make his or her competitive position stronger. But would his or her graduation, by itself, increase the number of available jobs? Clearly not. Although graduation may enable one to compete successfully for the available job, the applicant's success will leave someone else unemployed. If there is only one job and there are four applicants, no amount of educational improvement or redistribution will succeed in leaving fewer than three persons unemployed. Education may influence who gets the available jobs, but the demand for labor will determine how many jobs there are.

FRAZZ   *BY JEF MALLETT*

Source: Frazz comic strip by Jef Mallett.

---

[7]Cited in *Playboy*, December 1971, p. 26.

Bumping Down

The use of diplomas as admission tickets to jobs has another implication. As the supply of educated workers increases, employers may ratchet up hiring prerequisites. In the process, college graduates will take an increasing share of the jobs lesser-educated workers would have performed. Economists Frederick Pryor and David Schaffer assert that this process of bumping down explains why less-educated individuals have had increasing difficulty finding and holding low-skill jobs. It isn't that low-skill jobs are disappearing, but that higher-skilled workers are taking them. As the supply of educated workers has grown faster than the demand for them, more educated workers have moved down occupational ladders.[8]

Confusion about the causal significance of education comes from the failure to distinguish between individual and group dynamics. Observing that individual incomes are related to educational attainments easily leads to the supposition that raising the educational attainments of all the poor will eliminate poverty. Yet bestowing a high school diploma, or even a Ph.D., on all the poor will do little to alter the number or kinds of jobs available. A few more vacancies might be filled, but the greatest impact would be to alter the composition of the poor and to raise their educational attainments. By itself, such a degree-awarding bonanza would do little to reduce the extent of poverty in the short run.

THE CONTENT OF EDUCATION

The foregoing discussion says nothing about the content of education. Instead, the term has been used to refer to schooling in general. Accordingly, some of the most vital and controversial issues relevant to the education-income nexus have been neglected. Among the more salient of those issues are the questions of how much vocational content should be offered in school curricula and who should provide it. Training in specific skills might be especially valuable to those who are not going to pursue higher education. One study suggests that the incomes of black workers are particularly sensitive to the degree of vocational instruction in their high school curriculum.[9] Greater earning potential could be generated by simply *restructuring* educational curricula rather than by extending them. Critics worry, however, that such a restructuring of curriculum content would solidify class and race barriers.

Of even greater importance for policy consideration is the question of access to education. Because educational attainments significantly determine who will be poor in any given economic situation, we must also determine who receives the necessary credentials and why. Some consideration of these issues is taken up in Chapters 11 and 12. For the present, we may note that neither the issue of educational content nor that of access materially alters the conclusions previously cited. Regardless of what is taught or who it is taught to, education by itself can do very little to alter the number of jobs available at any given moment.[10]

[8]Frederick L. Pryor and David L. Schaffer, *Who's Not Working and Why: Employment, Cognitive Skills, Wages, and the Changing U.S. Labor Market* (Cambridge, U.K.: Cambridge University Press, 1999).

[9]Alan C. Kerckhoff and Robert A. Jackson, "Types of Education and the Occupational Attainments of Young Men," *Social Forces* (September 1982).

[10]Over a longer period of time, rising educational attainments may increase national productivity and employment, even if there is little immediate impact on the level of poverty.

ABILITY AND INCOME

Ability, like education, is presumed to be an important determinant of income. As Figure 10.1 illustrated, ability can affect income *directly* or *indirectly* through educational attainment. In either case, most people expect the distribution of incomes to reflect the distribution of productive abilities. We are accustomed to thinking that greater ability merits richer rewards and, indeed, that material success is visible proof of ability.

The presumption that ability breeds economic success finds empirical support in longitudinal studies. The National Longitudinal Survey of Youth (NLSY) has been tracking a cross section of individuals who were aged 14 to 23 in 1978. That sample is now in its forties. By looking at their experiences over time, one can distinguish the many different influences on adult incomes. One of the more interesting observations is summarized in Table 10.3. This table offers a multidimensional view of the relationships between education, family background, ability, and adult poverty. Each individual is first classified by (a) the poverty status of their family in 1978 (when they were teenagers) and (b) their ability ranking, as tested at that time. Twelve years later (1990) these same individuals are classified by (c) their educational attainments, and (d) their own poverty status (at ages 26–29).

Two salient observations stand out in Table 10.3. First, we see further confirmation that increased education reduces the risk of poverty. For youth from poor families the risk of adult poverty recedes from 50.3 percent for high school dropouts to 8 percent for college graduates. For youth from nonpoor families the correlation is equally strong. Youth from nonpoor families who complete college have virtually no chance (0.7 percent) of being poor in their late twenties.

The second noteworthy observation in Table 10.3 is the *independent* influence of ability on income. Each row of Table 10.3 refers to individuals of the *same* family background and educational attainment. As you move toward the right across the rows, you see how adult poverty rates decline as ability test scores (from their youth) rise. Hence,

TABLE 10.3 Poverty Rates, by Ability, Education, and Family Background (percent)

(a) Family Background (1978)	(c) Own Education (by 1990)	Total, all abilities	(b) Ability Ranking in 1979				
			Lowest Quintile	2nd Lowest Quintile	Middle Quintile	2nd Highest Quintile	Highest Quintile
Poor	All poor	32.5	48.5	22.3	13.0	15.0	14.4
	High school dropout	50.3	56.1	—	—	—	—
	High school grad	30.5	45.2	28.9	12.5	—	—
	Some college	14.4	23.4	11.2	—	—	—
	College grad	8.0	—	22.1	—	—	—
Not Poor	All nonpoor	9.9	28.4	15.5	6.5	3.8	2.8
	High school dropout	28.0	40.5	21.0	—	—	—
	High school grad	12.3	23.3	17.6	9.1	3.5	—
	Some college	5.9	8.0	8.0	4.8	5.8	3.3
	College grad	0.7	—	3.3	0.5	1.0	0.7

Source: Confronting the Youth Demographic Challenge: The Labor Market Prospects of Out-of-school Young Adults (Sar Levitan Center for Social Policy Studies) by Andrew Sum, Neeta Fogg, Garth Mangum, Neal Fogg, Sheila Palma. (Baltimore: Johns Hopkins University Press, Oct. 2000), Table 7-8.

measured ability exerts an independent effect on income, as suggested by the link *d* in Figure 10.1.[11]

As comforting as Table 10.3 might be for those who want to justify their relatively high income, there are some concerns about drawing too strong a conclusion from these observations. One concern is entirely normative. Why *should* the distribution of income and poverty reflect relative abilities? Why, for example, should a man who inherits the capacity to learn to steer rockets through space command a higher income than the man who is born with the capacity to drive buses? Are justice and equity any better served when rewards are distributed according to inherited genes rather than according to inherited dollars?

WHICH ABILITY MATTERS?

There is also a practical issue to consider here. In Chapter 9, we encountered some of the difficulties that engulf discussions of individual ability. The term *ability,* as it is commonly employed, incorporates elements of both innate capacity and developed performance. Accordingly, there is a certain vagueness in the question whether the income distribution reflects the ability distribution. If we refer to *innate* abilities, then we really have no means for answering the question. Despite impressive discoveries in molecular biology, we still don't know precisely what innate abilities are or how to measure them. When we instead focus on developed performance (e.g., the performance test scores used in Table 10.3), we must recognize that we are departing from the pattern of innate abilities because all individuals do not share equal opportunity to develop their capacities. An income distribution based on performance abilities may not meet our standards of equity.

Another problem with the measurement of performance ability is the fact that no single, all-inclusive performance criterion exists. The ability to sing or to run is distributed differently from the ability to solve complex mathematical problems. There are literally hundreds, if not thousands, of varied abilities, all uniquely distributed among the population. Determining whether incomes accurately reflect performance ability is impossible. At most, one could assert that the distribution of incomes reflects the distribution of abilities valued highly in the marketplace. But even that cautious assertion masks a tautology. One could assert that *any* income distribution reflects the same thing. There is no objective means for determining whether a given income distribution departs from the distribution of abilities. In the face of this impasse, we usually proceed in reverse. That is, we *infer* the distribution of abilities from the distribution of incomes: People with more money are *assumed* to be more able. In this way the income distribution justifies itself.

In view of these considerations, there is little foundation for objectively assessing the fairness or appropriateness of any existing income distribution. At most, we may simply observe how well the distribution reflects certain specific kinds of attainments or characteristics. We must then resort to our own values to determine how appropriate these criteria are and how equitably they are reflected in incomes. The inherent subjectivity of this approach does not render it impracticable, but it does make consensus difficult.

[11]Another longitudinal NLSY study revealed the direct links of IQ to school performance and its indirect links to delinquency behavior; see Jean Marie Megloin, Travis Pratt, and Jeff Maahs, "Rethinking the IQ-Delinquency Relationship," *Justice Quarterly* (September 2004), pp. 603–635.

IQ AND SCHOOLING

Two kinds of abilities continue to attract the most attention in discussions of income distribution—measured IQ and educational attainment. IQ is of interest both because it gauges highly valued performance abilities; such as perception and problem solving, and because, despite admonitions to the contrary, it is assumed to reflect innate capacities. As we saw in Chapter 9, IQ differences are also the focus of debates about race and class differences in income. Educational attainment is of interest for much the same reasons. Schooling is assumed to impart valuable skills and thus to differentiate the "deserving" rich from the "undeserving" poor. Accordingly, we may ask how well the existing income distribution reflects these criteria. Figure 10.4 provides an answer to this question.

The first thing to notice in Figure 10.4 is the different shape of the IQ, education, and earnings distributions. IQ tests are scored to conform to a smooth bell-shaped curve (the "normal" distribution). The distribution of educational attainments, however, is characterized by huge discontinuities at high school completion and college graduation. Finally, the income distribution looks like a disfigured bell with a long tail extending to the right. These different-shaped distributions suggest that the links

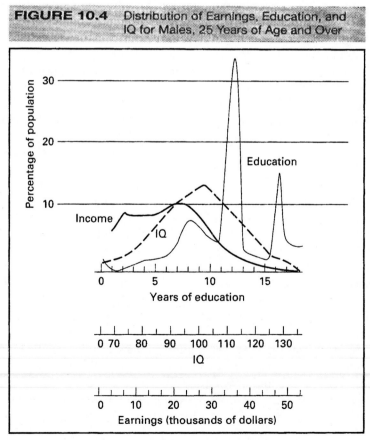

FIGURE 10.4 Distribution of Earnings, Education, and IQ for Males, 25 Years of Age and Over

Source: Adapted from Lester C. Thurow, *Poverty and Discrimination* (Washington, DC: Brookings Institution, 1969), p. 68; 1992 data from U.S. Census Bureau.

between ability and income are far from perfect. At the extremes of the distributions, the differences are particularly evident. There is a higher concentration of low incomes than either low IQ or low education. At the other end of the scale, the opposite is true: High educational attainments are more common than high incomes or high IQ.

Some interesting implications follow from Figure 10.4 and our previous discussions of ability and education. We have already suggested that high IQ scores are not equally accessible to all individuals of similar genetic capacity (see Chapter 9). Minority children, for example, have less of an opportunity to develop their innate capacities into performing abilities. This implies the income distribution is even less representative of innate capacities than is suggested by its observed relationship to IQ. Similarly, we should note that educational attainments depart considerably from the IQ distribution, suggesting that access to, and the quality of, education are not uniform.[12] These observations are considered further in Chapter 11.

Summary

Individuals with greater educational attainments unquestionably earn more money, on average, than persons with less education. Persons with highly valued abilities also tend to earn larger incomes. Accordingly, it is hardly surprising to discover that the poor have less education and fewer marketable skills than the nonpoor. While the evidence reviewed in this chapter demonstrates that these relationships are not perfect, they do have a general validity. More important than the question of association, however, is that of causality. What we really seek to discover is not whether the poor are undereducated or underskilled, but whether a lack of education or skills is responsible for their poverty.

Education does operate as a powerful mechanism in determining the distribution of poverty. Investments in human capital via the school system result in higher productivity and earnings. In addition to these absolute gains, more education also bestows an important relative advantage. Educational degrees are an important signal of motivation, commitment, and ability. As such, they are a cheap and convenient instrument for deciding whom to hire. When good jobs are in short supply, this "sheepskin" effect can give more educated job seekers a critical advantage in the competition for jobs. This queuing effect enhances the productivity-based returns to educational investments.

The relationship between education and poverty is not so simple on an aggregate basis, however. The competitive position of all workers cannot be raised simultaneously; if one individual's relative educational position rises, someone else's falls. Education cannot be a cause of aggregate poverty unless low levels of schooling preclude employment at wages that would prevent poverty. There is little evidence that such structural unemployment is severe enough to explain a substantial amount of poverty.

The relationship of ability to poverty is also more complex than commonly assumed. Because we lack unambiguous definitions and measurements of innate ability, there is no firm basis for declaring that the poor are inherently less able. At most, such

---

[12]Richard Herrnstein and Charles Murray assign a more prominent role to IQ, suggesting that IQ differences create a meritocracy in which high-IQ individuals uniformly excel; see their *The Bell Curve: Intelligence and Class Structure in American Life* (New York: Free Press, 1994). Among the many critiques of their work, see Claude S. Fischer et al., *Inequality by Design: Cracking the Bell Curve Myth* (Princeton, NJ: Princeton University Press, 1996); and John Cawley, J. Heckmon, and E. Vytlacil, "Meritocracy in America: Wages Within and Across Occupations," *Industrial Relations* (1999), pp. 250–297.

an observation means only that the poor make less money. Even when confined to measures of performance, such as IQ, the relationship of ability to income is oblique. The distribution of incomes diverges considerably from educational or IQ distributions and even further from the distribution of innate talents.

Further Reading

Herrnstein, Richard J., and Charles Murray, *The Bell Curve: Intelligence and Class Structure in American Life*. New York: Free Press, 1994.

Jencks, Christopher, et al., *Who Gets Ahead? The Economic Determinants of Success in America*. New York: Basic Books, 1979.

Jencks, Christopher, and Meredith Phillips, *Closing the Black White Test-Score Gap*. Washington, DC: Brookings Institution, 1998.

Jensen, Arthur, *The g Factor*. Cambridge, MA: Harvard Graduate School of Education, 1996.

Levy, Frank, and Richard Murnane, "Earnings Levels and Earnings Inequality: A Review of Recent Trends and Proposed Explanations," *Journal of Economic Literature* (September 1992), pp. 1333–1381.

Mayer, Susan E., and Paul E. Peterson, eds., *Earning and Learning: How Schools Matter*. Washington, DC: Brookings Institution, 1999.

Murnane, Richard J., "Education and the Well-Being of the Next Generation," in *Confronting Poverty*, eds. S. Danziger, G. Sandefur, and D. Weinberg. Cambridge, MA: Harvard University Press, 1994.

Murray, Charles, "The Inequality Taboo," *Commentary* (September 2005), pp. 13–22.

Sum, Andrew, Neeta Fogg, and Garth Mangum, *Confronting the Youth Demographic Challenge*. Baltimore, MD: Johns Hopkins University Press, October 2000.

Web Links

University of Michigan Population Studies Center. Ongoing research studies on education; related topics: www.psc.isr.umich.edu

U.S. Bureau of the Census. Detailed data on earnings by race, gender, and education: www.bls.census.gov/cps/ads/sdata.htm

CHAPTER 11

DISCRIMINATION
IN EDUCATION

᪥

Education appears to have a major impact on the distribution, if not necessarily the extent, of poverty. Anyone denied equal opportunity to education therefore has an increased probability of being poor. In other words, discrimination in education helps determine who will be poor.

Discrimination in labor markets has similar effects. To achieve nonpoverty status, an individual must be able to employ his or her abilities in the labor market. Acquisition of acceptable characteristics alone is no guarantee of escape from poverty. If there exist forces that prevent or limit access to the labor market, the rewards to human-capital development are never realized.

Barriers to either the development or utilization of human capital are the subject of this and the following chapter. The discussion in this chapter begins by considering the meaning and nature of *discrimination* and ends with an examination of discriminatory barriers in the educational system. Chapter 12 focuses on discrimination in the labor market.

DISCRIMINATION

The terms *discrimination, prejudice,* and *racism* are widely used. Seldom do they fail to evoke emotional, often heated responses. Although most people do not always understand what is meant by these concepts, they stand forever ready to deny or proclaim the significance of each. The report of the National Advisory Commission on Civil Disorders (the "Riot Commission") in early 1968 provided a striking example of this volatility. In searching for an explanation of the urban strife that was then erupting in American cities, the commission concluded that white racism was a principal source of injustice and unrest. Very few white Americans, President Johnson included, were ready to accept the commission's sweeping indictment. White Americans generally felt neither significantly prejudiced nor sufficiently involved in the ghetto to be responsible for the conditions therein. After the 1992 Los Angeles riots, some of the same questions about racial injustice and its consequences were again fiercely debated.

One of the obstacles to meaningful debate is the highly charged content of the term *racism.* For many people, racism means burning school buses, racial taunts, or protesting equal opportunity. Relatively few Americans identify easily with such characterizations. Racism, however, has other meanings. As used by the Riot Commission, the concept transcends the attitudes and behavior of individuals. The commission's indictment referred to broad patterns of racial interaction and the institutional character of much discrimination. A survey of students at Stanford University revealed that black students easily identified with this institutional definition of racism while white students thought of racism primarily in interpersonal terms. In other words, whites thought people but not institutions could be racist, while blacks felt institutions could be racist even if individuals were not.[1]

ATTITUDES VERSUS ACTION

To understand the nature of racism, we must begin by distinguishing between attitudes and actions. People often think differently than they act. As a result, they may adopt patterns of behavior that are injurious to others without consciously wishing to inflict injury. Conversely, they may harbor hostile feelings toward particular individuals or groups but refrain from acting them out due to personal, moral, or legal inhibitions. The term *prejudice* refers to the unfavorable feelings and attitudes that people harbor against others, especially other population groups. These are to be distinguished from unfavorable actions or behavior, which fall under the heading of discrimination. Prejudiced individuals may or may not discriminate, and discrimination does not necessarily imply the existence of prejudice.[2]

While people's prejudices are often the origin of discriminatory behavior and may be appropriate targets for public policy, they are relevant to our discussion only insofar as they find expression in behavior. Accordingly, we focus on the nature of discrimination. We may note here, however, that the broader term *racism* encompasses the concepts of both prejudice and discrimination.

The concept of discrimination need not convey notions of injustice or injury. In general, it refers only to the differential treatment of persons. Few people get upset when we assign the tallest boys to the basketball team or when we cheer for the local football team. Yet, both acts are a form of discrimination. But few people associate such discrimination with the willful exclusion of minority persons from higher-status jobs or classrooms. Clearly, a general concept of discrimination encompassing both situations is too anemic for practical use. But how, then, are we to distinguish the kind of discriminatory treatment that merits policy concern?

THE RELEVANCY STANDARD

We can move closer to an operational concept of discrimination by recognizing the criteria on which differential treatment is based. Assigning taller boys to a basketball team, for example, serves a very specific and productive function. In this case, the criterion of selection is directly relevant to the task at hand. The same cannot be said for the selection of a less qualified white competing with a more qualified black. Here the basis of selection—color—is irrelevant to the task at hand, and the resultant choice is actually counterproductive. Hence, we could refine our concept of discrimination by incorporating the relevancy of selection criteria. Discrimination based on irrelevant or nonproductive criteria would then be considered injurious to the public welfare.

The U.S. Supreme Court employed this relevancy concept when it restricted the use of aptitude tests for job seekers. The Court observed that intelligence tests and other hiring criteria used by the Duke Power Company were not related to job performance. That is, the tests performed no useful economic function. Yet they were effective in screening out black job seekers. In *Griggs* v. *Duke Power Company* (1971), the Court ruled that such practices were unfairly discriminatory.

---

[1]John H. Bunzel, "Black and White at Stanford," *The Public Interest* (Fall 1991), pp. 61–77.

[2]Glenn Loury suggests that an unconscious "racial stigma" may affect both attitudes and behavior; see his *The Anatomy of Racial Inequality* (Cambridge, MA: Harvard University Press, 2001).

Unfortunately, even this refinement does not provide a completely workable definition of discrimination. There remain many choices we would consider socially injurious that are not identifiable by the criterion of relevancy. The choice of one's neighbors is an example: The only obviously relevant criterion in choosing neighbors is one's own desires and satisfaction. Thus, the choice of a white neighbor over a black one conforms to a certain standard of relevancy. Nevertheless, we have come to regard racial discrimination in housing as a socially pernicious practice. On what grounds do we distinguish this kind of individual choice from others? Are there fundamental differences between the situation where a homeowner chooses a white neighbor and, say, the situation where you choose to listen to a rock singer rather than an opera singer?[3] Both situations reflect the free expression of individual choice.

There are few objective grounds for distinguishing between the choice of the selection decision: The opera singer loses potential income and the black home seeker loses a potential residence. Our distinction between the two situations rests instead on more subjective grounds. Racial discrimination in housing is singled out for special attention because it violates common notions of social justice. Against a combined background of religious, moral, legal, and historical considerations, we have collectively determined that racial discrimination is a particularly deleterious form of individual choice.

An important factor in our subjective judgment about the nature of racial discrimination is our perception of its effects. Where all whites discriminate against all blacks, the expression of free choice becomes especially pernicious. The black home seeker is denied not one potential home, but all potential homes in white areas. Free choice for whites thus implies restricted choice for blacks and, hence, violates a basic dimension of freedom. Other choices that are less uniform or pervasive are not equally worthy of public concern. Racial discrimination itself would cease to be a public concern were it the practice of only a relatively few, scattered whites. Yet many black Americans believe they are denied equal opportunity in housing, education, and employment. As Figure 11.1

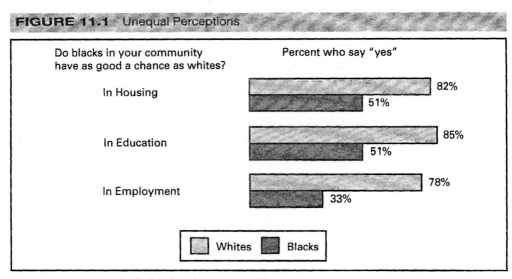

FIGURE 11.1 Unequal Perceptions

Do blacks in your community have as good a chance as whites?

Percent who say "yes"

In Housing — Whites 82%, Blacks 51%
In Education — Whites 85%, Blacks 51%
In Employment — Whites 78%, Blacks 33%

Whites   Blacks

Source: Adapted from the Gallup Social Audit Poll, 2001.

---

[3] This analogy was put forth by Milton Friedman in *Capitalism and Freedom* (Chicago: University of Chicago Press, 1962), Chapter 7.

documents, relatively few white people perceive such unequal access. In fact, a 2001 survey revealed that seven out of ten white people believe blacks have equal *or better* opportunities in America.[4]

COSTS AND BENEFITS OF DISCRIMINATION

While it is obvious that blacks, Hispanics, Muslims, and other targets of discrimination may suffer real and intangible losses from the practice of racial discrimination, it is not so apparent whether or how the white community gains. Psychologically, many whites may feel better off for having subordinated someone else. And if the majority white individuals actually feel uncomfortable around minorities, on the job, in school, or at home, we may conclude that they are even happier as a result of discrimination.[5] But the *economic* costs and benefits that may accrue to the white community are our immediate concern.

Many whites do reap tangible benefits from the practice of discrimination. When blacks and Hispanics are discriminated against in the labor market, for example, they will receive lower wages than white workers who possess equal qualifications. As a result, two groups gain. White workers who are shielded from the competition of minority workers obtain higher wages than otherwise. In addition, those employers (laundries, hotels, farms, for example) who actually hire minority workers benefit by getting higher-quality labor than they are, in fact, paying for. In the educational field, white children gain from discrimination by monopolizing better facilities and teachers. As long as racial discrimination is practiced, white children of lesser ability are also released from the necessity of competing with more able minority children in the quest for admissions.

Not all whites gain directly, however, from racial discrimination; some, in fact, actually lose. White workers who cannot escape menial occupations suffer from increased competition from minority workers. The wages of white laundry, hotel, and farm workers, for example, will be held down by the large number of blacks, Hispanics, and Asians excluded from other occupations. This relationship is illustrated in Figure 11.2. Some employers, too, will suffer losses. In a segregated community, employers will often incur higher labor costs through the use of lesser-qualified whites. In the field of education, many whites will suffer from racial discrimination. Not all whites can flee the inner city. Those left behind, primarily the poorest, will be trapped in increasingly inferior educational systems, unable to enjoy the fruits of suburban white monopolies. They, like their black and Hispanic neighbors, will find their human capital potential underdeveloped.[6]

On an individual basis, then, some whites gain and some lose as a direct result of discrimination, making it difficult to calculate the net microeconomic gain or loss to the white community. No such ambiguity attaches to the indirect losses that are incurred on an aggregate, or macroeconomic, level, however. Where discrimination against minorities is pervasive, society as a whole loses potential human capital. The abilities

---

[4]National survey conducted jointly by the *Washington Post,* Kaiser Foundation, and Harvard University in March–April 2001.

[5]The perception of psychological benefits may, of course, rest on prejudices, in which case the nature of benefits could be altered by illuminating and reducing racial stereotypes.

[6]Evidence that inner-city whites may fare worse than blacks is examined in Thomas A. LaVerst and Katrina Bell McDonald, "Race, Gender, and Educational Advantage in the Inner City," *Social Science Quarterly* (September 2002), pp. 832–852. Some whites may also suffer from policies designed to eliminate vestiges of discrimination against blacks: where blacks are given *preferential* (not just equal) access to schools or jobs, some whites suffer *reverse* discrimination. Reverse discrimination is discussed in Chapter 16.

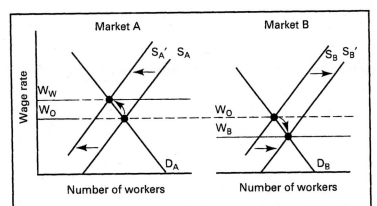

Suppose there are only two kinds of jobs, those in Market A and those in Market B. If everyone is allowed to move freely from one market to another, the equilibrium wage will end up at W_O in both markets. Why? Because if wages were higher in A than B, people would move out of B and into A, thereby lowering wages in A while raising them in B. Hence, freedom of movement between Markets A and B assures an equality of average wage rates.

Now suppose minority workers in A are kicked out and sent to Market B, making A a "whites only" preserve. This has the effect of shifting the labor supply curve in A to the left (to S_A') and the labor supply curve in B to the right (to S_B'). The net result of these supply shifts is to raise wages in A (to W_W) and to lower wages in B (to W_B). Thus, minority workers and any white workers trapped in Market B suffer lower wages, while the white workers in Market A end up with higher wages.

FIGURE 11.2 Wage Effects of Discrimination

and creativity of the minority communities remain underdeveloped and underemployed. Hence, total output of goods and services is less than it would be in the absence of discrimination. Estimates of the size of this loss run into hundreds of billions of dollars a year.[7] In addition, much of the output we do produce is directed to relatively unattractive uses such as the surveillance of homes, streets, jails, and welfare caseloads. Thus, whatever direct gains or losses individual whites incur are overwhelmed by the very large indirect losses to the economy as a whole.[8]

PROVING DISCRIMINATION

Given the potential socioeconomic cost of discrimination, it is clearly in society's interest to recognize its existence and eliminate it. The identification of discrimination is not always easy, however. Consider a situation where a white worker and a Hispanic

[7]Andrew Brimmer, "The Economic Cost of Discrimination," in Margaret Simms, ed., *Economic Perspectives on Affirmative Action* (Lanham, MD: University Press of America, 1995).

[8]White workers as a class may also lose if racial discrimination weakens worker solidarity, reducing labor's share of total income. See Michael Reich, "Who Benefits from Racism? The Distribution Among Whites of Gains and Losses from Racial Inequality," *Journal of Human Resources* (Fall 1978); and his "Changes in the Distribution of Benefits from Racism in the 1960s," *Journal of Human Resources* (Spring 1981).

worker both apply for the same job. The white applicant is accepted, and the Hispanic applicant claims that he was unfairly discriminated against. What grounds do we have for accepting the charge of discrimination, as opposed to, say, the charge that the Hispanic applicant is simply a poor loser?

The easiest cases of discrimination to prove are those that involve blatant discrepancies in treatment. If the Hispanic applicant was required to take special tests or possessed identifiably superior qualifications, the issue is readily resolved. The same simplicity exists where black children are confined to dilapidated schools or a prospective black home buyer is turned down after offering to pay the full retail value of a house.

But the practice of discrimination is not always so apparent. Indeed, with the public eye focused on discrimination, those who engage in discriminatory practices are likely to develop great subtlety. Accordingly, evidence of discriminatory treatment may have to rest on the observation of end results. If a company in a multiracial community has 4,000 employees, none of whom is black or Hispanic, there exists a strong presumption that its hiring procedures are not impartial. So it is with the schools: If blacks and whites go into the educational system comparatively equal but come out with gross disparities in achievement, we may conclude that they were treated differently somewhere along the line. Evidence of discriminatory treatment may be gathered by direct observation of treatment or by inference from results. Both types of evidence will be considered in our discussion of the educational and labor-market systems.

RACIAL DISCRIMINATION IN EDUCATION

Discrimination in the American educational system was once both blatant and pervasive. In the eighteenth and early nineteenth centuries, the teaching of slaves was barred in most southern states. In 1885, California adopted a school segregation law allowing the exclusion of Chinese and Mongolian children from white public schools. A county school superintendent in Texas proclaimed that "our Mexicans" were better off transplanting onions than going to school. In 1876, a black student admitted to the University of Pennsylvania Medical School was asked to sit behind a screen in the classroom, so as not to offend the white students. White students at Harvard University simply ejected the black entrants.[9]

The U.S. Supreme Court effectively condoned all this behavior by declaring in 1896 that "separate, but equal" education was constitutional (*Plessy* v. *Ferguson*). Even separate but unequal was tolerable, as long as the inequalities were not motivated by racial hostility (*Cumming* v. *Richmond County Board of Education*, 1899).

DISPARATE OUTCOMES

Discrimination still exists in American schools, even though it is much less pervasive or blatant than in the past. While this assertion will surprise very few readers, it is worthwhile to review the evidence on which it is based. Blacks and whites go into the educational system more equal than they come out.[10] By the time they are nine years old, majority

---

[9] These and other historical examples are cited in U.S. Commission on Civil Rights, *Toward Equal Educational Opportunity: Affirmative Admissions Programs at Law and Medical Schools* (Washington, DC: U.S. Government Printing Office, 1982).

[10] They don't start school on an *equal* footing, however. See A. Rathbern, J. West, and E. G. Hausken, *From Kindergarten through Third Grade* (Washington, DC: National Center for Education Statistics, 2004).

white students score 5 to 8 percent higher than black and Hispanic students on reading, science, and math tests. These disparities continue to grow, so that by age 17 black students are reading at the level of white 13-year-olds.[11]

Dropout Rates

Strong as these grounds are for believing that the education provided whites and blacks is not equal, they tend to understate disparities in black and white educations. The ability comparisons of black and white high school seniors, for example, necessarily exclude those students who dropped out of school before reaching the twelfth grade. Yet, the decision to quit school may itself reflect inferior educational opportunities and recognition of widening achievement disparities.[12] Seen in this light, minority dropout rates are especially disturbing. While over 93 percent of white students now graduate from high school, only 89 percent of black students and 74 percent of Hispanic students graduate.[13]

Illiteracy

Perhaps the most complete statement of black educational deficiencies is the rate of functional illiteracy among black youth. In 1975, the U.S. Office of Education sponsored a survey of the nation's 17-year-olds still in school. Students were asked to respond to 86 questions on reading items encountered in everyday life (for example, street signs, telephone directories, store coupons). Ninety-two percent of all white 17-year-olds were rated as functionally literate, having answered correctly at least three-fourths of all the questions. By contrast, only 58 percent of the black 17-year-olds were considered functionally literate. A 2005 survey revealed similar literacy gaps between white and minority teenagers.[14]

College Grads

Figure 11.3 offers one final perspective on the outcomes of the educational process. This figure shows the percentage of different groups that complete at least four years of college. One-third of all whites graduate from college. Only one out of five blacks and even fewer Hispanics attain that much education. If minorities and whites really do enter the educational system with equal potential, these differences in educational outcomes require further explanation.

---

[11]National Center for Education Statistics, *The Condition of Education, 2001* (Washington, DC: U.S. Government Printing Office, 2002). For more evidence, see John F. Kain and Kraig Singleton, "Equality of Educational Opportunity Revisited," *New England Economic Review* (May–June 1996).

[12]Congressional Budget Office, *Inequalities in the Educational Experiences of Black and White Americans* (Washington, DC: U.S. Government Printing Office, 1977), pp. x–9. Recent studies suggest that these disparities are shrinking; see Lyle Jones, "White-Black Achievement Differences: The Narrowing Gap," *American Psychologist* (November 1984), pp. 1207–1213.

[13]See U.S. Department of Education, *Dropout Rates in the United States: 2002 and 2003* (Washington, DC: U.S. Government Printing Office, 2006). For further analyses of dropout rates, see Gary Orfield, ed., *Dropouts in America* (Cambridge, MA: Harvard Education Press, 2004); also Jonathan Crane, "Effects of Neighborhoods on Dropping Out of School and Teenage Childbearing," and Susan E. Mayer, "How Much Does a High School's Racial and Socioeconomic Mix Affect Graduation and Teenage Fertility Rates?" both in *Urban Underclass,* eds. C. Jencks and P. Peterson (Washington, DC: Brookings Institution, 1991).

[14]The U.S. Department of Education now computes disaggregated indices of prose, document, and quantitative literacies rather than a composite index of functional literacy. See U.S. Department of Education, *Youth Indicators 2005* (Washington, DC: U.S. Government Printing Office, 2006).

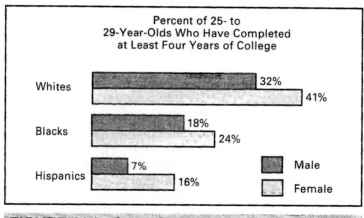

FIGURE 11.3 College Completion Rates, by Race and Sex

Source: U.S. Bureau of the Census (2005 data).

SCHOOL SEGREGATION

The indirect evidence on school discrimination is highly suggestive. In fact, the observed disparities in achievement between white and black students are so great that direct evidence of discrepancies in educational opportunity should be easy to find. Segregation of facilities provides one such example: Where separate schools are maintained for whites and blacks, the documentation of inequalities is simple.

Measuring Segregation

Before looking at the extent of continuing racial segregation in American schools, we need to establish some perspective on the meaning of segregation. When most people refer to *integrated schools,* they are encompassing all schools serving both whites and minority students. Such a definition is deceptive, however. Consider the case of a city with only two high schools: School A has 2,000 students, only one of whom is black; School B's 1,000 students are all black. By the usual criterion of biracial enrollment, School A would be regarded as integrated. Indeed, from an aggregate point of view, it would appear that half of this city's school system was integrated. But such conclusions are unwarranted. Surely, the racial isolation common to both schools is of greater significance than School A's dubious claim to biracial enrollment.

A more meaningful concept of integration must refer to the *proportion* of students attending school with children of another race. Complete integration would be a situation where all minority students attended school with white children, and vice versa. By this stricter definition of integration, the distinction between School A and School B disappears. For the city as a whole, we may say that only 0.1 percent of the black population attends school with whites. This is far more descriptive than saying that 50 percent of the city schools are integrated.

This broader concept of integration has tremendous significance for our perceptions of educational desegregation. Ten years after the Supreme Court's historic order to desegregate, the state of Florida boasted that nearly a third of its schools were integrated. Closer scrutiny revealed, however, that only 2.65 percent of Florida's black pupils were attending school with whites. Progress was even slower in other southern states.

TABLE 11.1 Segregation in Public Schools

PERCENT OF BLACK AND HISPANIC STUDENTS
IN SEGREGATED SCHOOLS

	School at Least 50% Minority		*School at Least 90% Minority*	
Year	*Blacks*	*Hispanics*	*Blacks*	*Hispanics*
1968–1969	76.9	54.8	64.3	23.1
1980–1981	62.9	68.1	33.2	28.8
1991–1992	66.0	73.4	33.9	34.0
2003–2004	73.0	77.0	34.0	39.0

Source: Adapted from Gary Orfield & Chungmei Lee, *Racial Transformation and the Changing Nature of Segregation* (Cambridge, MA: Harvard University, The Civil Rights Project, 2006.) http://www.civilrightsproject.harvard.edu/research/deseg/Racial_Transformation.pdf.

Recent Trends

Table 11.1 summarizes the extent of school segregation in American schools for both black and Hispanic students. The table shows the percentage of black or Hispanic students attending schools that are either predominantly (over 50 percent) or exclusively (over 90 percent) attended by other minority students. First notice that most black students and even a higher proportion of Hispanic students attend schools that are predominantly minority in enrollment. A third of all black and Hispanic students attend schools that are virtually all-minority institutions. Although segregation of black students,has diminished greatly since 1968, the segregation of Hispanic students has intensified. Even for black students there was a trend reversal in the 1990s that increased school segregation. Whether he or she lives in the North or the South, in the city or on a farm, a black, Hispanic, or other minority child is very unlikely to attend a truly integrated school. Racial isolation in the schools is still the hallmark of the American educational system.

Classroom Segregation

Even if *schools* were more integrated, *classrooms* might not be. The concept of integration we have offered goes no further than the outer walls of the school. Yet even an ostensibly integrated school may be severely segregated within. Students may be assigned rooms, teachers, and facilities within the school on an explicitly racial basis. An extreme illustration of such internal segregation was encountered in Milwaukee. Like most other cities, Milwaukee was prodded by the courts to integrate its schools. In part, integration was achieved by busing black pupils to previously white schools. The substance of educational opportunity was little changed, however. The bused-in black pupils were maintained in separate classrooms and bused back and forth to their old schools for lunch. Black students who lived close to the white schools were even required to proceed to the more distant black schools for bus transportation to the receiving schools!

Not all internal school segregation is as explicit and extreme as was the case in Milwaukee. Nevertheless, *classrooms* remain more segregated than *schools*.[15] A popular and subtle form of classroom segregation is embodied in the so-called *tracking systems,*

---

[15]See Office of Civil Rights, U.S. Department of Education, 1986 Elementary and Secondary School Civil Rights Survey: National Summaries (December 1987).

under which the more able students are separated from the rest and provided special opportunities to advance, while the least able students are held back for intensive remedial work. What makes the system so racially discriminatory is the fact that black pupils have received inferior education prior to integration, so that using IQ tests or other achievement examinations to allocate pupils serves to perpetuate racial separation.[16] A still subtler form of segregation within the classroom may prevail where teachers or white students regard minority pupils as innately or culturally incapable of attaining success.[17]

EQUALITY OF FACILITIES

The statistics of Table 11.1, together with our observations on the nature of integration, provide a sobering view of our efforts to provide equal opportunity "with all deliberate speed," as the Supreme Court ordered in 1954. In light of that background it may be argued that blacks and Hispanics still attend school separately from majority whites. How equal, then, are their separate opportunities?

A comparison of educational opportunities at the local level is easily made: Visit any black (or Hispanic) school and any white (Anglo) school in the same city. You can readily detect enough qualitative differences in their educational environments to judge the relative attractiveness of the minority school. These local observations of school quality cannot be expanded across the country, however. It would be too expensive and time-consuming to visit all the school districts across the nation in order to assess the average quality of black, Hispanic, and white schools. Even if we had enough time and money, our judgments would depend on the perspectives and standards of many different observers. Finally, any conclusions we reached would be limited to such statements as "white schools are better (or very much better)," with no clear indication of how great existing inequalities are. Accordingly, we are compelled to seek more objective, easily quantified measures of school quality.

The Coleman Report

In the most comprehensive survey of educational facilities ever undertaken, the U.S. Office of Education employed 67 separate measures of school quality. These measures ranged from the number of books in the school library to the education of the teachers' mothers. They represented a concerted effort to capture and measure every dimension of the educational environment that might distinguish white schools from black schools. What the Office of Education discovered is that black and white schools differ on a multitude of separate measures but that such individual differences were relatively small. The only clear pattern to emerge from their mountain of statistics was that black schools tended to be most deficient in primarily academic facilities such as science labs, textbooks, and debate clubs.

---

[16]See Angelia Dickens, "Revisiting *Brown* v. *Board of Education:* How Tracking Has Resegregated America's Public Schools," *Columbia Journal of Law and Social Problems* (Summer 1996); see also Tom Loveless, *The Tracking Wars* (Washington, DC: Brookings Institution, 1999); and David Figlio and Marianne Page, "School Choice and the Distributional Effects of Ability Tracking" (Cambridge, MA: National Bureau of Economic Research, Working Paper No. 8055, 2001).

[17]The impact of more subtle racism on the college experiences of black students is examined in Joe R. Feagin, "The Continuing Significance of Racism: Discrimination against Black Students in White Colleges," *Journal of Black Studies* (June 1992), pp. 546–578.

In assessing these results, the Office of Education recognized many limitations in their approach. They reported that:

> The school environment of a child consists of many things, ranging from the desk he sits at to the child who sits next to him, and including the teacher who stands in front of his class. Any statistical survey gives only the most meager evidence of these environments, for two reasons. First, the reduction of the various aspects of the environment to quantitative measures must inherently miss many elements, tangible and more subtle, that are relevant to the child. The measures must be comparable from school to school; yet the elements which are experienced as most important by the child will likely differ from one school to another, and may well differ among children in the same school.
>
> Second, the child experiences his environment as a whole, while the statistical measures necessarily fragment it. Having a teacher without a college degree may indicate an element of disadvantage; but in the concrete situation, a school-child may be taught by a teacher who is not only without a college degree, but who has grown up and received his schooling in the local community, who has never been out of the State, who has 10th-grade vocabulary, and who shares the local community's attitudes.
>
> For both these reasons, the statistical examination of difference in school environments for minority and majority children will give an impression of lesser differences than actually exist.[18]

The Texas Study

More recent studies have used better measures of school inputs to quantify the dimensions of school quality. One such study tracked 1.8 million elementary pupils in 4,500 Texas elementary schools for five years (1990–1994). Like the earlier Coleman study, the Kain-Singleton study documented racial achievement gaps that increased with years of school. Unlike the Coleman report, however, the Kain-Singleton study identified differences in school quality that contributed to those achievement disparities. Specifically, the study found that minority-dominated schools had teachers with lower achievement test scores, education, and experience than those in predominantly white (Anglo) schools.[19] The minority schools also had higher student/teacher ratios. Hence, the separate schools of white and minority children were demonstrably unequal.[20]

Even the Kain-Singleton study failed, however, to provide a summary measure of school quality, much less a definitive assessment of how much differences in school quality explain achievement disparities.[21] All we can say with certainty is that our everyday

---

[18]U.S. Office of Education, *Equality of Educational Opportunity* (The Coleman Report) (Washington, DC: U.S. Government Printing Office, 1966), p. 37.

[19]See John F. Kain and Kraig Singleton, "Equality of Educational Opportunities Revisited," *New England Economic Review* (May–June 1996).

[20]For a synopsis of research on school inequalities, especially teacher quality, see Linda Darling-Hammond, "Unequal Opportunity: Race and Education," *The Brookings Review* (Spring 1998), pp. 28–32. Also review the studies in J. A. and C. A. Banks (eds.), *Handbook of Research on Multicultural Education* (New York: Simon and Schuster, 1995).

[21]A similar conclusion is reached by Valentina Bali and R. Michael Alvarez, "Schools and Educational Outcomes; What Causes the 'Race Gap' in Student Test Scores?" *Social Science Quarterly* (September 2003), pp. 465–507.

observations agree with more formal surveys that find tangible (and intangible) differences in black and white educational facilities. We have no summary measure, however, of how large or how important those differences are.[22]

INHERENT INEQUALITIES

The Supreme Court provided a way out of this statistical ambiguity in 1954 by determining that segregated facilities were *inherently* unequal. In *Brown* v. *Board of Education,* the Court declared that "to separate them [black children] from others of similar age and qualifications solely because of their race generates a feeling of inferiority as to their status in the community that may affect their hearts and minds in a way unlikely ever to be undone."[23] The Court thus relegated the issue of tangible facilities to one of distinctly secondary importance. Even ostensibly "equal" schools for blacks and whites could never generate equal educational opportunity.

There were several specific considerations that led the Supreme Court justices to their landmark decision. They recognized that black pupils in segregated schools would have low self-esteem, knowing they were surrounded by failures and in schools regarded as inferior. Moreover, they would acquire a personal sense of futility knowing that, regardless of their individual attainments, they would always be identified by the community as members of a group viewed as less able, less successful, and less acceptable. Hence, the individual black child would see little reason to develop his or her individual talents. Community views would also affect the attitudes of teachers. Aware of, and probably sharing, the white community's low regard for blacks, teachers attached to black schools would tend to accept and transmit low expectations. They would not teach as much, or as well, to children deemed less teachable.

Impressive evidence in support of the Court's judgment was assembled by the U.S. Commission on Civil Rights in 1967. The commission discovered that black pupils of similar backgrounds performed quite differently in varying racial situations. In particular, it found that black educational achievements increased substantially where schools were more thoroughly integrated. In addition to the fact that white schools were generally better, it was observed that black pupils benefited from integration by believing that their opportunities had improved and by seeing others succeeding around them. Discrimination, then, and more especially school segregation, were seen to be major determinants of black achievements and status.[24]

CLASS DISCRIMINATION IN EDUCATION

While blacks do suffer from serious discrimination in the educational system, there is no reason to believe that they alone are singled out for substandard treatment. On the contrary, it is clear that other minority groups, among them Hispanics and American Indians, confront barriers at least as formidable as do blacks. Accordingly, nearly

---

[22]Michael A. Boozer, Alan B. Kruger, and Shari Wolkon, "Race and School Quality since *Brown* v. *Board of Education,*" *Brookings Papers on Economic Activity,* special issue on microeconomics (1992), pp. 269–326.

[23]*Brown* v. *Board of Education,* 347 U.S. 483 (1954).

[24]Further support for the Court's view is contained in Congressional Budget Office, *Inequalities in the Educational Experiences of Black and White Americans* (Washington, DC: U.S. Government Printing Office, 1977), pp. 10–11.

everything we have said about racial discrimination against blacks applies with equal force to other minority groups. But including other minority groups in our discussion does not completely cover the subject of discrimination. Racism has its counterpart in what has become known as *classism*. Poor individuals as a group, irrespective of their ethnic origin, are provided substandard educational facilities and opportunities in America.

ECONOMIC SEGREGATION

We have already noted that many whites lose out as a result of racial discrimination in education, namely, those who are not able to escape predominantly black neighborhoods and schools. But even where minority groups are not present, poor whites may be confined to separate and substandard schools. Neighborhoods are even more likely to be homogeneous by income classes than by race; that is, poor families will be confined to distinct neighborhoods of any city. Moreover, because school expenditures and decisions are determined by administrative bodies composed largely of the nonpoor, schools in low-income neighborhoods are likely to receive less than equal facilities.

SCHOOL FINANCES

Inequality of educational opportunities across income classes tends to be reinforced by the way schools are financed. Slightly over half of all elementary and secondary school expenditures are financed by local property taxes, with most of the remainder financed out of state revenues (only 10 percent of elementary and secondary school expenditures are financed out of federal revenues). This implies that children in poorer states and poorer school districts are provided with fewer resources. And so they are: In 2002, for example, average per pupil expenditure varied across states by nearly $7,000 (from a low of $4,900 in Utah to $11,793 in New Jersey). Within states, disparities across school districts have often been just as large. In Georgia, Connecticut, Massachusetts, and California, high-spending school districts spent more than twice as much per pupil as did the school districts with lowest per pupil expenditure. In New York State, the wealthiest school district spent $17,853 per pupil, while the poorest district spent only $9,000. In Montana, the spending per student ranged from $17,000 to $4,946. Because expenditures *within* a school district may also be distributed unequally, educational opportunities are unlikely to be the same for all income classes.

Jonathan Kozol has described in vivid terms how these differences in spending affect the school environment. Schools in poor districts have ill-equipped labs, erratic heating and cooling, broken playground equipment, and a shortage of textbooks. Students in those schools are often taught by uncertified teachers and frequently by substitutes. By contrast, schools in wealthier districts have new equipment, computer labs, attractive environments, Internet access, and certified teachers. As a result of these "savage inequalities" the quality of a child's education depends on the wealth of his or her parents and neighbors.[25]

The analogy of class discrimination to racial discrimination goes beyond differences in school facilities. Like minority children, poor white children tend to be surrounded by

[25]Jonathan Kozol, *Savage Inequalities: Children in American Schools* (New York: Crown, 1991).

families that have failed to achieve material success. Poor white children see few demonstrations of personal aspiration and talent leading to higher socioeconomic status. Furthermore, they are aware that society regards material success as a mark of personal worth and thus see themselves and their families as stigmatized by the larger community. They know, too, that their schools are inferior and that completion of their studies will leave them ill prepared to compete in the labor market. As a consequence, they are likely to internalize a sense of futility and inferiority.[26]

EDUCATIONAL ATTAINMENTS

The cumulative impact of class discrimination is apparent in the educational attainments of lower-class children. Poor children drop out of high school at over twice the rate of nonpoor children. Even more startling is the fact that a substantial number of poor children leave the educational system even *before* they enter high school. And those relatively few lower-income children who do manage to make it through until high school graduation cannot depend on their abilities to get them into college. College admissions are still reserved primarily for those who can support themselves or can afford to forgo several years of employment income.

College Attendance

Table 11.2 provides some perspective on the barriers to higher education imposed by low incomes. This table includes all families with at least one child 18 to 24 years old. Within this group of families, the table indicates the percentage of families within each income class who have at least one child attending college full-time. For example, 56 percent of all high-income ($50,000 plus) families have at least one child in college. Among the lowest-income families (under $10,000), only 21 percent have a child in college. As the first row of Table 11.2 reveals, the likelihood of attending college increases markedly with family income.

Another notable feature of Table 11.2 is the absence of significant racial differences *within* income classes. Look at the group of families with incomes of $40,000–49,999,

TABLE 11.2 Percent of Families with Children (aged 18–24) in College Full-Time, by Family Income and Race (1999)

	Total	Under $10,000	$10,000–$19,999	$20,000–$29,999	$30,000–$39,999	$40,000–$49,999	$50,000 and Over
				Family Income			
All	41.2	20.9	26.3	32.9	41.4	45.4	56.4
White	42.9	18.6	25.7	34.3	42.4	44.6	59.5
Black	28.1	17.9	24.1	25.2	33.5	39.2	50.0
Hispanic	24.3	15.3	17.3	20.0	34.0	45.6	40.1

Source: U.S. Department of Education.

[26]Some evidence of this vicious cycle is confaimed in N. Mcardle, *Racial Equity and Opportunity in Metro Boston Job Markets* (Cambridge, MA: Harvard Civil Rights Project, 2004).

for example. Within this income class, Hispanic youth are actually *more* likely to attend college full-time than are (Anglo) white youth. Within other income classes, racial differences are also relatively small. This suggests that *racial* differences in educational opportunity may, in fact, reflect *class* differences. From this perspective, blacks and other minorities do worse than whites in the educational system because their families' incomes are generally lower.[27]

THE QUESTION OF ABILITY

It is generally assumed by the nonpoor that poor children do not attain higher educational status because they are uniformly less able. There are some obvious weaknesses in this assumption, however. Very talented poor youngsters have no control over family finances. Hence, if the family cannot afford either to forgo their earnings or even to supply them with school clothes and lunches, they will not be able to take advantage of "free" high school education. Furthermore, there are no scholarship or loan programs for high school students. As a result, many talented poor children will never complete high school. Even for those who do attain high school diplomas, college admission will be barred by similar financial obstacles and by a legacy of inferior schooling.

It is not easy to determine how many bright, poor children are denied higher education because of their poverty. IQ tests remain our only standardized measure of ability, and those tests create problems for poor whites similar to those for blacks. Because their schools are substandard, poor whites fall increasingly far behind the nonpoor in educational performance. Hence, they demonstrate decreasing IQs over time, making it difficult to discern how many originally bright children existed among the poor. And yet, even on the restrictive criterion of IQ tests, we can identify a large number of poor and able high school graduates who never attained a college degree.

Table 11.3 displays the college attendance rates of youth, cross classified by family income and ability. The observations are based on a sample of roughly 15,000

TABLE 11.3 College Attendance by Family Income and Ability			
	Achievement Score (ability)		
Family Income	*Low*	*Middle*	*High*
Low	29.1	49.4	74.7
Middle	46.6	68.1	86.1
High	63.6	80.8	95.2

Source: Mathtech, Inc., *Factors Related to College Enrollment* (Washington, DC: Mathtech, 1998).

---

[27]The overlap of racial and economic segregation is documented in Gary Orfield and Chungmei Lee, *Why Segregation Matters: Poverty and Educational Inequality* (Cambridge, MA: Harvard Civil Rights Project, 2005). See also Stephen Cameron and James Heckman: The Dynamics of Educational Attainment for Black, Hispanic, and White Males," *Journal of Political Economy* (2001), v. 109, pp. 455–499 and Donald Heller, *Condition of Access: Higher Education for Lower Income Students* New York, NY: Praeger, 2002.

eighth-graders, first interviewed in 1988. These same youth were interviewed several times, including an interview in 1994. By that time, most of these young people had been out of high school for two years. Table 11.3 shows which students had enrolled in college by then.

Overall, two-thirds of the youth had enrolled in college by 1994. But the probability of enrollment was strongly influenced by family income. Notice, for example, the fate of high-ability students, as measured by standard reading and math tests. As the last column in the table shows, high-ability students from high-income families were almost certain (95.2%) to attend college. By contrast, only three out of four similarly able students from low-income families were attending college.

Even more striking is the higher college-attendance rates of children with mid-level ability but high-income parents. Indeed, these rich, mid-ability students were more likely to attend college (80.8%) than high-ability students from *low*-income families (74.7%). Even low-ability students from high-income families were very likely (63.6%) to attend college.

Table 11.3 understates the disadvantages of lower-income children. By the time the eighth graders in that study were tested, they had already been disadvantaged by inferior schools. Hence, their test scores probably understated their ability. Also, Table 11.3 doesn't distinguish the type or quality of college attended. In fact, low-income students are more likely to attend community colleges than four-year universities. Finally, Table 11.3 doesn't convey college *graduation* rates. Other studies have shown that *graduation* rates are even more strongly correlated with family income than are college *attendance* rates.[28]

Class discrimination in education, then, is a strong force in the educational system and helps to determine the distribution of poverty.[29] Whatever aggregate level of poverty exists, we may confidently predict that the children of the poor will be heavily overrepresented in the poverty statistics. It is also possible that class discrimination has become a stronger force in American society than racial discrimination. The U.S. Commission on Civil Rights, for example, found that schools were severely segregated by socioeconomic class and that the social class composition of schools is a stronger determinant of achievement than race.[30] Moreover, there is mounting evidence that middle-class whites, if forced to choose, would prefer as neighbors middle-class blacks to poor whites. Poor persons, of whatever color, are least accepted by the larger society. This will be of little comfort to poor blacks and other minorities, of course, who are likely to be the subject of both racial and class discrimination. As

---

[28]See Andrew Sum, Neeta Fogg, and Garth Mangum, *Confronting the Youth Demographic Challenge* (Baltimore, MD: Johns Hopkins University Press, October 2000), p. 163; also Bruce Eckland and Louis Henderson, *College Attainment—Four Years after High School* (Durham, NC: Research Triangle Institute, June 1981).

[29]Richard Herrnstein and Charles Murray claim that such class discrimination has all but disappeared, so that a meritocracy based on intelligence now determines access to education: see their *The Bell Curve: Intelligence and Class Structure in American Life* (New York: Free Press, 1994). Their view is challenged in Claude S. Fischer et al., *Inequality by Design: Cracking the Bell Curve Myth* (Princeton, NJ: Princeton University Press, 1996).

[30]Similar evidence is presented in S. Mayer, "How Much Does a High School's Racial and Socioeconomic Mix Affect Graduation and Teenage Fertility Rates?" Table 4.

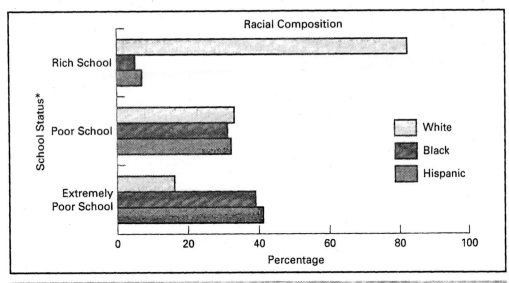

FIGURE 11.4 Class and Race Overlaps

*School status measured by percentage of poor students in attendance, as "rich" (less than 10% poor), "poor" (50–100%), and "extremely poor" (over 90% poor).

Source: Adapted from Gary Orfield and Chungmei Lee, *Why Segregation Matters: Poverty and Educational Inequality.* (Cambridge, MA: Harvard Education Press, 2005), Tables 8, 9, 10. http://www.civilrightsproject. harvard.edu/research/deseg/Racial_Transformation.pdf.

Figure 11.4 illustrates, minority children are the most likely to attend the very poorest schools.

SEX DISCRIMINATION IN EDUCATION

The educational handicaps of minority and lower-class groups are reasonably easy to document, but the disadvantages that women confront in the educational system are more subtle, at least in the early grades. The sex barriers that characterize primary and secondary educational systems consist of sex-typing certain kinds of curricula. Girls are encouraged to take home economics, foreign languages, and art, while gently discouraged from taking math, business courses, and science. The barriers emanate both from school counselors—who want to be "realistic" about occupational goals—and, perhaps more importantly, from parents and peers attuned to certain expectations with respect to male and female roles in society. As the Carnegie Commission on High Education noted:

> Almost from the moment of birth, boys and girls are subject to a wide variety of cultural influences that tend to prepare them for differentiated roles in life. Little girls are typically given dolls or miniature cooking utensils for toys; boys are generally given trucks and electric trains and mechanical toys. School readers show pictures of father going off to work and mother waving good-bye at the window, or of father playing baseball with his sons while mother bakes cookies. Girls play jump rope or tag on the school playground, while boys play ball. At about the seventh or eighth grade, boys take a course in manual training, while girls are taught cooking and sewing.

We are not suggesting that matters ought to be reversed, or that little girls should be forbidden to play with dolls, but rather that there ought to be more freedom of choice. Girls who show signs of a mechanical bent should be given an opportunity to play with mechanical toys and to enter the course on manual training. Boys should not be barred from courses on cooking and sewing if they are interested.[31]

GENDER SEGREGATION

This kind of acculturation—what the Sadkers call "educational sexism"[32]—tends to restrict the educational aspirations of female students and to frustrate them when they challenge those restrictions. One of the manifestations of this educational sexism is the "glass wall" that partitions women from men in college curricula. Although women are a bit more likely than men to attend college, they are not likely to be found in science or engineering classes. Only 30 percent of the students who major in physics, chemistry, or computer science are women. In engineering, the female presence drops to 20 percent. College coeds are more likely to major in home economics (89 percent of all degrees go to women), health sciences (87 percent), or general liberal arts (68 percent). This gender segregation reflects not only the persistent reinforcement of gender stereotypes from childhood, but also the gender bias in instruction and testing.[33]

Graduate Degrees

Equally explicit manifestations of sex discrimination in education have been apparent at the postcollege level. As suggested earlier, female college graduates have had difficulty gaining access to the professional schools that confer the necessary credentials for many desirable jobs. Secretarial schools have always been easy to get into, but law schools, medical schools, and business schools have often been a different story. Figure 11.5 depicts the proportion of different educational degrees awarded to women in 2005. As is evident, women accounted for a very substantial percentage of graduate enrollments in education schools, but were poorly represented in law or medicine, and virtually nonexistent in engineering schools.

To a large extent, this pattern of graduate education is the consequence of sex-differentiated roles and expectations nurtured from the crib to the campus. As the Council of Economic Advisers observed:

> Even more striking are the differences in the courses taken. At both the undergraduate and advanced levels, women are heavily represented in English, languages, and fine arts—the more general cultural fields. They are poorly represented in disciplines having a strong vocational emphasis and promising a high pecuniary return.[34]

---

[31]Carnegie Commission on Higher Education, *Opportunities for Women in Higher Education* (New York: McGraw-Hill, 1973), pp. 42–43.

[32]Myra and David Sadker, *Failing at Fairness: How America's Schools Cheat Girls* (New York: Scribners, 1994).

[33]Ibid., for extensive documentation.

[34]*Economic Report of the President* (Washington, DC: U.S. Government Printing Office, 1973), pp. 101–102.

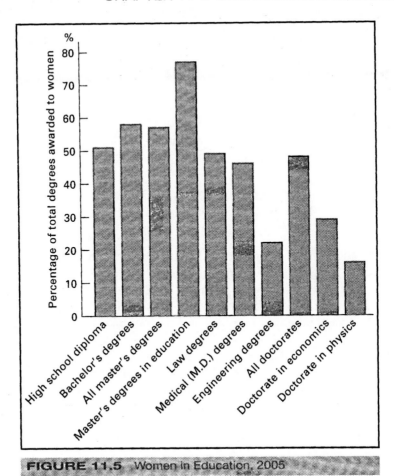

FIGURE 11.5 Women in Education, 2005

Source: U.S. Department of Education.

Vocational Education

Gender segregation is even more apparent in vocational school curricula. For youth who don't go to college, vocational schools can be an important springboard to better jobs. As Table 11.4 reveals, however, women are overwhelmingly enrolled in traditional female occupations, where wages are much lower than in traditional male jobs. In 2002, the National Women's Law Center asked the U.S. Department of Education to investigate the sources of this gender segregation.

Poor Prospects

The implication of this pattern of sex discrimination is that women will enter the labor market with less valuable human capital than men.[35] As a consequence, a disproportionate number of women, especially those trying to raise families on their own, will end up in poverty.

---

[35]This point was underscored by a 1975 report of the Carnegie Council on Policy Studies in Higher Education that identified underrecruitment of women to appropriate graduate programs as the major obstacle to greater equality of jobs in higher education. Although women still lag behind men in many graduate degrees, the enrollment gap has narrowed substantially in the last decade.

TABLE 11.4 Gender Segregation in High School Career and Technical Education Programs

Course of Study	Percentage Female Enrollment	Median Wage (hourly)
Engineering	16	$22.26
Construction	10	$17.99
Automotive worker	9	$16.87
Cosmetologist	98	$9.52
Child care worker	87	$8.06

Source: National Women's Law Center (2005 data).

Summary

Discrimination on the basis of race, income class, or sex violates commonly accepted standards of social justice. Where discrimination is pervasive, the freedom of minority groups is severely restricted, as are their opportunities for achievement. Such limitations harm not only those discriminated against, but also the larger community. Talents go undeveloped, potential output is irrevocably lost, and markets are unnecessarily restricted.

In the American educational system, racial discrimination has resulted in a pattern of segregated and inferior schools for blacks and other minorities. Over one-third of all minority students continue to attend virtually all minority elementary and secondary schools. The inferiority of the education these children receive derives not only from disparities in school facilities but, more importantly, from a sense of isolation and subjugation. The consequences of this discrimination are manifest in the low educational attainments of minority youth.

As serious and pervasive as discrimination against minorities is, it is not the only kind of discrimination practiced in the educational system. Poor children, in particular, are maintained in schools segregated largely by socioeconomic class and provided with substandard facilities. They and their families are also stigmatized by the larger community for failure to attain material success. As a result, children of poor families drop out of school at alarming rates and generally lag behind nonpoor children in demonstrated achievement. Even those relatively few poor children who do demonstrate high levels of achievement are denied high levels of education. Class discrimination, then, is directly analogous to discrimination against racial or minority groups.

Finally, we must recognize that women are discriminated against in the educational system as well, even if such discrimination is more subtle. To the extent that such discrimination restricts later job opportunities, particularly for those women who end up as heads-of-household, it too contributes to the level and distribution of poverty.

Because educational attainments are a prime determinant of the distribution of poverty, those discriminated against in the schools are most likely to be among the poor. For whatever level of aggregate poverty exists, the children of yesterday's poor, minority households, and female-headed families will be overrepresented in the poverty statistics. Children of poor minority families headed by women will be the most disadvantaged, as they may be subject to all three forms of discrimination.

Further Reading

ON THE NATURE
OF DISCRIMINATION

Clotfelter, Charles, *After Brown: The Rise and Retreat of School Desegregation,* Princeton, N.J.: Princeton University Press, 2006.

Dovidio, John, Peter Glick, and Lourie Rudman, eds., *On the Nature of Prejudice: Fifty Years' after Allport.* Malden, MA: Blackwell, 2005.

Hurley, Jennifer A., ed., *Racism.* San Diego, CA: Greenhaven Press, 1998.

Loury, Glenn, *The Anatomy of Racial Inequality.* Cambridge, MA: Harvard University Press, 2002.

Massey, Douglas S., and Nancy A. Denton, *American Apartheid: Segregation and the Making of the Underclass.* Cambridge, MA: Harvard University Press, 1993.

Pager, Devah, "The Dynamics of Discrimination," University of Michigan, National Poverty Center Working Paper #06-11, June 2006.

Williams, Mary E., ed., *Discrimination.* San Diego, CA: Greenhaven Press, 1997.

Wu, Frank H., *Yellow: Race in America Beyond Black and White.* New York, NY: Basic Books, 2002.

Zuriff, G.E., "Inventing Racism," *The Public Interest* (Winter 2002), pp. 114–128.

ON DISCRIMINATION
IN EDUCATION

Collins, W. J. and R. A. Margo, "Historical Perspectives on Racial Differences in Schooling in the United States." Cambridge, MA: National Bureau of Economic Research, June 2003.

Hochschild, Jennifer, "Social Class in the Public Schools," *Journal of Social Issues* (2003), pp. 821–840.

Kain, John F., and Kraig Singleton, "Equality of Educational Opportunity Revisited," *New England Economic Review* (May–June 1996).

Kozol, Jonathan, *The Shame of the Nation: The Restoration of Apartheid Schooling in America.* New York: Crown, 2005.

Orfield, Gary, and Chungmei Lee, *Why Segregation Matters: Poverty and Educational Inequality.* Cambridge, MA: Harvard Educational Press, 2005.

Rothstern, Richard, *Class and Schools.* Washington, DC: Economic Policy Institute, 2004.

Sadker, Myra and David, *Failing at Fairness: How America's Schools Cheat Girls.* New York: Scribners, 1994.

U.S. Department of Education, *The Condition of Education.* Washington, DC: Government Printing Office, annual.

Ward, Nadia L., "Improving Equity and Access for Low-Income and Minority Youth into Instructions of Higher Education," *Urban Education* (January 2006), pp. 50–70.

Web Links

Harvard University. Summary of reports on school segregation by the Civil Rights Project: www.civilrightsproject.harvard.edu

U.S. Department of Education, National Center for Education Statistics. Data on school enrollments and attainments by race and gender: http://www.nces.ed.gov

CHAPTER 12
DISCRIMINATION IN THE LABOR MARKET

In 1927, a clothing manufacturer in New York City advertised for help with the following wage offer: "White Workers $24: Colored Workers $20."[1] His offer embodied one of the most flagrant forms of racial discrimination in the labor market: namely, the payment of unequal wages for equal work. Few employers are so blatant today, and certainly no one advertises such discriminatory practices in print anymore. Nevertheless, as we observed in Chapter 11, minority workers and even many white workers believe unequal treatment in the labor market is still the norm. As Figure 12.1 reveals, one out of four blacks and one out of five Hispanics believe they have *personally* suffered from discrimination in the labor market.

If minority workers are discriminated against in the labor market, they are denied full use of their productive abilities. As a consequence, their incomes will be depressed, and they will be overrepresented in the ranks of the poor. Hence, racial discrimination in the labor market tends to affect both the distribution and extent of poverty. In this chapter, we examine the consequences, forms, and practices of discrimination in the labor market.[2] As in Chapter 11, we begin with a discussion of racial discrimination, then consider the phenomena of class and sex discrimination.

RACIAL DISCRIMINATION IN THE LABOR MARKET

We know that there are tremendous disparities between the incomes of blacks and whites. In Chapter 3, we noted that 1 out of nearly 4 blacks and Hispanics is poor compared to only 1 out of 12 whites. In Chapter 9, we observed that average incomes for black and Hispanic families are $20,000 less than white family incomes. Moreover, we have observed that racial or cultural theories cannot explain these inequalities. Thus, there are strong grounds for assuming that blacks and Hispanics continue to be the subject of discrimination, despite the lack of advertising to that effect.[3]

---

[1]Cited by Orley Ashenfelter, "Changes in Labor Market Discrimination over Time," *Journal of Human Resources* (Fall 1970), pp. 403–430. An assessment of explicitly race-based help-wanted ads that appeared in major U.S. newspapers in 1960 appears in William Darity Jr. and Patrick L. Mason, "Evidence on Discrimination: Codes of Color, Codes of Gender," *Journal of Economic Perspectives* (Spring 1998), Table 1.

[2]For analysis of labor-market discrimination in other nations, see William A. Darity Jr. and Jessica G. Nembhard, "Racial and Ethnic Economic Inequality: The International Record," *American Economic Review* (May 2000).

[3]For a dialogue on this, see Mary E. Williams, ed., *Discrimination* (San Diego, CA: Greenhaven Press, 2003), chapter 1.

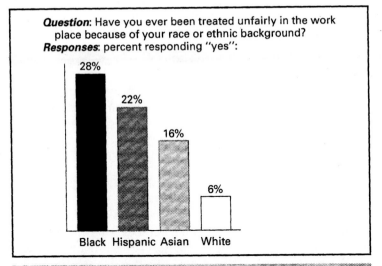

Question: Have you ever been treated unfairly in the work place because of your race or ethnic background?
Responses: percent responding "yes":

FIGURE 12.1 Perceived Labor-Market Discrimination

Source: "Race and Ethnicity: Attitudes, Perceptions and Experiences–Toplines/ Survey," (#3143), *The Washington Post*/The Henry J. Kaiser Family Foundation/ Harvard University, September 2001. This information was reprinted with permission from the Henry J. Kaiser Family Foundation. The Kaiser Family Foundation, based in Menlo Park, California, is a nonprofit, private operating foundation focusing on the major health care issues facing the nation and is not associated with Kaiser Permanente or Kaiser Industries.

LOCUS OF DISCRIMINATION

Nonmarket Discrimination

It would be mistaken, however, to conclude that all existing income inequalities can be explained by discriminatory practices in the labor market. We know, for instance, that blacks and Hispanics enter the labor market with less human capital than whites as a result of racial discrimination in the schools. Accordingly, a labor market that rewarded all individuals only on the basis of demonstrated achievement would still provide less income for minority individuals than for majority whites. A high proportion of blacks also continue to live in the South, where employment levels and wages are generally lower. As we noted in Chapter 9, blacks and Hispanics also tend to be spatially isolated in low-income neighborhoods. As a result they have less access to jobs and a lower probability of getting them.[4] Hence, income disparities alone do not prove the existence of racial discrimination in the labor market; they simply create a presumption that discrimination will be discovered if sought.

Past Labor-Market Discrimination

Even if we find that income disparities continue to exist after we have accounted for educational and geographic differences, we cannot necessarily conclude that discriminatory practices are rampant in the labor market. If discrimination against minority workers ceased altogether, they would still be handicapped by past labor-market

---

[4]For more evidence on this, see Katherine M. O'Regan and John M. Quigley, "Teenage Employment and the Spatial Isolation of Minority and Poverty Households," *Journal of Human Resources* (Summer 1996), pp. 692–702.

discrimination. They would be less skilled and experienced and lower on seniority ladders, for example. As in the area of education, minority workers would remain disadvantaged by past discrimination, even if present discrimination were eliminated.

Current Labor-Market Discrimination

The observed income disparities between white and minority workers, then, are potentially the result of three forces: nonmarket discrimination, past labor-market discrimination, and current labor-market discrimination. What we seek to identify in this section is that portion of existing income disparities attributable solely to continuing racial discrimination in the labor market.

DISPARITIES IN EARNINGS

White families have accumulated vast amounts of wealth in the form of property, savings accounts, bond holdings, and stock ownership. Stockholders' equity alone now amounts to more than $10 trillion, while another $40 trillion is tied up in savings, cash, government bonds, and other financial assets. Black families have comparatively little access to this wealth, as they have been denied equal opportunity to earn and accumulate money in the past. Thus, the median white family has over seven times as much wealth as the median black or Hispanic family.[5] Such disparities in wealth tend to overwhelm differences in income.

For the most part, these differences in wealth do not reflect current *labor-market* discrimination. Current income includes not only labor-market earnings, but also money derived from accumulated wealth, especially money received in the form of dividends, interest, and capital gains. Accordingly, *total* income differences between blacks and whites are much larger than differences in *earnings,* that is, income derived from labor-market activity. To assess the impact of racial discrimination in the labor market, then, we need to focus on racial disparities in earnings alone.

In 2005, the mean earnings of white male workers over age 25 were $58,215. For black workers, the average was only $37,586, just two-thirds of white earnings. The

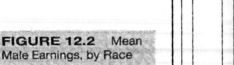

FIGURE 12.2 Mean Male Earnings, by Race

Source: U.S. Bureau of the Census (2005 data for males 25 years old and older).

---

[5]Maury Gittleman and Edward N. Wolff, "Racial Wealth Disparities: Is the Gap Closing?" *Journal of Human Resources* (Winter 2004); also Ana Aizcorbe, A. Kennic Kell, and K. Moore, "Recent Changes in U.S. Family Finances," *Federal Reserve Bulletin* (January 2003), pp. 1–32.

earnings of Hispanic workers were lower still, as Figure 12.2 illustrates. In absolute terms, the earnings gap between (Anglo) white and minority workers was roughly $22,000 per year.

How much of this earnings difference was due to discrimination in the labor market? To isolate the impact of racial discrimination on this disparity, we need to identify the influence of other earnings determinants. Education, skills, age, and geographic location all influence a person's earnings. Only by controlling for these other factors can we perceive the *independent* influence of racial discrimination in the labor market.

EDUCATIONAL DIFFERENCES

We have already noted the tremendous importance of educational attainments for income. Therefore, we must control for the influence on earnings of the nonmarket discrimination suffered in schools. This may be done by observing the comparative earnings of workers with equal educations. If there were no racial discrimination in the labor market, blacks, Hispanics, and whites with equal education should command approximately equal incomes.

Years of Schooling

As Table 12.1 shows, this isn't the case. However, the earnings of white, black, and Hispanic men with equal years of schooling are closer than the unadjusted comparisons. As Figure 12.2 illustrates, the "raw" Hispanic earnings are only 58 percent of average white earnings. However, Hispanic college graduates earn 77 percent of what white college graduates earn. Hence, once schooling differences are taken into account, the earnings gap between Hispanics and whites is cut substantially. The same kind of schooling adjustment reduces the black and white gap.[6] This reduces the potential explanatory power of pure labor-market discrimination considerably.

Quality of Schooling

Further adjustments in the gross earnings comparisons are needed to identify white, black, and Hispanic workers possessing equal human capital. Table 12.1 adjusts only for the *quantity* of schooling. But what about the *quality*? As we observed in Chapter 11, years of schooling do not have the same educational significance for blacks and whites. A complete adjustment for nonmarket discrimination would have to control for the significant differences in the *quality* of education received by each group. We must

TABLE 12.1 Male Earnings, by Race and Education

Education	Average Earnings of White Workers	Earnings as Percent of White Average, for	
		Black Workers	Hispanic Workers
High school dropout	$31,451	67.5	78.6
High school graduate	$40,893	73.3	78.4
Some college	$48,015	76.3	77.0
College graduate	$73,198	72.5	76.6

Source: U.S. Bureau of the Census (2005 data for males 25 years old and older).

---

[6]The relative education gains of blacks has also narrowed the black-white earnings gap; see Kenneth Couch and Mary C. Daly, "Black–White Wage Inequality in the 1990s: A Decade of Progress," *Economic Inquiry* (January 2002), pp. 31–42.

recognize that a typical black high school graduate comes to the job with as little educational preparation as the typical white high school dropout. When this additional control for nonmarket discrimination is imposed, observed labor-market disparities shrink further. Black workers of equivalent educational backgrounds, including both quantity and quality of schooling, earn incomes approximately 90 percent as large as their white counterparts.[7]

Current Discrimination

It appears, then, that most of the earnings disparity between whites and blacks can be attributed to prior (nonmarket) discrimination in the schools. This means that only a small share of the observed earnings disparity can be explained by current labor-market discrimination. Indeed, the combined influence of other factors, including skills, age, and region, reduce the disparity further. Recent studies of discrimination have estimated that only about one-fourth of existing earnings disparities are directly attributable to discriminatory labor-market practices.[8] As a rough approximation, then, we may say that two-thirds of the $22,000 earnings disparity is due to nonmarket discrimination (education, residence); one-sixth due to past market discrimination (work skills and experience); and one-sixth to current labor-market discrimination.[9]

While nonmarket discrimination apparently overwhelms other types of discrimination, some caution is necessary in interpreting these conclusions. Clearly, these are only rough approximations to the relative impact of various handicaps. They are best viewed as orders of magnitude, not precise estimates. Even if the allocation of the gross racial earnings gap is correct, current labor-market discrimination still exacts a significant toll: One-sixth of the gross earnings gap amounts to a "tax" of over $3,600 on the annual earnings of minority workers. Racial discrimination in the labor market is, thus, a large and important racial barrier, even if outstripped by discrimination in education.

---

[7]This conclusion is reinforced by the finding that black and white workers with similar literacy skills—an outcome of the quantity and quality of education—have similar employment probabilities; see Francisco L. Rivera-Batiz, "Quantitative Literacy and the Likelihood of Employment among Young Adults in the United States," *Journal of Human Resources* (Spring 1992), pp. 313–328.

[8]See Derek Neal and William Johnson, "The Role of Premarket Factors in Black-White Differences," *Journal of Political Economy, 104*:5 (1996), pp. 869–895; Nan Maxwell, "The Effect of Black-White Wage Differences in the Quantity and Quality of Education," *Industrial and Labor Relations Review* (January 1994), pp. 249–264; David Card and Alan K. Krueger, "School Quality and Black-White Relative Earnings: A Direct Assessment," *Quarterly Journal of Economics* (February 1992), pp. 151–200; June O'Neill, "The Role of Human Capital in Earnings Differences Between Black and White Men," *Journal of Economic Perspectives* (Fall 1990), pp. 25–45. Even lower estimates are found in Donald R. Deere, "Trends in Wage Inequality in the United States," in Finis Welch, ed., *The Causes and Consequences of Increasing Inequality* (Chicago, IL: University of Chicago Press, 2001), pp. 9–36, and are *completely* eliminated in Satoshi Kanzawa, "The Myth of Racial Discrimination in Pay in the United States," *Managerial and Decision Economics, 26* (2005), pp. 285–294.

[9]This estimate is consistent with conclusions in Joseph G. Altonji and Rebecca M. Blank, "Race and Gender in the Labor Market," in *Handbook of Labor Economics*, Vol. 3c, eds. O. Ashenfelter and D. Card (Amsterdam: Elsevier, 1999); William Darity, David Guilkey, and William Winfrey, "Explaining Differences in Economic Performance Among Racial and Ethnic Groups in the USA: The Data Examined," *Journal of Economics Sociology* (October 1996), pp. 411–426; and Peter Gottschalk, "Inequality, Income Growth, and Mobility," *Journal of Economic Perspectives* (Spring 1997), pp. 21–40. By contrast, Richard Herrnstein and Charles Murray claim that measured IQ accounts for the entire earnings gap between white and black workers employed year-round, leaving no discriminatory residual; see their *The Bell Curve: Intelligence and Class Structure in American Life* (New York: Free Press, 1994). Among the many critiques of their argument are Claude S. Fischer et al., *Inequality by Design: Cracking the Bell Curve Myth* (Princeton, NJ: Princeton University Press, 1996).

Furthermore, it cannot be assumed that these proportions are fixed. If, in fact, the quality and quantity of schooling for blacks and Hispanics increase—as they have in recent years—we have no assurance that minority educational attainments will continue to be rewarded at the same rate. As more educated black and Hispanic workers emerge, racial discrimination in the labor market may intensify. Some potential discrimination in the labor market is now averted due to the fact that relatively few blacks and Hispanics are able to compete directly with whites. As minority educational attainments—and thus labor-market competition—increase, the situation may change dramatically.[10] Accordingly, we have no firm basis for predicting a linear reduction of earnings disparities as educational opportunities become more equal. These calculations illustrate where the locus of discrimination is now; they cannot predict where it will be in the future.

COMPONENTS OF EARNINGS DISPARITIES

While the image is provocative, it is mistaken to picture a thief called Discrimination openly robbing minority workers of $22,000 each year, even though the effect may be the same. Instead, we must realize that this earnings loss emerges from several dimensions of the labor-market process. Minority workers are not robbed of their earnings outright. Very little of the discrimination that takes place in the labor market is of the sort exemplified by the New York garment manufacturer who paid different wages to white and black workers. Aside from being illegal, the visibility of such practices makes them especially vulnerable to public scrutiny and civil rights action. In addition, such overtly inequitable treatment violates the consciences of most employers. Rather, minority workers are hired less often, for fewer hours, for less desirable jobs, and at lower wages (see Figure 12.3). They are also offered less training on the job. The sum total of these different forces leaves the minority worker poorer. A more thorough

FIGURE 12.3 The Sources of Earnings Disparities

---

[10]Asian men apparently experience this kind of higher-level discrimination; see Harriet Orcutt Duleep and Seth Sanders, "Discrimination at the Top: American-Born Asian and White Men," *Industrial Relations* (Fall 1992), pp. 416–432. A similar pattern has been observed for black women in Deborah Anderson and David Shapiro, "Racial Differences in Access to High-Paying Jobs and the Wage Gap Between Black and White Women," *Industrial and Labor Relations Review* (January 1996), pp. 273–286. Evidence for upwardly mobile black workers is in Eric Grodsky and Pager Devah, "The Structure of Disadvantage: Individual and Occupational Determinants of the Black–White Wage Gap," *American Sociological Review* (August 2001), pp. 542–567.

TABLE 12.2 Unemployment of Male Workers, by Race

	Whites	Blacks	Hispanics
Unemployment rate (percent)	4.4	10.5	5.4
Average duration of unemployment (weeks)	17.6	22.6	16.0

Source: U.S. Bureau of Labor Statistics (2005 averages).

understanding of discrimination is attained by considering the relative importance of each of these forces.

Employment

Because minority workers are less educated, less experienced, and less attractive to most employers than available white workers, they are least likely to be hired. In any given job situation, white workers will be hired first and laid off last. Hence, the frequency of employment and the number of hours worked will differ for minority and white workers as the combined result of nonmarket and market racial discrimination. Indeed, a significant part of the observed earnings disparity derives not from the decision to pay minority workers lower wages but from the decision to employ them less often.[11] Table 12.2 shows that black workers are more than twice as likely to be unemployed as are white workers. Black workers also tend to remain unemployed for a longer time. Hispanic workers also experience unemployment more frequently, although for shorter periods of time.

Occupation

Of still greater significance to the observed earnings disparity is the decision to employ black and Hispanic workers at different kinds of jobs. Once again, all forms of discrimination take their toll. Minority workers are denied entrance to many occupations because they lack necessary educational attainments or credentials. They also often lack required work skills and experience. And finally, whites regard many jobs as being inappropriate for blacks and therefore exclude them. Social work, athletics, garbage collection, and bus driving are regarded as acceptable minority occupations; retail sales, management, or even teaching are less appropriate. And many whites are reluctant to use the services of a black doctor or lawyer (not to mention a female one of any race). Accordingly, most minority workers are largely excluded from full participation in the more pleasant and remunerative occupations. Table 12.3 indicates the general nature of existing occupational patterns.

White workers of either sex are much more likely to hold white-collar jobs than are minority workers. The very small percentage of black and Hispanic workers in managerial and administrative jobs is especially noteworthy. Apparently, minority workers seldom have the opportunity to be the boss. Indeed, black and Hispanic men are more likely to be nonfarm laborers than managers or administrators. Yet white men are three times as likely to be in a management position (16 percent) as in nonfarm labor (5.2 percent).

---

[11]Supply effects are relevant also. Confronted with discrimination in the labor market, minorities may choose to drop out of school or withdraw from the labor market. See M. Baldwin and W. G. Johnson, "The Employment Effects of Wage Discrimination Against Black Men," *Industrial and Labor Relations Review* (January 1996), pp. 312–316.

TABLE 12.3 Occupational Status, by Race and Sex (percent)

Occupational Status	Male Workers			Female Workers		
	White	Black	Hispanic	White	Black	Hispanic
White collar	**49.5**	**37.3**	**27.7**	**73.9**	**63.8**	**55.4**
Professional and technical	16.3	12.1	7.0	25.2	20.4	14.4
Managers and administrators	16.3	8.9	6.6	13.6	10.0	7.9
Sales workers	11.3	8.5	7.5	12.5	7.5	12.3
Clerical workers	5.9	9.8	6.6	22.6	22.4	20.7
Blue collar	**38.1**	**40.7**	**52.9**	**7.0**	**8.9**	**14.1**
Craftspeople	20.3	14.2	30.0	1.1	0.9	2.0
Operatives	3.4	10.2	11.1	4.0	5.3	8.5
Transport drivers	4.2	6.7	4.7	0.2	0.2	0.3
Nonfarm laborers	5.2	9.6	7.1	1.7	2.5	3.3
Service workers	**12.1**	**20.0**	**19.5**	**19.0**	**27.2**	**30.5**
Farm workers	**1.1**	**0.5**	**2.8**	**0.4**	**0.2**	**1.0**

Source: U.S. Bureau of Labor Statistics (2005 annual averages). See also Barbara H. Woofton, "Gender Differences in Occupational Employment," *Monthly Labor Review* (April 1997), pp. 15–24.

Occupational disparities are further aggravated by the fact that minority workers who do gain access to the better occupations end up in the lowest and least desirable jobs *within* each occupational group. Within the professional, technical, and managerial class, for example, white workers tend to be lawyers, doctors, engineers, and social scientists. Black workers, on the other hand, are more likely to be funeral directors, welfare workers, and teachers in segregated schools. The same situation exists in the other occupational categories, sometimes in even more extreme forms. For example, among clerical workers are grouped both white insurance adjusters and black postal clerks, among sales workers both white stockbrokers and Puerto Rican sales clerks. In other words, the disparities evident in broad-based occupational distributions reveal only a relatively small proportion of the job barriers that actually confront minority workers.

At the bottom of the occupational ladder, the respective concentrations of blacks and whites are, of course, reversed. As Table 12.3 reveals, two-thirds of all black workers are concentrated in the lower occupational categories, and, again, the disparities in actual jobs are great. Black women are maids in private homes or maids in hotels and office buildings. Black men are day laborers, bus drivers, and janitors. The better service and blue-collar jobs, including firefighters, police, bartenders, and teamsters, are largely reserved for whites. The fact that minority workers are employed less often and for fewer hours is of relatively little significance in comparison with this uneven distribution of occupational opportunities.[12]

Wages

Job disparities *within* occupational categories are reflected in wages. Table 12.4 displays the weekly earnings of whites, blacks, and Hispanics working in the *same* occupational

---

[12]Kimberly Bayard, Judith Hellerstein, David Neumark, and Kenneth Troske, "Why Are Racial and Ethnic Wage Gaps Larger for Men Than for Women? Exploring the Role of Segregation," Cambridge, MA: National Bureau of Economic Research, March 1999.

TABLE 12.4 Weekly Earnings, by Occupation and Race

Occupational Status	Median Earnings ($) of Male Workers		
	White	Black	Hispanic
White collar			
Professional	1,074	722	873
Managers and administrators	1,201	801	859
Sales workers	788	426	590
Clerical workers	625	517	513
Blue collar			
Craftspeople	637	570	480
Operatives	618	539	452
Transport drivers	587	508	474
Nonfarm laborers	408	390	360
Service workers	492	421	393
Farm workers	371	361	356

Source: U.S. Bureau of Labor Statistics (2005 data for full-time wage and salary workers).

category. Within professional occupations, for example, the typical majority white worker earns $1,074 per week, substantially more than blacks ($722) or Hispanics ($873) working in the same broad occupational category. These disparities reflect the facts that minority workers (1) hold different *jobs* within a given occupation; (2) are likely to be more concentrated in certain *industries*; and (3) may be paid less for the same work.[13]

Training

Another disparity between majority and minority workers relates to training. Workers in the U.S. economy get most of their skill training on the job. This on-the-job training (OJT) provides the basis for both job security and later advancement. In general, the more training an employer "invests" in a worker, the faster the worker is likely to advance on the job. The additional human capital acquired also makes a worker more attractive to other employers.[14]

The amount of training actually received by whites is nearly double that received by minority workers. White workers report that they are more likely to receive on-the-job training and to get it for a longer period of time.[15] As a consequence, observed disparities in occupations and earnings may understate eventual income differences.

WHO DISCRIMINATES?

It is not easy to visualize so much discrimination taking place in the labor market. It is even more difficult to picture those persons or groups who actually engage in discrim-

---

[13] Some evidence of pure wage discrimination is contained in Major G. Coleman, "Job Skill and Black Male Wage Discrimination," *Social Science Quarterly* (December 2003), pp. 892–205.

[14] For the theory and experience of training programs, see Orley Ashenfelter and Robert LaLonde, eds., *The Economics of Training* (2 vols.) (Lyme, NH: Edgar Reference Collection, 1996).

[15] Saul D. Hoffman, "On-the-Job Training: Differences by Race and Sex," *Monthly Labor Review* (July 1981). For more recent estimates, see Jonathan Veum, "Training Among Young Adults: Who, What Kind, and for How Long," *Monthly Labor Review* (August 1993), pp. 27–32.

ination. Very few of us can readily identify anyone as an outright racist. The whole notion of purposeful maltreatment simply runs counter to the way we are accustomed to viewing ourselves or the marketplace. Nevertheless, employers, unions, employees, employment agencies, and training programs are all implicated in the charge of labor-market discrimination. To understand how so many individuals and groups are involved, we must return to the nature of discrimination.

Institutionalized Discrimination

Much market discrimination is unintended. Even persons free of prejudice or animosity may engage in discriminatory patterns of behavior. Although such unintentional practices make fewer headlines, their impact on minority employment opportunities is no less important. Traditional company recruitment practices provide a simple illustration. Most companies, large or small, rely heavily on existing employees for new recruits. If new jobs open up, present employees usually are able to locate friends or relatives who want the new positions. Such word-of-mouth recruitment systems are remarkably efficient. Present employees know the company, the jobs, and the applicants; therefore, they are in a position to match jobs and people accurately. Word-of-mouth recruitment is also inexpensive; no outside agencies need be contacted, and advertisement costs are kept to a minimum. Large companies are so impressed with this recruitment system that they offer bonuses to employees who bring in new workers.

Word-of-mouth recruitment practices, although efficient, tend to exclude minority workers from better jobs. Would-be minority applicants do not have a network of friends in better employment positions. Accordingly, they are seldom aware of developing opportunities and are rarely brought to the attention of recruitment personnel. Even in the absence of willful discrimination, they are effectively cut off from new jobs.[16]

Recruitment outside the firm does not always assure equal access either. Companies are generally unfamiliar with the people and skills available in minority residential areas, especially ghetto areas. They do not know who, how, or where to recruit. As a result, they tend to rely on traditional sources and agencies of recruitment more readily accessible to whites.[17] Would-be minority applicants also experience a certain hesitancy in approaching unfamiliar companies or employment agencies. Knowing that prejudice exists and having possibly confronted explicit discrimination themselves, minority job seekers are often reluctant to risk embarrassment or harassment. They rely, instead, on familiar sources and companies with established reputations in the community for fair treatment. Recent converts to equal employment opportunity have difficulty communicating their new intentions.

Overt Discrimination

While these institutionalized patterns of behavior constitute a barrier to truly equal employment opportunity, we cannot ignore the impact of overt discrimination. Not all

---

[16]Informal (e.g., word of mouth) job searching is particularly disadvantageous for Hispanic job seekers according to Gary P. Green, Leann M. Tigges, and Daniel Diaz, "Racial and Ethnic Differences in Job-Search Strategies in Atlanta, Boston, and Los Angeles," *Social Science Quarterly* (June 1999), pp. 263–278. For a detailed analysis of hiring patterns, see Philip Moss and Chris Tilly, *Stories Employers Tell: Race, Skill, and Hiring in America* (New York: Russell Sage, 2001).

[17]See Kathryn M. Neckerman and Joleen Kirschenman, "Hiring Strategies, Racial Bias, and Inner-City Workers," *Social Problems* (November 1991), pp. 433–447, for more discussion of how blacks and low-income job seekers are disadvantaged in the hiring process.

TABLE 12.5 Perceptions of Racism (percent)

Question: In general, how much of a problem do you think racism in the workplace is for black families today?

Responses	White	Black
Big problem	25	46
Somewhat of a problem	43	34
Not a problem	22	12
Don't know	10	8

Source: Nationwide *Newsweek* poll conducted by Princeton Survey Research Associates, April 1999.

discriminatory practices are innocent; some exclusionary practices are motivated by outright racism. As Table 12.5 indicates, a majority of both whites and blacks recognizes the existence of such overt discrimination. Here we can only review some historical examples.

LABOR UNIONS

Labor unions have often come under attack as instruments of racial discrimination. Because labor unions are often large and highly visible, they are easy to target. They also tend to control access to the better-paid jobs in crafts or industries for which minority job seekers are at present most qualified. High-status employment areas of lesser union strength, among them clerical, technical, and professional work, tend to require higher educational credentials. Hence, unions are sometimes in a position to provide a fast route to improved economic status.

AFL

Unions haven't always made that route available to minority workers. In fact, the early history of labor unions was marked by overt discrimination. Although the American Federation of Labor (AFL) was founded on the principles of racial and worker solidarity, its practices quickly departed from that philosophy. As early as 1895, nine years after its inception, the AFL compromised on the issue of racial equality by admitting deliberately discriminatory unions. By 1899 the AFL was even admitting unions whose constitutions explicitly forbade black membership, thereby forsaking even the pretense of racial equality. This development was particularly damaging to black workers because the AFL was strongest in those areas where black employment skills were concentrated, namely, the crafts, such as carpentry, blacksmithing, and mechanical arts. Indeed, at the time of the Civil War black workers dominated craft employment in the South, outnumbering white craftspeople five to one. As the craft union movement grew, however, blacks lost their foothold in the job market. Black craftspeople were forced out of their jobs and denied access to new ones. Apprenticeship programs were also closed, thereby eliminating future opportunities for employment.

While racial prejudice was at the root of much union discrimination, economic motivations were dominant. The nascent unions knew that their strength and welfare depended on their ability to control job entry. Any potential craftsperson was viewed as a direct economic threat. The AFL unions not only sought to eliminate competition from blacks but also worked vigorously to restrain all immigration from abroad.

The Chinese were viewed as "people of vice and sexual immorality who were incompatible with our moral concepts."[18] Japanese and Koreans were no less undesirable. Even European immigrants were viewed as a threat to economic security and organizational strength. Hence, it is probably fair to conclude that the AFL was egalitarian in its discriminatory practices; that is, it discriminated against all potential competition with little regard to race, creed, or color! Where racial arguments were employed, their primary purpose was to camouflage narrower economic interests. Nevertheless, black workers were most harmed, since they were the largest and closest competition.

CIO

The Congress of Industrial Organizations (CIO) emerged in 1935 in a changed economic climate and with a different constituency. Whereas the AFL had focused on craft labor, the CIO directed its attentions to the mass of workers on assembly lines and in less skilled jobs. These jobs generally required less training and experience and were concentrated more in the North. Not only were blacks significantly represented in these jobs, they also constituted an enormous threat to future union strength. If excluded from the industrial unions, black workers could be used by employers as strike-breakers to undercut union power. The same possibility did not exist in craft unions because specific skills were required for available jobs. Hence, the CIO had a powerful economic incentive to lower racial barriers to union entry. This combined with the egalitarian outlook of its leaders, especially John L. Lewis, led the CIO to establish nondiscriminatory membership policies.[19]

AFL-CIO'

The AFL-CIO merger in 1955 did not revolutionize union practices. While the new union organization was founded on stronger antidiscrimination principles, it did little to alter the actual practices of local affiliates. After the splintering of the AFL-CIO in 2005 (by breakaway unions that formed the Change to Win Coalition), the AFL-CIO had even less control over local unions. The national AFL-CIO organization, however, has remained a strong lobbying force for civil rights legislation and economic issues (e.g., minimum wages) that are important to minority workers.

EMPLOYERS

Like unions, business management tends to reflect the interests and attitudes of its members: Some employers harbor racial prejudices and stereotyped views of minority workers. Even more prevalent, however, is a general reluctance to engage in actions that are controversial or merely tangential to primary business pursuits. Employers are hesitant to challenge traditional hiring practices or to confront what they regard as the community's racial attitudes. Hence, employers will often ignore potential minority workers, not as a result of their own prejudice, but because they fear that such hiring

---

[18]Cited by Herbert Hill in *Employment, Race, and Poverty,* eds. Arthur M. Ross and Herbert Hill (New York: Harcourt Brace Jovanovich, 1967), p. 389.

[19]The tendency of craft unions to be more discriminatory was also documented in the 1970s; see Orley Ashenfelter, "Racial Discrimination and Trade Unionism," *Journal of Political Economy* (May 1972); and Duane E. Leigh, "Racial Discrimination and Labor Unions," *Journal of Human Resources* (Fall 1978). The general impact of unions on racial inequality is examined in E. M. Beck, "Labor Unionism and Racial Inequality: A Time-Series Analysis of the Post–World War II Period," *American Journal of Sociology, 85* (1980).

will trigger the prejudices of white employees or customers.[20] Employers have very little incentive to stir up racial troubles or even to bother determining whether such troubles would actually emerge. Profits, politics, recreation, and even local charities command more attention and commitment. As a result, only the most cautious antidiscriminatory actions are undertaken, and then usually only as a result of economic or social pressures, such as boycotts or legal action.[21]

Another barrier to more affirmative action on the part of business management arises from the nature of collective bargaining. Where management does, in fact, decide to hire minority workers on a more equal basis, the unions are likely to demand reciprocal concessions. Unions tend to view management initiatives as an encroachment on their own prerogatives. Altered hiring practices are interpreted as a concession to management, so the union seeks compensation in other areas, such as wages or working conditions. Thus, the cost of affirmative action escalates, and management is even less likely to press for the elimination of discriminatory employment patterns.

Hiring Practices

Finally, even "objective" hiring practices of employers may have discriminatory effects. We have already observed how word-of-mouth recruitment and traditional advertising tends to exclude minority workers. Another obstacle emerges from the use of employment tests and other credentials as hiring criteria. All too often, tests and educational credentials used to screen out prospective employees exclude a disproportionate number of minority workers. Moreover, such tests may have no direct relationship to job performance. Under such circumstances, the tests simply reduce an employer's hiring costs by reducing the number of extended interviews. In the process, however, many minority workers lose potential job opportunities. Such nonfunctional tests were outlawed by the U.S. Supreme Court in 1972 (*Griggs* v. *Duke Power Company*) but have not been eliminated completely.

Statistical Discrimination

Even if all such tests were eliminated, minority workers would still suffer from *statistical discrimination*. Employers never know for sure which job seekers will turn out to be the best employees. Tests and educational credentials help reduce such uncertainty. If all such screening criteria are eliminated, employers may rely more on racial characteristics. Because white workers have, on average, more education, skill, and experience than minority workers, an employer is statistically "safer" in hiring white workers. In other words, screening out minority workers on the basis of their lower *average* qualifications may be an efficient recruitment technique, particularly if no other screening mechanisms are available. In this case, minority workers are excluded

---

[20]The productivity of white males may also decline if newly hired minority upset traditional on-the-job social relations; see Barbara Bergmann and William Darity Jr., "Social Relations, Productivity, and Employer Discrimination," *Monthly Labor Review* (August 1981).

[21]Evidence of overt employer discrimination in the hiring process is offered by Genevieve M. Kenney and Douglas A. Wissoker, "An Analysis of the Correlates of Discrimination Facing Young Hispanic Job-Seekers," *American Economic Review* (June 1994), pp. 674–683. A much more exhaustive analysis of employer hiring practices is contained in Philip Moss and Chris Tilly, *Stories Employers Tell* (New York: Russell Sage, 2001).

from equal consideration on statistical grounds, not because of employer prejudice.[22] Of course, to the minority job seeker, the end result is the same.

Finally, it must be noted that managers tend to hire people like themselves. This may be human nature. It becomes discrimination, however, when managers are predominantly white males.

Competitive Pressures

In a highly competitive market, employers who discriminated in these ways would be at an economic disadvantage. Employers who routinely hired white workers over more qualified minority workers would have higher costs and lower productivity. By contrast, equal-opportunity employers would reap the benefit of the cheaper, more productive minority workers shunned by discriminating employers. As a result, nondiscriminating employers would reap larger profits and increasing market share. In a *perfectly* competitive market, discriminating employers would eventually be driven out of business.

In reality, markets aren't *perfectly* competitive. Information on the productivity of both current and prospective employees is imperfect. As a result, even nondiscriminating employers may engage in statistical discrimination. Furthermore, firms with strong brand identity (market power) can typically absorb the higher costs of discriminatory hiring practices. Finally, the costs of continuing discrimination may be small relative to the total costs of operating a business. In that case, competitive pressures may not be sufficient to wipe out discriminatory practices.[23]

CLASS DISCRIMINATION IN THE LABOR MARKET

Minority racial groups are not the only workers who suffer discrimination in labor markets. Racial discrimination has a counterpart in class discrimination. In this case, individuals from low-income backgrounds are consistently denied equal access to better jobs and pay.

Employers, like the larger society, tend to have low estimates of the capabilities of job applicants who are poorly dressed or from "bad" neighborhoods. There is an underlying conviction that poverty reflects personal inadequacy (Flawed Character). As a result, poor applicants are viewed differently than others and must exhibit exceptional talents to obtain competitive jobs. As a result, if their talents are only equal to, say, middle class applicants, then prejudice is likely to deny employment to the poor.

These discriminatory practices are often institutionalized in the recruitment procedures of companies. As we noted earlier, corporations seldom recruit in poverty areas. They know virtually nothing about available talent in poor neighborhoods and expend little effort to increase their knowledge. As a consequence, poor job seekers and company

---

[22]The concept of *statistical discrimination* is discussed in Edmund S. Phelps, "The Statistical Theory of Racism and Sexism," *American Economic Review* (September 1972); and Dennis J. Aigner and Glen G. Cain, "Statistical Theories of Discrimination in Labor Markets," *Industrial and Labor Relations Review* (January 1977). More recent evidence is examined in Gerald S. Oettinger, "Statistical Discrimination and the Early Career Evolution of the Black-White Wage Gap," *Journal of Labor Economics* (Winter 1996), pp. 52–78.

[23]For more discussion of market-based discrimination see Kenneth J. Arrow, "What Has Economics to Say About Discrimination?" and Glenn C. Loury, "Discrimination in the Post–Civil Rights Era: Beyond Market Interactions," *Journal of Economic Perspectives* (Spring 1998). For evidence on the relationship of firm-level market power and the extent of discrimination, see Judith K. Hellerstein, David Neumark, and Kenneth R. Troske, "Market Forces and Sex Discrimination," *Journal of Human Resources* (Spring 2002), pp. 353–380.

recruiters seldom make contact. The same kind of isolation results from the word-of-mouth recruitment practices previously mentioned. Like blacks and Hispanics, poor whites tend to have comparatively few friends or acquaintances employed at higher-status jobs. They thus have little knowledge of or access to good jobs that are opening up. What jobs they hear of are those they have always encountered: dirty, low-paid, and menial.

Class discrimination in the labor market, then, means that poor job seekers have less chance to obtain employment than nonpoor job seekers of equal ability. Racial discrimination has the same effect for blacks and other minority groups, sex discrimination the same effect for women. In all cases, discrimination takes place as a result of individual prejudices and institutionalized practices. The poor, like blacks and Hispanics, have many personal characteristics and backgrounds unfamiliar to middle-class employers, employment agencies, and even unions. Conduct, speech, and dress are among those factors that create communication barriers. Employers tend to see these differences as indicators of ability rather than as the result of socioeconomic environment. It is assumed that the poor will not be as able or dependable on the job. Workers are not sought from poorer areas and, when they come forth, are unfavorably considered.[24]

SEX DISCRIMINATION IN THE LABOR MARKET

The same forces that tend to constrain the earnings of minorities and lower-income classes also operate to limit the employment and income opportunities of women. Here again, we must take into account the fact that women enter the labor market with less human capital than men do, especially when measured in terms of advanced degrees. They also tend to be trained for different kinds of work, as a result of both societal pressures and overt discrimination in the educational system. These handicaps help explain why women exhibit less labor force participation, inferior occupations, and lower pay. But such handicaps do not provide a complete explanation: Female workers additionally suffer from limited access to jobs for which they are otherwise qualified.

OCCUPATIONAL SEGREGATION

As we noted in our discussion of racial discrimination (see Table 12.3), occupational segregation is a significant source of earnings disparities. This mechanism is especially important for women as well, as they tend to be relegated to a limited number of occupations and an even more limited number of jobs within each occupation. According to estimates by Heidi Hartmann and Donald Treimann, occupational segregation accounts for over a third of the wage gap between men and women.[25]

---

[24]These kinds of class barriers may help explain the handicap of low-income backgrounds on later income, as observed in Mary Corcoran, R. Gordon, D. Laren, and G. Solon, "The Associations Between Men's Economic Status and Their Family and Community Origins," *Journal of Human Resources* (Fall 1992), pp. 575–601.

[25]Heidi Hartmann and Donald Treimann, eds., *Women, Work, and Wages: Equal Pay for Jobs of Equal Value* (Washington, DC: National Academy Press, 1981). For an analysis of *why* female-dominated occupations pay lower wages, see David A. Macpherson and Barry T. Hirsh, "Wage and Gender Composition: Why Do Women's Jobs Pay Less?" *Journal of Labor Economics* (1995). Aggregate measures of occupational segregation are discussed in Mary C. King, "Occupational Segregation by Race and Sex, 1940–88," *Monthly Labor Review* (April 1992), pp. 30–36. Thomas Wells shows how within-occupation segregation declined significantly in the 1980s and more slowly in the 1990s; see his "Changes in Occupational Sex Segregation During the 1980s and 1990s," *Social Science Quarterly* (June 1999), pp. 370–379.

TABLE 12.6 A Nonliberated Labor Force

	Traditional Jobs for Women	Percent of Jobs Held by Women	Nontraditional Jobs for Women	Percent of Jobs Held by Women
Professional and technical	Home economics teachers	100	College economics teachers	12
	Librarians	84	Engineers	11
	Registered nurses	93	Lawyers	29
	Elementary teachers	84	Dentists	17
	Dental hygienists	99	Clergy	14
	Dietitians	84	Pilots	3
Managers and administrators	Personnel	69	Funeral directors	18
	Insurance	69	Construction	11
Sales workers	Demonstrators	69	Sales representatives	40
Clerical workers	Secretaries	99	Mail carriers	32
	Bank tellers	90	Meter readers	10
	Telephone operators	92	Dispatchers	46
Craftspeople	Dressmakers	90	Electricians	2
	Decorators	58	Telephone lineworkers	7
Operatives	Sewing machine	80	Taxicab drivers	13
	Laundry/dry cleaning	64	Printers	17
	Typesetters	62	Truck drivers	5
Service	Nurses' aides	90	Police officers	17
	Waiters/Waitresses	77	Bartenders	50
	Child care workers	98	Firefighters	2

Source: U.S. Bureau of Labor Statistics, unpublished data from 1999 Current Population Survey.

The statistics in Table 12.6 provide a clue as to how high the sex barriers are when one begins to examine the labor market in detail. Within the "professional and technical" occupational category, for example, we discover that there are clearly "female jobs" and "male jobs": 93 percent of all registered nurses are women, while only 11 percent of our engineers are women. The same kind of imbalance is evident throughout the list.

Nor is this the end of the story. Even within the more detailed occupations of Table 12.6, men and women tend to be employed at different kinds of jobs, in different industries, or in different work settings. Consider just one example, that of waiters and waitresses. Women comprise 77 percent of that category, but how many of them are employed in the best restaurants (where prices and tips are highest, incidentally)? Very few.

These male–female job disparities *within* occupational groups result in sharply different wages for men and women. The median weekly earnings of full-time female workers ($585 in 2005) is only four-fifths of male workers ($722). The same kind of differential exists within most occupations.[26] Like minorities, women are also less likely to receive OJT training that will increase their responsibilities and wages.

---

[26]Within-occupation segregation may actually be increasing, according to William E. Spriggs and Rhonda M. Williams, "A Logit Decomposition Analysis of Occupational Segregation," *Review of Economics and Statistics* (May 1996), pp. 348–355.

TABLE 12.7 Global Gender Wage Gaps

In the United States women's wages are only 75 percent of men's wages. Much smaller "gender gaps" exist in Scandinavia and the South Pacific. Japan, however, has a much wider gender gap.

Country	Female-to-Male Hourly Wage Ratios (%)
Sweden	90
Australia	88
Norway	87
Denmark	83
France	81
New Zealand	81
Finland	78
United States	**75**
West Germany	74
United Kingdom	72
Canada	71
Switzerland	67
Japan	50

Source: Data for various years in the 1990s, as reported in Jane Weldfogel, "Understanding the 'Family Gap' in Pay for Women with Children," *Journal of Economic Perspectives* (Winter 1998), pp. 137–186.

The "gender gap" in pay is not unique to the United States. But as Table 12.7 illustrates, the U.S. gender gap is larger than in many other industrialized nations.

Job Interruptions

A popular explanation for these job and pay disparities is the lesser labor force attachment of women. Most women who do work either start their careers after having children or interrupt their careers for that purpose. The job interruption that typically accompanies childbirth translates into lost job experience and thus less human capital development. Can this "natural" barrier to female productivity explain occupational and income differentials? Partially, but *only* partially. As the President's Council of Economic Advisers observed:

> One important factor influencing the (earnings) differential is experience. The lack of continuity in women's attachment to the labor force means that they will not have accumulated as much experience as men at a given age. The relatively steeper rise of men's income with age has been attributed to their greater accumulation of experience, of "human capital" acquired on the job.
>
> [But] a differential, perhaps on the order of 20 percent, between the earnings of men and women remains after adjusting for factors such as education, work experience during the year, and even lifelong work experience.[27]

---

[27] *Economic Report of the President* (Washington, DC: U.S. Government Printing Office, 1973), pp. 104–106.

More recent estimates, using panel data and improved methodology, suggest that the residual discrimination differential is considerably smaller.[28] However, the existence of a sex-based differential is undisputed. Accordingly, we cannot dismiss occupational and earnings differentials between men and women on the basis of the "natural" responsibilities of childbirth. Discrimination is clearly at work here: The pay and job status of women workers are being constrained by exclusionary employment practices. Moreover, we must take care to note that the same kind of negative feedbacks that constrain the human capital development of minority workers affect women, too. Why should a woman postpone childbirth or pursue a lengthy and difficult course of study if it appears that she will not receive commensurate rewards in the labor market? Role differentiation and labor-market discrimination tend to reinforce each other.[29]

Summary

Minority racial groups, women, and the poor generally start out in the labor market at a distinct competitive disadvantage, largely as a result of discrimination in the educational system. Their handicaps do not end there, however. In the labor market itself, these groups do not have equal opportunity to make the best of their disadvantaged beginnings. Prejudice and institutional employment practices combine to handicap them still further.

Racial and class discrimination in the labor market takes many forms. Some employers and unions willfully exclude blacks, Hispanics, and other minority workers. Other employers rely on recruitment procedures that have the same effect on minority racial groups, women, and the poor. Doubts about the capabilities of individuals who fall into any of these categories also limit employment and promotional possibilities. Notions of what kind of work is "proper" for minority workers and fear of employee or community disapproval restrains even unprejudiced, but profit-maximizing, employers from providing equal opportunity. The cumulative impact of these practices is evident: Members of minority or poor populations end up working less often, for fewer hours, at less attractive jobs—and, ultimately, for less income.

---

[28] Stephen Jarrell and T. D. Stanley, "Declining Bias and Gender Wage Discrimination: A Meta-Regression Analysis," *Journal of Human Resources* (Summer 2004), pp. 828–836; also Sharmila Choudhury, "Reassessing the Male-Female Wage Differential: A Fixed Effects Approach," *Southern Economic Journal* (October 1993), pp. 327–340.

[29] For an analysis of feedback effects, see David Neumark and Michele McLennan, "Sex Discrimination and Women's Labor Market Outcomes," *Journal of Human Resources* (Fall 1995), pp. 713–746. A study of business-school seniors, however, found no negative feedback effects on women's labor supply; see Francine D. Blau and Marianne A. Ferber, "Career Plans and Expectations of Young Women and Men," *Journal of Human Resources* (Fall 1991), pp. 581–607. The theoretical problem of assessing causation in similar situations is discussed in Glen G. Cain, "The Uses and Limits of Statistical Analysis in Measuring Economic Discrimination," in *Essays on the Economics of Discrimination*, ed. E. Hoffman (Kalamazoo, MI: Upjohn Institute, 1991).

Further Reading

Bergmann, Barbara R., *In Defense of Affirmative Action*. New York: Basic Books, 1996, Chapters 2 and 3.

Blau, Francine D., Marianne A. Ferber, and Anne E. Winkler, *The Economics of Women, Men, and Work*, 5th ed. Upper Saddle River, NJ: Prentice-Hall, 2005.

Darity, William Jr., ed., *Economics and Discrimination* (2 vols.). Lyme, NH: Edgar Reference Collection, 1995.

Darity, William A., and Patrick L. Mason, "Evidence on Discrimination in Employment: Codes of Color, Codes of Gender," *Journal of Economic Perspectives* (Spring 1998), pp. 63–90.

Dyer, Susan K., ed., *Behind the Pay Gap*. Washington, DC: American Association of University Women, April 2007.

Jacobsen, Joyce P., "Trends in Work Force Sex Segregation, 1960–1990," *Social Science Quarterly* (March 1994), pp. 204–211.

Jarrell, Stephen, and T. D. Stanley, "Declining Bias and Gender Wage Discrimination: A Meta-Regression Analysis," *Journal of Human Resources* (Summer 2004), pp. 828–838.

Massey, Douglas, *Categorically Unequal: The American Stratification System*, New York: Russell Sage, 2007.

McCall, Leslie, "Sources of Racial Wage Inequality in Metropolitan Labor Markets: Racial, Ethnic, and Gender Differences," *American Sociological Review* (August 2001), pp. 520–541.

Moss, Philip, and Chris Tilly, *Stories Employers Tell*. New York: Russell Sage, 2001.

Rose, Stephen, and Heidi Hartman, "The Long-Term Gender Gap," *Challenge* (Sept./Oct. 2004), pp. 30–50.

Welch, Finis, ed., *The Causes and Consequences of Increasing Inequality*. Chicago, IL: University of Chicago Press, 2001.

Web Links

U.S. Bureau of Labor Statistics. Data on earnings by age, race, gender: http://www.stats.bls.gov

National Bureau of Economic Research. Occasional studies on discrimination: http://www.nber.org

CHAPTER 13
WELFARE PROGRAMS
༺๑༻

Public policy toward the poor has been plagued by a persistent dilemma. Should we provide poor people with enough income to buy essential shelter, food, and clothing, or should we instead focus on improving opportunities for the poor to *earn* more income? In a nutshell, should public policy emphasize *welfare* or *work*?

The choice of policy emphasis is rooted in views of poverty causation. If the poor have Flawed Character, then welfare benefits might be viewed as an inappropriate "reward" for moral turpitude. Indeed, the Big Brother view of poverty contends that more generous welfare provisions actually *encourage* socially destructive behavior, thus increasing the incidence of poverty. President Ronald Reagan went so far as to assert that welfare is "a cancer that is destroying those that it should succor and threatening society itself."

Others have a more benign view of welfare. They contend that a lack of jobs, good education, and training prevents the poor from achieving financial independence. Until the fetters of Restricted Opportunity are eliminated, the poor will need direct financial support.

There is plenty of room between these opposing views to "fine-tune" welfare policies. Indeed, it is in this broad middle ground that most of the details of welfare policy are settled. Even the historic welfare reforms of 1996—the reforms that President Clinton had promised would "end welfare as we know it"—reflected elements of the Flawed Character, Restricted Opportunity, and Big Brother perspectives. The Flawed Character perspective led to time limits on welfare eligibility and toughened work requirements. Increased funding of child care and medical assistance were motivated by the concern over Restricted Opportunity. A sense that Big Brother was getting in the way prompted Congress to turn more program and funding decisions over to the states.

This chapter examines the motivations for these and earlier welfare reforms. We first look at how welfare is distinguished from other income transfer programs, then describe the major cash and in-kind programs that comprise the welfare system. As we will see, the many federal, state, and local programs that provide income assistance to the poor are less a welfare "system" than a collage of overlapping activities. The 1996 welfare reforms accentuated this diversity by reducing the federal role in program design and funding. The reforms themselves were a response to the conflicting goals that make all public assistance initiatives so complex and controversial.

WELFARE VERSUS SOCIAL INSURANCE

An important starting point for any discussion of welfare policy is a clear delineation of what constitutes a "welfare" program. The federal government spends a trillion dollars a year on income transfers, and state and local governments spend billions more. Not all of these transfers are "welfare" payments, however.

TYPES OF INCOME TRANSFERS

Means Testing

What distinguishes welfare programs from other income transfers are the eligibility conditions for benefit receipt. Eligibility for welfare benefits is based on income and assets; only poor people qualify. That is to say, all welfare programs are *means-tested* income transfers.

Event Eligibility

The Social Security program is twice as large as all the welfare programs combined. Unlike welfare, however, Social Security retirement benefits are not conditioned on current income or assets: Both rich people and poor people get Social Security benefits. The only conditions for benefit receipt are age and work history. Once a person with at least ten years of work experience reaches retirement age, he or she can start collecting monthly Social Security benefits.

Other transfer programs that are conditioned on *events* rather than *means* are Medicare and unemployment insurance. Once individuals reach age 65, they automatically qualify for Medicare assistance. Individuals who lose their jobs qualify for weekly unemployment benefits if they satisfy specific work-experience requirements. Generally, all event-conditioned transfers are referred to as *social insurance* programs because they insure against income losses that result from specific events. As Figure 13.1 illustrates, social insurance programs overwhelm welfare programs in the federal budget.

EITC

One program depicted in Figure 13.1 is the Earned Income Tax Credit (EITC). Because the refundable tax credits paid out in the EITC program are means-tested, the EITC program is unquestionably a welfare program. In fact, it has become the nation's most expensive welfare program. Much of its benefits go to people who are *near*-poor, however, rather than poor. Furthermore, the benefits one receives from EITC depend on how much an individual *works*. Because EITC benefits are conditioned on wages, that program is reviewed in Chapter 15 ("Employment Policies"). Social insurance programs are reviewed in Chapter 14.

FIGURE 13.1 Federal Income Transfers: Welfare versus Social Insurance

WELFARE
Food Stamps
TANF
EITC
SSI
Housing aid
Child nutrition
Medicaid

SOCIAL INSURANCE
Social Security
Medicare
Unemployment Insurance
Child Support Enforcement

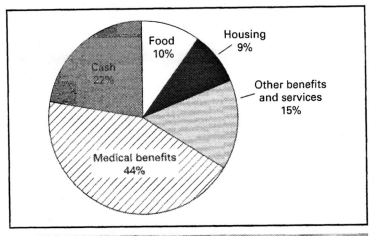

FIGURE 13.2 Welfare Spending by Type of Benefit

Note: Includes federal, state, and local spending on means-tested benefits and services.

Source: U.S. Congress, House Ways and Means Committee, *2004 Green Book,* Appendix K (Washington, DC: U.S. Government Printing Office, 2004).

Cash versus In-Kind

Although welfare programs are generally smaller than the major social insurance programs, they are far more numerous. In 2005, there were at least 80 different means-tested programs. One way to fashion some order out of this array is to distinguish among programs by the type of benefit they provide. Some programs provide outright *cash* assistance ("welfare checks"), while others provide *in-kind* assistance—items like housing, food, and medical assistance—rather than cash. Figure 13.2 shows that only a fourth of all public assistance is conveyed in cash. Most federal, state, and local welfare spending is on in-kind benefits, particularly medical assistance (e.g., Medicaid), food (e.g., food stamps), and housing (e.g., rent subsidies). We will first examine the major cash welfare programs, then turn to means-tested programs that offer in-kind benefits and services.

WELFARE: THE CASH ASSISTANCE PROGRAMS

Table 13.1 provides a summary view of the major programs that provide cash assistance to the poor. The four programs listed in the table are directed to very different population groups. The federal Supplemental Security Income (SSI) program was established for the aged, the blind, and the permanently disabled. It was introduced in July 1973, taking the place of three previous programs.[1] As of 2005 it was providing cash assistance to 7 million people at an estimated annual cost of approximately $37 billion. The federal-state Temporary Aid to Needy Families (TANF) program (formerly, the Aid to Families with Dependent Children [AFDC] program) was serving 4.4 million people in the spring of 2005, at an annual cost of roughly $17 billion, of which $10 billion was in

---

[1]The SSI program was enacted as part of the 1972 Social Security Act Amendments and consolidated the Old Age Assistance (OAA), Aid to the Blind (AB), and the Aid to Permanently and Totally Disabled (APTD) programs.

TABLE 13.1 Cash Assistance Programs (2005)

Program Target Group	Number of Current Recipients (millions)	Average Benefit per Recipient ($ per month)	Total Annual Payments ($ billions)
SSI: Supplemental Security Income			
Aged and disabled poor	7.2	452	37
TANF: Temporary Aid to Needy Families			
Poor families with children	4.4	150	10
EITC: Earned Income Tax Credit			
Working Poor	21.1	154	39
GA: General Assistance			
Poor people not covered elsewhere	1.4	190	3

Source: U.S. Department of Health and Human Services; U.S. Office of Management and Budget; U.S. Social Security Administration. Total outlays include administrative expenses.

cash benefits. As noted earlier, the EITC program provides cash benefits to *working* poor households. The fourth program, General Assistance (GA), is operated solely under state and local auspices to provide help to those who are poor but do not fit one of the other three categories (mostly childless couples and individuals).[2]

INADEQUACIES

The statistics provided in Table 13.1 suggest that we are giving a lot of money to a lot of people. Expenditures on just the four cash programs listed in the table approach $90 billion per year. If other cash programs and all state/local outlays were included, the total would exceed $100 billion. To a lot of taxpayers, the enormity of these outlays suggests that welfare payments must be financing a pretty good life for a whole lot of people. Hard-working taxpayers are apt to conclude that they are being "ripped off" by being forced to finance the "good life" for so many nonworkers.

The realities of welfare are quite different, however. Although $100 billion is a lot of money, there are also lots of poor people. In early 2005, nearly 37 million Americans were officially designated as poor—even *after* receiving welfare benefits. Moreover, the poverty gap that remained after the distribution of welfare checks was approximately $120 billion. Hence, it would take a lot more cash to eliminate poverty. As it is, the $100 billion in annual benefits works out to less than $3,000 per poor person. Hence, a family wholly dependent on welfare benefits would have an income well below official poverty thresholds.

The $100 billion of cash welfare benefits aren't distributed equally across the poverty population, of course. How much welfare a household receives depends on what program it qualifies for and how much nonwelfare income it receives. The typical TANF family (mother and two children), for example, received only $4,800 of cash assistance in 2005. That was less than half the amount the government had determined such families need. A budget that small simply does not go far, no matter how thinly it is spread. Just

---

[2]For an overview of the GA program see L. Jerome Gallagher et al., *State General Assistance Programs, 1998* (Washington, DC: Urban Institute, 1999).

recall how little food, shelter, and clothing are provided by the much larger poverty budget (roughly $15,600). It would be a strange individual who forsook any but the poorest paying and most loathsome job for such a "free ride."

In light of the meager cash benefits available to TANF recipients, it seems unlikely that wage earners, even low-paid ones, would rush to the welfare rolls. To guard against this possibility, however, most states set limits on how much property (e.g., home equity, car, bank balance) a recipient may own. Hence, a person whose *income* falls may be forced to sell her *assets* in order to get welfare benefits. Even then, the "free ride" on welfare doesn't last long. Federal rules set a five-year limit on welfare receipt and require recipients to engage in some work activity after two years of TANF benefit receipt. States can be more generous with *state*-financed welfare programs, but few are.

A discussion of welfare programs must begin, then, from the observation that financial dependence on public assistance is not comfortable. Families that depend on cash welfare benefits as their *sole* source of income will have a standard of living well below levels society otherwise deems minimally adequate.

INEQUITIES

In addition to providing inadequate levels of income maintenance, the welfare system is also beset with inequities. Less than 10 million people received cash assistance in 2005, even though nearly 37 million people were counted as poor in that year. Clearly, the welfare system provides some help to many, but none at all to others. The question is: Who is denied help and for what reasons?

Two-Parent Families

Conspicuously missing from the welfare rolls in nearly every state are male-headed poor families. As we noted earlier, the SSI program aids the aged, the blind, and the disabled, while the TANF program is supposed to provide help to families with children. But of the 20 million poor people in families with children in 2005, only 4.4 million were receiving TANF assistance at any one time (Table 13.1). Thus, being poor in a family with children was not sufficient qualification for receiving welfare support; a further distinction was made between the deserving and the undeserving poor. In this case, the deserving are those children whose fathers are absent from the home. The presence of a male adult in the home is taken as prima facie evidence that the family is capable of its own support. TANF payments are largely reserved for fatherless homes, regardless of whatever needs male-headed poor families may have.

In principle, poor families with both parents present may receive welfare benefits under the TANF program. However, limitations on owned property and earnings exclude most intact families counted as poor. Prior to 1989, the individual states could elect not to provide any welfare benefits for two-parent families, and half of the states chose that option. In 1988 Congress passed legislation that requires all states to provide benefits. Most intact families remain ineligible for TANF benefits, however, due to asset and earnings limitations.[3]

---

[3]For a description of state-specific asset limitations and other eligibility conditions, see U.S. Department of Health and Human Services, *TANF Annual Report to Congress;* also see James P. Ziliak, "Income Transfers and Assets of the Poor," *Review of Economics and Statistics* (February 2003).

TABLE 13.2 TANF Payments in Selected States, 2003

Maximum Monthly Benefit for Three-Person Family	
High-benefit states	
Alaska	$ 923
California	786
Hawaii	712
Wisconsin	673
Low-benefit states	
Arkansas	204
Tennessee	185
Mississippi	170
Alabama	164

Source: U.S. Department of Health and Human Services, *TANF: Fourth Annual Report to Congress* (Washington, DC: Government Printing Office, January 2007).

Inter-Program Disparities

Even among those families poor enough to receive welfare payments, there are tremendous disparities in the amount of support provided. Notice in Table 13.1, for instance, how differently recipients of SSI and TANF are treated: SSI recipients receive on average nearly three times as much aid as TANF recipients. This disparity arises in part from taxpayers' sympathy for the aged and disabled, combined with their distrust of younger poor families. The distrust of TANF families stems largely from the assumption that they could support themselves if they so chose. Not only are the adults who benefit from TANF relatively young but their marital status—which the program itself constrains—is suspect. Public distrust of the program is heightened by the fact that large numbers of blacks, Hispanics, families headed by women, and illegitimate children participate in the program. Thus, provision of TANF benefits usually begins against a background of public mistrust and resentment.

Inter-State Disparities

Further inequities in the cash assistance programs arise from the different levels of benefits received by families in identical situations. Each state sets its own benefit levels under the TANF program. Although the "average" TANF family of three received approximately $4,800 in cash assistance in 2006, actual benefits varied widely across states: Some families in Alaska, California, and Hawaii received over $8,000 per year in welfare payments, while similar families in Mississippi received less than $1,500. Table 13.2 indicates how maximum benefits varied in other states.

Differences in state benefit levels not only imply unequal treatment of poor people, but may also alter residence decisions. People in high-benefit states may be reluctant to seek job opportunities elsewhere. Conversely, families in low-benefit states may be induced to migrate in search of higher benefits. Although the evidence on such immigration effects is mixed, the issue sparks considerable concern in high-benefit states.[4]

---

[4]See Paul E. Peterson and Mark C. Rom, *Welfare Magnets* (Washington, DC: Brookings Institution, 1990); for a different view, see William Berry, Richard Fording and Russell Hanson, "Reassessing the 'Race to the Bottom' in State Welfare Policy," *Journal of Politics* (May 2003), pp. 327–349.

Disparities in support reflect far more than differences in the cost of living. In essence, they reflect the ability and willingness of taxpayers in each state to provide for the needy. Welfare payments in Mississippi, for example, are low, both because there is little public or private money in the state and because many white Mississippians have been reluctant to spend what little there is in providing for the poor, many of whom are black.[5]

FAMILY DISINCENTIVES

While the low and uneven level of welfare benefits clearly limits their antipoverty effectiveness, those benefits may also threaten family stability. As we observed, cash welfare benefits are largely reserved for female-headed families. This targeting of benefits may affect family decisions in ways that increase the number of such families. Specifically, the number of female-headed families may increase if:

- Fathers in intact poor families leave in order to make the remaining family members eligible for welfare.
- Wives view welfare as an alternative source of economic support and so are more likely to divorce or separate in the wake of marital discord.
- Unmarried women view welfare as a source of economic support after child-rearing and so are less reluctant to become single mothers.
- Unwed mothers who previously lived with relatives use welfare benefits to establish their own households.

Critics of cash welfare have argued that such family disincentives are at the heart of America's welfare crisis. They contend that Big Brother's welfare rules have undermined the family stability of low-income families and created a growing population of female-headed families that remain impoverished and dependent. By one estimate, some 2.5 million additional children have been added to the U.S. poverty rolls by such behavioral changes—what Lowell Gallaway calls "poverty by choice."[6] A Canadian study showed that welfare benefits there affected a poor single mother's decision to marry or cohabit.[7]

Despite the evident inducement for female-headed families, there is little concrete evidence that welfare payments actually change family behavior. As Ellwood and Summers point out, the number of female-headed families has grown much faster than the number of welfare families. Furthermore, the real value of benefits *declined* in the 1980s while welfare rolls were increasing. They argue that the feminization of family structures is more a product of social values than welfare rules.[8]

---

[5]See Larry Orr, "Income Transfers as a Public Good," *American Economic Review* (June 1976); and Bradley R. Schiller, "Income Transfers as a Public Good: Comment," *American Economic Review* (December 1978).

[6]Lowell Gallaway and Richard Vedder, *Poverty, Income Distribution, the Family, and Public Policy,* a study for the Joint Economic Committee, U.S. Congress (Washington, DC: U.S. Government Printing Office, December 19, 1986). Charles Murray also highlights this family disincentive as a root cause of increased dependency; see "Does Welfare Bring More Babies?" *The Public Interest* (Spring 1992), pp. 17–30.

[7]Pierre Lefebvre and Philip Merrigan, "The Impact of Welfare Benefits on the Conjugal State of Single Mothers in Canada," *Journal of Human Resources* (Summer 1998), pp. 742–757.

[8]David Ellwood and Lawrence Summers, "Is Welfare Really the Problem?" *The Public Interest* (Spring 1986).

Although the evidence is mixed, a consensus of expert opinion appears to agree that welfare does have *some* effect on family stability.[9] Of greatest concern is the encouragement that welfare gives to unwed mothers to establish their own house-holds—households that are most likely to be poor and dependent for a long time.[10]

SAVING DISINCENTIVES

The risk of long-term dependency is heightened by the asset limits on welfare eligibility. As noted earlier, states place low ceilings on the amount of assets a welfare recipient can own. As a consequence, saving money can put welfare eligibility at risk. In other words, the very kind of prudent behavior we want to encourage is *dis*couraged by welfare regulations. Apparently, such regulations do affect behavior: when cars are exempted from the asset limitation, car ownership does increase among welfare recipients.[11]

WORK DISINCENTIVES

Family and saving disincentives are not the only problems associated with welfare. Welfare benefits also create *dis*incentives for working. In the absence of welfare bene-fits, a family would have to work or seek assistance from family, friends, or community charities. The pressure to find a job would be enormous. The availability of welfare benefits relieves that pressure. A family that does not participate in the labor market won't forsake all income: Welfare benefits will provide financial support. While not exactly the "good life," the assured flow of welfare benefits may dampen the desire to find a job.

The work disincentive implicit in any offer of welfare benefits is compounded by the way in which a family's welfare benefits are calculated. When a family applies for welfare, it is obliged to report any income at its disposal. A woman with small children, for example, might earn $150 a month by baby-sitting for neighbors. Up until 1967 wel-fare authorities subtracted any such income from the family's needs, as determined by those same authorities, and provided the difference. Suppose the welfare authorities concluded that Ms. Jones and her three children needed $400 a month: They paid her only $250, knowing that she could provide the rest.

---

[9]See Marianne Bitler, Jonah Gelbach, and Hilary Hoynes, "Welfare Reform and Children's Living Arrangements," *Journal of Human Resources* (Winter 2006), pp. 1–27. For earlier research summaries, see Robert Moffitt, "Welfare Benefits and Female Headship in the U.S. Time Series," *American Economic Review* (May 2000), pp. 373–377; "Incentive Effects of the U.S. Welfare System: A Review," *Journal of Economic Literature* (March 1992), pp. 1–61; also McKinley Blackburn, "Welfare Effects on the Marital Decisions of Never-Married Mothers," *Journal of Human Resources* (Winter 2000), pp. 116–142.

[10]Philip K. Robins and Paul Fronstin found evidence that young women were more prone to having a first child when they knew welfare benefits were available; see their "Welfare Benefits and Family-Size Decisions of Never-Married Women" (Madison, WI: Institute for Research on Poverty, 1993). T. Paul Schultz also emphasizes the importance of distinguishing the responses of various welfare subgroups to different kinds of benefits. The *average* effect of welfare on family structure may not be that meaningful. See his "Marital Status and Fertility in the United States: Welfare and Labor Market Effects," *Journal of Human Resources* (Spring 1994), pp. 637–669. Also relevant is Marianne Bitler, Jonah Gelbach, and Hilary Hoynes, "The Impact of Welfare Reform on Living Arrangements" (Cambridge, MA: National Bureau for Economic Research, February 2002).

[11]James X. Sullivan, "Welfare Reform, Saving, and Vehicle Ownership," *Journal of Human Resources* (Winter 2006), pp. 72–105; see also Erik Hurst and James P. Ziliak, "Do Welfare Asset Limits Affect Household Saving," in the same journal.

Marginal Tax Rates

Although the foregoing procedure for calculating welfare benefits might appear reasonable, it destroyed all monetary incentives to work. To appreciate the dynamics of this situation, imagine that Ms. Jones was offered regular part-time employment—as a nurse's aide, for example—at $8 an hour for ten hours a week. Ms. Jones might be reluctant to leave her small children in the care of others, but she could certainly use the money. Consequently, she is inclined to accept the new job rather than continue baby-sitting, especially if transportation problems (she has no car) and child care arrangements can be worked out. But what happens to her income if she takes this step toward self-improvement? Absolutely nothing. The welfare authorities simply note that she is earning $320 a month rather than $150, and reduce her welfare payment to $80. Her family's income remains at $400 whether or not the family head finds employment and regardless of how hard she strives for self-improvement. From Ms. Jones's perspective, work clearly does not pay.

Table 13.3 summarizes the problem. On row A, Ms. Jones is not working at all, and getting $400 per month in welfare benefits. If she baby-sits (row B) she earns $150, but her welfare benefit declines by the same amount. As a nurse's aide, (row C) she earns more ($320), but still has a monthly income of $400.

The reduction in welfare benefits that took place when Ms. Jones accepted the nurse's aid job amounted to an implicit tax on her earnings. An *explicit* tax comes out of a person's paycheck or tax return. As a result of the tax, a person is left with less income to spend. An *implicit* tax has the same effect: Every wage dollar is "taxed" in the form of an offsetting reduction in welfare benefits. The dollar-for-dollar benefit reduction is effectively a 100 percent tax on earnings. Thus, the *marginal tax rate* turns out to be 100 percent in this case: Ms. Jones loses one dollar in welfare benefits for every additional dollar she earns. Faced with such a high tax rate, how many people would seek additional employment? Very few, which is the heart of the work incentive problem.

The Social Security Amendments of 1967 alleviated the work incentive problem by reducing the marginal tax rate. The significance of this change is illustrated in Figure 13.3. Consider the case of Ms. Jones again.

If she does not work at all, she will receive $4,800 a year ($400 a month) from welfare, a situation designated by point A. Now suppose she is offered the nurse's aide job, for 500 hours a year (ten hours a week). If she accepted the job under the old system, she would move to point E, working more but with no change in total income (as shown in Table 13.3). Under the 1967 regulations, however, she moved to point D and increased her well-being by working. Point D is obviously more desirable than E, as it represents more income for the same amount of effort. Hence, whatever Ms. Jones's feelings about work, she was more likely to take a job under the post-1967 system than the old one. In this sense, the revised system provided a greater incentive to work.

TABLE 13.3 Wages, Benefits, and Income			
	Wages +	*Benefit* =	*Income*
A. No work	0	$400	$400
B. Baby-sitting	$150	$250	$400
C. Nurse's aide	$320	$80	$400

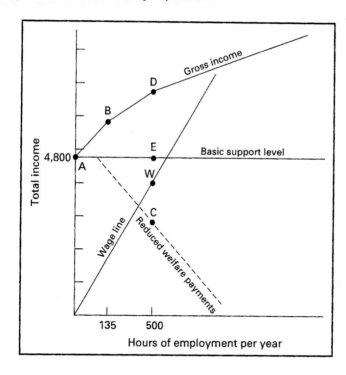

FIGURE 13.3 Work Incentive Provisions Under 1967 AFDC Reforms

Disregards

How did Ms. Jones get to point D under the post-1967 system? First, the welfare authorities recognized that there are certain costs associated with working, such as transportation expenses, work wardrobe, and added meal expenses. In Ms. Jones's case, these costs amounted to $60 a month (or $720 a year). To assure that Ms. Jones took home at least enough income from her new job to cover these costs and thus to eliminate the possibility of her incurring a net loss from working, the welfare department "disregarded" that much income in calculating her welfare benefits. Whereas they would have deducted $720 from her welfare checks under the old system, they now deducted nothing, thus enabling her to receive both the $4,800 in welfare benefits and the first $720 she earned.

To give Ms. Jones still more incentive to work, the welfare authorities also disregarded an additional $30 per month ($360 per year). Ms. Jones could then earn a total of $1,080 in wages before experiencing *any* reduction in welfare benefits. In effect, the marginal tax rate, the rate at which welfare benefits are reduced as earnings increase, on the first $1,080 of earnings dropped from 100 percent to 0 percent. As a result, Ms. Jones could work 135 hours per year earning $1,080 and move to point B without welfare department interference.

Only as Ms. Jones's earnings exceeded $1,080 a year did the welfare department begin to take notice of her added income and reduce her welfare check. Accordingly, beyond point B, Ms. Jones's total income rose more slowly than her increased earnings. But it did rise, because the welfare department no longer reduced her benefits by a dollar for every additional dollar she earned. That is, they no longer imposed a 100 percent marginal tax on earnings beyond point B, but instead allowed her to keep something for herself. Under the revised system the marginal tax rate was 67 percent, so that the welfare department reduced her benefit check by only 67 cents for every additional dollar she earned. The remaining 33 cents increased Ms. Jones's total income, thus providing a financial incentive to work. The incentive was still modest, to be sure, but nevertheless greater than the one that existed prior to the 1967 reform.

Total Income

The total income of Ms. Jones and her family at point D is easily computed. The post-1967 welfare benefit formula was

$$\text{Welfare benefit} = \$4,800 - (0.67 \times \text{Earnings in excess of } \$1,080)$$

If Ms. Jones worked all year (500 hours) at her new job, she received the following amount: her wages ($4,000 at point W) plus a welfare check reduced by two-thirds of her wages in excess of $1,080. In this case, she received a welfare check in the amount of $2,852 (point C). Her total income at point D was thus $4,000 from working plus $2,852 from welfare, or $6,852. By her own modest efforts, then, she managed to substantially increase her family's economic status.

CONFLICTING WELFARE GOALS

The benefit computation got more complicated after 1967. But the bottom line was clear: Welfare recipients had more economic incentive to work. In Ms. Jones's case, she now had the opportunity to increase her family income from $4,800 to $6,852 by working ten hours per week. Under the previous system, she could have worked also, but her *income* wouldn't have increased. She now had a financial *incentive* to get a job.

If a reduced marginal tax rate creates an incentive to work, why not drop the implicit tax even further? Why not let Ms. Jones keep a little more of the money she earns from making beds, emptying bedpans, and distributing medications? After all, the life of a nurse's aide is not exactly glamorous and Ms. Jones obviously needs the money. So why not lower the marginal tax rate from 67 percent to, say, 25 percent, or even zero? That would clearly solve the work incentive problem while giving Ms. Jones a real chance to make a few bucks.

Trade-Offs

The difficulty with this solution to the work incentive problem is that it conflicts with other goals. Three distinct goals are commonly associated with welfare systems:

- income provision
- work incentives
- cost minimization

To the extent that we want to protect people from the indignities of poverty, we should provide a high income floor (or guarantee). If we desire to encourage employment and self-improvement, we must impose low marginal tax rates (allow recipients to keep a substantial share of their earnings above the minimum). And if we desire to hold program costs down to a reasonable level, we must limit the coverage of the program to those in need. All these objectives are worthwhile. Unfortunately, they are mutually exclusive; we cannot move in all three directions at once.

Suppose that we actually eliminated the marginal tax rate on Ms. Jones's earnings, thus allowing her to keep everything she earns. In that case, her total income would rise to $8,800 ($4,800 in benefits plus $4,000 in wages). Still no life of luxury, but improving. Now suppose that the hospital technicians form a union and pay scales are increased. Ms. Jones is offered a raise to $10 an hour, provided that she works 1,000 hours a year (20 hours a week). Because we no longer reduce her welfare benefits as her earnings increase, this stroke of good fortune will give Ms. Jones the opportunity to take home a total income of $14,800. Terrific! But should we still be providing $4,800 in welfare payments to someone who earns $10,000 on her own? How about someone earning $15,000? $20,000? Or, to make a long story short, where should we draw the line?

Break-Even Level

The crux of the problem here is a trade-off between work incentives and program costs. A marginal tax rate of 100 percent destroys the incentive to work. On the other hand, a marginal tax rate of zero makes everyone eligible for full welfare benefits. If we let people keep receiving all their welfare benefits after they start working, program costs soar.

The conflict between the goals of income provision, work incentives, and cost minimization can be summarized in a simple equation:

$$\text{Break-even income level} = \frac{\text{Income floor}}{\text{Marginal tax rate}} + \text{Disregarded income}$$

The break-even income level refers to the amount of money a person can earn before losing all welfare benefits. In Ms. Jones's case, the break-even point under the post-1967 AFDC system was

$$\$8,280 = \frac{\$4,800}{0.67} + 1,080$$

Beyond that level of earnings, she would have been on her own. If the marginal tax rate were 100 percent as under the pre-1967 system, the break-even point would be $4,800 ($4,800/1.00), meaning that people who earned $4,800 on their own would get no assistance from welfare. Under our aborted proposal to lower marginal tax rates to zero, the break-even point would rise to infinity ($4,800/0), and we would all be on welfare.

As is apparent from this arithmetic, a lower break-even income level can be achieved only by sacrificing a high income floor or low marginal tax rates. Hence, cost minimization can be fulfilled only by sacrificing income provision or work incentives. More generally, fulfillment of any two objectives necessitates sacrificing the third.

THE GOAL COMPROMISE

Whatever compromise we strike between the goals of income provision, work incentives, and cost minimization, it is not going to please everyone. More important, however, we should note that the same compromise is not necessarily appropriate for all population groups. For those people incapable of working, income provision is more urgent than work incentives. On the other hand, high-income guarantees for people who are capable of working might seem unnecessary. Hence, it would make sense to strike a different compromise of welfare goals for two distinct groups: those who can work and those who cannot.

Unfortunately, it is not always possible to draw such a neat distinction. A 92-year-old woman confined to a wheelchair would seem to have very few employment opportunities; for her, work incentives would be irrelevant. But what about the father of four children who loses his job? Or the mother who is left with a five-year-old child when her husband skips town with the next-door neighbor? Or what about the teenager who got pregnant and is now trying to raise a child on her own? Are work incentives irrelevant in these cases? Our collective response, as reflected in welfare regulations, has been "no."

Although it is often difficult to distinguish the potentially employable from the rest of the poor, we attempt to approach this distinction by segregating needy families into different welfare classifications. This is why we have a separate welfare program (SSI) for the aged, the blind, and the handicapped, a program that provides higher income guarantees and smaller work incentives. In the process, of course, many younger families temporarily unable to find or accept employment end up at the margins of deprivation.

President Reagan introduced another welfare rule to help alleviate these goal conflicts. He argued that once welfare recipients got a foothold in the job market, they would advance up the income ladder. Most jobs offer more than just entry wages; they also offer opportunities for training, promotion, and pay increases. Even entry-level jobs can provide contacts and experience that lead to better-paying opportunities. The key to success, therefore, is to get welfare recipients into jobs quickly. From that perspective, work-incentive provisions need not be permanent. Accordingly, the rules were changed to eliminate work-incentive provisions after a four-month period of employment. After 1982 AFDC recipients confronted a 67 percent marginal tax rate only for the first four months of employment. Thereafter they faced a total loss of benefits. In principle, the implied marginal tax at the end of four months could exceed 100 percent (if the benefit loss exceeded the wage gain). This was a great disincentive to working, especially for welfare recipients who were not likely to advance up the wage scale quickly. Given the risk of unexpected job loss and the inevitable delay in reestablishing welfare, many recipients concluded that work simply did not make sense. After the 1982 rules went into effect, fewer families combined work and welfare.[12]

WELFARE REFORMS, 1982–2002

The Omnibus Budget Reconciliation Act of 1981 was the first initiative in a series of significant reforms to cash welfare programs.

STATE EXPERIMENTS, 1982–1988

The Omnibus Budget Reconciliation Act of 1981 not only altered *federal* benefit computations, but also gave *states* increased authority to reshape welfare regulations. States used this authority to change eligibility conditions, work requirements, and other welfare rules. In the process, the "national" welfare program (AFDC) became an increasingly diverse set of state programs.

---

[12]Alternatively, welfare families may have responded by simply reporting less of their labor-market activity; see S. Mayer and C. Jencks, "Recent Trends in Economic Inequality in the United States: Income versus Expenditures versus Material Well-Being," in *Poverty and Prosperity in the U.S.A. in the Late Twentieth Century*, eds. D. Papadimitriou and E. Wolff (New York: St. Martin's Press, 1993).

THE FAMILY SUPPORT ACT OF 1988

After nearly a decade of state experiments with various welfare initiatives, Congress came to three conclusions. First, welfare recipients had to assume more responsibility for achieving financial independence. Second, financial *incentives* weren't sufficient to get welfare recipients working; work *requirements* were needed, too. Third, an eclectic mix of services was more likely to succeed than any unidimensional intervention. The Family Support Act (FSA) of 1988 revamped national welfare legislation to reflect these conclusions. The most notable features of that Act are described in the following paragraphs.

Child Support

The increased self-responsibility envisioned by the FSA was manifest in provisions for child support and program participation. Title I of the act strengthened procedures for obtaining child support from noncustodial parents. States were required to establish paternity for welfare children, to enforce guidelines for support awards, and to with-hold support payments from the paychecks of noncustodial parents. Taken together, these provisions were designed to emphasize the responsibilities of parenthood while reducing the need for public assistance.

JOBS Program

To "encourage and assist" recipients to get off of welfare, the Family Support Act also imposed greater activity requirements on adult recipients. A major premise of the FSA was that welfare should be a short-term transition rather than a long-term solution. To help assure this, the FSA created the Job Opportunities and Basic Skills (JOBS) training program. While the educational and vocational services offered by JOBS are similar to those of previous programs, the provisions for participation were different. Participation in some JOBS activity was *mandatory* for most adult welfare recipients without children under age three. States could even extend that participation requirement to parents of children at least one year old.

The JOBS program also included a workfare component: States were required to demand at least 16 hours of community service per week from one parent in two-parent households. Single parents who failed to find a regular job after completing training could also be required to perform community service.

Work Incentives

The "stick" of mandatory activity requirements was accompanied by a "carrot" of enhanced work incentives. As we observed earlier, the loss of benefits that accompanies increased employment is a financial disincentive to working. The severest disincentive occurs at that juncture (point M in Figure 13.7) where Medicaid coverage ceases. The FSA addressed this concern by extending Medicaid eligibility for one full year after a recipient left welfare and went to work. The FSA also guaranteed child care for recipients who participated in JOBS or became employed.

AFDC-UP

The FSA also required all states to offer welfare benefits to *two*-parent families. Prior to 1989, states could choose whether to implement the AFDC-UP (unemployed parent) program. Only about half of the states did so, thereby leaving a gap in welfare eligibility that encouraged single-parent families. Congress closed that gap by making AFDC-UP a required program. However, more stringent eligibility rules and limits on benefits kept the AFDC-UP program very small.

Funding Limitations

The ambitions of the FSA were constrained by budget considerations. Congress appropriated relatively little money for the program and many services were dependent on cost-sharing by the states. When the economy slipped into the 1990–1991 recession, the states could not afford their share of program costs. As a result of these funding limitations, participation in the JOBS program remained below legislative targets.

STATE WAIVERS, 1991–1995

Neither the provisions nor the funding levels of the FSA satisfied the quest for welfare reform. Many critics were particularly concerned that the FSA gave individual states so little authority to tailor programs to their own needs. In response to this concern, the U.S. Department of Health and Human Services granted "waivers" to individual states. The waivers permitted states to amend the provisions of federal welfare law (FSA).

Between 1991 and 1995, 35 states obtained federal waivers. These waivers spawned a diverse array of state welfare "demonstrations." The demonstrations set time limits on welfare dependency, added new eligibility conditions, altered work requirements, restricted benefits for children born to welfare mothers ("family caps"), and modified work incentives.

At the same time that states were conducting their welfare demonstrations, welfare caseloads dropped sharply. Between January 1993 and January 1997, the national AFDC caseload plunged by 20 percent—the largest decline ever. Lots of governors were quick to credit their state-initiated reforms. However, the economy was growing steadily and unemployment rates were declining sharply. Hence, the economy, not state reform, was the principal cause of caseload declines.[13] Nevertheless, the apparent contribution of state reforms to the caseload decline rekindled the demand for more comprehensive federal reform. President Clinton responded to that demand, promising to "end welfare as we know it."

PRWORA: THE 1996 WELFARE REFORMS

After four years of intense debate and negotiations, in 1996 Congress passed a truly historic welfare-reform law. The Personal Responsibility and Work Opportunity Reconciliation Act (PRWORA) of 1996 ended a 60-year federal entitlement and turned the primary responsibility for welfare over to the states.

The End of Entitlements

The 1996 reforms terminated the AFDC program. Since its inception in 1935, AFDC had been a federal *entitlement*. Anyone who satisfied its eligibility requirements was entitled to a welfare check. As a result, the amount spent on welfare each year was unforeseeable, since it depended on the flow of welfare applicants.

---

[13]For an analysis of the 1992–1998 caseload decline, see Council of Economic Advisors, *The Effects of Welfare Policy and the Economic Expansion on Welfare Caseloads: An Update* (Washington, DC: The White House, August 1999); Bradley R. Schiller, "State Welfare Reform Impacts: Content and Enforcement Effects" (Washington, DC: American University, May 1997); and James Ziliak et al., "Accounting for the Decline in AFDC Caseloads," *Journal of Human Resources* (Summer 2000), pp. 570–586.

TANF Block Grants

In place of the AFDC entitlement, Congress created block grants to help finance the welfare system. Congress authorized a fixed amount ($16.4 billion per year) to be turned over to the states, who would then deliver whatever benefits and services they felt appropriate. The new program is called Temporary Assistance for Needy Families (TANF).

State Flexibility

TANF gave the states permanent authority to design their own welfare programs. Congress set a "maintenance of effort" rule that forbids states from reducing their own welfare spending very much. But it gave states wide discretion to decide who is eligible for welfare, how much aid they get, and what services and work requirements accompany a welfare check. As a result, it is much more difficult today to summarize the features of the "national" welfare program.[14] Although all states confront the same trade-offs and behavioral risks endemic to welfare, they are free to resolve these problems as they deem appropriate.

Time Limits

Although states enjoy unprecedented program authority with TANF, Congress did set some national rules. One of these is a time limit on welfare dependency. TANF has a *lifetime* eligibility cap of five years. This time limit is intended to break the cycle of dependency. However, Congress gave the states a couple of loopholes. States can exempt 20 percent of their welfare caseload from the five-year limit. They can also continue to use *nonfederal* funds to extend welfare benefits beyond the threshold.

Work Requirements

Congress also laid down new work requirements for welfare recipients. Within two years of welfare receipt, adult recipients had to engage in some work-related activity. In addition, states were required to have a rising percentage of recipients in work programs for at least 30 hours per week. The work participation requirement began at 25 percent in 1997 and rose five percentage points a year. Thus, by 2002, half of adult recipients were supposed to be in some form of work activity (a job, job search, education, or training).

Child Care

To facilitate work activity, the 1996 reforms substantially increased funding for child care. Indeed, the legislation created *two* block grants, one for welfare benefits and a second for child care. The Child Care and Development Block Grant (CCDBG) provided for over $20 billion in federal support over the first six years of the TANF program (1997–2002). With such funding, states could virtually guarantee child care for any welfare parent who wanted to go to school, work, or participate in training.

Transitional Assistance

To further encourage recipients to work, TANF guarantees continued Medicaid coverage to families that leave welfare to take a job. States are required to continue Medicaid benefits for one full year for such families.

---

[14]For a look at post-1996, state-level variability in just one dimension of benefit computations—the earnings disregard—see Philip K. Robins and Charles Michalopoulos, "Using Financial Incentives to Encourage Welfare Recipients to Become Economically Self-Sufficient," *Economic Policy Review* (Federal Reserve Bank of New York, September 2001), pp. 105–134.

Nonmarital Births

The PRWORA of 1996 also created new incentives and rules to reduce nonmarital births. The law requires teenaged mothers to live in a home with a responsible adult. This provision closes off the use of welfare by teenagers to establish their own households. Teen moms are also required to attend school. All unmarried welfare mothers are required to help identify fathers and establish paternity responsibilities. To prod states to enforce these edicts, Congress set up various financial incentives and penalties for state performance.

Noncitizens

Last, but not least, the 1996 reforms sharply limit noncitizen access to welfare. Illegal immigrants were always ineligible for welfare. The 1996 law extended that exclusion to most *legal* immigrants as well. All noncitizens are barred from Supplemental Security Income (SSI) and food-stamp benefits. In addition, states can deny TANF benefits to legal immigrants as well.

OBSERVED EFFECTS

As Figure 13.4 documents, the general public overwhelmingly approved key features of the 1996 welfare legislation. The strongest support was expressed for time limits on

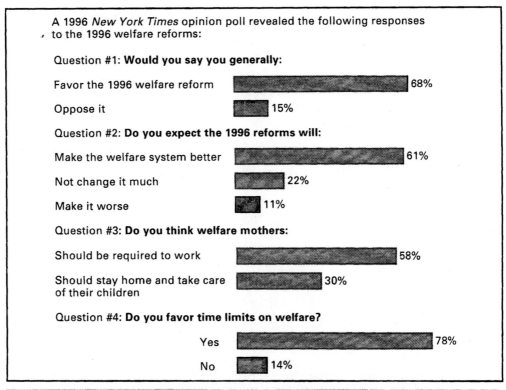

FIGURE 13.4 Public Support for Welfare Reform

Source: Adapted from *The American Enterprise* (March–April 1997), p. 91.

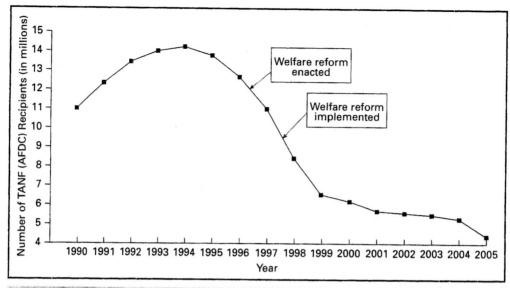

FIGURE 13.5   Welfare Caseloads, 1990–2004

Source: U.S. Department of Health and Human Services.

welfare receipt, while a 2-to-1 majority also favored requiring welfare mothers to work. An even larger majority (61 percent) expected the 1996 reforms to improve the welfare system.

During the first five years after the passage of the 1996 welfare reforms, welfare caseloads declined dramatically. As Figure 13.5 illustrates, the national AFDC/TANF caseload declined from 13 million in 1996 to less than 6 million at the end of 2001. Proponents of those reforms—including President Clinton—were quick to hail this sharp caseload decline as proof of their reform success.

Caseload Decline

Although it is tempting to credit the 1996 reforms for the post-1996 caseload decline, such a conclusion is not entirely defensible. First of all, the decline in welfare caseloads began *before* the PRWORA Act was even signed (July 1996), much less fully implemented (July 1997). Notice in Figure 13.5 that the caseload decline actually began in 1994.

The new time limits on welfare receipt were even less of a factor in the caseload decline. The 1996 legislation set a five-year, lifetime limit on welfare receipts. Hence, the time limit didn't affect any welfare recipients until 2002. And even then, the states had the discretion to exempt some recipients from the federal time limits or move recipients to wholly state-funded programs. Hence, TANF time limits can't very well explain the observed 1994–2000 caseload reduction.[15]

Work requirements probably had a more significant effect on welfare exits. The two-year "trigger" in TANF required welfare recipients to engage in some sort of

---

[15]A more sanguine conclusion is reported in Jeffrey Grogger, "The Effects of Time Limits, the EITC, and Other Policy Changes on Welfare Use, Work, and Income Among Female-Headed Families," *Review of Economics and Statistics* (2003) and in J. Grogger and Charles Michalopoulos, "Welfare Dynamics under Time Limits," *Journal of Political Economy* (April 2003).

work-related activity as a condition of continued eligibility. This requirement started becoming effective in 1998 (and in some state experiments even earlier). Recipients who didn't comply with new work requirements could be sanctioned with loss of benefits. Many welfare recipients may have concluded that it made more sense to get a paid job off welfare than to engage in a nonpaid work activity while on welfare. Some observers also suggested that the TANF work requirement helped "smoke out" recipients who were already engaged in unreported employment.

Finally, the period 1996–2000 was a boom time for the U.S. economy. Strong economic growth pushed the national unemployment rate to its lowest levels in a generation. This job growth created opportunities for welfare recipients to leave the welfare rolls that had nothing to do with the specifics of welfare reform.

Eventhough the U.S. economy slumped briefly in 2001, welfare caseloads kept declining—albeit at a slower rate. In fact, welfare caseloads declined for twelve years in a row. By 2006, the national TANF caseload was down 60 percent from 1996. In Wyoming, Virginia, Illinois, and Louisiana the caseload decline exceeded 80 percent!

This dramatic decline in welfare caseloads was a testament to the success of the 1996 reforms. But the caseload reductions were not *entirely* due to new rules and regulations. The Pesident's Council of Economic Advisors tried to isolate the impact of welfare reform itself on caseload reductions. The Council concluded that only a third of the observed welfare decline was due to legislated reforms.[16] To reach this conclusion, however, the Council had to argue that the caseload declines that occurred *before* 1997 were the result of welfare recipients *anticipating* time limits and work requirements.[17] Critics said this assumption was unfounded and therefore the Council's estimate of reforms effects was too large.[18] Later studies, however, attributed as much as *half* of the caseload reduction to welfare reform.[19]

Notwithstanding these complications, the public has credited the 1996 reforms with the 1996–2002 caseload reduction. As Figure 13.6 indicates, 62 percent of the public attributed the caseload decline to new rules that "forced" people to go to work. Only 23 percent of the general public credited the strong economy. Interestingly, the views of *poor* people were even more lopsided in their praise for work requirements.

Poverty Impact

Whatever the ultimate caseload effects turn out to be, the emphasis on caseload dynamics may be misplaced. The ultimate goal of social policy is to reduce *poverty*, not welfare caseloads. If we terminated all welfare programs tomorrow, caseloads would drop to zero. But poverty would probably increase. Hence, caseload reduction should

[16]Council of Economic Advisors, *The Effects of Welfare Policy and the Economic Expansion on Welfare Caseloads: An Update* (Washington, DC: White House, August 1999).

[17]Empirical support for this argument is provided in Jeffrey Grogger, "Time Limits and Welfare Use," *Journal of Human Resources* (Spring 2004), pp. 405–424.

[18]For more discussion of the problems of estimating reform effects see Bradley R. Schiller, "State Welfare-Reform Impacts: Content and Enforcement Effects," *Contemporary Economic Policy* (April 1999), pp. 210–222. For a summary and discussion of more recent assessments of economic and reform effects, see Federal Reserve Bank of New York, *Economic Policy Review* (September 2001), pp. 25–63.

[19]Jacob Klerman and Steven Hander, "A Stock-Flow Analysis of the Welfare Caseload," *Journal of Human Resources* (Fall 2004), pp. 865–886.

Question: The number of Americans receiving public assistance has dropped significantly over the last few years. Do you think this is mainly because:

(a) Changes in the welfare laws have forced people to go to work?

All respondents answering "yes"

62%

Respondents in poverty answering "yes"

73%

(b) The strong economy has created lots of new jobs in the past few years?

All respondents answering "yes"

23%

Respondents in poverty answering "yes"

16%

FIGURE 13.6 Public Opinion on Caseload Decline

Source: NPR Kaiser Kennedy School poll of January–February 2001, as reported in *The American Enterprise* (June 2002), p. 62. This information was reprinted with permission from the Henry J. Kaiser Family Foundation. The Kaiser Family Foundation, based in Menlo Park, California, is a nonprofit, private operating foundation focusing on the major health care issues facing the nation and is not associated with Kaiser Permanente or Kaiser Industries.

not be viewed as the sole measure of policy performance. Critics of the 1996 reforms worry that when recipients are pushed off the welfare rolls by work requirements and time limits, they will be worse off than before.[20]

Six years after the PRWORA was implemented there was little evidence of such a calamity. The great majority (60–75 percent) of welfare mothers who left welfare in 1996–2001 found jobs. Although their wages were relatively low ($7–$8 an hour), the combination of earnings, wage supplements (the EITC), and noncash benefits (e.g., Medicaid) lifted family incomes above welfare levels. As a result, child poverty rates declined along with numbers of welfare caseloads.[21] By 2000, poverty among black children was at its lowest-ever rate and among Hispanic children, the lowest in 20 years.

WELFARE: THE IN-KIND PROGRAMS

Virtually all of the welfare reforms of the 1980s and 1990s focused on the *cash* welfare programs. Relatively few reforms were directed at the *in-kind* programs. Yet, as we saw earlier (Figure 13.1), the in-kind programs are larger than the cash programs. Moreover, the goal conflicts that lie at the heart of cash-benefit programs also bedevil the in-kind programs. In fact, when welfare recipients are eligible for *both* cash and in-kind programs, the goal conflicts become even more acute. The *combination* of cash and

---

[20]An evaluation of an earlier state demonstration (the San Diego Saturation Work Initiative Model) showed that work requirements decreased caseloads but not poverty; see Daniel Friedlander and Gayle Hamilton, "The Impact of a Continuous Participation Obligation in a Welfare Employment Program," *Journal of Human Resources* (Fall 1996), pp. 734–756.

[21] The contribution of welfare reforms to this decline is highlighted in Rebecca Blank and Robert Schoen, "Changes in the Distribution of Children's Family Income over the 1990's," *American Economic Review* (May 2003), pp. 304–308.

in-kind benefits tends to diminish further the economic incentive to work and to create additional inducements for single parenthood.

In the following paragraphs, we review a few of the major in-kind programs, then look at their impact on welfare adequacy, cost, and work incentives.

FOOD STAMPS

Food stamps are the most familiar in-kind welfare benefit. Food stamps are simply coupons ("stamps") that allow a person to buy food. The stamps are "spent" at the grocery store, where they are accepted at face value in the form of electronic debits or paper coupons. The grocer, in turn, deposits the food stamp coupons or credits at a bank, taking payment from the government. In effect, then, food stamps are a direct substitute for cash. Food stamps are not fully equivalent to cash, however, since they may be used only for food purchases.

Food stamps are distributed to poor families on the basis of need. The value of stamps given to a family depends on its income and family size. The maximum monthly benefit in 2006 was $408 for a three-person family without other income. Average benefits are much lower—around $264 per month (about $1.00 per meal per person). The value of food-stamp transfers is automatically increased each year to account for higher food prices.

MEDICAID

Even larger than the food-stamp program is Medicaid, the program that provides medical services to the poor. Under Medicaid an eligible person can use the services of a doctor or hospital just like anyone else. The difference is that the Medicaid patient simply passes the bill on to the government, rather than paying for it directly or submitting it to a private insurance company. Obviously, the amount of benefit a poor family gets from Medicaid depends on how often it requires medical treatment. Nearly all public welfare recipients make some use of Medicaid, as do many others who have incomes just above the poverty standard. The average value of the services received varies tremendously, however. Most Medicaid assistance goes to the aged, blind, and disabled recipients of Supplemental Security Income; they have average medical costs in excess of $10,000 per year. Less than a fifth of Medicaid benefits go to younger families with children, most of whom also receive cash benefits. A typical three-person welfare family receives about $3,000 a year in Medicaid benefits.

HOUSING ASSISTANCE

In addition to food and medical services, a poor family can also receive housing assistance. In many cases, such assistance is provided in the form of public housing, usually large housing projects owned and operated by the government. In a public housing project the tenants enjoy cheap (subsidized) rents, although not a great deal more in terms of quality of environment. Nevertheless, the fact that they are paying less than the market value of their apartments means that they are effectively receiving an income transfer, which on average works out to approximately $2,000 a year.

In addition to public housing projects, there are also housing assistance programs for low-income people who are renting or even buying their apartments and homes in the private market. In these programs, the rent or mortgage payment is reduced, with the government (the Department of Housing and Urban Development, or HUD) making up the difference.

TABLE 13.4 In-Kind Welfare Programs, 2005

Program	Number of Recipients (millions)	Average Benefit per Recipient per Month ($)	Total Annual Cost ($billions)
Food stamps	27	94	38
Medicaid	55	386	258
Housing assistance	11	183	23
School lunch program	30	30	7
Women, Infants, and Children (WIC)	8	37	5
Total			331

Source: U.S. Bureau of the Census and Office of Management and Budget. Totals include administrative costs. Medicaid includes state cost sharing.

NUTRITION PROGRAMS

In addition to the "big three" in-kind programs—food stamps, Medicaid, and housing assistance—there are scores of other means-tested programs. Table 13.4 displays two more, both intended to assure greater nutrition for low-income children. The school lunch and breakfast programs provide free or subsidized meals. The Women, Infants, and Children (WIC) program provides food vouchers (like food stamps) to pregnant women and infants.

THE WELFARE PACKAGE

As Table 13.4 documents, we spend a lot of money on in-kind welfare programs. Spending on just the five programs listed in Table 13.4 exceeded $300 billion in 2005, more than three times what was spent on cash benefits (Table 13.1).

When in-kind benefits are combined with cash benefits, the value of the "welfare package" increases substantially. As we noted earlier, a typical welfare family of a mother and two children gets less than $5,000 a year in welfare checks (cash). But food stamps can bring in another $3,000 and housing subsidies another $4,000 of benefits. Medicaid can cover all medical expenses, and the nutrition programs can supply a lot of free meals. If a welfare family got all of these benefits, it would have a standard of living worth at least $15,000 a year. They wouldn't be rich, but they wouldn't be nearly as destitute as their cash income ($5,000) implied.

Few welfare families get all of these benefits. And virtually none get the *maximum* value of each benefit. However, most welfare families do get two or more benefits. As Table 13.5 reveals, 81 percent of AFDC recipients also get food stamps; nearly all of them make use of Medicaid. The median value of the resulting welfare package is about $12,000.

REVISITING THE GOAL CONFLICT

Tables 13.4 and 13.5 clearly demonstrate that in-kind welfare programs substantially raise the standard of living for the poor; they do so, however, at the expense of certain identifiable costs. Obviously, they involve a substantial amount of public expenditure—over $320 billion in 2002. Less obvious, but perhaps more important, is

TABLE 13.5 Multiple Benefit Receipts

Percentage of Welfare (TANF) Households Receiving:

Food stamps	81%
Medicaid	99
Housing assistance	38
School lunch program	62
WIC	35

Source: U.S. Congress, Committee on Ways and Means, *2004 Green Book* (Washington, DC: U.S. Government Printing Office, 2004).

the impact of these in-kind programs on the goal compromise we observed earlier. As we noted, cash assistance programs tend to sacrifice more of the income-provision goal in order to better fulfill the work-incentive and cost-minimization goals. That compromise has been altered by the availability of food stamps, Medicaid, and housing assistance.

Although it might seem that the in-kind programs are a way of meeting all three of our welfare goals simultaneously—of filling in the gaps left in our earlier compromise—that is only an illusion. The three goals remain irreconcilable, and the provision of in-kind assistance serves only to strike a new compromise, not to render the three competing welfare goals more compatible.

Higher Income Guarantees
The impact of in-kind programs on our policy compromise can be seen in Figure 13.7. In this figure we reconstruct the opportunities available to Ms. Jones under the cash welfare program (TANF). As we noted earlier, Ms. Jones had an incentive (albeit limited) to take a job while on welfare, as she could increase her standard of living (move to points B and D) by so doing.

The new and higher line in Figure 13.7 represents the opportunities available to Ms. Jones and her family from the combined provisions of cash welfare (TANF) benefits, food stamps, Medicaid, and housing assistance. We will assume Ms. Jones qualifies for $2,000 each of food stamps, housing subsidies, and medical payments. As is evident, Ms. Jones's family enjoys a much higher standard of living when it gets not only welfare checks but lives in subsidized housing and gets free medical services and food stamps as well. Even if Ms. Jones chose not to work at all, her total real income would be $4,800 in welfare benefits plus $6,000 in in-kind benefits. This combined income of $10,800 is represented by point A* in Figure 13.7. This is far superior to the cash (TANF) income available at point A.

Reduced Work Incentives
There is another change in Figure 13.7. Notice what happens to her total gross income as she works more hours. Her gross income rises slowly at first, then not at all. From point A* to B* her gross income is rising, but beyond point B* the gross income curve flattens out. Ultimately (at point M), her gross income actually *falls* as her work effort increases! Not only does Ms. Jones now feel less *need* to work as a result of her greater public subsidy, but she now confronts less *incentive* to work. The attainment of greater income provision has been achieved at the sacrifice (opportunity cost) of work incentives. That is not

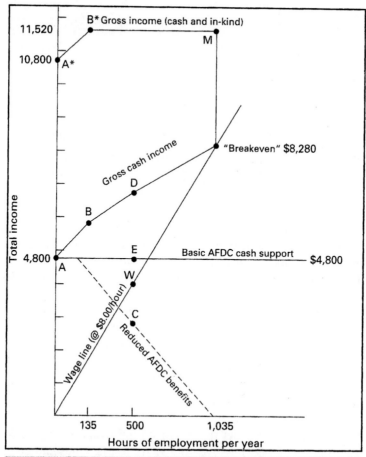

FIGURE 13.7   Effect of In-Kind Benefits on Income and Work Incentives

to say that the new compromise is any better or worse than the old one, but simply to point up the fact that the old goal conflict still exists.

Cumulative Marginal Tax Rates

The reduction in work incentives comes about from an increase in the implicit marginal tax rate. The rules for cash benefits haven't changed: Ms. Jones can still keep 100 percent of the first $1,080 she earns (the disregards) and 33 percent of any additional wages. Now, however, she loses some of her in-kind benefits when her earnings increase.

Recall that the value of a family's food-stamp allotment depends on a family's income. Families with higher incomes get fewer stamps. Hence, part of what Ms. Jones earns is effectively taken away in the form of food-stamp losses; this acts as a tax on earnings. For food stamps the implicit marginal tax rate is 30 percent; that is, the family's stamp allotment declines by 30 cents for each dollar of earned income.

The same kind of implicit tax accompanies housing subsidies. The size of the rent subsidy depends on how much income a family has. In general, the subsidy declines by 25 cents for each additional dollar of family income.

The arithmetic of work disincentives should be coming clear at this juncture. A welfare recipient who earns an additional dollar of wages might lose 67 cents in cash benefits, 30 cents worth of food stamps, and 25 cents of rent subsidies.[22] In other words, an individual might lose *more* in welfare benefits (cash and in-kind) than she earns in wages! In this worst-case scenario, the *cumulative* marginal tax rate exceeds 100 percent.

Figure 13.7 depicts a slightly more optimistic situation. In this case, the cumulative marginal tax rate beyond point B* is *only* 100 percent. This assumes that the implicit tax on cash benefits is 67 percent and the implicit tax (benefit-reduction) rate on in-kind benefits is 33 percent. When Ms. Jones increases her earnings from $0 to $1,080, TANF (cash) benefits are unaffected but she loses $360 worth of food stamps and housing assistance. This moves her from point A* to point B*. Her income is increasing as she starts working, but more slowly than her wages.

To the right of point B* work incentives diminish further. Once her wages exceed the $1,080 disregard, Ms. Jones starts losing TANF benefits. The *combined* marginal tax rate is now 100 percent—67 percent in TANF "taxes" and another 33 percent from food stamps and housing assistance. The gross income line flattens out to the right of B*; further work effort does not result in higher real income. There is no financial incentive to work more than 135 hours per year (point B*) in this case. More generally, there is no incentive to earn more than $1,080 per year. In other words, the benefit-reduction rules associated with food stamps and rent subsidies eliminate even the small work incentive that TANF alone contained.

A still greater blow to work incentives occurs at point M. At point M, Ms. Jones has achieved the break-even point and so no longer qualifies for cash benefits. When she stops receiving cash benefits, however, her Medicaid eligibility is at risk as well. In most states persons receiving TANF benefits are automatically eligible for Medicaid. If they leave the (cash) welfare rolls, however, families may lose their Medicaid benefits. This may happen immediately or may take as long as a year. In any case, the loss of Medicaid eligibility means that this family loses $2,000 of in-kind benefits if its wages reach the (cash) welfare breakeven level. At the margin this means that $1 of additional wages *reduces* family income by $2,000. An experience like that could seriously diminish a person's desire to work![23]

CONTINUING WELFARE REFORMS

To a large extent, the welfare reforms of the last 20 years diminished the potency of these work disincentives. Disincentives are relevant only if an individual has some degree of choice about whether to work or not. Since 1981, however, welfare rules have shifted the focus from work *incentives* to work *requirements*. The process began with

---

[22]Effective tax (benefit-reduction) rates are typically less than these nominal rates due to underreporting of income and administrative discretion in determining "countable" income; see Terra McKinnish, Seth Sanders, and Jeffrey Smith, "Estimates of Effective Guarantees and Tax Rates in the AFDC Program for the Post-OBSRA Period," *Journal of Human Resources* (Spring 1999), pp. 312–345. The net effect of increased wage rates on a recipient's income is analyzed in Gregory Acs et al., *Does Work Pay? An Assessment of the Work Incentives under TANF* (Washington, DC: Urban Institute, 1999).

[23]Significant impacts of Medicaid on employment behavior are estimated in Anne E. Winkler, "The Incentive Effects of Medicaid on Women's Labor Supply," *Journal of Human Resources* (Spring 1991), pp. 308–377; and Robert Moffitt and Barbara Wolfe, "The Effect of the Medicaid Program on Welfare Participation and Labor Supply," *Review of Economics and Statistics* (November 1992), pp. 615–626.

the *workfare* programs proposed by President Reagan. Reagan wanted to compel all adult welfare recipients to work, either in private sector employment or, if necessary, community service jobs. Although Congress refused to pass a national workfare program, it did authorize the states to experiment with the concept. Between 1982 and 1988, over half of the states decided to take this approach. In most cases, however, the state legislatures simply passed the buck to their respective counties, letting them decide whether to impose a workfare requirement. Relatively few counties implemented the program, and participation rates were always low. As a consequence, only 1 to 2 percent of the national welfare caseload participated in workfare.[24] In most cases, mandatory community service (called the Community Work Experience Program, or CWEP) was one of many employment-related options recipients confronted.

Despite the low level of workfare utilization, the program seemed to be effective in reducing caseloads. In addition, the program proved to be popular not only among taxpayers but among welfare recipients as well.[25]

The Family Support Act of 1988 and the Personal Responsibility and Work Opportunity Reconciliation Act of 1996 increased the emphasis on work *requirements* rather than work *incentives*. Recall that the 1996 reforms require early work activity and place time limits on welfare receipt. There is little discretion for individual labor-supply decisions in those statutes.

TRANSITIONAL ASSISTANCE

In an effort to bolster both work incentives and income provision, Congress has provided for greater transitional assistance to recipients leaving welfare roles. Most importantly, families leaving (cash) welfare are assured access to Medicaid for some period of time. In 1997, Congress also authorized more funds for the states to expand Medicaid eligibility (the State Children's Health Insurance Program, or SCHIP). These changes helped eliminate the perverse income reduction that occurred at point M in Figure 13.7. Transitional assistance also helps assure that poverty reduction keeps pace with caseload reduction.

Transitional assistance is not a panacea for welfare conflicts. In a sense, transitional assistance only postpones the day of reckoning. An individual still confronts the abrupt income fall-off at point M. The confrontation now occurs at the end of the transition period (typically a year later) rather than on the day of welfare exit. Liberals worry that families will end up worse off—back in poverty—when that day comes.

Conservatives emphasize that income rises with work experience. The welfare mom who takes a first postwelfare job at $7 to $8 an hour is likely to be earning higher pay a year later. She is also likely to be covered by employer-based health insurance. Hence, few welfare leavers will still need Medicaid coverage a year later. Those that do will most likely qualify for their state's Medicaid program. Accordingly, extending mandatory Medicaid coverage beyond the first year is unnecessary and would be too expensive.

The same arguments apply to food stamps and other welfare supplements. Liberals want to assure continued access to those in-kind benefits for welfare leavers. They are

---

[24]Bradley R. Schiller and C. Nielson Brasher, "Workfare in the 1980s: Successes and Limits," *Policy Studies Review* (Summer 1990).

[25]See Bradley R. Schiller and C. Nielson Brasher, "The Effects of Workfare Saturation on AFDC Caseloads," *Contemporary Policy Issues* (January 1993).

particularly concerned about the sharp drop in food stamp receipt that accompanied declines in (cash) welfare caseloads. They fear that the new emphasis on work requirements has deterred many poor people from visiting welfare offices to pursue their noncash benefits.

CONTINGENCY FUNDS

Liberals have also expressed concern about the impact of an economic downturn on welfare leavers, especially those who have exhausted their eligibility time limit. Although states have the flexibility to offer services and benefits from their own funds, critics fear that their budgets will be depleted in a serious recession. That would leave former welfare recipients with nowhere to turn.

WORK REQUIREMENTS

Although there has been a massive shift from welfare to work since 1994, conservatives want to strengthen work requirements further. They say that the track record of welfare-to-work transitions proves the efficacy of this approach. They want to strengthen work requirements in two ways. First, they want more recipients engaged in actual paid employment rather than in "work-related" activities like education, training, and job search. Second, they want to raise state thresholds for required participation. Liberals resist these changes, fearing that they would drive the hardest-to-employ recipients off welfare and deeper into poverty.

FAMILY FORMATION

One of the most contentious issues in ongoing welfare policy development is the effect of welfare on family structure. The 1996 legislation put significant emphasis on family structure. The PRWORA encouraged states to direct more services to family structure, including reductions in teen pregnancies and nonmarital births. The PRWORA also encouraged states to direct more services to developing stable marriages (e.g., marital counseling). However, states spent less than 1 percent of their available funds on such activities in the first six years of the TANF program. President Bush led the demand for greater attention to family formation services and incentives. Critics argued that such matters were largely beyond the control of welfare offices, whatever services or economic incentives they offered.

2005 REAUTHORIZATION

All of these issues came to a head in 2002, when the six-year authority of the PRWORA was set to expire. The Republican-led House of Representatives passed a reauthorization bill that incorporated most of the reforms favored by conservatives. Of particular concern to the conservatives was the amount of work activity required of welfare recipients. The 1996 law required half of all adult recipients to work at least 30 hours per week. But the states would count welfare *leavers* in the caseload computation. Because so many people left welfare in the 1990s, that work requirement was effectively rescinded. Hence, the Bush administration wanted to recast the state-level work requirement and also narrow the definition of "work" activities (excluding school enrollment and limiting vocational training and drug treatment, for example).

The debate over these and other welfare provisions dragged on for three years. Finally, in an omnibus deficit-reduction bill passed in December 2005, the state-level work requirements were toughened. States must now get half their welfare recipients working within one year or face funding penalties. In June 2006 the Bush administration also tightened the definition of "work" and required states to verify actual hours of community service and other jobs.

THE LIMITS OF WELFARE

The reality of welfare reform is that it begets no simple answers. The U.S. Congress effectively conceded this point with the passage of the landmark 1996 welfare reforms. In effect, the Congress admitted that it couldn't design a national program that would satisfy all parties. So it turned over to the individual states that responsibility for program design and implementation. Now the "national" cash welfare system is a quilt of 50 separate state programs.

As state TANF programs evolve we will surely learn more about which welfare rules work and which don't. But consensus on a "model" program is likely to remain elusive. To a large extent, the continuing controversy reflects the diverse goals that people have for welfare reform. The effects of the 1996 reforms are also certain to vary with the condition of the local economy and the unique circumstance of different welfare families.[26]

Despite the complexity of the welfare problem, the American people continue to prod elected officials to fashion a "silver bullet" that will end the welfare problem. Welfare reform is a politically appealing position, particularly when it promises a reduction in welfare caseloads and associated costs. As reformers soon learn when they try to grapple with the complexities of welfare, however, few reforms come cheaply.

In the midst of this frustration, simpler visions have a certain appeal. One of the most extreme suggestions is simply to eliminate welfare altogether. Charles Murray asserts that the very existence of a welfare system has nurtured the socially destructive behavior that traps people in poverty. If the promise of welfare support were withdrawn, teenagers would exercise greater birth control. Without the option of welfare support, teenage women who did have children would have to look to the child's father or their own families for support. Fathers would not feel they needed to abandon their families so they could get welfare and would be reluctant to leave if no benefits were available. The abolition of welfare could spark a revolutionary change in family relationships that restores the two-parent family to social and economic primacy.[27] The elimination of welfare would also put an end to the work-incentive issue, since publicly supported nonwork would no longer be an option.

Some people could not cope without welfare, of course. Some families and parents are so dysfunctional for a variety of cultural, psychological, or physical reasons

---

[26]The variability of reform impacts on individual families is documented in Marianne Bitler, Jonah Gelbach, and Hilary Hoynes, "What Means Miss: Distributional Effects of Welfare Reform Experiments" *American Economic Review* (September 2006), pp. 988–1012; see also Domenico Parisi, D. McLaughlin, S. Grice, and M. Taquino, "Exiting TANF: Individual and Local Factors and Their Differential Influence Across Racial Groups," *Social Science Quarterly* (March 2006), pp. 76–90.

[27]This expectation—and the primary responsibility of families to support their own members—is emphasized in James Payne, *Overcoming Welfare* (New York: Basic Books, 1999).

that they cannot achieve economic security even when the opportunity exists. Without a welfare system, the children in such families would be particularly vulnerable. Rather than keeping the welfare system intact "for the sake of the children," however, Murray proposes that society assume direct responsibility for such children by placing them in orphanages or nonparental adoption. If parents cannot or will not provide a safe and secure environment for their children, Murray argues, the children would be better off in nonparental care. This severing of parental rights would break the intergenerational cycle of underclass behavior that breeds dependency.

According to public opinion surveys, less than one out of ten Americans would be willing to take the gamble that Charles Murray proposes.[28] His suggestions, however, help underscore the limits of welfare reform. Modest adjustments in eligibility rules, benefit formulas, or service offerings are unlikely to transform the parameters of the welfare problem. People enter and exit welfare rolls for a variety of reasons, most of which are related to family formation and (re)marriage rather than narrower economic considerations like marginal tax rates and eligibility rules.[29]

The only lasting solution to the welfare problem will have to come from outside the welfare system. The solution lies in more and better jobs, more and better schooling, more stable families, and reduced teenage pregnancy. These are enormous challenges that must be approached from a much broader platform than welfare policy. What welfare reform can best accomplish in these circumstances is to encourage, assist, and sometimes compel individuals to move in these directions.

Summary

Welfare programs are part of a much larger collection of income transfers. What distinguishes welfare transfers is the use of means-testing as a condition of eligibility. By contrast, social insurance programs are conditioned by events and thus available to rich and poor people alike.

There is no single welfare system in the United States. What is referred to as the welfare system is actually a conglomeration of diverse means-tested programs offering cash and in-kind assistance. Since the reforms of 1996, which gave states greater program authority, the welfare "system" has become even more diverse.

Prior to 1997, the largest cash welfare program was Aid to Families with Dependent Children (AFDC). AFDC was a federal entitlement, jointly financed by the federal and state governments. AFDC has been replaced with Temporary Assistance for Needy Families (TANF). TANF provides federal block grants to the states, which then fashion their own welfare programs. Federal TANF rules include a five-year limit on welfare dependency, stricter work requirements, and stepped-up child support enforcement. An accompanying block grant assures child care availability.

---

[28]Clancy Shulman Yankelovich, poll results reported in *The American Enterprise* (September–October 1993), p. 86.

[29]The interaction of personal, economic, and administrative variables on welfare behavior is explored in C. Michelle Piskulich, "Toward a Comprehensive Model of Welfare Exits: The Case of AFDC," *American Journal of Political Science* (February 1993), pp. 165–185.

In addition to cash benefits, most welfare families also get in-kind benefits like food stamps, Medicaid, nutrition programs, and housing assistance. These in-kind programs have expanded rapidly and now pay out far more in benefits than the cash programs. The combined "welfare package" of benefits has a median value of at least $12,000 per year for a mother and two children.

The central dilemma of welfare policy is the conflict among goals of adequacy, work incentives, and cost containment. As welfare benefits rise, the incentive to work is reduced and program costs increase. Low marginal tax (benefit-reduction) rates encourage work but raise program costs. Recent welfare reforms have used various rules (i.e., time limits, work requirements, denial of aid to teen moms living alone) to forge a politically acceptable compromise of the three policy goals. The general thrust of recent reforms has been to emphasize work *requirements* rather than work *incentives*. At the same time, more funds and services (e.g., child care, transitional assistance) have been made available to support ex-recipients' work efforts.

The 1996 welfare reforms were a huge success, in almost every dimension (caseload reduction, greater employment, reduced poverty). Debates continue, however, about what rules, services, and incentives will further reduce dependency, lessen poverty, and strengthen low-income families. The 2003 reauthorization left most of these challenges to state welfare administrators.

It is unlikely that any single welfare reform will solve the welfare problem. People are driven onto the welfare rolls by a variety of social, demographic, and economic forces and exit welfare for as many diverse reasons. The "big" solutions to welfare are likely to lie in these larger socioeconomic dynamics rather than in the details of welfare rules and services. In this context, continuing welfare reforms are likely to generate only modest changes in welfare caseloads and costs.

Further Reading

Bane, Mary Jo, and David Ellwood, *Welfare Realities*. Cambridge, MA: Harvard University Press, 1994.

Blank, Rebecca, "Evaluating Welfare Reform in the United States," *Journal of Economic Literature* (December 2002), pp. 1105–1166.

Duncan, Greg, Aletha Huston, and Thomas Weisner, *Higher Ground: New Hope for the Working Poor and Their Children*. New York: Russell Sage, 2007.

Ellwood, David T., "Anti-Poverty Policy for Families in the Next Century: From Welfare to Work," *Journal of Economic Perspectives* (Winter 2000), pp. 187–198.

Grogger, Jeffrey, and Lynn A. Karoly, *Welfare Reform: Effects of a Decade of Change*. Cambridge, MA: Harvard University Press, 2005.

Haley, James, ed., *Welfare*. San Diego, CA: Greenhaven Press, 2003.

Haskins, Ron, *Work over Welfare*. Washington, DC: Brookings Institution, 2006.

Katz, Michael B., *In the Shadow of the Poorhouse: A Social History of Welfare in America*. New York: Basic Books, 1986.

Moffitt, Robert, ed., *Means-Tested Transfer Programs in the United States*. Chicago, IL: University of Chicago Press, 2003.

Murray, Charles, *In Our Hands: A Plan to Replace the Welfare State*. Washington, DC: AEI Press, 2006.

Payne, James L., "Welfare's Fatal Attraction," *The Public Interest* (Winter 1998), pp. 126–133.

Turner, Lesley, S. Danziger, and K. Seefeldt, "Failing the Transition from Welfare to Work," *Social Science Quarterly* (June 2006), pp. 227–247.

U.S. Congress, Ways and Means Committee, *2004 Green Book*. Washington, DC: Government Printing Office, 2004. Appendix L: "Assessing the Effects of Welfare Reform Initiatives."

U.S. Department of Health and Human Services, *Indicators of Welfare Dependence*.

Washington, DC: U.S. Government Printing Office, annual.

Wilson, Laura A., Robert P. Stoker, and Dennis McGrath, "Welfare Bureaus as Moral Tutors: What Do Clients Learn from Paternalistic Welfare Reforms?" *Social Science Quarterly* (September 1999), pp. 473–486.

Web Links

Brookings Institution. Research studies and policy briefs on welfare.
www.brook.edu

Center on Budget and Policy Priorities. Analyses of Safety net programs.
www.cbpp.org

Joint Center for Poverty Research. Research studies on all dimensions of welfare.
www.jcpr.org

Manpower Development Research Corporation. Evaluations of welfare and related programs.
www.mdrc.org

Urban Institute. Welfare rules database and many welfare studies.
www.urban.org

U.S. Department of Agriculture. Information on food stamp program.
www.fns.usda.gov/fsp

U.S. Department of Health and Human Services.
(1) Assistant Secretary for Planning and Evaluation. Research studies on welfare and related issues.
http://aspe.os.dhhs.gov

(2) Administration for Children and Families. Data and studies on welfare and related issues.
www.acf.dhhs.gov

(3) Center for Medicare and Medicaid Services. Information on Medicaid.
http://cms.hhs.gov/medicaid

U.S. General Accounting Office. Periodic research reports on welfare programs.
www.gao.gov

CHAPTER 14
SOCIAL INSURANCE PROGRAMS

❧

The welfare system is designed to provide financial assistance to people who have fallen into poverty. By contrast, the social insurance system is designed to *prevent* families from falling into poverty. Social insurance is intended to cushion income losses from specific events that might otherwise push people below poverty thresholds.

As we noted in Chapter 13, expenditures on social insurance programs greatly exceed welfare expenditures. They are also vastly more effective in reducing poverty. This is hardly surprising, given the failure of welfare programs to provide income support in excess of poverty thresholds and the unique mission of social insurance in preventing poverty. It is instructive, however, to consider how much poverty might exist if the United States had no social insurance programs.

In this chapter three major social insurance programs—Social Security, Medicare, and unemployment insurance—are examined. The major features of each program are described and their special impacts on poverty are assessed. Proposals to expand the government's role in child support are also discussed.

SOCIAL SECURITY

Social Security is by far the largest income transfer program in the United States. Unlike welfare, however, Social Security benefits are not reserved for those in need. Tax contributions rather than need establish eligibility for benefits. Anyone who has paid Social Security payroll taxes for a prescribed number of years is eligible to receive Social Security benefits at retirement age. Thus, the program is neither intended nor operated as an antipoverty mechanism. The majority of the 50 million individuals who receive Social Security benefits have never experienced poverty. Yet they receive nearly $600 billion in annual payments, triple the size of combined annual expenditures on cash welfare, food stamps, and housing assistance.

OASDHI PROGRAMS

Social Security is really a mixture of three distinct programs that share a common source of financing. The original Social Security Act of 1935 created only one program for older Americans—the Old Age Insurance (OAI) program. The purpose of OAI was to assure a basic floor of retirement income after older workers left the labor force. Four years later, Congress amended the act to authorize payment of benefits to survivors and dependents of workers who died (survivors' insurance). The combination of old age and survivors' coverage (OASI) is the essential *retirement* program of Social Security.

In 1956 the coverage of Social Security was extended to disabled workers, creating a second major benefit program (disability insurance) for American workers. A third program of health insurance (HI) was added in 1965, creating the Medicare program.

FINANCING

All three major Social Security programs are financed by a common payroll tax levied on wages and salaries—a tax euphemistically referred to as a "contribution" toward Social Security benefits. Most people mistakenly believe that their "contributions" accumulate in their personal accounts during their working years. They envision a savings "balance" from which retirement, disability, and health benefits are later paid. In reality, people do not accumulate any savings in the Social Security program. There is no huge pool of savings being set aside for future retirees. Instead, the Social Security system is a pure income transfer program, financed on a pay-as-you-go basis. The system uses the *current* contributions of workers to pay *current* benefits to retirees. By contrast, a conventional savings program uses *current* income to finance *future* payments. Accordingly, the availability of benefits for retirees depends on the continued ability and willingness of workers to make Social Security contributions.

The FICA Payroll Tax

The contributions of current workers to benefits for Social Security recipients are actually a tax on payrolls. The Social Security tax is deducted directly from employee paychecks, along with income tax withholding. This special payroll tax is popularly known as the FICA deduction in recognition of the law (Federal Insurance Contributions Act) that requires employers to withhold these Social Security contributions.

In addition to the employee's contribution, employers are taxed as well. Employers not only withhold the FICA tax from employee paychecks but also make an additional contribution of equal size. Thus, the revenues of the Social Security program come from payroll taxes on both employers and employees. Self-employed persons must pay both sides of the tax.

Tax Rates

The FICA tax covers not only contributions to the Social Security retirement (OASI) and disability insurance programs (DI), but also to health insurance (HI) programs (primarily Medicare) authorized by the Social Security Act. In 2006, the total FICA payroll tax was 7.65 percent. As Table 14.1 shows, the lion's share of this tax went to the retirement program (OASI) and disability benefits (DI). HI tax receipts fund Medicare. To a taxpayer, the bottom line is a total Social Security tax of 7.65 percent.

The Wage Base

The FICA tax is a tax on wages. However, not every dollar of wages is taxed. Congress sets a *ceiling* on taxable wages; only wages below the ceiling are taxed. For the OAS

TABLE 14.1 Components of Social Security Tax

Program	Tax Rate
OASI (old age and survivors' insurance)	5.60%
DI (disability insurance)	0.60
Subtotal, OASDI	6.20
HI (health insurance)	1.45
Total FICA tax	7.65%

and DI programs, the wage ceiling—called the wage base—was $97,500 in 2007. Accordingly, the *maximum* OASDI tax an individual paid was

$$\text{Maximum annual contribution for OASDI programs} = \text{OASDI tax rate} \times \text{wage base}$$
$$= .062 \times \$97,500$$
$$= \$6,045$$

The FICA tax also includes a contribution for health insurance (at a rate of 1.45 percent). There is no ceiling on taxable wages for HI, however; all wages and salaries are taxed to pay for Medicare. Recall that the employer pays an identical amount and a self-employed worker pays both parts (15.3 percent) of these taxes.

The ceiling on OASDI taxable wages ($97,500) makes the Social Security tax *regressive*. A person earning up to $97,500 pays 7.65 percent in taxes on every dollar earned. But a person earning twice that much pays no more in payroll taxes. Hence, the effective tax rate *declines* as earnings increase beyond $97,500.

BENEFITS

Although the payroll tax that finances Social Security is regressive, the distribution of benefits is very much *progressive*. That is to say, lower income workers get a higher "return" on their payroll taxes than do high-income workers. As we'll see, this progressivity is a critical mechanism for reducing poverty among the aged.

Early versus Normal Retirement

The basic retirement benefits of Social Security are available under two age-related options:

- *Normal retirement*—a worker born before 1937 who retires at age 65 is eligible for full retirement benefits. For workers born after 1960, the normal retirement age will be 67.[1]
- *Early retirement*—a worker may retire at ages 62 to 64 and receive smaller monthly benefit checks.

The early retirement alternative is designed to pay just as much in lifetime benefits. Because the expected retirement period is longer, however, the monthly benefit checks are smaller. Despite this disadvantage, most Americans choose the early retirement option.

Benefit Levels

The size of the benefit check depends on a worker's employment history. Workers receive a credit for every calendar quarter they are employed. To be eligible for retirement benefits, a worker must accumulate at least 40 credits, or the equivalent of ten years of employment.[2]

The amount of benefits a retired worker receives depends on the wages he or she earned. The relationship between wages and benefits is not linear, however. Workers

---

[1]Since 2000, the normal retirement age increases by two months each year, until it reaches age 67 in the year 2022. Early retirement will still be available at age 62 but at proportionately reduced benefit levels.

[2]Quarterly credits are actually based on annual earnings. In 2006, a worker got one calendar quarter of credit for every $980 earned during the year (up to a maximum of four credit quarters).

with low wages get *proportionately* higher benefits. The benefit award in 2006 was calculated as

- 90 percent of the first $656 of average monthly earnings plus
- 32 percent of the next $3,299 of average monthly earnings, plus
- 15 percent of average monthly earnings over $3,955.

A private insurance program would pay benefits in proportion to wages. The Social Security system instead uses a manifestly *progressive* benefit formula. The formula shown above gives low-wage workers a higher wage-replacement rate. A minimum-wage worker, for example, might earn an average of only $1,000 per month. Upon retirement his benefit would be computed as:

90% of first $656	=	$590
32% of next $344	=	$110
Monthly benefit	=	$700

Hence, his retirement benefit would amount to 70 percent of his paycheck.

A high wage worker gets a much smaller wage-replacement rate. Consider someone earning an average of $8,000 per month. This individual's retirement benefit would be

90% of first $656	=	$ 590
32% of next $3,229	=	$1,056
15% of wages above $3955	=	$ 607
Monthly benefit	=	$2,253

for a total of $2,253. Although this is a much larger benefit than the minimum-wage worker gets ($700), it is a smaller proportion (28%) of previous wages. Hence, as wages increase, the wage-replacement rate declines. This makes the *post*retirement distribution of income more equal than the *pre*retirement distribution.

The progressiveness of the Social Security benefit formula is reinforced with a ceiling on benefits. In 2007, the *maximum* benefit was $2,116 per month. As a result, the high-income worker described above can't collect $2,253 in benefits, but only $2,116. This benefit ceiling further narrows postretirement income differences.

The benefit formula is increased automatically each year at the rate of inflation. Congress also changes the formula and age thresholds on occasion. In the 1960s and early 1970s Congress made the formula more generous, causing Social Security benefits to rise much faster than inflation.

Benefit Adjustments

The benefits computed by the foregoing formula are "full" benefits for a worker retiring at the "normal" age (65–67, depending on year of birth). A worker who chooses early retirement at age 62 would get only 80 percent of the full benefit amount. As noted earlier, this reduction is due to the fact that the retirement period is lengthened by early retirement.

Social Security also provides benefits to nonworking spouses. A 50 percent supplement is added to the monthly benefit check if the retiree has a spouse who is not eligible for his or her own benefits (or whose own benefits would be less than the 50 percent supplement). Widow(er)s and children of workers who die may also receive survivor benefits.

The Earnings Test

Workers needn't actually *retire* in order to get Social Security retirement benefits. Instead, an individual may elect to collect both a paycheck and a retirement benefit. At ages 62–64, a worker can earn as much as $12,480 and still keep his or her full retirement benefit as computed above. That wage limit—called the "earnings test" in bureaucratic jargon—rises each year with inflation.

Only after wages exceed the earnings test does the Social Security Administration start reducing monthly benefits. Every dollar earned beyond the earnings test reduces Social Security benefits by fifty cents. Hence, a worker who was eligible for $12,000 in annual Social Security benefits could earn $12,480 in wages and still get full benefits. But someone earning $25,000 in wages would only collect $5,740 of those Social Security benefits ($12,000 − 0.5 ($25,000 − $12,480)).

Beneficiaries

Over 50 million individuals receive some form of Social Security benefits. Nearly three out of four beneficiaries are retired workers or their survivors (old age and survivors insurance). In 2006, the average benefit for a worker retiring at age 65 was approximately $1,100 per month.

Workers who become disabled before reaching retirement age can also receive Social Security benefits. In this case, benefits are paid from the DI (disability insurance) part of the program. More than 8 million individuals were receiving DI benefit checks in 2006. Once DI recipients reach retirement age, they start getting regular (OASI) retirement benefits.

POVERTY IMPACT

The lion's share of Social Security benefits goes to people who are not poor. Even though the benefit formula is progressive, individuals who earned higher wages when in the labor force also receive larger benefit checks when they retire. Table 14.2 shows how benefit amounts vary by income class. Retirees whose *total* income places them in the top quintile of aged households got median Social Security benefits of $13,111 per year in 2004. This was twice as much as retirees in the lowest income quintile received. Although the Social Security benefit formula is progressive, it clearly doesn't equalize retirement benefits.

Despite the high proportion of benefits paid to the nonpoor, Social Security is still a highly effective antipoverty mechanism. Its antipoverty effectiveness results from the massive amount of income that is transferred and from the fact that virtually all older

TABLE 14.2 Median Social Security Benefits by Income Quintile

Income Quintile	Median Social Security Benefits (per year)	
	Nonmarried Persons	Married Couples
Top fifth	$13,111	$19,799
Second fifth	12,487	20,186
Third fifth	12,355	20,078
Fourth fifth	9,655	19,646
Bottom fifth	6,511	14,198

Source: Susan Grad, *Income of the Population 55 or Older, 2004* (Washington, DC: U.S. Government Printing Office, May 2005).

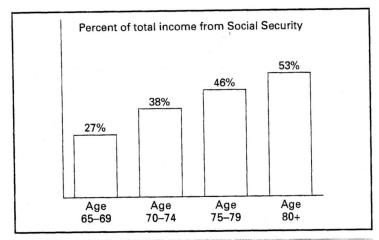

FIGURE 14.1 Dependence on Social Security, by Age

Source: Social Security Administration. Office of Policy. Office of Research, Evaluation, and Statistics. 2006. Income of the Population 55 or Older, 2004. Washington, DC: SSA.

people receive Social Security benefits.[3] Even though most of the money goes to people who were never poor, there is still enough to keep millions of others out of poverty.

Income Dependence

The first indicator of Social Security's pivotal antipoverty role is the proportion of *total* income that comes from that source. As we first observed in Chapter 7 (Figure 7.3), Social Security benefits account for nearly 40 percent of all the income received by aged households. That dependence on Social Security grows even larger as retirees get older. As Figure 14.1 illustrates, over half of the income of people over age 80 comes from Social Security. As other income sources (e.g., earnings) disappear, Social Security benefits become ever more important.

The importance of Social Security for preventing poverty is even more apparent when the distribution of benefits across income classes is considered. In the two lowest income quintiles of aged households, Social Security benefits represent over 80 percent of total income, as Figure 14.2 illustrates. For these lower-income aged households, Social Security benefits are *the* mainstay of financial support.

Poverty Prevention

Table 14.3 illustrates how critical Social Security is in preventing older Americans from falling into poverty. In 2005, one of 10 older Americans was poor, even while receiving Social Security benefits. Were Social Security benefits to cease, almost half of all older Americans would fall into poverty. Hence, for four out of ten older Americans—more than 12 million individuals—Social Security benefits provide the margin of financial security that keeps them out of poverty. Table 14.3 shows how this margin of security becomes increasingly important as people age. Nearly 60 percent of all individuals over age 80 would be poor without Social Security benefits.

---

[3]Ninety percent of older Americans receive Social Security benefits. Those who don't are either still working or receiving retirement benefits from another public pension program (federal, state, or local government; railroad retirement).

Income quintile	Percent of total income from Social Security
Top fifth	19%
Second fifth	48%
Third fifth	67%
Fourth fifth	84%
Bottom fifth	83%

FIGURE 14.2 Dependence on Social Security, by Income Quintile

Source: Social Security Administration. Office of Policy. Office of Research, Evaluation, and Statistics. 2006. Income of the Population 55 or Older, 2004. Washington, DC: SSA.

Behavioral Responses

Although the Social Security program is undoubtedly the foremost safety net for older Americans, 13 million people would not necessarily fall into poverty if benefits ceased. Table 14.3 illustrates how many older people would be poor if they lost their Social Security benefits and *nothing else changed*. In reality, people would behave differently if there were no Social Security program. Without Social Security, people would stay in the workforce longer. When a worker becomes eligible for Social Security benefits, work is much less a necessity.

Social Security not only provides a retirement cushion, but also discourages continued work. Recall the work *incentive* problem we encountered with welfare benefits (Chapter 13). Benefit reductions acted like an implicit tax, discouraging welfare recipients from working. The Social Security benefit formula has the same effect. For workers aged 62–64, every dollar of wages above the earnings test ($12,480 in 2006) reduces Social Security benefits by 50 cents. Hence, the implicit tax rate on wages is 50 percent. When combined with income and payroll taxes, the implied burden on an older worker's wages exceeds 75 percent. This makes continued work unprofitable. Like

TABLE 14.3 Antipoverty Impact of Social Security

Subgroup	Percent in Poverty	
	With Social Security	**Without Social Security**
All aged persons	8.4	48.9
White	7.2	48.1
Black	20.4	63.1
Hispanic	16.5	56.7
Persons aged 65–74	7.1	35.2
aged 75–79	8.5	52.3
aged 80+	10.7	59.3
Married couples	2.6	41.5
Nonmarried persons	15.3	57.7

Source: U.S. Social Security Administration (2005 data).

welfare recipients, older workers opt for more leisure rather than more work when confronted with such work disincentives.[4]

In the absence of Social Security people might also save more during their working years so as to accumulate larger nest eggs for retirement. Fewer retirees would live on their own, choosing instead to live with relatives or friends in order to reduce expenses. These behavioral changes might not make up for the loss of Social Security benefits, but they would lessen the poverty impact. To the extent that Social Security benefits now *substitute* for these income alternatives, their antipoverty impact is exaggerated.

REFORM OPTIONS

Several suggestions have been made for enhancing the antipoverty impact of Social Security.

More Progressivity

Although people would undoubtedly work and save more if there were no Social Security, the program has done a remarkable job of reducing the number of aged poor and of alleviating the condition of those who remain poor. Nevertheless, there are many observers who argue that we could further reduce poverty by increasing Social Security benefits. Across-the-board increases in benefits would extend to the poor and nonpoor alike, of course. Thus, if we wanted to aid the aged poor while holding down program costs (and payroll taxes!), *minimum* benefit levels would have to be raised faster than average benefit levels.

There are strong objections to raising minimum benefit levels faster than average benefit levels or, for that matter, raising any benefit levels at all. The primary objection is that the Social Security system should retain as much of its *insurance* character as possible, and not become a straightforward *welfare* program.[5] What is feared is that the further substitution of welfare (income redistribution) objectives for insurance objectives will undermine the popular support that the Social Security system enjoys. Thus, Congress walks a thin line when it seeks to aid the aged poor while maintaining broad public support.

Some people have also suggested reducing, or even eliminating, Social Security benefits for wealthy retirees. Why give income transfers to people who don't need it? By using an income or wealth ceiling for benefit eligibility, more funds would be available for low-income retirees. However, this proposal runs into the same argument that opposes higher *minimum* benefits; any means testing for benefits converts Social Security into a welfare program. Upper-income workers will feel cheated out of the benefits they "earned." The broad political base of the program would erode.

---

[4] See Leora Friedberg, "The Labor Supply Effects of the Social Security Earnings Test" (Cambridge, MA: National Bureau of Economic Research, Working Paper #7200); also see Cordelia Reimers and Marjorie Honig, "Responses to Social Security by Men and Women," *Journal of Human Resources* (Spring 1996), pp. 359–382. Canada's Income Security program has similar effects, according to Micheal Banker, Jonathan Gruber, and Kevin Milligan, "The Retirement Effects of Canada's Income Security Programs" (Cambridge, MA: National Bureau of Economic Research, Working Paper #86583). A global survey of incentive effects is provided in Jonathan Gruber and David Wise, "Social Security Programs and Retirement Around the World: Micro Estimation" (Cambridge, MA: National Bureau of Economic Research, Working Paper #9407, 2003).

[5] In reality, the redistributional component of Social Security overwhelms its annuity component; see Edward N. Wolff, "Social Security Annuities and Transfers," in *Poverty and Prosperity in the U.S.A. in the Late Twentieth Century,* eds. D. Papadimitriou and E. Wolff (New York: St. Martin's Press, 1993).

More Work Incentives

Retirees resent the benefit reductions that occur when they continue to work past retirement age. As we observed earlier, any wages above the "earnings test" threshold ($12,480 in 2006) are offset by a cut in current Social Security benefits, for workers aged 62 to 64. This 50 percent implicit tax rate is such a strong work disincentive that few retirees earn above the earnings test threshold. In 2000, Congress eliminated the earnings test for workers over age 65. But by that age most people have left the workforce. Younger retirees want similar relief from the earnings test. If the earnings test were eliminated, however, the costs of the Social Security program would increase substantially. This is the now familiar goal conflict.

Privatize

In recent years, critics have proposed an even more radical reform for Social Security—eliminating the program altogether. Instead of a tax-funded *public* retirement program, they favor a wholly *private* system of retirement savings. The argument for *privatization* springs from several observations. First, the "returns" (benefits) on people's Social Security "investments" (taxes) are low and getting worse. Individuals could get a higher return by investing their money in stocks, bonds, or other assets. Second, compulsory Social Security leaves individuals with little choice about how and when to save or retire. Third, the Social Security system confronts severe financial strains when the baby boomers (born 1946–1960) start retiring in 2008. So the current program can't continue without major changes anyway.

Defenders of the program point out that individual investing is uncertain and risky. What would happen to people who didn't save enough or whose investments soured? Inevitably, a new means-tested program would have to be created if the Social Security safety net were withdrawn. Furthermore, any diversion of payroll taxes to private investments would worsen Social Security's financial position. The baby boomers will need (and expect) their Social Security benefits even if young workers are permitted to rely on privatized savings plans. The biggest challenge for the next 20 years will be to secure enough funds (via higher payroll taxes or general revenues) to pay those benefits.

MEDICARE

Like welfare recipients, older Americans receive not only *cash* transfers but also *in-kind* transfers. The most important of these come from the Medicare program. Like other forms of social insurance, the benefits of Medicare are available to all older Americans without consideration of income or wealth. Medicare benefits come in two forms: basic hospital insurance and a supplemental medical insurance option.

HOSPITAL INSURANCE

The core of the Medicare program is universal hospital insurance (HI) for people over age 65 (and younger disabled recipients of disability insurance). The HI program provides for

- inpatient hospital care
- skilled nursing care
- home health care
- hospice care

Although its scope is broad, the HI program provides full coverage of related expenses for very limited time periods. After 60 days of hospital care or 20 days in a skilled nursing facility, patients must pay a significant share of their own bills (up to $101.50 a day). After 100 days, all HI coverage ceases.

SUPPLEMENTAL MEDICAL INSURANCE

Because HI coverage is so limited, Medicare gives older Americans the option of purchasing subsidized insurance for additional medical costs. The supplemental medical insurance (SMI) program offers very broad coverage for a low monthly premium ($93.50 in 2007). Beginning in 2007, high-income households had to pay higher premiums ($106 to $162), giving the program a touch of progressivity. With SMI coverage, an older person pays a small annual deductible ($111 in 2007) and 20 percent of covered medical expenses. Virtually all older Americans enroll in the SMI program.

Since 2005, Medicare has also offered supplemental coverage for prescription drugs. The so-called "Part D" program is an insurance option offered by private companies with a government subsidy. For a premium of roughly $32 a month, seniors pay 25 percent of prescription drug costs in the range of $250 to $2,250 and only 5 percent of costs that exceed $5,000 a year.

POVERTY IMPACT

In 2005, the Medicare program paid out $300 billion in benefits. Only $33 billion was collected from older Americans in the form of SMI premiums. Hence, Medicare generated a net transfer to the aged that was worth over $270 billion. About two-thirds of this transfer was financed by the FICA payroll tax; the rest came out of the federal government's general revenues.

The in-kind Medicare transfer of $270 billion amounts to roughly $6,000 per year for every older American. Although the amount of benefits actually received depends on an individual's health status, the average transfer puts perspective on the relative importance of Medicare for financial security. The median *money* income of an older couple was approximately $35,000 in 2005; for aged persons living alone the median was $14,000. Accordingly, the in-kind Medicare transfer increased *real* incomes of the aged by 17 to 40 percent.

Because Medicare is an in-kind benefit, it does not directly affect the official poverty count, which focuses exclusively on *cash* income. The Medicare subsidy, however, reduces the expenses of the aged and so allows them to stay above poverty living standards even if their cash income falls short of official poverty thresholds. According to Census Bureau estimates, approximately 1 million older people now officially counted as poor would not be so if the value of Medicare benefits were taken into account. Millions more older Americans enjoy a higher living standard (and better health) due to Medicare as well.

UNEMPLOYMENT INSURANCE

The Social Security and Medicare programs are principally sources of social insurance for retired workers. For younger individuals still active in the labor force, social insurance against income loss is far less extensive. To a large extent, this gap reflects the conviction that people should work to support themselves (work incentives).

TABLE 14.4 Major Social Insurance Programs	
Program	**Benefits Paid in 2005**
Social Security	
Old Age and Survivors' Insurance	$415 billion
Disability Insurance	78 billion
Medicare	
Hospital Insurance	168 billion
Supplemental Medical Insurance	135 billion
Unemployment Insurance	35 billion
Workers' Compensation	58 billion
Veterans' Benefits	57 billion

Source: U.S. Office of Management and Budget.

There are two major social-insurance programs for active workers: unemployment insurance and workers' compensation. As Table 14.4 indicates, the combined benefits of these two programs amount to less than one-eighth of the social-insurance benefits paid to older Americans.

Despite the relatively small amount of money set aside for unemployment insurance (UI), that program could be an important factor in preventing poverty. As we observed in Chapter 5, unemployment is a major cause of poverty. By replacing some of the income lost during spells of unemployment, the UI program reduces slippage into poverty. How effective the UI program is in preventing poverty depends on how much it offers in benefits and to whom.

ELIGIBILITY CONDITIONS

The UI system created in 1935 was not designed to provide benefits for everyone who experiences unemployment. Rather, the program was targeted more narrowly to experienced workers who lose their jobs through no fault of their own. Graduating students just looking for their first full-time job don't qualify for UI benefits. Nor do workers who quit their jobs or who get fired for cause.

Because each state runs its own UI program, there is no uniform set of eligibility conditions for UI benefits. However, all states require that UI applicants

- have certain amounts of recent work experience and earnings,
- demonstrate an ability and willingness to seek and accept suitable employment, and
- have lost their jobs through no fault of their own.

Over 95 percent of the *employed* workforce is covered by UI. However, only about a third of all *unemployed* persons are covered due to the work experience and job-loss conditions.

BENEFITS

If eligible for UI insurance, an unemployed worker can collect a weekly UI benefit check. Generally, the UI benefit amounts to 50 to 70 percent of the former wage, up to a specified maximum. There is tremendous variation among the state programs, however. An unemployed worker in Hawaii could have gotten as little as $5 a week in 2006. In

TABLE 14.5 Variations in State UI Benefits (2006)

State	Minimum Benefit	Maximum Benefit	Average Benefit
High benefits			
Hawaii	$ 5	$459	337
Massachusetts	31	826	357
New Jersey	75	521	336
Minnesota	38	515	321
Low benefits			
Arizona	60	240	195
Alabama	45	230	182
Mississippi	30	210	186
Louisiana	10	258	192

Source: U.S. Department of Labor, Employment and Training Administration.

Massachusetts, an unemployed worker could have received as much as $826 per week. Table 14.5 illustrates some of this variation in benefit levels.

Although there is great interstate variation in weekly benefit levels, the duration of benefit eligibility is more uniform. Federal legislation authorizes a basic 26-week program, funded completely out of state payroll tax receipts. Federal law also authorizes an additional 13- or 26-week period of benefits when state unemployment rates exceed certain thresholds. The second period of eligibility is jointly funded by the federal and state governments.[6] In severe national recessions, Congress has also authorized a third period of extended benefits, paid exclusively out of federal revenues.

POVERTY IMPACT

Most UI benefits are not paid to poor people or even to people who are at high risk of becoming poor. This is hardly surprising, given our earlier observation (Chapter 5) that most people who experience unemployment are not poor.

The family income of UI recipients is typically kept substantially above poverty levels by the presence of other workers in the household. Nearly two-thirds of all UI recipients are married, and most of these married recipients have a working spouse.

The financial security of many UI recipients is also buttressed by the nature of their job loss. A sizable proportion of UI recipients is employed in industries where recurrent layoffs are common. Typically, the jobs are in manufacturing or construction and are often unionized. Over a third of all UI recipients end up getting recalled to their former jobs in a relatively short amount of time.

As emphasized in Chapter 5, unemployment poses the greatest risk of poverty if it continues for a long period of time. Most of the people who receive UI benefits don't stay unemployed very long. In 2005, the median duration of UI receipt was only 15 weeks. During that period, the average UI recipient received $4,000 in benefits.

The UI recipients most likely to be at risk of poverty are those who remain unemployed until their UI eligibility is exhausted. About 30 percent of all UI recipients

---

[6]All state and regular federal extended benefits are financed by a net payroll tax of 0.8 percent on the first $7,000 of annual wages.

exhaust their regular benefits. Although nearly half of these exhaustees find employment shortly after their UI benefits run out, their post-UI jobs often pay less than their former employment. Even more at risk are those UI exhaustees who remain unemployed for months longer after their UI benefits cease. Although these unemployed "UI exhaustees" are a small fraction of all UI recipients, their risk of poverty is high: about one in three are poor. Only about 6 percent of UI exhaustees end up on welfare and 10 percent receive food stamps. Accordingly, the UI program is an important element in the social safety net—keeping middle-class families from falling into poverty. Without UI, a lot more unemployed workers would be poor.[7]

CHILD-SUPPORT ENFORCEMENT

Child support has long been viewed as a family law issue to be resolved by local courts. Over time, however, state and federal governments have taken an increasingly aggressive role in the establishment and enforcement of child-support obligations. Prior to 1984, state and federal governments largely restricted their enforcement efforts to welfare (AFDC) cases. Since 1984, however, states are *required* by federal laws to offer child-support enforcement to *all* parents who request it. Further federal legislation in 1988 (the Family Support Act) established mandatory wage withholding for child-support obligations and national guidelines for child-support awards. With these and other changes, child-support enforcement has evolved from a means-tested welfare service to something more akin to social insurance. In the process, it has also become a more effective mechanism in preventing poverty.

CHILD-SUPPORT GAPS

The impetus for public child-support initiatives comes from the recognition that more and more children grow up in single-parent families, often with no financial support from the absent parent. In 1970, only 12 percent of all children (under age 18) lived in a one-parent family; today, nearly 30 percent do so and roughly 50 percent will do so before reaching age 18. As discussed in Chapter 8, this revolutionary change in family structure has affected rich and poor and all racial and ethnic groups.

The financial security of single-parent families often depends on support contributions from the absent parent. It is widely believed that absent parents also have a moral and social obligation to provide child support, even in cases where financial insecurity is not present. This societal expectation for child support is often not met, however. In 2005, there were nearly 14 million women raising children in the absence of their natural fathers. Fewer than 8 million of these mothers received any child-support payments from absent fathers. Accordingly, over 6 million mothers—and their children—had to get along without child-support payments. (Another 3 million children live with their custodial father, but few statistics are collected on them.)

---

[7]For more information on the characteristics and experiences of UI recipients, see Congressional Budget Office, *Family Income of Unemployment Insurance Recipients* (Washington, DC: Government Printing Office, March 2004); also Karen Needels, Walter Corson, and Walter Nicholson, *Left Out of the Boom Economy: UI Recipients in the Late 1990s* (Princeton, NJ: Mathematica Policy Research, October 2001); also Walter Corson and Mark Dynarski, *A Study of Unemployment Insurance Recipients and Exhaustees* (Princeton, NJ: Mathematica Policy Research, 1990).

TABLE 14.6 Child-Support Payments, by Marital Status of Single-Parent Poor Mothers

Marital Status	Number (%)	Percent Entitled to Support	Percent Receiving Support	Average Payment	Average Income
All poor mothers	2,823,000	56	37	$3,078	$7,604
Remarried	216,000 (8%)	59	44	$2,664	$3,593
Divorced	763,000 (27%)	64	47	$3,767	$8,036
Separated	479,000 (17%)	48	33	$3,663	$7,941
Never married	1,343,000 (48%)	52	31	$2,389	$7,955

Source: U.S. Congress, Committee on Ways and Means, *2004 Green Book,* Table 8-6.

Table 14.6 shows how the gap in child support affects poor families. Two-thirds of all *non*poor custodial mothers and just 56 percent of all poor custodial mothers are supposed to receive child support from noncustodial fathers, either by court order or agreement. In both income groups, child-support entitlement is common among remarried and divorced mothers but relatively rare among never-married mothers. Indeed, the low child-support entitlement among poor women is largely due to the fact that nearly half of them never married the father of their children.

Only about two out of three custodial mothers who are legally entitled to get child support actually receive *any* payments. Only one out of three receive the *full* amount due.[8] This gap is particularly evident among poor families, where only one out of three custodial mothers gets any child support. Here again, the likelihood of actual support depends greatly on marital status, with never-married mothers least likely (31 percent) to get *any* child support. Even when they do get some support, the amount of money is very low (average of $2,389 per year). That's just under $200 a month. As Table 14.6 shows, the *total* cash income of these single mothers—even with child support—is far below poverty thresholds.

Table 14.6 documents that millions of custodial mothers are raising their children without any significant financial support from absent fathers. These unsupported women and children are at high risk of poverty and have swelled welfare caseloads in every state.

ENFORCEMENT POLICIES

To increase parental support, government at all levels has expanded the government's role in child-support enforcement. The 1975 amendments to the Social Security Act (Title IV, part D) strengthened enforcement mechanisms by providing the states with federal matching funds for:

- enforcing child-support obligations
- locating absent parents
- establishing paternity
- obtaining support awards

[8]For more detail, see U.S. Census Bureau, *Custodial Mothers and Fathers and Their Child Support: 2003* (Washington, DC: Government Printing Office, July 2006).

Title III of the 1996 welfare reform legislation (PRWORA) went beyond federal offers of financial aid to *mandatory* state programs. To get TANF block grants states must maintain paternity-establishment and child-support collection programs. Any custodial parent who applies for federally funded welfare must agree to help collect child support and also assign all rights to support payments to the welfare agency. In return, the state is required to initiate a paternity investigation (including mandatory genetic testing), to seek and enforce support obligations, and to implement guidelines for support awards. Since 1994 states have also been required to impose automatic withholding of support payments from the paychecks of noncustodial parents. To find absent parents and enforce support obligations, the states are authorized to access all government databanks including tax records, motor vehicle registrations, Social Security records, and the Selective Service System.

As noted earlier, federal law has required the states since 1984 to make these child-support enforcement services available to *all* custodial parents, regardless of income. The states can charge a fee of no more than $25 to nonwelfare parents. Even this fee can be charged to the noncustodial parent or paid by the state itself if it chooses.

POVERTY IMPACT

In theory, child-support payments could be an important antipoverty mechanism. In practice, however, they are more effective in preventing slippage into poverty than facilitating poverty exits. More than $20 billion a year in child-support payments is received by nonpoor mothers.

Single mothers already in poverty clearly don't fare as well. To some extent, their poverty reflects the failure to collect support payment from absent fathers. The gap between collections and entitlement is not wide enough, however, to explain much poverty. In 2001 there were 2.8 million single-parent moms in poverty of whom 1.6 million were legally entitled to a child-support award. As Table 14.6 showed, less than two out of three of these mothers actually received any child support and what they got was meager. Yet, even if *full* payment had been made on those awards, only 200,000 of those families—one out of nine—would have had incomes above the poverty threshold. Hence, child-support enforcement is a fairly ineffective mechanism for reducing poverty; it serves, however, as a substantial safety net for keeping low-income families from falling into poverty.[9]

Reform Proposals

The primary weakness of child-support enforcement as an antipoverty mechanism originates in the status of the poor child's parents. The problem starts with never-married mothers and fathers. Nearly 60 percent of the poor women who don't receive child support are never-married mothers, typically in their late teens and early twenties. Without a marital union, they confront greater obstacles to obtaining child support. They must be willing and able to identify the father and, if necessary, to establish legal paternity in the courts or administrative agencies. Many young mothers may be hesitant to do so. They may be hopeful of maintaining a household with the father, and

---

[9]There is evidence that the prospect of enforcement may deter low-income couples (especially fathers) from divorcing; see Lucia A. Nixon, "The Effects of Child Support Enforcement on Marital Dissolution," *Journal of Human Resources* (Winter 1997), pp. 159–181.

reluctant to antagonize him. Alternatively, they may regard the father as a poor marital or parenting prospect and prefer to avoid further contact with him.[10] Since the welfare agency gets any support payments collected, the economic incentive to pursue paternity and child support is also weak.

Poor Fathers

Regardless of the mother's feelings or incentives, there is also little expectation of substantial support in many cases. The sexual partners of teenage mothers are typically teenage boys with little work experience, modest education, and little income.[11] Although these fathers may have a moral and social obligation to support their children, it is not evident how that obligation can or should be enforced. Should a teenage father be compelled to quit school and take a job? Should he be imprisoned if he can't or won't pay? Aside from abstinence, there are no easy answers for the economic security of children born to teenage parents.

Child-support collections are also inhibited by the tangle of red tape. There are substantial administrative costs associated with child-support enforcement. Even though such activities appear to be highly cost-effective, limited public budgets typically require a rationing process. As administrative delays lengthen, the probability of establishing and enforcing child-support obligations diminishes. If a noncustodial parent moves to another state, the process of enforcement becomes much more costly and success much less likely.

Child-Support Assurance

Professor Irwin Garfinkel and others have urged that the present system of child-support *enforcement* be replaced with a system of child-support *assurance*. In effect, the federal government would guarantee a certain threshold of child support to children of absent parents. Just as Social Security insures against the death or disability of a breadwinner, so would a child-support assurance system insure against the absence of a parent. With such a system *all* single parents would receive assured child support. The government would assume full responsibility for collecting child-support obligations from noncustodial parents, according to fixed guidelines (e.g., 17 percent of gross income for one child, 25 percent for two children, and so on) and using mandatory wage withholding.

A child-support assurance system could have a dramatic effect on poverty rates and welfare caseloads. According to simulation estimates, assured annual support of $1,000 to $3,000 per child would reduce the poverty gap by 13 to 24 percent.[12]

---

[10]An experiment in Ohio revealed that nearly half of all unmarried welfare mothers refused to identify their children's fathers; see Charles Adams, David Landsbergen, and Larry Cobler, "Welfare Reform and Paternity Establishment," *Journal of Policy Analysis and Management* (1992), pp. 665–687.

[11]See Maria Cancian and Daniel Meyer, "The Economic Circumstances of Fathers with Children on W-2," Focus (Summer 2002), pp. 19–24; Ronald Mincy and Elaine Sorensen, "Deadbeats and Turnips in Child Support Reform," *Journal of Policy Analysis and Management* (Winter 1998); Maureen Piroq-Good and David Good, "Child Support Enforcement for Teenage Fathers: Problems and Prospects," *Journal of Policy Analysis and Management, 14* (1994), pp. 15–42; Robert Lerman and Theodora Ooms, eds., *Young Unwed Fathers: Changing Roles and Emerging Policies* (Philadelphia, PA: Temple University Press, 1993).

[12]Irwin Garfinkel, "Child Support Assurance: An Addition to Our Social Security Menu," in *Security for America's Children,* eds. P. Vande Water and L. Schorr (Dubuque, IA: Kendall/Hunt, 1992), pp. 57–70. Lower estimates of potential welfare reduction (including observations on welfare *reentry*) are contained in Daniel R. Meyer, "Child Support and Welfare Dynamics: Evidence from Wisconsin," *Demography* (February 1993), pp. 45–62, and Wei-Yin Hu, "Child Support, Welfare Dependency, and Women's Labor Supply," *Journal of Human Resources* (Winter 1999), pp. 71–103.

Although a child-support assurance system might significantly *reduce* poverty among single-parent families, such an approach is not universally welcomed. One objection emerges from cost considerations. Universal child-support assurance could cost up to $5 billion per year. Costs would come down only if the government could substantially increase collections from absent parents. Since most of the absent parents of poor children are poor themselves, the prospects for increased collections (and lower net costs) are not good.

Another objection is based on family values. Many critics fear that further government intrusion into family matters will weaken already tenuous family bonds. The administrative and legal procedures entailed in public child-support assurance may antagonize parents and diminish chances of reconciliation. Public resources would be better spent, they say, in promoting parent access, family formation, and employability than in focusing on financial collections. There is some evidence, however, that stronger child-support enforcement actually *reduces* the probability of marital breakup, especially for women who would otherwise end up on welfare.[13] Hence, the family effects of better child support may differ for never-married and other mothers. Finally, critics fear that assured child-support payments would increase the incentives for childbirth already associated with the more onerous welfare system.[14]

As the larger issues entailed in a child-support assurance system continue to be debated, incremental changes in the present system are advocated. Given the demonstrated efficacy of child-support enforcement efforts, proponents want enforcement budgets increased. They also want to increase the efficiency of enforcement efforts by requiring more coordination across state boundaries. If child-support enforcement became more certain, voluntary support payments might increase. There might even be a greater reluctance to have children one didn't plan to support.[15]

Summary

Social insurance programs are the largest component in the U.S. income transfer system. They are distinguishable from welfare programs by the absence of income or wealth eligibility conditions (means testing).

The Social Security programs of retirement, survivors', and disability insurance are the largest expenditure item in the federal budget. Social Security is a pay-as-you-go system, with current benefits financed by current payroll taxes. Eligibility and benefit levels are determined by age and earnings history. Social Security is the nation's most effective antipoverty program, providing nearly 40 percent of all retirement income.

The Medicare program also provides substantial in-kind income to older Americans. The health insurance subsidies of Medicare substantially reduce the cash

---

[13]Lucia A. Nixon, "The Effect of Child Support Enforcement on Marital Dissolution," *Journal of Human Resources* (Winter 1997), pp. 159–181.

[14]Anna Aizer and Sara McLanahan, "The Impact of Child Support Enforcement on Fertility, Parental Investments, and Child Well-Being," *Journal of Human Resources* (Winter 2006), pp. 28–45.

[15]Another alternative is to assure quality child care rather than direct financial support; see Barbara Bergmann, "Curing Child Poverty in the United States," *American Economic Review* (May 1994), pp. 76–80. Bergmann compares the French and American systems of child support in *Saving Our Children from Poverty* (New York: Russell Sage, 1996).

expenses of older Americans, eliminating real poverty for close to 1 million older Americans and raising real living standards for millions more.

Unemployment insurance (UI) is available to workers with recent work experience who lose their jobs because of layoffs, plant closings, and other nonpersonal reasons. Although benefits vary widely across states, they average from 50 to 70 percent of previous wages. Because most experienced workers who have a spell of unemployment are not poor, the UI program is not a major antipoverty mechanism. Most at risk of poverty are individuals who remain unemployed for several months after their UI benefits cease.

Child-support enforcement has evolved into a quasi-social insurance program. In principle, any single parent can access government services to establish and enforce child-support obligations. Present child-support payments fall far short of universal coverage, however, leaving millions of single parents and their children in poverty. More aggressive enforcement activity has significant potential to increase payments. However, its antipoverty potential is limited by the youth and low income of absent fathers who were the sexual partners of never-married mothers. Reform proposals range from a child-support assurance system that guarantees support payments to more modest administrative changes that would increase support collections.

Further Reading

Aizer, Anna, and Sara McLanahan, "The Impact of Child Support Enforcement on Fertility, Parental Investments, and Child Well-Being," *Journal of Human Resources* (Winter 2006), pp. 28–45.

Cogan, John, and Olivia Mitchell, "Perspectives from the President's Commission on Social Security Reform," *Journal of Economic Perspectives* (Spring 2003), pp. 149–172.

Congressional Budget Office, *Family Income of Unemployment Insurance Recipients*. Washington, DC: Government Printing Office, March 2004.

Egendorf, Laura K., ed., *An Aging Population*. San Diego, CA: Greenhaven Press, 2002.

Freeman, Richard B., and Jane Waldfogel, "Dunning Delinquent Dads," *Journal of Human Resources 36:2* (Spring 2001), pp. 207–225.

"The Future of Medicare," a symposium, *Journal of Economic Perspectives* (Spring 2000), pp. 21–98.

Huang, Chien-Chung, Irwin Garfinkel, and Jane Waldfogel, "Child Support Enforcement and Welfare Caseloads," *Journal of Human Resources* (Winter 2004), pp. 108–134.

Pirog, Maureen, and Kathleen Ziol-Guest, "Child Support Enforcement: Programs and Policies, Impacts and Questions," *Journal of Policy Analysis and Management* (September 2006), pp. 943–990.

Schulz, James H., *The Economics of Aging,* 7th ed. Westport, CT: Auburn House, 2001.

U.S. Census Bureau, *Custodial Mothers and Fathers and Their Child Support: 2003,* Washington, DC: Government Printing Office, July 2006.

U.S. Congress, Committee on Ways and Means, *Green Book,* Washington, DC: U.S. Government Printing Office, occasional.

U.S. Congressional Budget Office, *The Outlook for Social Security,* Washington, DC: Government Printing Office, June 2004.

Web Links

Center for Law and Social Policy. Occasional studies and policy briefs: www.clasp.org

National Bureau of Economic Research. Ongoing Studies on social security and related topics: www.nber.org

Urban Institute. Ongoing studies, including the Sorenson, Zibman study noted previously, from New Federalism project: www.urban.org

U.S. Department of Labor. Data on unemployment insurance program: www.doleta.gov

U.S. Social Security Administration. Data on Social Security program: www.ssa.gov

Administration for Children and Families. Data and research bibliography on child support enforcement: www.acf.dhhs.gov

Medicare program. www.medicare.gov

CHAPTER 15
EMPLOYMENT POLICIES
꩜

If meaningful and long-term solutions to the problem of poverty are to be implemented, public policy must venture beyond income maintenance. As recent welfare reforms have recognized, employment is a necessary condition for the financial security of nonaged households. But it's not sufficient to require welfare recipients to search for work. The jobs must also be there. And they must provide enough income to keep families out of poverty. When those conditions are fulfilled, poverty and the need for income maintenance will be at a minimum.

The government has several alternatives at its disposal for expanding employment opportunities. At the most general level, it may seek to increase the demand for labor by stimulating aggregate demand. A variety of fiscal and monetary measures are available for that purpose. Rather than raise the general demand for labor, the government might instead try to increase the demand for specific groups of workers (e.g., low-income workers; welfare recipients). This may entail tax credits or other financial incentives for hiring target groups. Or the government might take still more direct action by creating jobs itself via public employment programs.

The government can also influence the *supply* of labor. Rather than stimulate new demand, government policy may focus on training unemployed workers for jobs already available. Still another possibility is to make labor markets more efficient in matching available workers with vacant jobs. The government can also increase the financial *incentive* to work, by raising minimum wages or supplementing low wages (e.g., with tax credits). Or, as we noted in Chapter 13, the government can *compel* people to work as a condition of continuing income transfers.

These various strategies for increasing employment reflect the disparate Restricted Opportunity, Flawed Character, and Big Brother perspectives that underlie all antipoverty policies. As with other approaches, public attitudes and policies have shifted over time. In the 1930s a heavy emphasis was put on public employment. After World War II the government placed primary reliance on aggregate economic policies to provide the necessary job opportunities. Only in the late 1950s and early 1960s did an awareness emerge that other approaches were also necessary to provide a requisite number of jobs; at that time, a variety of training programs was introduced. The whole sequence started again in the 1970s. First there was an expansion of public employment programs, especially in the mid-1970s. Then the primary importance of aggregate demand policies was emphasized, along with an increasing concern for aggregate supply. This concern led to a preference for training over public jobs and a search for new ways to improve the match between job seekers and job vacancies.

In the 1980s there was an increasing emphasis on the obligation of welfare recipients to work or improve their employability prospects (e.g., via human capital investment). The recession of 1990–1991 helped shift attention back to the adequacy of the social safety net. As the economy recovered, greater emphasis was directed toward the nature of available jobs and government policies that, in President Clinton's words, would "make work pay." By the end of the 1990s this goal had largely been achieved with greatly expanded tax credits (the EITC) for low-income workers. This chapter reviews the nature, history, and potential of these many different dimensions of employment policy.

AGGREGATE DEMAND POLICIES

Most people believe that the United States could have averted the Great Depression were we as knowledgeable in 1930 as we are now about the workings of the economy. This belief stems from the conviction that economists can now manage the economy to a degree formerly unheard of. Present-day arguments between economists concentrate not on the issue of whether the level of demand can be affected, but on how much success can be achieved by such policies.

DEMAND MANAGEMENT

The claims of modern economists inspire hope for the plight of the poor. If we really can manage aggregate demand, we can provide enough jobs for the unemployed, the underemployed, and the discouraged poor. Anyone who has ever skimmed through an introductory economics textbook can provide an outline for action. Fiscal policies can expand demand through increased government expenditures, consumer tax cuts, or enhanced tax incentives for investment. Monetary policy may provide a stimulus to demand by making access to credit easier and cheaper. Together, such policies could potentially move millions of persons out of poverty.

As enticing as the notion of complete demand management might appear, it is evident that the economy has not performed as well as such management capability would imply. The economy continues to suffer periodic recessions. Although the 1990s ended with a prolonged economic expansion and record-setting low unemployment rates, few people believed economic downturns were a thing of the past.

The first two years of the twenty-first century in fact demonstrated again how economies can flounder. Although the 2001 recession was relatively mild, it still eliminated millions of job opportunities. As the national unemployment rate drifted upward, the odds of falling into poverty increased. It also became more difficult for welfare recipients to gain financial independence.

FULL EMPLOYMENT VERSUS PRICE STABILITY

Although no one claims that economic recessions can be eliminated completely, the role of policy in *fostering* recessions must be recognized. Creating jobs for the poor isn't the sole goal of macroeconomic policy. The goal most often in conflict with full employment is price stability. By making goods and services more expensive, inflation squeezes people's budgets. Even if their incomes increase at the same pace, consumers don't like paying higher prices for the goods and services they buy. Too much inflation can also erode confidence in a nation's currency, its economy, and ultimately its government. To avert these problems, government policy seeks to hold price-level increases in check.

Unfortunately, the pursuit of price stability often causes an increase in unemployment. This happens because the primary strategy for keeping price levels in check is to restrain aggregate demand. If total spending is restrained, there will be less demand-side pressure on prices. Hence, the easiest way to curb inflation is to restrain consumer, investor, and government spending. Unfortunately, when spending slows, so does job growth.

This is certainly what happened in 2001–2002, in 1990–1991, and again in 2005–2006. In all three cases, the Federal Reserve Board feared that the economy was growing so rapidly that inflationary pressures were building up too much. So the "Fed" raised interest rates, making it more expensive for market participants to purchase goods and services. As investment, consumption, and government spending slowed, unemployment rates rose.

THE PHILLIPS CURVE

The Fed isn't unmindful of the unemployment pain it causes when it reins in aggregate demand. But it feels it has no choice. The willingness to tolerate high levels of unemployment is based on a historical relationship between inflation and unemployment. As Figure 15.1 suggests, lower rates of unemployment have generally been accompanied by higher rates of inflation. This tendency, first observed in England by A. W. Phillips, has been found to prevail in scores of countries.[1] Accordingly, the Phillips curve not only summarizes a historical relationship between unemployment rates and inflation rates but appears to offer policy makers a finite set of choices. As long as the curve is an accurate description of economic performance, then full employment and price stability are not attainable at the same time. Instead, some point on the curve, a distinct compromise between the two goals, must be selected as a policy target. And so it happens that some policy makers choose to sacrifice full employment in the hopes of achieving lower rates of inflation.

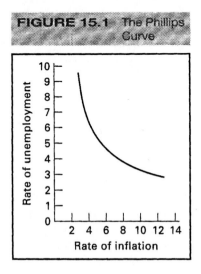

FIGURE 15.1 The Phillips Curve

---

[1] For international observations, see Marina Malinov and Paul Sommers, "A New Line on the Phillips Curve," *Social Science Quarterly* (September 1997), pp. 740–746, and the subsequent discussion in *Social Science Quarterly* (March 1999), pp. 193–196.

Shifting Trade-Offs

Although the Phillips curve appears to present policy makers with a finite set of trade-offs, we must not be too quick in rejecting the goal of full employment. At best, the Phillips curve is a generalization of historical experience; in fact, we have experienced scores of inflation–unemployment combinations that lie both above and below the curve depicted in Figure 15.1. In the 1980s and the early 1990s, the policy consensus was that a national unemployment rate below 5.5 percent would cause wages and prices to accelerate. So policy makers were reluctant to stimulate the economy too much. Despite these fears, however, the unemployment rate fell below 4 percent in 2000 without any acceleration of inflation. Hence, one should not view any particular Phillips curve as an absolute constraint on full employment. At a minimum, one has to recognize that whatever trade-off exists between unemployment and inflation depends on the circumstances (e.g., structural rigidities, international trade, labor union strength, productivity).

The reasoning behind the Phillips curve is also suspect, resembling as it does certain structural unemployment arguments. Nearly everyone agrees that an expansion of aggregate demand is necessary to reduce high levels of unemployment. The proponents of the Phillips curve theory argue that comparatively few benefits of increased spending actually reach the unemployed because they have the wrong skills, are too young or old, live in the wrong places, or are simply unaware of new opportunities. Accordingly, demands for new output are met by overworking existing employees rather than by hiring new workers. Wage rates, and then prices, go up while unemployment rates change little. The greater the effort to reduce unemployment, the faster the rate of inflation.

Transitional Trade-Offs

Even a fixed (unmovable) Phillips curve need not necessitate a permanent sacrifice. The element of time is important. Suppose, for example, that an increase in the demand for goods and services occurred. To satisfy this demand, producers will have to hire additional workers or employ their existing labor forces more fully. Other workers may not be immediately available, however, and they are likely to require training or orientation before they can contribute to output. As a result, producers probably will have to rely primarily on their existing workers for an initial expansion of output. Such reliance is expensive, however, as overtime wage rates are high; productivity is likely to decline with longer hours; and workers will feel in a better position to demand higher base wages. Producers will have a large and increasing incentive to locate and train new workers as expanded output continues. As time passes, producers will substitute new labor for overtime labor, thus reducing costs.

The labor-market adjustment process described here implies that expansion of demand will, indeed, lead to higher prices but that the increased rate of inflation may be a temporary phenomenon. As new workers are absorbed into the production process, the pressure on prices may abate. What the Phillips curve may portray on an aggregate level is the rate of inflation necessary to evoke the required labor force adjustment. The curve should not necessarily be understood to mean that the same high rate of inflation will continue once the adjustment is made. Not only may the price increase be temporary, but it is an integral feature of the adjustment mechanism. Hence, we might be able to say that an 8 percent rate of inflation is necessary to reduce the unemployment rate from 6.0 to 5.5 percent, but we have no firm reason for anticipating continuing high rates of inflation once the lower level of unemployment is reached. High rates of inflation could continue, of course, but they would be the consequence of actions other than the initial effort to reduce employment.

Expectations

Inflationary expectations are often the source of continued wage–price escalation. When people see prices rising, they may come to expect inflation to continue. Prodded by such expectations, they may themselves demand higher wages and prices, thereby making inflation more permanent. To the extent that structural factors or expectations create a trade-off between unemployment and inflation, attaining full employment is obviously more difficult. This does not mean, however, that we are stuck with any particular trade-off. Policies that reduce structural bottlenecks or restrain inflationary expectations can shift the Phillips curve to the left. In so doing, they make it less costly (in terms of inflation) to reach the goal of full employment. If, for example, the move toward full employment is slowed by the fact that unemployed workers possess skills in small demand or live in the wrong areas, further expansion of demand might be channeled more specifically in their direction. The pattern of demand, both occupationally and geographically, will affect the speed of adjustment and, thus, the dynamic trade-off. Accordingly, there is no unchangeable relationship of inflation to unemployment. The relationship depends on the capability and determination of policy makers to alter the pattern of demand as they expand it.

Politics

Even if one were to design a policy package that promised more employment with no more inflation, its pursuit would still entail risks. There would be an economic risk that the trade-off didn't improve. There would also be a political risk. Even a successful transitional program would entail some inflationary pressure. And that could backfire politically. The reality is that the politics of the unemployment–inflation trade-off don't favor the poor. Inflation tends to hurt the middle class and older Americans, depending on fixed-income sources (e.g., interest on bonds, private pensions). They will favor policies that shield them from the threat of inflation. Even when the national unemployment rate is relatively high, the number of *employed* individuals far exceeds the number of *unemployed*. Accordingly, the commitment to full employment may waver once prices start rising.[2] When that happens, the president, the Congress, and the Fed are all likely to fret more about the interests of the middle class than the needs of the poor.

THE QUALITY OF JOBS

Fear of inflation has not been the only obstacle to more effective aggregate demand policies. In the general euphoria of our discovery that we could manipulate aggregate demand, we neglected some simple truths. The way in which aggregate demand is stimulated has significant impact on the economy. A large reduction in interest rates, for example, will stimulate the housing and lumber industries, where interest charges are a

[2]For more discussion of the politics of the full employment–price stability trade-off, see Robert Pollin, "Class Conflict and the 'Natural Rate of Unemployment,'" *Challenge* (November–December 1999), pp. 103–111.

major component of total cost. Investment credit allowances, on the other hand, benefit manufacturers of steel, airplanes, and heavy machinery with little impact on housing production. More generally, tax cuts expand the private sector while increases in government spending expand the public sector. Indeed, every fiscal or monetary action will affect the distribution of output, as well as its volume.

Some observers claim that the content of our economic growth has actually worsened job prospects for the poor. They see the manufacturing sector declining and the service sector expanding. In the process, they assert, "good" jobs are disappearing and "bad" jobs are proliferating. Without access to the higher-wage jobs in manufacturing, more workers are likely to be poor at any given level of aggregate unemployment.[3]

Paradoxically, other observers assert that recent job growth has been disproportionately in "good" jobs. As they see it, the jobs created in today's economy require advanced education and technical skills. Middle-class workers have the prerequisites, but poor people don't. As a consequence, college graduates quickly and easily get on the financial fast track. By contrast, job seekers with few skills and little education get left at the starting gate. From this perspective, the proliferation of good jobs widens wage inequalities and does little to reduce poverty.[4]

Although these two perspectives on the labor market are very different, they come to similar policy conclusions. In either case, low-skilled job seekers face bleak prospects. Either they confront an abundance of bad jobs (the first view) or no jobs at all (the second view). To remedy this problem, more attention must be paid to the *structure* of demand, rather than simply its *level*. Some policies provide more jobs for the poor with little effect on prices, while others do just the reverse. The trick is to find the right ones. This will require that policy makers explicitly incorporate antipoverty objectives into their budget plans and look more closely at the impact of alternative policy strategies on the distribution of job opportunities.[5]

However, even truly enlightened full employment policies will not provide decent jobs for all who need them. As unemployment levels drop, it becomes increasingly difficult—and socially expensive—to reach those who still need employment. Accordingly, expansionary fiscal and monetary policies alone cannot wholly eliminate poverty among those who are presently or potentially in the labor force. But it is even more important to emphasize that without determined full employment policies all other efforts to eliminate poverty are rendered impotent. In 1991–1992, for example, more money was spent on welfare, training, education, and other antipoverty efforts than in earlier years. Nevertheless, the number of people in poverty grew by 4.5 million because unemployment levels rose sharply. A similar scenario unfolded in 2000–2004. Clearly,

---

[3]For discussion of the "good" versus "bad" jobs issue, see Bennett Harrison and Barry Bluestone, *The Great U-Turn* (New York: Basic Books, 1988); Gary Loveman and Chris Tilly, "Good Jobs or Bad Jobs?" *International Labor Review, 129* (1988), pp. 593–611; Gary Burtless, ed., *A Future of Lousy Jobs?* (Washington, DC: Brookings Institution, 1990).

[4]For analyses of widening wage inequalities see the symposium in the Spring 1997 *Journal of Economic Perspectives;* also S. Danziger and P. Gottschalk, *America Unequal* (Cambridge, MA: Harvard University Press, 1995).

[5]This kind of industrial policy is advocated by Richard Caputo, "Family Poverty, Unemployment Rates, and AFDC Payments: Trends Among Blacks and Whites," *Families in Society* (November 1993), pp. 515–526.

the demand for labor, especially labor provided by the poor, must be kept at high levels if the poor are to gain financial independence. All other efforts are secondary.[6]

TRAINING PROGRAMS

As every freshman economist knows, both supply and demand forces operate in the labor market. Hence, to many observers it seems as logical to adapt supply to demand as to proceed the other way around. On the supply side is the option of skill training. As public-opinion polls consistently reveal, there is a broad support for this policy option.

STRUCTURAL UNEMPLOYMENT

The potential of training programs to reduce poverty is rooted in the concept of structural unemployment. As we observed in Chapter 5, there are always lots of job vacancies, even when there are millions of unemployed workers. Part of the problem is a mismatch between the skills possessed by the unemployed workers and the skill requirements of available jobs. Hence, it seems eminently reasonable to expect skill training programs to close the skills gap and thereby reduce structural unemployment.

In reality, the skills gap is an ever-changing phenomenon. Changes in the level of aggregate demand affect it, as do changes in technology, investment, and expenditure patterns. As a consequence, any skill training program—especially one run by a third party (like a government agency)—runs the risk of obsolescence.

We also have to recognize that most skill training occurs on the job and not in the classroom. Rarely is a worker hired who is totally job-ready. Even if a new hire has substantial general training in a specific occupation, there is always a void of employer-specific knowledge that must be filled. Moreover, the demands of the job—and the job itself—are likely to evolve over time. To attain higher levels of productivity, employers typically provide a continuum of training, both on the job and, less often, in the classroom.

The amount of upfront training employers have to provide varies inversely with unemployment rates. When the unemployment rate is high, there are more experienced and skilled job seekers in the labor force. Therefore, the need for upfront training is less. By contrast, when unemployment rates are low, those individuals still seeking jobs are most likely to have the greatest skill and experience gaps. Hiring and training them is a more expensive proposition.

The countercyclical nature of the skills gap puts a lid on the potential for government training programs. Poverty is at its worst when unemployment rates are high. Yet that is also the time when training the neediest job seekers is least likely to succeed. There are simply too many other more-qualified job seekers at such times. Training the most needy job seekers may improve their competitive position, but then runs the risk of leaving someone else unemployed. Conversely, when unemployment rates are low,

[6]This conclusion is supported in Robert Haveman and Jonathan Schwabish, "Economic Growth and Poverty: A Return to Normalcy?" (Madison, WI: Institute for Research on Poverty, 1999), and by Hilary Hoynes, Marianne Pace, and Ann Huff Stevens, "Poverty in America: Trends and Explanations," *Journal of Economic Perspectives* (Winter 2006), pp. 47–68.

there is less need for government-provided skill training, since employers are more likely to offer it themselves.[7]

Finally, we must recognize that the desired set of skills is not immediately visible. Employers typically hire workers based on the *expectation* of adequate productivity. That expectation may be influenced, however, by gender, race, and class biases that undervalue the skill potential of the neediest workers.[8] This makes closing the skills gap for poor job seekers that much harder.

PROGRAM EXPERIENCE

In view of all these considerations, expectations for the efficacy of vocational training programs as an antipoverty mechanism are typically too high. The track record of such programs largely bears this out.

MDTA

The first full-scale government training program was established in 1962 under the Manpower Development and Training Act (MDTA). Persistently high rates of unemployment in the period 1958–1961, coupled with fears of advancing automation, led many observers to conclude that a basic mismatch existed between people and jobs. The only way to approach fuller employment, it seemed, was to provide the unemployed with the new skills demanded by advancing technology. Accordingly, Congress provided for a national effort to retrain displaced and unemployed workers in new skill areas.

In the years since the establishment of the MDTA program, the federal government has introduced and operated scores of training programs, with various services and for different target groups (the young, the old, the skilled, the unskilled, welfare recipients, high school dropouts, and so on). Several of those programs are particularly significant because they illustrate different approaches to skill training.

The CETA Program

The Comprehensive Employment and Training Act (CETA) of 1974 was the centerpiece of employment policy in the 1970s. A unique feature of CETA was its transfer of program responsibilities from the federal government to state and local governments.

Another feature of CETA was its increasing focus on disadvantaged (low-income and minority) workers and youth. In its final year (fiscal 1983) over 95 percent of CETA participants were disadvantaged. This focus maximized the program's antipoverty effectiveness. To further assure that disadvantaged workers could participate in CETA, the program paid participants a stipend while they were enrolled in education and training classes. Although small, these stipends enabled people with little other income to acquire needed skills.

A third and most distinctive feature of CETA was its increasing emphasis on public sector employment. President Carter concluded that providing new low-skill jobs in the public sector was the fastest and surest way to employ disadvantaged job seekers. By 1981, one third of all CETA expenditures was going to public service employment rather than to skill training, basic education, or other job services.

---

[7]For evidence from employers, see Harry Holzer, "Will Employers Hire Welfare Recipients? Recent Survey Evidence from Michigan," *Journal of Policy Analysis and Management* (Summer 1999), pp. 449–472.

[8]For a discussion of how employer perceptions affect hiring decisions, see Philip Moss and Chris Tully, *Stories Employers Tell: Race, Skill, and Hiring in America* (New York: Russell Sage, 2001), Chapters 3 and 4.

Although CETA had served over 30 million people in its nine-year history, the program was terminated by the Reagan administration in 1983. In part, the termination of CETA was simply part of the Reagan administration's general retrenchment of social spending. In addition, CETA's heavy emphasis on public sector employment (PSE) was regarded as a failure. PSE jobs were viewed as extraordinarily expensive "make-work" jobs that taught few skills, seldom led to private sector employment, and were too easily corrupted by local political interests. Critics also argued that CETA undermined the work ethic by paying people to rake leaves or attend classes. Although defenders of the program pointed to its success in serving the truly needy, they were unable to demonstrate that the public service employment programs were having any lasting impact on skills or employment.[9]

JTPA Programs

CETA was replaced by the Job Training Partnership Act (JTPA) of 1982. Like CETA, JTPA provided for a variety of employment and training services. There were important differences, however, in JTPA's focus, content, and administration.

Under CETA, employment and training funds were allocated to local prime sponsors, often bypassing state governments. In the process, a whole new bureaucracy was created. JTPA eliminated this level by distributing funds directly to governors to allocate within their own states. At the same time, JTPA gave local private industry councils veto power over JTPA expenditures. This cemented the "partnership" dimension of the program, and provided some assurance that the program would be responsive to business needs.

Whereas CETA provided a mix of training and public sector employment, JTPA focused more on training. The only job creation occurred in the summer jobs program for youth. JTPA was seen more as a long-term solution to structural unemployment, rather than as a short-run response to cyclical unemployment.

The focus of JTPA was broadened to include dislocated workers as well as the disadvantaged workers who were the target of CETA. Dislocated workers are those who have lost jobs because of plant closings and permanent layoffs, and who have little chance of returning to their old jobs. They need not be low-income or minority status, as are disadvantaged workers. JTPA tried to get dislocated workers back into employment by providing skills, (re)training, job search assistance, and other services.

At its peak, approximately half a million people participated annually in JTPA training programs at a cost of roughly $1.5 billion. Most of these participants were disadvantaged and about a fifth were on welfare. Overall, however, the training provided had only very modest effects on the earnings of adult welfare recipients and no impact on out-of-school youth.[10]

Workforce Investment Act

The JTPA program expired in 2000. It was replaced by the Workforce Investment System (WIS). The key difference between earlier employment training programs and

---

[9]For a review of CETA performance, see Sar Levitan and Garth Mangum, eds., *The "T" in CETA* (Kalamazoo, MI: Upjohn Institute, 1980); and Laurie Bassi, "The Effect of CETA on the Post-Program Earnings of Participants," *Journal of Human Resources* (Fall 1983). A review of these and other studies with an emphasis on methodological evaluation issues is contained in Burt Barnow, "The Impact of CETA Programs on Earnings," *Journal of Human Resources* (Spring 1987).

[10]See Howard S. Bloom et al., "The Benefits and Costs of JTPA Title II-A Programs," *Journal of Human Resources* (Summer 1997), pp. 549–576.

the WIS was the establishment of one-stop delivery systems. By forcing local governments to consolidate various training, educational, and counseling services at a single location, WIS hopes to achieve an improved match between available services and client needs. WIS also broadened the definition of dislocated workers to include displaced homemakers.

The WIN Program

A frequent criticism of JTPA, WIS, and other mainstream programs is that they fail to serve adequately the neediest individuals. The number of available training and employment slots is always less than the number of unemployed workers. Hence, some deliberate choices must be made about whom to serve. Under these circumstances, program administrators often prefer to serve those individuals who are most job-ready. The least needy individuals are likely to provide the greatest success stories for program administrators. Unfortunately, this tendency to "cream" from the pool of potential program participants leaves many of the neediest job seekers to fend for themselves.

The failure of mainstream training programs to provide adequate help to the neediest led to the creation of another major training program in the 1970s, the Work Incentive Program (WIN). What distinguished WIN from the outset was the fact that it served only those receiving public assistance: Program participation was specifically limited to adult recipients of AFDC assistance. Moreover, all adult recipients were *required* to register for WIN services, unless exempted for reasons of health or the care of preschool children. This provision resulted from the widespread conviction that welfare recipients avoid employment (see Chapter 9). On a more positive note, the program attempted to provide the supplemental services necessary for successful program completion. These ranged from day care services and work orientation to medical examinations, transportation allowances, counseling, and job placement.

Although WIN seemingly offered all the ingredients for successful movement into employment, the program was not regarded as a success. Funding levels fell far short of program requirements, rendering the promise of comprehensive services impossible to fulfill. As a result, only welfare recipients without child care, transportation, or training needs were likely to get through the program.

A second problem was that welfare recipients were required to *register* for the program but not required to *participate*. This created a mass of paper shuffling and fostered widespread cynicism about program goals. In 1986, 1.6 million welfare recipients were registered for WIN services, but only about 220,000 individuals actually received any services.[11]

The WIN program also exempted from registration and participation welfare mothers with preschool children (under age six). This effectively meant that young women just turning to welfare wouldn't get any employment-related services for years.

The JOBS Program

After 21 years of activity, the WIN program was replaced in 1989 by the Job Opportunities and Basic Skills (JOBS) training program. Like the earlier WIN program, the JOBS program offered an array of employment and support services to hasten the

---

[11]Mary Jo Bane and David T. Ellwood, *Welfare Realities* (Cambridge, MA: Harvard University Press, 1994), p. 20. For more description of WIN services and outcomes, see Bradley R. Schiller, "Lessons from WIN: A Manpower Evaluation," *Journal of Human Resources* (Fall 1978).

movement from welfare to work. There were important differences in the design of JOBS, however. To begin with, there was much greater emphasis on the obligation of welfare recipients to *participate* and on the obligation of states to enforce participation requirements. At least one adult in every two-parent welfare family was required to participate. Mandatory participation was also extended to mothers whose children were at least three years old (versus six years old under WIN). States could even stretch that requirement to mothers whose youngest child was only one year old. Under JOBS, the requirement was to *participate* in some self-help activity (e.g., education, training, work experience), not just register for the program.

The JOBS program also put more emphasis on mandatory community service (workfare) than earlier programs. State demonstrations of alternative program activities during the 1980s had revealed that workfare and job-search assistance activities were effective in reducing welfare caseloads.[12] JOBS not only authorized all states to implement workfare programs but made that activity one of four employment options from which states had to choose at least two. (The other work-related options were on-the-job training, job search, and wage subsidies.)

Like earlier efforts, JOBS was hobbled by funding constraints. Congress offered the states $1 billion in initial matching funds. The 1990–1991 recession squeezed state budgets so tightly, however, that the states were unable to allocate enough of their own funds to secure the federal matching grants. Even if they had, a billion dollars in matching funds would not have stretched very far.

State Block Grants

The welfare reforms of 1996 (see Chapter 13) terminated the JOBS program. Rather than specify a federal program design for the states, Congress decided instead to give the states block grants that they can use for training, job placement, or other services for welfare (TANF) recipients. Since July 1997 states have had much greater flexibility in deciding how much money to spend on training programs and what kind of training services to provide. The decentralization of training activity, however, has also made definitive assessments of program outcomes more difficult.

GENERIC PROBLEMS

As states fashion their own training programs for the poor, they confront the hard realities noted earlier. Traditional skill training programs are expensive and their performance is marginal, particularly for disadvantaged participants. Typically, successful graduates of such programs earn only a few hundred dollars more than they would have without training.[13] That isn't enough to get most off welfare, much less to raise their living standards significantly. Rarely are such programs cost-effective.[14]

---

[12]See Bradley R. Schiller and C. Nielson Brasher, "Workfare in the 1980s: Successes and Limits," *Policy Studies Review* (Summer 1990) and "The Effect of Workfare Saturation on AFDC Caseloads," *Contemporary Policy Issues* (January 1993); also, Judith M. Gueron and Edward Pauly, *From Welfare to Work* (New York: Russell Sage, 1991).

[13]See Howard S. Bloom et al., op. cit.; also, June O'Neill, "Can Work and Training Programs Reform Welfare?" *Journal of Labor Research* (Summer 1993), pp. 265–279; and Gueron and Pauly, *From Welfare to Work.*

[14]Stephen H. Bell and Larry L. Orr, "Is Subsidized Employment Cost Effective for Welfare Recipients?" *Journal of Human Resources* (Winter 1994), pp. 42–61.

In addition to the macro problems noted earlier, the performance of traditional training programs is also constrained by information gaps. The administrators of government training programs often have limited knowledge of job opportunities in the private sector. They simply respond to offers of training services from vocational schools and other institutions whose business is to train people, not hire them. Program participants are also ill-informed about the kinds of jobs that are available, what skills they require, or how much they pay. Accordingly, the training decision is often the outcome of an agreement between two individuals (a trainee and program administrator) who are acting on the basis of incomplete information.

Job-search and workfare programs help address this problem by exposing participants (and administrators) to real jobs. Ideally, a job-search program will find someone a job. Even if it doesn't, however, it will give program participants a better sense of what jobs are available and the kinds of skills employers seek. Workfare programs give participants not only work experience but also expose them to a variety of specific jobs. If the workfare experience is successful, it can also generate a job reference—a valuable asset in competitive labor markets. Job-search and workfare activities can be particularly beneficial for individuals with little or no work experience. A 1995 evaluation of the JOBS program concluded that programs that emphasized labor force attachment (e.g., work experience) were much more successful than programs that emphasized human capital development.[15] The post-1996 experience with mandatory state welfare-to-work programs seems to confirm this view.[16]

Even when employment is secured, movement out of poverty is not assured. As we observed in Chapter 6, there are lots of people who are working *and* poor. *Accessing* a job is only the first step in escaping poverty. As noted in earlier chapters, a critical issue is upward mobility. For low-wage workers the key to upward mobility is job retention and advancement.[17] For single welfare mothers, the demands of child-rearing (e.g. sick days, transportation problems) often results in too many missed work days.[18] Pursuing additional training outside of the job is a remote, if not impossible option. This makes *holding* a steady job difficult and job advancement is even less likely. According, the transition from welfare to work is often slow and difficult even when jobs are available.

"LIVING WAGE" LAWS

Some people argue that the failure of training programs to reduce poverty is not an indictment of skill training but rather the result of structural wage inequalities. They argue that low-skill workers lack the power and organization to command higher

---

[15]See S. Freidman and D. Friedlander, *The JOBS Evaluation: Early Findings on Program Impacts at Three Sites* (New York: Manpower Demonstration Research Corp., 1995); also U.S. Government Accounting Office, *Welfare to Work: Most AFDC Training Programs Not Emphasizing Job Placement* (Washington, DC: GAO, 1995).

[16]Judith Gueron and Gayle Hamilton, "The Role of Education and Training in Welfare Reform," in Isabel Sawhill et al., eds., *Welfare Reform and Beyond* (Washington, DC: Brookings Institution, 2002).

[17]Harry Holzer and Karin Martinson, "Can We Imporve Job Retention and Advancement among Low-Income Working Parents?" (Madison, WI: Institute for Research on Poverty, 2005), and Gregory Acs and P. Loprest, *Leaving Welfare: Employment and Well-Being of Families That Left Welfare in the Post-Entitlement Era* (Kalamazoo, MI: Upjohn Institute, 2004).

[18]See Ajay Chaudry, *Putting Children First: How Low-Income Working Mothers Manage Child Care* (New York: Russell Sage, 2004).

wages. Competition from foreign workers—via both imports and outsourcing—further depresses their wages. To overcome these obstacles, it is argued, the government must take direct action to raise wage thresholds. Increases in the federal minimum wage are one response to these demands. Advocates would like to see the government go even further and set wage thresholds at a "living wage" standard. A living wage would be high enough so that a full-time worker could support a four-person family at a non-poverty level. At present, this would require a living wage threshold of $11–12 per hour, far above the federal minimum wage.

To date, only individual cities have legislated living wage ordinances. Even in those cities, the living wage law only applies to employers who do contract work for the city. Accordingly, only a relatively small number of jobs have been affected. The major constraint on living wage ordinances is the recognition that they may reduce job opportunities, particularly for the lowest-paid workers. This *dis*employment phenomenon is particularly important at the local level since employers can always move into the suburbs or even to other states.[19] Cities also worry that they will end up paying more for goods and services, with little positive impact on poverty.

EMPLOYMENT TAX CREDITS

The tax system offers alternative antipoverty strategies that don't reduce the number of job openings. Rather than using tax revenues to pay higher (living) wages or to fund government training programs, we can use the tax system to subsidize *private* sector training. The policy mechanism here is tax credits. By offering tax credits to employers, the government can encourage the training and hiring of low-income workers, thereby altering the *demand* for such workers. The government can also use tax credits to increase the *supply* of low-income workers by increasing the reward for working.

EMPLOYER CREDITS

The goal of employer job tax credits is to increase the number of hires, especially among low-income workers and other disadvantaged groups.

Targeted Jobs Tax Credit
The Targeted Jobs Tax Credit (TJTC) of 1978 illustrates the potential of the credit approach. The TJTC was designed to increase the employment and training of specific (targeted) groups, including disadvantaged youth, ex-convicts, veterans, and welfare recipients. Companies hiring from these groups could claim a tax credit equal to 40 percent of the first $6,000 of wages paid. Thus, the implicit subsidy for hiring a disadvantaged targeted person was $2,400. An employer could also get credit for hiring disadvantaged targeted youth in summer jobs. Such credits reduce the cost of hiring labor and thus encourage more hiring and training of the poor.

Although tax credits have a lot of appeal, they also have important limitations. To be effective, the tax credits must stimulate a net increase in the employment and training of disadvantaged workers. Otherwise, the credits become just a general

---

[19]For a review of local experiences, see Scott Adams and David Neumark, "The Effects of Living Wage Laws: Evidence from Failed and Derailed Living Wage Campaigns" (Cambridge, MA: National Bureau of Economic Research, Working Paper No. 11343, May 2005).

subsidy to firms that were already employing disadvantaged workers. This was a case in the early years of the TJTC program, as indicated by the fact that three-fourths of the credits were certified retroactively, after employment decisions had already been made.[20]

Tax credits are also weakened by an inherent goal conflict. The more specifically tax credits are targeted on certain groups or activities, the more complex they become. This increases the administrative cost of using them, especially for small firms. Workers, too, are often reluctant to reveal their disadvantaged status to prospective employers.[21] Nevertheless, as many as 1 million credits were used in a single year, mostly for youth and welfare recipients. Because there was little evidence of net employment growth, however, Congress let the TJTC credit expire at the end of 1994.

Work Opportunity Tax Credit

Despite the apparent failure of the TJTC to increase employment, a similar tax credit was introduced in 1996. Like the TJTC, the Work Opportunity Tax Credit (WOTC) offered employers a 40 percent subsidy tax credit on the first $6,000 of wages paid to targeted workers (including welfare recipients). Hence, it would cost an employer only $4.80 an hour to hire an $8-an-hour worker. To improve the *net* hiring impact of the tax credit, Congress required employers to obtain written certification of a worker's eligibility at least one day before hiring. Employers, especially small ones, complained that getting those certifications was too burdensome, especially if they were hiring only one or two targeted workers.

Welfare-to-Work Tax Credit

In 1997, Congress narrowed the hiring target to long-term welfare recipients and gave employers even greater financial incentive to hire them. In the first year of employment, employers can get a credit of 35 percent for the first $10,000 of wages. To encourage the job retention of former welfare recipients, the credit jumps to 50 percent in the second year.

Although the TJTC, the WOTC, and the Welfare-to-Work tax credit offered increasingly generous incentives for hiring welfare recipients and other low-income workers, evidence of positive employment effects is hard to find. In fiscal year 1999, less than $200 million in tax credits were taken, and no study has yet shown that targeted employment actually increased beyond what would have occurred anyway.[22] Accordingly, most observers have concluded that employer tax credits are more of a general business subsidy than an effective antipoverty tool.[23]

---

[20]Frederick Tanney argues, however, that even retroactive certifications increased job tenure and long-run wages; see his "Targeted Jobs Credit and Labor Market Experience" (Washington, DC: Employment Policies Institute, June 1998).

[21]The conflict between general and targeted tax credits is discussed in Dave M. O'Neill, "Employment Tax Credit Programs: The Effects of Socioeconomic Targeting Provisions," *Journal of Human Resources* (Summer 1983).

[22]For experience with the WOTC, see Ellen Tenenbaum, *Employers' Use of WOTC* (Rockville, MD: Westat, Inc., Summer 2000).

[23]For a more optimistic view, see Timothy Bartik, "Poverty, Jobs, and Subsidized Employment," *Challenge* (May–June 2002), pp. 100–111.

EMPLOYEE CREDITS: THE EITC

Employer tax credits are intended to increase the *demand* for low-skilled labor. An alternative approach is to encourage a greater *supply* of labor. As we observed in Chapter 13, welfare benefits create a work disincentive by offering an alternative source of financial support and imposing high marginal tax rates. A low-wage worker who not only pays payroll and income taxes, but also loses 30–70 cents of welfare benefits for every dollar earned, doesn't have much incentive to work. The implied marginal tax rate is so high that supplying additional labor makes little sense. To help overcome these disincentives, the government can reward low-income workers with favorable tax treatment. That is the basic idea behind employee tax credits.

The Earned Income Tax Credit (EITC) was first authorized in 1975. The general idea of the EITC is simple. A low-income worker gets a tax credit for every dollar of wages earned. Currently, a low-income worker with two or more children is eligible for $4 of tax credits for every $10 he or she earns. Thus, the federal government supplements a low-income worker's paycheck with a tax credit at the subsidy rate of 40 percent. A worker employed for $8 an hour gets an additional $3.20 an hour from Uncle Sam. Table 15.1 also shows the credits available to low-income workers who either are childless or have only one child.

Work Incentives

What makes the EITC tax credit unique is that it is *refundable*. In fact, it's the only refundable credit in the tax code. Other (*non*refundable) tax credits can only be used to reduce an individual's tax bill. This wouldn't do much for low-income workers, who have minimal tax liability. So the U.S. Treasury instead mails EITC recipients a check for the amount of the EITC credit. Hence, the EITC is a cash income transfer. It's not pure welfare, however. Even though it is means-tested (see wage ceilings in Table 15.1), it is also event-conditioned (a person must work to get it).

The antipoverty benefits of the EITC are clear. First, the EITC substantially increases the income associated with low-income jobs. A household head working year-round at $8 an hour earns only $16,000 a year—less than the poverty threshold for a family of four. The EITC kicks in another $4,536, however, lifting that family out of poverty. Hence, the EITC significantly reduces the number of working poor (Chapter 6).

Because the EITC increases the reward to working so much, it also encourages more poor people to seek jobs. Hence, the EITC increases the likelihood of employment, then reduces the risk of poverty for those who work. In 2006 more than 22 million households received EITC credits averaging $1,800 per year. With total credits now exceeding

TABLE 15.1   EITC Provisions, 2006

Number of Children	Credit Rate	Wage Ceiling for Maximum Credit	Maximum Credit	Phase-Out Begins*	Phase-Out Rate	Breakeven Wage
0	7.65%	$5,380	$412	$6,750	7.65%	$12,120
1	34.00%	$8,080	$2,747	$14,810	15.98%	$32,001
2	40.00%	$11,340	$4,536	$14,810	21.06%	$36,348

*Phase-out thresholds for nonmarried worker; married thresholds and breakeven wage levels are slightly higher.
Source: Office of Tax Analysis, U.S. Treasury.

$36 billion a year, the EITC is the largest cash-transfer program directed at the poor. The federal EITC alone is credited with reducing poverty by nearly 5 million persons in 2005.[24]

Work Disincentives

Although the EITC has done a remarkable job in reducing poverty, it is not without faults. Like other income transfer programs, it must contend with the goal conflicts between income provision, work incentives, and program cost. If the EITC were available to everyone, even Bill Gates would be getting a tax credit and the program would cost trillions of dollars. To contain costs, a limit must be set on eligibility. As Table 15.1 shows, the EITC eligibility limits are a combination of wage ceilings and family size. Thus, a parent with two children could get the 40 percent subsidy for only the first $11,340 of wages.

The dilemma for program design is in how to limit the EITC to workers earning less than that wage ceiling. If everyone got a credit for their *first* $11,340 of wages, we'd have the Bill Gates problem already noted. If we withdrew eligibility completely for anyone earning more than $11,340, we'd create a horrific incentive problem. In that case, a worker earning exactly $11,340 would have an income of $15,876 ($11,340 in wages plus a $4,536 EITC credit), but a worker earning just a dollar more in wages would end up with $4,536 less. This would discourage people from earning wages above the EITC ceiling.

What we have here is the work disincentive problem discussed at length in Chapter 13. To control program costs, the EITC credit must be reduced as wages rise above the eligibility ceiling. If we reduce the EITC by a dollar for every extra dollar of wages, the implied marginal tax rates would be 100 percent. Hence, there would be no financial incentive to work unless one could earn *more* than the wage ceiling plus the maximum EITC credit. In 2006, that threshold was $15,876 for a two-child family (Table 15.1). Working for wages in the range of $11,340 to $15,876 simply wouldn't have added to family income.

To improve incentives for working beyond the EITC wage ceilings, the program reduces the EITC credit at a slower rate. It does this by letting recipients keep the maximum EITC credit for a while after their wages exceed the EITC ceiling. For a two-child family this disregard zone was $11,340 to $14,810 in 2006. Beyond that zone, the additional wages begin to reduce the EITC credit. The phase-out rates shown in Table 15.1 are the marginal tax rates confronting EITC recipients who earn more than the wage ceiling. In 2006, a two-child family confronted a phase-out rate of 21.06 percent. Hence, it could continue to receive at least some EITC credit until it reached the breakeven wage threshold, in this case:

$$\text{Breakeven wage level} = \frac{\text{Maximum EITC}}{\text{Phase-out rate}} + [\text{Wage ceiling} + \text{Disregard zone}]$$
$$= \frac{\$4,536}{0.2106} + [\$11,340 + \$3,470]$$
$$= \$36,348$$

The phase-out rate creates the work-incentive problem. Although relatively low (Table 15.1), these EITC phase-out rates come on top of explicit payroll and income tax

---

[24]Many states have introduced EITC credits of thier own, further enhancing the antipoverty effectiveness of this approach; see Nicholas Johnson, "A Hand Up: How State Earned Income Tax Credits Help Working Families Escape Poverty in 2001" (Washington, DC: Center on Budget and Policy Priorities, 2000, www.cbpp.org).

rates. Hence, the *cumulative* tax burden can be substantial for low-income workers. This increased tax burden may induce people in the phase-out range of income to work *less*.

The EITC thus has two contrary effects on labor supply. It encourages people with very low incomes to work more. But it also encourages workers earning higher wages to work less. The net effect therefore depends on how these two incentives compare. Because there are more than twice as many eligible households in the phase-out range ($14,810 to $36,348) than the subsidy range ($1 to $11,340), negative labor-supply effects outweigh the positive effects. The General Accounting Office came to such a conclusion after estimating that "phase-out households" would work 70 hours less a year, while "subsidy" households would only work an additional 48 hours per year.[25]

Another concern relates to the enhanced incentives for tax fraud created by the more generous EITC. Usually the Internal Revenue Service worries that people *understate* their incomes. The EITC, however, creates an incentive to *overstate* income. A nonworker with two children who claims to have earned $11,340 is eligible for a $4,536 EITC payment. Even if a person paid Social Security payroll taxes on this nonexistent income, the net return would exceed $2,000. Neighbors could even collude, paying each other $11,340 a year to care for each others' children. *Reported* income and employment could increase significantly, even if low-income workers chose to work less.

The EITC also creates an incentive for taxpayers to claim more children than they have. A childless worker got a maximum credit of $412 in 2006 (Table 15.1), while a one-child worker received $2,747. According to one study, one-third of male household heads claiming the EITC lacked the prerequisite children.[26] These and other errors result in 15–20 percent of all EITC payments being unjustified.

Despite the evident work disincentives and fraud potential, the EITC has been a highly effective antipoverty tool. Because it transfers so much income (over $30 billion per year), it provides a significant cushion that keeps many *low-income* workers from being *poor*. For millions of other recipients, EITC payments reduced their poverty gap even if they weren't sufficient to move the family out of poverty completely.

Although both liberals and conservatives have supported the EITC, the program is not faultless. Like all other antipoverty programs, the EITC must continually confront trade-offs between goals of income security, work incentives, and program cost.[27]

---

[25]For additional evidence, see Nada Eissa and Hilary W. Hoynes, "The Earned Income Tax Credit and the Labor Supply of Married Couples" (Cambridge, MA: National Bureau of Economic Research, April 1999); and Jeffrey B. Liebman, "The Impact of the Earned Income Tax Credit on Incentives and Income Distribution," in *Tax Policy and the Economy*, ed. J. Poterba (Chicago, IL: University of Chicago Press, 1999). On the other hand, the EITC did increase the hours worked by poor single women with children—the core of welfare caseloads; see Bruce D. Meyer and Dan T. Rosenbaum, "Welfare, the Earned Income Tax Credit, and the Labor Supply of Single Mothers" (Cambridge, MA: National Bureau of Economic Research, September 1999). Limiting the EITC to full-time work might increase positive employment effects; see Phillip K. Robins and Charles Michalopoulos, "Using Financial Incentives to Encourage Welfare Recipients to Become Economically Self-Sufficient," *Economic Policy Review* (Federal Reserve Bank of New York, September 2001), pp. 105–132.

[26]Jeffrey Liebman, "Who Are the Ineligible Earned Income Tax Credit Recipients?" in *Making Work Pay*, eds. B. Meyer and D. Holtz-Eakin (New York: Russell Sage, 2001).

[27]The EITC affects not only incentives to work, but also to marry or have children; see David T. Elliwood, "The Impact of the Earned Income Tax Credit and Social Policy Reforms on Work, Marriage, and Living Arrangements" in *Making Work Pay*, eds. Bruce Meyer and Douglas Holtz-Eakin (New York: Russell Sage, 2001). For a different view, see Stacy Dickert-Conlin and Scott Hauser, "EITC and Marriage," *National Tax Journal* (March 2002), pp. 25–37.

Because the EITC has become the largest cash antipoverty program, those trade-offs are particularly important.

FAMILY POLICY

While tax credits create greater financial incentives for both hiring and supplying labor, incentives alone may not be enough to get more poor people into the economic mainstream. Recall that over one-third of all poor persons and nearly all recipients of cash welfare live in female-headed families. As we discussed in Chapter 8, single-parent families have unique obstacles to employment. As such, antipoverty strategies may have to move beyond traditional training and incentive programs to create more work opportunities for single moms.

Maternity leave and child care are two mechanisms that can substantially improve the earnings potential of single mothers. Maternity leave permits a new mother to return to her previous job without loss of pay or tenure. Child care services help her stay on the job. Both policies can be critical in expanding job opportunities and increasing earnings potential for a very vulnerable subgroup of the poor.[28] The 2005 TANF reauthorization set aside nearly $3 billion per year for child care. It also allocated $150 million for programs to promote stable marriages and responsible fatherhood.

Flexible leave time may also be a significant factor in helping low-income parents hold onto their job when the children are sick. The federal Family and Medical Leave Act of 1993 requires businesses that have 50 or more employees to allow up to 12 weeks of *unpaid* family leave. But the U.S. Department of Labor says that four out of five workers who need family leave don't take it because they can't get by without a paycheck. In 2002, California introduced a program of *paid* family leave. Under that program, a worker can get 55 percent of pay (up to maximum of $728 per week) for as long as six weeks to provide at-home care for a family member.

A COORDINATED APPROACH

Aggregate demand policy, training programs, work requirements, tax credits, and family policies are not mutually exclusive alternatives. Instead, they must be perceived and implemented as complementary dimensions of a single, coordinated employment policy. High aggregate demand reduces the need for, and improves the outcome of, training programs. By the same token, training programs make expansionary macroeconomic policy more effective by reducing skill bottlenecks. The two approaches are complementary, not contradictory. Likewise, tax credits may do little to reduce poverty unless ample training and job opportunities exist.[29]

---

[28] An international assessment of maternity leave is provided in Jane Waldfogel, "Understanding the 'Family Gap' in Pay for Women with Children," *Journal of Economic Perspectives* (Winter 1998), pp. 137–156.

[29] A demonstration program in Washington state revealed that work incentives may not be an adequate substitute for mandatory participation in work-related programs; see S. Long, D. Nightingale, and D. Wissoker, *The Evaluation of the Washington Family Independence Program* (Washington, DC: Urban Institute, 1994).

In attempting to assess the potential effectiveness of employment policies for eliminating poverty, then, one must perceive the whole spectrum of policy options. We must recognize that no single approach will bring about full employment or eliminate poverty—at least not without enormous social costs. Government training efforts illustrate the point most vividly. Government training programs enrolled over 4 million individuals in 1991, at a federal cost of nearly $10 billion. Nevertheless, they failed to make a significant dent either in unemployment or poverty. Restrictive fiscal and monetary policies undercut all employment programs and plunged the economy into recession. Even in more favorable economic conditions, the potential of training programs to reduce poverty is limited by the tangle of forces that affect family structure and employment. Moreover, training programs may need to be accompanied by a mix of education and support services to be fully effective for some target groups.[30] This implies a level of budget expenditures that taxpayers may not support.[31] This makes it all that much more important to maintain job-creating aggregate demand policies that both reduce the need for training and increase the effectiveness of such training.

The end product of a coordinated employment policy should be an abundance of jobs that provide decent wages and advancement opportunity. The benefits of such jobs are as obvious as is the necessity for them. They will provide the incomes necessary to lift families out of poverty, to keep them together, and to give them promise of a secure future. Their benefits will reach to the children of the poor, who will have the means and incentive for staying in school. Employment policy has the potential, then, of minimizing both present and future poverty.

Summary

The major components of employment policies are macroeconomic fiscal and monetary actions, training programs, public service employment, and tax credits. While each of these components has its own character and purpose, they are all interdependent. No one component can succeed alone. At the same time, effective action in any one area enhances the potential for success in the others. One reason government employment policy has not been more effective in the past is that these components have been viewed more as alternatives than as complements.

The track record of government training programs is not impressive. The prerequisites for successful training efforts are (1) a strong economy, with ample job vacancies, and (2) efficient matches between participant skills and employer needs. All too often, neither prerequisite is fulfilled. As a result, even programs that offer a comprehensive array of incentives and support services typically generate only modest employment gains and minimal welfare reduction.

Job-search assistance and mandatory community service (workfare) activities have become more common in welfare-to-work and other training programs. One

---

[30]For a review of different employment-service configurations and their impact, see U.S. Department of Health and Human Services, *Evidence from Employment, Education, and Training Programs for Welfare Recipients* (Washington, DC: Office of Assistant Secretary for Planning and Evaluation, December 1994); and S. Freidman and D. Friedlander, *The JOBS Evaluation,* op. cit.

[31]James Heckman estimates the cost of a true antipoverty training effort to exceed $200 billion; see "Is Job Training Oversold?" *The Public Interest* (Spring 1994).

advantage of these activities is that they expose participants to the job market, thereby encouraging more informed decisions on training and employment. These activities are also far less expensive than vocational training.

Public service employment has been regarded as the unwanted stepchild of employment policy. It suffers from distorted memories of the 1930s and widespread fears of make-work and government expansion. Workfare programs overcome some of these fears by requiring welfare recipients to perform community service, at little additional taxpayer cost. More explicit programs (e.g., the CETA) entail potentially unacceptable budget outlays or, if underfunded, the certainty of unfulfilled promises.

Tax credits can be used as subsidies for labor supply or demand. The Earned Income Tax Credit (EITC) offers a substantial wage supplement to low-income workers. It has moved millions of poor people out of poverty and closed the poverty gap for millions of other working poor families. In the process, it has become the largest means-tested transfer program. However, it also creates work *dis*incentives for workers above the program's wage ceilings.

Although no employment policy offers a perfect solution, employment policies are the key to poverty reduction. Coordinated and comprehensive employment policies could sharply diminish existing and future poverty. Jobs—in abundance and of good quality—are the most needed and most permanent solution to the poverty problem.

Further Reading

Andersson, Fredrik, Harry Holzer, and Julia Lane, *Moving Up or Moving On: Who Advances in the Low-Wage Labor Market?* New York: Russell Sage, 2006.

Bainbridge, Jay, Marcia Meyers, and Jane Waldfogel, "Child Care Policy Reform and the Employment of Single Mothers," *Social Science Quarterly* (December 2003), pp. 771–791.

Bell, Stephanie, and L. Randall Wray, "The War on Poverty Forty Years On," *Challenge* (September–October, 2004), pp. 6–29.

Edin, Kathryn, and Laura Lein, *Making Ends Meet*. New York: Russell Sage, 1997.

Eissa, Nada, and Hilary Hoynes, "Behavioral Responses to Taxes: Lessons from the EITC and Labor Supply," Cambridge, MA: National Bureau of Economic Research, Working Paper No. 11729, November 2005.

Friedlander, Daniel, David Greenberg, and Philip Robins, "Evaluating Government Training Programs for the Disadvantaged," *Journal of Economic Literature* (December 1997), pp. 1809–1855.

Handler, Joel F., and Lucie White, eds., *Hard Labor: Women and Work in the Post-Welfare Era.* New York: M. E. Sharpe, 1999.

Heckman, James J., "Is Job Training Oversold?" *The Public Interest* (Spring 1994), pp. 91–115.

Hotz, Joseph, and John Scholz, "The Earned Income Tax Credit," in R. Moffitt, ed., *Means-Tested Transfer Programs in the United States.* Chicago, IL: University of Chicago Press, 2003.

Web Links

Center for Budget and Policy Priorities. Lots of EITC studies.
www.cbpp.org

Earned Income Tax Credit (EITC).
www.irs.ustreas.gov/individuals/index.html

EPN News. Directory to current research reports from various think tanks and nonprofit organizations.
www.movingideas.org

Joint Center for Policy Research. Various studies on welfare–work issues.
www.jcpr.org

National Bureau of Economic Research (NBER). Various studies on employment, training, and tax-credit programs.
www.nber.org

CHAPTER 16
EQUAL OPPORTUNITY POLICIES

Earlier chapters have documented the disadvantaged status of minority groups in America. Not only do such groups command fewer resources now, but they have less chance to acquire resources in the future. They have less opportunity to attain higher educational levels or even good-quality schooling at lower levels. Even with appropriate educational credentials, they are not permitted to make maximum use of their attainments in the labor market. Such discrimination—both in schools and in the labor market—creates institutional barriers between people and jobs. Those barriers, in turn, alter both the size and composition of the poverty population.

In Chapter 12, a distinction was drawn among three different categories of discrimination. These were current market discrimination, prior market discrimination, and nonmarket discrimination. These disparate sources of inequality create a fundamental dilemma for corrective policy. Can we create "equal opportunity" just by eradicating all overtly discriminatory behavior from present-day job and educational markets? Or would minorities still be so disadvantaged by *past* discrimination in schools and jobs that they still could not reasonably "catch up" in a race- and gender-blind marketplace?

If minorities still carry the burden of past discrimination, how can the government reduce that burden? Should the government fund special training programs to provide skills and education earlier denied? Should it create new job opportunities? Should it redistribute access to schools and jobs via affirmative action or even rigid quotas?

Public opinion on the limits of "equal opportunity" policy is sharply divided. On the one hand, the vast majority of Americans favor the principle of equal opportunity. On the other hand, nearly as many people oppose programs that give special preference to past or present victims of discrimination. As Table 16.1 documents, nearly one out of two white Americans want *less* affirmative action than the government now pursues. This "principle-implementation gap" makes the design of equal opportunity policy particularly difficult. In this chapter we review past and present government policies and try to develop a sense of their potential effectiveness.

EQUAL EMPLOYMENT OPPORTUNITY POLICIES

Public concern with the employment status of black workers came to the forefront just prior to World War II. Frustrated with their inferior employment status in a generally depressed labor market, black workers threatened to march on Washington, D.C., in the spring of 1941. To forestall that march, President Roosevelt issued an executive order creating the first federal Fair Employment Practices Committee (FEPC). The stated purpose of the FEPC was to provide the machinery necessary to enforce the general provisions of the Thirteenth, Fourteenth, and Fifteenth Amendments to the Constitution,

TABLE 16.1 Affirmative Action?

Q: Do you favor affirmative action programs for racial minorities?

Responses:	Blacks	Hispanics	Whites
Yes	70%	63%	44%
No	21%	28%	43%

Source: Gallup poll, March 2003.

amendments that were thought to forbid discrimination in the labor market. The FEPC was to monitor and correct any such discriminatory practices.

Although Roosevelt's FEPC had little power or authority, it confronted persistent and decisive opposition in Congress. Congress twice dismantled the FEPC, finally burying it in 1945. Despite the FEPC's quick demise, its members nevertheless saw great potential for meaningful action. In their final report, the FEPC staff claimed that racial discrimination in employment could be ended if and when the federal government took decisive action.

No further equal employment opportunity action was taken until 1951. At that time, President Truman created a committee similar to the FEPC. That committee, too, had few powers and continued to exist quietly throughout the eight years of the Eisenhower administration.

The federal effort to promote equal employment opportunity first began to look serious in 1961. That was the year President John Kennedy issued an executive order committing the government to action. According to Kennedy's executive order, the federal government assumed specific responsibility to "promote the full realization of equal employment opportunity." The government pledged not only to eliminate discrimination within its own agencies and departments but to assure equal opportunity in all private firms that performed work for the federal government. Failure to eliminate discrimination, the government warned, would result in the termination of federal contracts. This threat was the first real power such a committee attained. An Office of Federal Contract Compliance—now called the Office of Federal Contract Compliance Programs (OFCCP)—was established to carry out the executive order.

THE EEOC

A parallel move toward equal employment opportunity took place in Congress shortly afterward. The historic Civil Rights Act of 1964 forbade discrimination in the labor market. Title VII of that act explicitly outlawed discrimination by corporations, unions, or any other labor-market participants. The enforcement of that prohibition was delegated to the newly created Equal Employment Opportunity Commission (EEOC).

The enforcement machinery and effectiveness of the EEOC and the OFCCP differ greatly. The EEOC has only limited enforcement power. It is directed by Congress to "endeavor to eliminate any discriminatory employment practice by informal methods of conference, conciliation, and persuasion." It may not impose sanctions, issue cease and desist orders, nor even make public the fact that discrimination is being practiced. It depends largely on the goodwill of the offender to bring about equal employment opportunity once a complaint is filed.

The potential effectiveness of the EEOC is limited by its procedural orientation. Before the EEOC can take any action at all, it must receive a sworn complaint from an individual. Once the complaint is received, the commission seeks to determine whether the allegation is reasonable. If the complaint appears well founded, the commission then approaches the offending employer, union, or employment agency for "conference, conciliation, and persuasion." If conciliation is not attained, the complainant and the EEOC may seek redress in the courts. This rarely happens, however.

This dependence of the EEOC on individual complaints has several drawbacks. First, it is tremendously expensive and time-consuming to review and process each complaint (over 70,000 complaints are filed each year). This results in a backlog of unprocessed complaints (45,000 in 2006) that saps the morale of the complainants and staff. A second procedural drawback is the lack of incentive: An aggrieved person has to report discriminatory actions. The complaint procedure subjects an individual to potential union or employer retaliation, costs him or her time and money, and yields little practical benefit. At best, a complaining individual is apt to gain employment, promotion, or back pay from a chastened and resentful employer.

Because the pursuit of individual cases is so cost-ineffective, the EEOC has also pursued "systemic" discrimination. Although these investigations also begin with individual complaints, their scope is enlarged to cover a broader pattern of company behavior. In one of the first such cases, the EEOC persuaded AT&T to pay nearly $50 million in compensation to its female employees, who had systematically been denied equal job opportunities. In June 2002, the EEOC concluded that black employees at Xerox Corporation's Cincinnati facility had been "subjected to a racially hostile environment," including racial slurs, the display of black dolls with nooses around their necks, and more frequent disciplining than white coworkers. That finding laid the groundwork for a (private) class-action lawsuit, led by the four Xerox employees who had initially lodged a complaint with the EEOC. In 2006, the EEOC convinced Cracker Barrel to pay $2 million to 51 employees who were victims of sexual harassment or racial discrimination.

Not all complaints to the EEOC end so dramatically. In 60 percent of its cases, the EEOC finds no basis for the discrimination complaint. Another 18 percent of the cases are closed for administrative reasons (e.g., failure to locate a witness). Most of the remaining 22 percent of EEOC complaints are settled, including the 10 percent in which the agency finds evidence of discrimination.

THE OFCCP

Stronger powers of initiative and enforcement have always been available to the OFCCP. The OFCCP may itself initiate investigations to determine whether discriminatory practices exist. It may also impose sanctions, such as contract termination, where discrimination is discovered. Furthermore, the OFCCP may require employers to take affirmative action to remedy past discrimination. These sanctions may be applied to all businesses that sell or service products to the government. Thus, the potential power of the OFCCP is as vast as the government's position in the economy.

While the potential power of the OFCCP to eliminate discriminatory practices and rectify past injustices is great, that power has been used rarely. The first constraint on the OFCCP is a lengthy administrative process. Once complaints are filed, they are adjudicated by administrative law judges within the U.S. Department of Labor. The decisions of these judges can then be appealed to the U.S. Secretary of Labor. Politically sensitive cases can lay buried in the secretary's office for years. When Robert Reich, President Clinton's first Labor Secretary, tried to clear up the backlog of cases in his office, he discovered that two dozen cases had been on appeal for an average of 7.5 years. In one case he turned down an appeal from Honeywell, against whom complaints had been filed 16 *years* earlier (when Reich himself had still been a student at Yale Law School). Even that ruling didn't end the case, since Honeywell could appeal Reich's decision in federal court.

Politics are largely to blame for these endless delays. Employers beset by the OFCCP always have recourse to other authorities. Should they command the sympathy of members of Congress or executive offices, OFCCP sanctions may be delayed or suspended. Bureaucratic interests also undermine the OFCCP's power. The Department of Defense, for example, regards weapons procurement as more vital to its mission than guidelines for equal opportunity. Hence, it may devote relatively little attention to compliance with OFCCP edicts and may even inveigh against contract cancellations that threaten orderly procurement. Accordingly, the power of the OFCCP remains largely on paper. Until 1979, not a single contract had been terminated or canceled to enforce equal opportunity. Moreover, the first big enforcement case against Uniroyale (the nation's third-largest rubber manufacturer, with $36 million in federal contracts in 1978) was based on the company's failure to cooperate with an OFCCP investigation of discrimination (begun in 1968!), not because of discrimination per se. In 2000, the OFCCP filed only 13 administrative complaints, nine of which were filed against just one employer.

In 2003, the OFCCP shifted its focus to systemic discrimination. Using statistical analysis of employment records, the agency tries to determine if a pattern of discrimination is likely to be found before taking further action. With this tool, the OFCCP was able to increase its recovery to $45 million in 2005, on behalf of nearly 15,000 workers.

QUOTAS AND GUIDELINES

Still stronger action has been taken by the government with regard to the nation's labor unions, especially the construction unions. As we saw in Chapter 12, blue-collar unions often have the potential to provide immediate access to remunerative employment. In addition, the government is a major force in the construction industry, purchasing up to one-third of total output. The Nixon administration used this leverage to establish guidelines for minority recruitment in the building trades. The first attempt, in Philadelphia, proposed to raise the proportion of new black recruits from 5 percent in 1970 to 25 percent in 1975. That attempt and later "Philadelphia plans" elsewhere were not notably successful, however. Unions have tremendous political strength and do not like interference. From their point of view, "plans" and "goals" look too much like quotas, especially when enforced by threats of contract termination. Furthermore, the slack economy of the early 1970s raised anxious questions about whose jobs would have to be sacrificed to make room for newly hired black workers, the same kind of "reverse discrimination" fear that later surfaced in other industries (including universities).

While there have been few stunning employment rights achievements from direct federal action, federal policy has had important indirect impacts. One of the most important side effects of federal legislation and pronouncements has been to stimulate private legal actions against discriminatory employers. Federal action has established a legal basis on which private individuals can build. Accordingly, much of the responsibility for implementing and enforcing equal employment opportunity has been taken over by individuals and the courts. And in a score of cases, including the major EEOC suit against AT&T in 1974, individuals have won substantial sums of money from their employers to compensate for the income they were denied as a consequence of discriminatory practices in hiring and promotion. More importantly, there is evidence that minority employment has risen as a direct and indirect result of affirmative action initiatives.[1]

REVERSE DISCRIMINATION

The employment successes that have been achieved with various forms of affirmative action have not eliminated discriminatory barriers. They have been effective enough, however, to arouse growing hostility to any form of special opportunities for women and minority workers. In large part, this hostility arises from the threat that affirmative action poses for already privileged positions. But this is not the only basis for decrying reverse discrimination. Critics also point to the basic contradiction between special hiring preferences and equal opportunity. Others contend that the existence of affirmative action casts a shadow over the real achievements of minority workers. Such achievements are too easily dismissed as the outcome of affirmative action rather than personal effort. Finally, there is concern that affirmative action will make the workplace less efficient, thereby slowing economic growth and reducing average incomes.[2] These kinds of considerations help explain why only a bare majority of even minority and women workers favor special preferences.[3]

Weber: "Manifest Imbalance"

The critics of affirmative action have taken their case to court. In a landmark complaint, Brian Weber, a white male employee of Kaiser Aluminum, sued Kaiser and his union, the United Steel Workers, for reverse discrimination. Weber had been rejected by a craft training program that reserved half its places for minorities. In the absence of such a privileged "set-aside," Weber argued, he would have been accepted for training. Lower courts agreed with Weber, noting that Kaiser could not use racial quotas except as a remedy for past discrimination at Kaiser. Since Kaiser itself did not admit to such prior discrimination, there was no legal basis for the special quotas. In 1979, the Supreme Court overruled the lower courts, however, arguing that preferential access to training is permissible when used to remedy "manifest racial imbalance."

[1]David Neumark and Wendy Stock, "The Labor Market Effects of Sex and Race Discrimination Laws," *Economic Inquiry* (July 2006), pp. 385–419; also Jonathan S. Leonard, "The Impact of Affirmative Action and Equal Employment Law on Black Employment," *Journal of Economic Perspectives* (Fall 1990), pp. 47–63.

[2]For debates on this issue, see the symposium in the March 1996 issue of *Society;* also contrast Peter Brimelow and Leslie Spencer, "When Quotas Replace Merit, Everybody Suffers," *Forbes,* February 5, 1993, with Frank McCoy, "Rethinking the Cost of Discrimination," *Black Enterprise* (January 1994). Evidence on how employers avoid productivity losses is assessed in Harry Holzer and David Neumark, "Assessing Affirmative Action," *Journal of Economic Literature* (September 2000), pp. 483–568.

[3]For public opinion trends on affirmative action, see Jack Citrin, "Affirmative Action in the People's Court," *Public Interest* (Winter 1996), pp. 39–58. Also review the results of the 2001 opinion survey on racial issues conducted by the Kaiser Family Foundation, Harvard University, and the *Washington Post.*

The Court broadened the basis for quotas in *Fullilove* v. *Klutznick* (1980). In this case a white contractor challenged a provision of the 1977 Public Works Act authorizing 10 percent of government funds to be "set aside" for minority employers. This provision clearly gave minority contractors preferential treatment even where neither past discrimination nor racial imbalance existed. The Court upheld the set-aside provision, however, arguing that such quotas were not an unjust burden to place on whites (even if they had not consciously committed discrimination) and were permissible ". . . as long as remedial classifications serve important governmental objectives, and are substantially related to the objectives."

Teal: "Disparate Impact"

In another case the Supreme Court made a decision that seemed to stretch the concept of affirmative action to its limits. Winnie Teal, a black female employee of the Connecticut Department of Public Welfare, had applied for the post of permanent welfare supervisor. She was required to take a written examination, which she failed. In fact, 46 percent of the blacks who took the exam failed, compared with only 26 percent of the whites. The department then hired 11 blacks, or 22.9 percent of the total black applicants, and 35 whites, or 13.5 percent of the total white applicants. It appeared, then, that the department had given blacks a decided advantage in hiring. Nevertheless, Winnie Teal sued the department, arguing that she had been discriminated against on the basis of race. In July 1982, the Court agreed with her, ruling that no step in the hiring process could manifest "disparate impact." This ruling (*Connecticut* v. *Teal*) appeared to proclaim that blacks had to be guaranteed a proportional share of jobs, regardless of qualifications or seemingly fair hiring criteria.

Reagan-Era Reversals

These and other court decisions were challenged by the Reagan administration. In 1983, William Bradford Reynolds, chief of the Justice Department's Civil Rights Division, publicly characterized affirmative action as a "racial spoils system" that violated basic American concepts of fair play. As Reynolds saw it, "Thus we come full circle—fighting discrimination with discrimination . . . an urgent need has been pressed and those intent on finding a quick fix rather than a lasting solution have reached for the loaded weapon— the so-called remedial use of racial discrimination."[4] The Reagan administration rejected this approach, and sought to eliminate quotas as an affirmative action tool. In pursuing this policy, the Justice Department sided with white Boston firefighters in their challenge to affirmative action. The case arose as a result of budget cuts that forced layoffs within the Boston Fire Department. Based upon the department's "last hired–first fired" seniority rule, minorities would have been laid off first and disproportionately. The NAACP argued, however, that a layoff of black firefighters would destroy the gains of earlier affirmative action. When lower courts agreed to shelter the blacks from seniority-based layoffs, the white firefighters took their case to the Supreme Court. The case was declared moot, however, when Boston provided the money needed to rescind the layoffs.

In 1989, the Supreme Court—dominated by Reagan appointees—again shifted the focus from disparate *outcomes* to discriminatory *processes*. In *City of Richmond* v. *J. A. Crosen Co.,* it ruled that the governments could require hiring quotas and set-asides

---

[4]William Bradford Reynolds, "Legitimizing Race as a Decision-Making Criterion: Where Are We Going?" lecture at Amherst College, April 29, 1983.

only if clear and precise evidence of past discrimination was apparent. Moreover, any subsequent affirmative action had to be "narrowly tailored" to that past discrimination. In that same year, the Court also ruled that individuals who complained of discriminatory treatment could not rely on statistical patterns of apparent inequality but had to offer evidence of discrimination in specific employment practices (e.g., hiring, promotion, or job-assignment procedures). In a third case, the Court ruled that whites could bring reverse discrimination claims against Court-approved affirmative action plans.[5] Those three decisions made it much more difficult to implement affirmative action.

1991 Civil Rights Act

Congress curbed the Supreme Court's 1989 rulings with the 1991 Civil Rights Act. That legislation shifted more of the burden of proof back to employers, who must justify employment practices that have disparate effects on women or minorities. The 1991 act also extended to women the right to claim monetary damages in the wake of intentional discrimination.

COMPARABLE WORTH

The conflict between the goals of equal opportunity (nondiscrimination) and affirmative action (reverse discrimination) has not been confined to racial issues. The same conflict has arisen in attempts to eliminate both past and present sex discrimination in hiring, occupational status, pay rates, pensions, and maternity leave.

Until the Civil Rights Act of 1991, sex discrimination battles had been fought on different battlefields. The first was the field of "equal pay for equal work." The Equal Pay Act of 1963 required employers to pay men and women equal pay for equal work. The courts enforced this act by providing compensatory damages to women whose pay was below that of men performing "identical" work in "similar" conditions.[6]

Critics argue, however, that this concept of equal pay is too restrictive. Because of occupational discrimination, few women hold jobs identical to men's. To assess "fair" wages, it is argued, "comparable" jobs, not identical ones, should be considered. By this standard, women should get equal pay for jobs *comparable* to men's. Comparability is measured in various ways, including skills, responsibility, mental and physical effort, importance, and the extent of training required. The Supreme Court gave impetus to comparable worth cases when it ruled that female prison guards had the right to sue over pay discrimination even though they weren't performing tasks identical to male prison guards (*County of Washington* v. *Gunther,* 1981).

Although the concept of comparable worth has obvious appeal, it suggests a radical departure from market economics. The forces of supply and demand have a major impact on the wages for different jobs. Wage differentials also encourage people to take jobs that society values highly. To the extent that wages are set instead by computations of comparable worth, labor markets will be less efficient. Critics also question

---

[5]The EEOC was itself sued for reverse discrimination in a 2002 class-action case (*Worth et al.* v. *HUD and EEOC*).

[6]These awards may have reduced job opportunities for women; see David Neumark and Wendy Stock, "The Labor Market Effects of Sex and Race Discrimination," *Economic Inquiry* (July 2006), pp. 385–419.

whether anyone really has the ability to make conclusive and objective computations of the "worth" of different jobs.[7]

CLASS-BASED PREFERENCES

Critics of both affirmative action and comparable-worth policies have proposed a wholesale shift of focus for equal opportunity policy. They argue that any preferences extended to individuals should be based on economic class, not race or gender. Not all blacks, Latinos, or women suffer from discriminatory treatment. Why, then, critics ask, should all of these individuals have access to contract set-asides, preferential hiring, or lower employment standards? Moreover, whites who are trapped in the same blighted neighborhoods as poor minority groups are unfairly denied similar preferences solely because of their race or gender. Preferences based on economic class, rather than race or gender, would provide more equal access to those who need it the most. In the process, affirmative action would become a more potent antipoverty tool. A class-based system of preferences might also defuse much of the sociopolitical tension that now envelops affirmative action policies.

While not opposed to greater inclusion of the poor in employment preferences, proponents of gender- and race-based preferences worry that the broader goals of social justice will be sacrificed by class-based preferences. The burden of discrimination isn't borne solely by the poor. Rather, its effects are apparent throughout the income distribution. The issue, therefore, isn't just the antipoverty effectiveness of affirmative action, but also the consequences for broader social justice.[8]

EQUAL EDUCATION OPPORTUNITY POLICIES

The controversies that accompany remedies for *employment* discrimination apply as well to *education* policies. Do minorities suffer from present-day discrimination within school systems, or do they bear the burden of past discrimination? What remedies might effectively relieve either burden? Can the government redress past or present wrongs without engaging in reverse discrimination? Who should pay the price, if any, for more "equal opportunity"?

LIMITS ON FEDERAL POLICY

Governmental policy in the field of equal educational opportunity is more difficult to characterize than in the field of employment opportunity. Politics and bureaucracy again take their toll, of course, as do complacency and inertia. What renders this subject especially complex, however, is the degree to which educational responsibilities

---

[7]For more views on comparable worth, see Paula England, *Comparable Worth: Theories and Evidence* (New York: Aldine de Gruyter, 1992); also Erica L. Groshen, "Comparable Worth: Is It a Worthy Policy?" *Journal of Economic Literature* (March 1996). The Canadian experience with comparable worth is discussed in Kenneth A. Kovach, "An Overview and Assessment of Comparable Worth Based on a Large-Scale Implementation," *Public Personnel Management* (Spring 1997).

[8]For a lucid defense of gender- and race-based affirmative action, see Barbara R. Bergmann, *In Defense of Affirmative Action* (New York: Basic Books, 1996). The judicial shift to class-based preferences is examined in Richard D. Kahlenberg, "Class-Based Affirmative Action," *California Law Review* (July 1996). See also David B. Oppenheimer, "Understanding Affirmation Action," *Hastings Constitutional Law Quarterly* (Summer 1996).

are shared by different levels of government. Educational policy has traditionally been a prerogative of the separate states. The federal government provides less than 10 percent of all educational expenditures and administers no schools. Consequently, it has less power to create equal opportunity in the schools. It cannot terminate contracts or open new job slots as it may do in the labor market. In general, it must instead rely on, and cooperate with, the states and the courts to abolish discrimination in the schools. Only in higher education, particularly among large, research-oriented universities, does federal grant money account for a significant enough share of total income to make direct federal action a more serious threat.

The most obvious form of discrimination in the educational system is school segregation. While discrimination can take place even in the absence of segregation, not even a pretense of equal opportunity is possible as long as segregated schools are maintained. The Supreme Court itself made this observation, as we saw in Chapter 11. To what extent, then, are governmental bodies endeavoring to abolish segregation?

DE JURE VERSUS *DE FACTO* SEGREGATION

A distinction is commonly made between two kinds of segregation. The first, *de jure,* refers to a situation where blacks and whites are legally constrained to attend separate schools. The second, *de facto,* refers to a situation where school segregation results, not from edict, but from circumstance. Such a case occurs where blacks, Hispanics, and whites live in different neighborhoods, thereby making school integration difficult.

While the distinction between *de facto* and *de jure* segregation is often useful, it creates a distinction that few victims of discrimination can appreciate. As Judge J. Skelly Wright noted in a 1967 ruling on District of Columbia schools: "Racially and socially homogeneous schools damage the minds of all children who attend them . . . whether the segregation occurs in law or in fact." The distinction between *de jure* and *de facto* also gives rise to a false aura of innocence. *De jure* segregation is commonly seen as the consequence of evil intent, while *de facto* segregation is seen as the innocent by-product of socioeconomic forces—especially in the housing market. Such a view obscures the fact that government bodies set the pattern for much *de facto* segregation. Segregation of the schools is rarely, if ever, a completely natural and unplanned circumstance.

Governments have two avenues of influence on *de facto* segregation. They may directly affect residential housing patterns, thereby enlarging or diminishing the foundation for *de facto* segregation; or they may alter the distribution of schools within established housing patterns, thereby facilitating or obstructing greater integration of the schools.

HOUSING PATTERNS

To a large extent existing residential patterns are the outcomes of millions of individual housing decisions, but free choice is not the only force operating in the housing market. The government, through its building and loan programs, has also participated in the establishment of segregated neighborhoods, and thus, must bear a significant responsibility for the *de facto* school segregation that results from neighborhoods isolated by race and class.

FHA Loans

The Federal Housing Authority (FHA) has been a major factor in the housing market since its creation in 1938. It had a particularly important role in establishing the housing patterns of the post–World War II housing boom, patterns that still predominate today. The power of the FHA to alter housing choices lies in its ability to insure or guarantee loans on residential construction. FHA support often determines whether a house can be purchased, at what location, and at what cost. During the housing boom of the late 1940s and 1950s, the FHA helped finance one-third of all new housing. Today's suburbs are, in large part, the product of FHA financing.

Given the power of the FHA in the housing market, its ability to foster or contain segregation is clear. For the most part, it chose to encourage and extend rigid racial and class segregation. The FHA Underwriting Manual of 1938 declared that "if a neighborhood is to retain stability, it is necessary that properties shall continue to be occupied by the same social and racial groups." Agency valuators, considering whether or not to make FHA loans, were warned to protect against "inharmonious racial groups." The FHA even composed and distributed a model racially restrictive covenant, prohibiting "the occupancy of properties except by the race for which they are intended." The FHA deemed it necessary and proper to create and maintain racially and socially homogeneous neighborhoods.

In 1962, President Kennedy issued an executive order that ended the explicitly segregationist practices of the FHA, but that order came too late and had too little force. The new FHA policy of nondiscrimination is limited largely to new housing. Thus, the established patterns of housing segregation are virtually unaffected.[9] Moreover, a July 2004 report by the U.S. Department of Housing and Urban Development (HUD) accused the two government-sponsored mortgage buyers (Fannie Mae and Freddie Mac) of continuing to underserve first-time home buyers, especially blacks and Hispanics.

Poor families of whatever color are further handicapped by the FHA's focus on middle-class families. Because loan applicants must be eligible for commercial loans, FHA insurance and guarantees benefit few, if any, poor families.

Federal efforts designed explicitly to improve the living conditions of the poor have likewise failed to promote residential integration. Public housing is almost always located in the poorest areas and most often segregated by race. Thus, it tends to intensify racial and economic isolation. The U.S. Commission on Civil Rights reports that, of the quarter of a million public housing units built in the nation's 24 largest metropolitan areas, only 76 units had located outside the central city. The result is not only residential segregation but *de facto* segregation of schools as well. Indeed, it appears that continuing residential segregation is the primary cause of continuing school segregation.[10]

---

[9]Local zoning ordinances can also enforce racial and class housing segregation and ultimately access to schools: See Raquel Fernandez and Richard Rogerson, "Keeping People Out: Income Distribution, Zoning and the Quality of Public Education," *International Economic Review* (Winter 1997). For evidence that racial discrimination in mortgage lending has abated, see U.S. Department of Housing and Urban Development, *All Other Things Being Equal: A Paired Testing Study of Mortgage Lending Institutions* (Washington, DC: Government Printing Office, April 2002).

[10]Steven G. Rivkin, "Residential Segregation and School Integration," *Sociology of Education* (October 1994), pp. 279–293. See also Emily Rosenbaum and Grigoris Argeros, "Holding the Line: Housing Turnover and the Persistence of Racial/Ethnic Segregation in New York City," *Journal of Urban Affairs*, 27:3 (2005), pp. 261–281.

School Zones

Although residential segregation explains most school segregation, there are other forces that keep racial and ethnic groups "separate and apart" in American schools. School authorities have broad discretion in defining the number and nature of school boundaries to be superimposed on residential patterns. Hence, local school authorities have the power to combat the segregation that exists in housing. Once again, however, this power has often been employed to intensify rather than to combat racial and economic isolation.

The power of local school authorities to encourage or resist school segregation is embodied in a variety of public decisions. Housing patterns alone do not define neighborhoods, much less school zones. Instead, the definition of a neighborhood is partly determined by the decisions of where and how to locate public schools. The number of schools to build, their size, and their geographic location are all decisions that help to shape neighborhoods. Building one large school between racially segregated housing areas, for example, does more to promote school integration than constructing two separate schools within racially homogeneous communities. Also important for the pattern of school integration is the number of grades to be served by each school and the actual specification of attendance zones. These decisions, too, can abet or overcome residential segregation.

To a large extent, existing school patterns reflect historical, rather than current, decisions. This fact does not exonerate school authorities from responsibility, however. Residential patterns are continually changing and schools are continually being built or rezoned. Hence, school authorities have discretion to alter the distribution of pupils or facilities and to counteract past decisions. Some of the tactics used to promote or impede integration include:

- *Gerrymandering* Gerrymandering refers to the purposeful restructuring of school attendance zones to foster specific attendance patterns. It is the oldest, simplest, and most blatant tactic available to local school authorities. Its visibility, however, has led to a decline in its use, especially where legal action has focused attention on the practice.

   The potential for gerrymandering is broadened when a school system is expanding or contracting. When a system is shrinking, some schools must be closed, and their students reassigned to other schools. In the process, entirely new attendance zones can be created. Those new zones can be designed either to foster or impede school integration.

- *Optional Zones* A tactic not far removed from gerrymandering is the use of optional attendance zones. An optional zone is a limited geographical area in which students are permitted to choose the school they will attend. In effect, optional zones are a more subtle and flexible tool to achieve either greater integration or segregation.

   In the South, *free choice* provisions are the counterpart of optional attendance zones. Students are permitted or required to state a preference for the schools they wish to attend. Priority is often given to those preferences, however, that are based on residential location, established school ties, or other correlates of race.

- *School Construction* The selection of a school site can have tremendous impact on the pattern of school segregation. Schools located within all-white or all-black residential areas solidify racial isolation. Schools located in fringe areas have the potential of accelerating integration. Unfortunately, site selection all too often conforms to segregationist practices. Of the 371 schools constructed in 16 cities from 1950 through 1965, over 80 percent opened nearly all white or all black.

- *Grade Structure*   Even when faced with established school locations and size, school authorities are not powerless to alter racial attendance patterns. One subtle but effective means for overcoming these obstacles is to redefine grade structures. Enlarging the number of grades a school will serve has the effect of shrinking its attendance zone. On the other hand, schools that serve only a few grades must reach out in all directions to enroll a sufficient number of pupils.
- *Selling the Schools*   School and government officials in Shaw, Mississippi, provide a final example of mechanisms for circumventing desegregation. In 1966, an all-white school board foresaw the inevitability of court-ordered desegregation in the public school system. To avoid this fate, the school board authorized the sale of selected public schools to private academies for a price of one dollar each. The private academies had more freedom to discriminate. This situation continued until 1983, when the school board acquired a 3 to 2 black majority, and voted 3 to 2 to repurchase the schools.

The many options local school boards have for creating or restructuring school attendance patterns greatly weaken the distinction between *de jure* and *de facto* segregation. In 1974, the federal courts explicitly noted the difficulty of maintaining this distinction in Boston. Boston had never been segregated by law. However, Judge W. Arthur Garrity Jr. observed that in the purchase and construction of new facilities, the assignment of staff and students to individual schools, and the use of open enrollments, the Boston School Committee was "at all times displaying an awareness of the potential racial impact of their actions. . . . The defendants have, with awareness of the racial segregation of Boston's neighborhoods, deliberately incorporated that segregation into the school system."[11]

BUSING

To reduce the segregation of Boston's school system, Judge Garrity ordered mandatory busing of pupils between white and black schools. In view of the extensive segregation of both neighborhoods and schools, busing was perceived as the shortest route to equality of educational opportunity. Proponents of busing argued that buses are the only sure access to equality of facilities and may help promote more complete social integration. The legal basis for using school buses to promote equal educational opportunity was firmly established by the U.S. Supreme Court in 1971 (in *Swann* v. *Charlotte-Mecklenburg*).

The reaction to interracial busing in Boston and other cities was hostile and often violent. Visions of masses of white children being bused into black or Hispanic ghettos stir the fears of most white parents. Anxiety is also expressed for the stamina of children who must be bused daily to their classrooms. What is seldom realized is that busing of children to school is a common phenomenon in the United States. Nationally, slightly more than 50 percent of all schoolchildren are bused to school. Most are bused

---

[11]Opinions of Judge Garrity in *Morgan* v. *Hennigan,* cited in U.S. Commission on Civil Rights, *Fulfilling the Letter and Spirit of the Law* (Washington, DC: U.S. Government Printing Office, 1976).

simply because such transportation is most convenient. Only 3.6 percent of all public school pupils are bused for desegregation purposes. Ironically, still others are bused to extend and enforce racial segregation.

The question of busing—especially when it is proposed for purposes of facilitating integration—touches a very sensitive nerve in most Americans. Three out of four Americans oppose mandatory busing, even though most still claim to support school integration. Indeed, the hostility to busing is so strong that many white families have fled the cities or schools where mandatory busing has been imposed.[12] In some cases, courts tried to compensate for white flight by forcing students to be bused between the central city and its suburbs. In June 1995, however, the United States Supreme Court ruled (*Missouri* v. *Jenkins*) that the Kansas City School System could no longer look beyond its city borders for remedies to racial isolation.[13]

Why is the opposition to busing so fierce? In part, the opposition to busing reflects fears for the safety and stamina of children. As noted earlier, however, this fear may be exaggerated. A more important concern may be the expectation that the quality of education will decline when mandatory busing is imposed. In part, this concern may simply manifest latent racial prejudices. Beyond that, however, white parents realize that their children already have a monopoly on better schools. To share these limited resources with bused-in black students implies a reduction in educational services. To be bused into a formerly black school implies an even larger reduction in educational services.

Finally, busing is almost always perceived as a direct threat to the cherished notion of a neighborhood school. Neighborhood schools are deemed desirable for two reasons. They are close to home and thus conveniently accessible. They also serve to foster community cohesiveness. Children who reside close together and attend a common school have more opportunity to interact and to establish enduring relationships. These two benefits, proximity and social integration, are the mainstays of neighborhood school support.

What is curious about arguments for neighborhood schools is not their potential benefits but their historical perspective. Arguments against economic or racial integration usually proceed from the assumption that integration is destroying the neighborhood school. There are three problems with this perspective. First, children have historically traveled quite far to school and continue to do so. More proximate schools have resulted from increasing population density rather than from an increased awareness of any "neighborhood" benefits. Second, we have already seen that there is considerable flexibility in defining a neighborhood school. School attendance zones themselves can create neighborhoods, and deliberate manipulation of school zones can even affect residential choice. Families will want to live near the schools they know they can attend. Finally, the narrow neighborhood concept has been repeatedly sacrificed to other social objectives. Every major city, for example, has at least one citywide school reserved for students of outstanding ability. In these cases, productivity and individual development

---

[12]See Lino A. Graglia, "The Triumph and Defeat of the Nondiscrimination Principle," *Society* (March 1996); also Charles T. Clotfelter, "School Desegregation, 'Tipping,' and Private School Enrollment," *Journal of Human Resources* (Winter 1976).

[13]For an assessment of the subsequent Kansas experience, see Donna Davis, "Merry-Go-Round: A Return to Segregation," *Urban Education* (July 2004), pp. 394–407.

are deemed more important than neighborhood cohesiveness. No one has argued that the attending students are in any way deprived. A high percentage of white parents send their children to distant private schools for exactly the same reasons.

The opposition to busing, then, is firmly based in both prejudice and privileged position. To overcome this opposition, school authorities would have to provide credible evidence that busing does not reduce the quality of education. School authorities may even have to "bribe" white students to stay in the public schools with improved facilities and programs.

The actual experience with court-ordered or "diversity"-driven busing failed to mollify white opposition. In the late 1990s, dozens of school districts were released from court-supervised busing policies. Then a federal court in Charlotte, North Carolina—the "home" of forced busing (*Swann* v. *Charlotte-Mecklenberg*)—ruled in 1999 that race could no longer be a consideration in school assignments. That decision effectively undercut the legal foundation for busing and raised fears of educational resegregation.

FISCAL DISPARITIES

As school districts grapple with new legal edicts, they are refocusing on the core problem of inequality in educational resources. Even if one rejects the notion of "separate but equal," one must recognize that greater equality of facilities would serve to promote integration. At least it would defuse some white opposition to school policies that "mixed" students from different neighborhoods.

As desirable as it sounds, greater equality of school resources is not easy to achieve. Much of this problem derives from the way schools are financed. Local communities continue to provide the bulk of their own school resources. In 2006 the federal government supplied only 8 percent of all educational expenditures and state governments contributed 48 percent; local governments provided the remainder. This means that the quantity and quality of educational resources in a community depends largely on the ability of the local populace to pay taxes. As a result, wealthier white enclaves in the suburbs can provide educational opportunities for their children that few cities can ever hope to match. There is ample evidence that this fiscal disparity is more important than race per se in suppressing minority educational attainments.[14]

It is easy to see how such disparities arise. In the suburbs the ratio of property values to school-age children is far higher than in the cities. Indeed, population density is ten times larger in urban ghettos than in surrounding areas. This means that residents of the city must support far more schoolchildren per square mile than people in the suburbs. Furthermore, the wealthier residents of the suburbs are better equipped to support public schools. They have the property and income on which school revenues depend.

The economics of local school financing encourages school districts to attempt to maximize their tax base while minimizing enrollment size. That is, they seek to include the wealthier and exclude the poorer, especially those with many children.

---

[14]See Linda Darling-Hammond, "Unequal Opportunity: Race and Education," *The Brookings Review* (Spring 1998), pp. 28–32. There is also empirical evidence that raising school quality is more effective than reallocating students among schools in raising minority achievements. See Steven G. Rivkin, "School Desegregation, Academic Attainment, and Earnings," *Journal of Human Resources* (Spring 2000), pp. 333–346.

The results are staggering. In California, for example, the poorest elementary school district had only $15,500 of assessed property per pupil in 1997. The richest district had over $47 million of property per pupil! This led to a lower tax rate for those most able to pay, an outcome of great benefit to the wealthier but of great disadvantage to the poor.

Given the nature of school financing, suburban communities have a tremendous incentive to insulate their school systems from the poor. They have little desire to impose higher tax rates on themselves to provide more educational opportunity for others. In some communities wealthier neighborhoods may even seek to incorporate independent school districts to dispose of responsibilities they already share. This tactic has taken on special significance as the courts have ordered opportunities to be equalized within, but not across, school districts.

To some extent, state and federal governments attempt to equalize the educational inequalities between richer and poorer communities. The Elementary and Secondary Education Act of 1965 is an example of such an attempt. Under this act the federal government distributes $10–$20 billion a year to the poorest schools, but even this infusion of funds is inadequate. Only two-thirds of the students eligible to receive aid from Title I of the Elementary and Secondary Education Act are actually served. This reflects a number of problems, including inadequate funding, poor selection procedures, and the lack of Title I programs at certain grade levels. Even those served by Title I programs only receive an additional $800 in educational services per year. The most absurd and distressing statistic of all is, perhaps, this: The wealthiest schools are more likely than the poorest schools to have subsidized milk or food programs! Many poor schools are denied such benefits because they cannot afford cafeterias, extra personnel, or their share of total costs. While the federal government is spending $10–$20 billion in special aid, over $400 billion is being spent on elementary and secondary education, with the biggest share still going to wealthier communities.

The subject of school financing highlights several important dimensions of the educational opportunity issue. The localized nature of school financing, for example, provides an independent motive for segregation. Even persons who harbor few racial prejudices are not immune to self-interest. On the contrary, most people seek to minimize their tax burden while providing well for their own children. Thus, they seek to exclude poor children, many of whom are Hispanic or black, from their school systems. This exclusionist tendency illuminates again the close ties of racial and class discrimination.

The class discrimination inherent in existing patterns of school financing has become a major judicial issue. In August 1971 the California Supreme Court acknowledged that fiscal disparities between school districts "make the quality of a child's education a function of the wealth of his parents and neighbors." Ruling that such discriminatory treatment violated the Fourteenth Amendment of the U.S. Constitution, the Court declared the state's entire system of financing public schools to be unconstitutional. However, the U.S. Supreme Court effectively overturned that decision in 1973 in a similar case originating in San Antonio, Texas. In its decision the Supreme Court admitted that the mechanisms for financing schools were "imperfect," but argued that it did not have the prerogative to bypass the legislative branch, much less overturn the wisdom and experience of state legislatures and educational administrators. Solutions to the inherent inequalities of school finance, the Court suggested, should be sought in state legislatures, not the courts.

Since then at least two dozen state school systems have been embroiled in legal disputes over disparate school finance. In 1994 a state judge ruled that New Jersey's method of funding public schools was unconstitutional. The state had 611 school districts of widely varying size, wealth, and spending levels. Since the 1970s the state had tried to reduce fiscal disparities between these districts by supplementing local property tax revenues with state sales tax revenues. Even with supplemental funds, however, poor school districts were still spending half of what the richest districts spent per pupil. The state supreme court ruled that such disparities created a separate class of students that was undereducated and isolated; it ordered the state to achieve spending equality.

When states attempt to equalize per-pupil spending across school districts, average spending and school quality may decline. High-income communities may decide that it no longer makes sense to support local schools (with property taxes) when they discover that *state* support declines whenever *local* support increases. In a pure equalization program, rich communities would simply be subsidizing poor communities with their property taxes. Under such circumstances, rich communities might prefer to reduce property tax rates and have more students attend private schools. In that case, inequalities and socioeconomic segregation might increase.[15]

To avoid this averaging-down effect, states would have to increase *total* school spending as they pursued equalization. In New Jersey, the state would have had to increase overall school spending by $500–$600 million per year to raise average per pupil expenditure to the level of the richer school districts. Although individual states have not moved that far toward fiscal equality, court-ordered finance reforms have significantly reduced within-state inequalities by spending more in the poorest districts while leaving spending in the richest districts unchanged. This has required states to raise taxes to fund increased education spending.[16] Local tax bases still exert substantial influence on interdistrict inequalities, however.

COMPENSATORY EDUCATION

An approach to equal education opportunity that has aroused relatively little hostility is compensatory education, the provision of added educational resources to children from poor or minority homes. Indeed, most of the federal money spent on elementary and secondary education is distributed to the lower-income school districts either by federal statute (Title I of the Elementary and Secondary Education Act, as reauthorized by the No Child Left Behind Act of 2001) or by allocation decisions made by the states that receive federal grants. The unspoken objective of these efforts is to improve the resources available to poor and minority groups without sharing those (via racial or class integration) available to upper-income groups. As we noted earlier, however, the total federal effort is small in relation to the size of the educational system.

---

[15]Some evidence of this response is provided in Caroline Hoxby, "All School Equalizations Are Not Created Equal," *Quarterly Journal of Economics* (November 2001).

[16]Sheila Murray, William Evans, and Robert Schwab, "Education-Finance Reform and the Distribution of Education Resources," *American Economic Review* (September 1998), pp. 789–812.

Head Start

Perhaps the most important form of compensatory education has been the preschool program, particularly Head Start. As the designers of Head Start observed:

> . . . the early years of childhood are a most critical point in the poverty cycle. During these years, the creation of learning patterns, emotional development and the formation of individual expectations and aspirations take place at a very rapid pace. For the child of poverty, there are clearly observable deficiencies in these processes, which lay the foundation for a pattern of failure, and thus a pattern of poverty, throughout the child's entire life.

To help such children get a more equal start in the education system, Head Start was created to provide educational, health, nutritional, and social services to disadvantaged children in their preschool years. Since its creation in 1964, over 25 million children have participated in Head Start. In 2006, a million children participated, almost all of them from poor families.

Evaluations of Head Start have consistently documented its success in raising preschool children's capabilities, interest, and aspirations. At the same time, however, observers noted that the program's impact tends to be short-lived: After a year or two in their regular school systems, Head Start children performed no better than their similarly disadvantaged classmates.[17] Critics of the program are quick to cite this as evidence of the basic genetic or cultural deficiencies of minority children. More sympathetic observers argue, however, that ghetto schools operated as levelers, that the higher motivation and aspirations of Head Start children were not being reinforced by their regular schools.[18]

COLLEGE ADMISSIONS

One very clear implication of our review of (un)equal opportunity in the preschool, elementary, and secondary school systems is that minority groups will be less prepared than others to enter colleges and universities. Because they are not provided full and equal opportunities to develop their skills earlier, they will not exhibit the required skills at the time of admission to higher education. This will be manifested not only in grade records, but even more clearly in standardized college entrance exams (the SAT or ACT, for example) that are a major screening mechanism for admissions applicants. Accordingly, if all college applicants were treated equally, we would expect a much lower proportion of minority applicants to gain entrance to higher education. The effect of such an "equal opportunity" policy would be to widen educational disparities between whites and minority youth and ultimately increase income inequalities as well.

The vestiges of prior discrimination thus raise very serious policy questions about our concept of equality and the appropriate role of educational institutions in fulfilling

---

[17]Alison Aughinbaugh, "Does Head Start Yield Long-Term Benefits?" *Journal of Human Resources* (Fall 2001), pp. 641–665. For an earlier review of the Head Start evidence, see Edward Zigler and Sally J. Styfro, "Head Start: Criticisms in a Constructive Context," *American Psychologist* (February 1994), pp. 127–132.

[18]Janet Currie and Duncan Thomas, "School Quality and the Longer-Term Effects of Head Start," *Journal of Human Resources* (Fall 2000), pp. 755–774. More positive long-term effects for white children are reported in Eliana Garces, Duncan Thomas, and Janet Currie, "Longer-Term Effects of Head Start," *American Economic Review* (September 2002), pp. 999–1012. See also Jens Ludwig and Deborah Phillips, "The Benefits and Costs of Head Start" Ann Arbor, MI: University of Michigan National Poverty Center, February 2007.

equal opportunity goals. On the one hand, it can be (and is) argued that *equal treatment* is the foremost policy goal and that schools should not be expected to exceed that mandate. From this point of view, the overriding goal of higher education is to enhance society's productivity by concentrating resources on the most able. So long as all applicants are treated equally, then the goals of efficiency and equality are both fulfilled.[19]

As we have noted, however, this "color-blind" admissions policy effectively "writes off" the talents of individuals who have been discriminated against in earlier stages of the school system. Hence, an alternative viewpoint stresses the importance of achieving *equality of status* between whites and blacks, rather than stopping at *equal treatment*. Proponents of this view also suggest that black and Hispanic applicants will prove their worth (demonstrate their latent abilities) once they have an opportunity to catch up. Thus, it is argued, minority students should be admitted to college and professional schools on a preferential basis (with lower test scores and grade point averages), a policy that will not only hasten the achievement of status quality, but will ultimately fulfill our goals of efficiency as well.

The Assault on Preferences

Clearly, there is considerable merit to the preceding argument, particularly if the preferentially admitted students do indeed catch up. But the merits of the case are not likely to impress those who end up paying the costs of such a policy—in particular, those white applicants who are denied admission to make room for minority groups. Such students have worked hard to meet college admission standards and are naturally resentful when others with fewer "qualifications" take their place.[20] Indeed, such students argue that they themselves are being denied equal opportunity—as the victims of reverse discrimination—and have sought appropriate relief from the courts.

A landmark case concerns a rejected applicant to the University of California's Medical School at Davis (*Regents of the University of California* v. *Alan Bakke*). Under a special admissions program, 16 of that school's 100 entry slots were set aside for minorities, a policy that was attacked on the basis of reverse discrimination. A superior court judge in the county ruled that the program did violate the equal protection clause of the U.S. Constitution, the corresponding provision of the California constitution, and Title VI of the U.S. Civil Rights Act of 1964. In June 1978, the U.S. Supreme Court also agreed with *Bakke*. The Court noted that race could be considered as one factor in the admissions process, but ruled that rigid quotas based on race were too discriminatory. Since then, universities and courts have been compelled to differentiate quotas from less rigid preference policies. In 1994, the U.S. Department of Education ruled that the preferential admissions policies at the University of California at San Diego were legal, even though they gave minority and low-income applicants a decided (but not conclusive) advantage. Rejected law school applicants sued the University of Texas in 1994, claiming that the admissions threshold for minority applicants was far below the reject threshold for white applicants. The white students ultimately prevailed in

---

[19]For a fuller discussion of this viewpoint, see the symposium on "Black Separation vs. American Integration," *Society* (March 1996); and the symposium "On Equality," *The Public Interest* (Fall 1982).

[20]Far more white students perceive themselves to have been "left out" than are in fact displaced by race-based preferences. Further, most preferential access has occurred at elite schools, not the ones most students attend. See Thomas J. Kane, "Racial and Ethnic Preference in College Admissions," in *The Black-White Test Score Gap,* eds. C. Jencks and M. Phillips (Washington, DC: Brookings Institution, 1998).

court (*Hopwood* v. *State of Texas*) in 1996, forcing the University of Texas to abandon its race-conscious admissions policy.

In that same year, California voters took to the polls, not the courts, to dismantle racial preferences. In 1996, Proposition 209 decreed that the state could not engage in any discrimination, including the reverse discrimination implied by preferential race policies. "Color-blind" admissions policies were mandated for the state's graduate schools in 1997 and for undergraduate admissions beginning in 1998.

The end of racial preferences had a dramatic effect on minority enrollments. At the University of Texas—which had produced more minority lawyers than any other school in the country—black and Hispanic admissions plummeted by 75 percent in 1997. At the Berkeley and UCLA law schools, black and Hispanic admissions fell by 50–80 percent.[21]

The precipitous decline of minority admissions with "color-blind" programs has intensified the debate over the nature of "equal opportunity." Critics of affirmative action cite the admissions drop-offs as proof of how unfair and inefficient the racial double standard was. Defenders respond that the admissions decline also demonstrates how disadvantaged minorities are by the racial and economic disparities that permeate the entire school system from preschool to college.

The legal battle over these issues took another turn in May 2001. A federal appeals court ruled that the University of Michigan Law School's race-conscious admissions policy was legal. This case (*Grutter* v. *Bollinger*) looked identical to the 1978 *Bakke* case. This time, a white female was suing because she had been denied admission to the law school while less qualified black applicants got in. Even the school acknowledged she would have gotten in without racial preferences. But the school argued it needed a "critical mass" of black students to assure everyone a voice in the classroom. The school also acknowledged that without racial preferences, less than 4 percent of its 350 new students would be black. Ms. Grutter argued that the school's "race-conscious" policy was effectively a rigid quota, admitting a 13.5–14.0 percent black share each year. In a hotly disputed decision, the appeals court approved, saying the school's policy was a "temporary" tool for achieving a specific purpose. In December 2002, the U.S. Supreme Court agreed to review the Michigan case and the evident conflict in lower court rulings.

In June 2003, the U.S. Supreme Court upheld the legality of the Michigan Law School's preference system. At the same time, however, it ruled that Michigan's undergraduate admissions preferences were illegal. Undergraduate admissions were based on a point system that automatically awarded 20 points to every minority applicant (more points than were awarded for writing skills and some other academic achievements). This point preference gave minorities an overwhelming advantage, as a score of 100 or more ensured admission. The Court concluded that those point preferences were too rigid and arbitrary. They preferred the law school's approach, which was less formulistic and encouraged individual-specific assessments.

Two months later, Michigan adopted a less rigid, holistic admissions policy, first introduced by the University of California in 2001. According to this "comprehensive evaluation" policy, every applicant is to be judged not just by prior academic achievements but

---

[21]Asian American enrollments *increased* significantly, however, thereby mitigating the decline in *minority* enrollments. See Stephan Thernstrom, "Farewell to Preferences?" *The Public Interest* (Winter 1998), pp. 34–49; also Martin Trow, "California after Racial Preferences," *The Public Interest* (Spring 1999), pp. 64–85.

by a litany of personal circumstances (e.g., raised by a single parent) and a personal essay justifying his or her admission. The resulting admissions evaluation seeks to create a more diverse and motivated student body. Critics contend that this policy is just a less explicit preference system that is both overly expensive (applicant files and essays must be read in detail) and arbitrary. Advocates defend it as a necessary step in ensuring both diversity and equal opportunity.

The U.S. Supreme Court took up this issue again in 2006. This time the focus was on race-conscious school assignments in elementary and secondary education. School administrators in Seattle and Louisville pursued racial diversity by giving preference in school assignments to minority students, thereby circumventing housing segregation. In the process, however, some white students had to be assigned to out-of-neighborhood schools. Their parents sued, arguing that the school districts exceeded the bounds of the Court's 2003 ruling with fixed numerical targets for racial balance (in the Louisville plan all schools were to have a minimum black enrollment of 15 percent and a maximum of 50 percent).

SCHOOL-BASED QUOTAS

An alternative approach to greater equality of educational opportunity is to use school-based quotas for college admissions. With school-based quotas, the top students at every high school are guaranteed admission to state colleges. In 1999, Governor Jeb Bush proposed this policy for Florida, offering guaranteed college admission for the top 20 percent of students from each high school in that state. California guarantees admission to the top 4 percent of each high school's graduates; Texas gives the top 10 percent of each high school automatic admission to the state college of their choice.

There are some evident advantages to school-based quotas. To begin with, they substitute for race-based quotas without sacrificing racial diversity in college enrollments. In fact, geographically based quotas would *increase* minority college enrollments in most states. Another advantage of school-based quotas is that they are easy to understand and enforce. They are also likely to be viewed as fair by both white-majority and minority populations since they explicitly link personal achievement to college admission.

School-based quotas might even reduce race and class segregation in secondary schools. White students with only marginal odds of college admission might opt to attend high schools with high proportions of minority and low-income students. By attending less competitive schools, they would increase their relative class ranking and thus the chances of college admission.

Although there are several advantages to school-based quotas, this approach also entails some problems. The first issue is money. School-based quotas will result either in (1) a substantial increase in college enrollments or (2) the displacement of students now admitted without geographic quotas (e.g., students who rank below the top 20 percent in better-quality high schools but still have high achievement levels or high family income). If less qualified quota students displace more qualified nonquota students, political opposition will increase and educational efficiency will decrease.

The quota-based students who are admitted to college may not be adequately prepared for college work. As we have observed, minority and low-income schools don't offer the same learning resources as majority-white schools. This implies that many quota-admitted students will not be able to satisfy college-level learning requirements. For them to succeed, an array of college-prep and tutoring programs might well be required.

Clearly, a school-based quota system won't succeed unless a lot more resources are allocated to both college and high schools. Recognizing this, Governor Bush proposed a 43 percent increase in state-funded minority scholarships and more school funding. To end racial and class disparities in educational opportunity, however, would require much more substantial increases in funding or dramatic (and politically unpopular) reallocation of existing resources. In the absence of such sweeping change, governments at all levels should at least commit far more resources to preparing minority students for college admissions. Even then, however, a delicate compromise must be struck between those claims to admission based on achievement and those based on denied opportunity (and thus potential achievement).

Summary

Equal opportunity policies can help eliminate poverty in two ways: They may provide access to educational credentials; and they may dismantle artificial barriers between people and jobs. Access to educational credentials is important to the extent that it opens new employment opportunities or redistributes existing ones.

The federal government's direct efforts to create equal opportunity in employment have not met with much success. Minority workers continue to suffer higher levels of unemployment and to be relegated to less desirable jobs. A major reason for this continuing discrimination lies in the nature of government efforts. For decades the federal government has had the power only to exhort employers to create equal employment opportunities. It was not until the early 1960s that the government acquired some meaningful powers to enforce its proclamations. The Office of Federal Contract Compliance Programs may terminate contracts of discriminatory employers, while the Equal Employment Opportunity Commission may facilitate legal action. Those powers have been used rarely, however, and then mostly as a threat. Political, bureaucratic, and economic interests continue to impede the attainment of equal employment opportunity; what progress has been achieved is largely the result of private legal action, building on public legislation (e.g., the Civil Rights Acts of 1964 and 1991).

In the educational system, equal opportunity has been just as elusive. Local and state governments have not demonstrated a consuming ambition to open school doors to all. On the contrary, they have often employed a variety of manipulative techniques to forestall school integration for as long as possible. The localized nature of school financing also creates a tremendous incentive for wealthier white communities to exclude poor minority children from their schools. Federal authority to alter the pattern of segregation resides primarily in the power to bestow or withdraw funds under the Elementary and Secondary Education Act. But the amount of funds involved is relatively small and the political pressure to maintain their flow great.

In the late 1990s some of the explicit tools of affirmative action were dismantled. Race-based busing was discontinued in many jurisdictions and race-based quotas and preferences were being discarded. The focus of equal opportunity policy was shifting to *economic* disadvantage rather than presumptive disadvantage related to race or ethnicity. To implement greater equality of opportunity in either dimension will require substantial increases or reallocations of school resources.

Further Reading

Bergmann, Barbara, *In Defense of Affirmative Action*. New York: Basic Books, 1996.

Bowen, William G., and Derek Bok, *The Shape of the River: Long-Term Consequences of Considering Race in College and University Admissions*. Princeton, NJ: Princeton University Press, 1998.

Clegg, Roger, "The Bad Law of 'Disparate Impact,'" *The Public Interest* (Winter 2000), pp. 79–90.

Galster, George, and Erin Godfrey, "By Words and Deeds: Racial Steering by Real Estate Agents in the U.S. in 2000," *Journal of the American Planning Association* (Summer 2005), pp. 251–268.

Holzer, Harry, and David Neumark, "Affirmative Action: What Do We Know?" Cambridge, MA: National Bureau of Economic Research, Working Paper No. 06-03, January 2006.

Hurley, Jennifer A., ed., *Racism*. San Diego, CA: Greenhaven Press, 1998, Chapter 3.

Loury, Glenn, *The Anatomy of Racial Inequality*. Cambridge, MA: Harvard University Press, 2001.

Powell, John A., Gavin Kearney, and Vina Kay, eds., *In Pursuit of a Dream Deferred: Linking Housing and Education Policy*. New York: Peter Lang, 2001.

Reskin, Barbara F., *The Realities of Affirmative Action in Employment*. New York: American Sociological Association, 1998.

U.S. Commission on Civil Rights, *With All Deliberate Speed, 1954–19??* Washington, DC: U.S. Government Printing Office, 1981.

Williams, Mary E., ed., *Discrimination*. San Diego, CA: Greenhaven Press, 2003.

Web Links

Education Trust. Annual reports on inequalities of school funding.
www.edtsust.org

Equal Employment Opportunity Commission. Data on discrimination complaints.
www.eeoc.gov

Gallup Organization. Social audit opinion polls.
www.gallup.com/poll/specialReports/socialAudits

National Conference of State Legislatures. Information and policy briefs on school finance.
www.ncsl.org/programs/educ/NCSLEducationFinance.htm

U.S. Commission on Civil Rights. Occasional studies and reports.
www.usccr.gov

U.S. Department of Education. The National Center for Education Statistics maintains data on school enrollments and finances.
http://nces.ed.gov/edfin

U.S. Department of Health and Human Services. Head Start program statistics.
www.acf.hhs.gov/programs/hsb and www.headstartinfo.org

U.S. Department of Housing and Urban Development. A bibliography on mortgage discrimination.
www.hud.gov

CHAPTER 17
DIRECTION AND PROSPECTS

According to official estimates, over 35 million Americans remain in poverty. Although these estimates are exaggerated by the neglect of in-kind transfers, it is evident that millions of Americans are poor. Millions more struggle with incomes just above official poverty thresholds, often with the critical help of income transfers. In a nation where the *average* family has an income that is more than three times the *poverty* threshold, such deprivation is hard to comprehend. This manifest disparity raises two simple questions: (1) Why are so many Americans poor? and (2) What policies will eliminate their poverty? The preceding chapters have provided much of the background material necessary to resolve these questions. This concluding chapter attempts to summarize the salient impressions of our inquiry.

THE CAUSES OF POVERTY

The most popular diagnoses of poverty focus on the personal characteristics of those who are poor. The poor are viewed as less able, less motivated, overly reproductive, too aged or sick, or otherwise handicapped. By inference or declaration, they are thus assumed to be responsible for their own impoverishment. This Flawed Character view of poverty, as we have called it, is reinforced by statistical profiles of the poverty population. Very high percentages of the poor are in families that *are* female headed, black or Hispanic, have large numbers of children, or headed by a nonworker.

We have seen how easy it is to infer *causation* from such *correlates*. We have also seen, however, that such inferences are often unjustified. To begin with, a large portion of the poverty population doesn't fit into any of these "suspect" categories. Over one-fourth of the poverty population lives in white, married-couple families. Another 2 million poor persons are over age 65 and living alone. Furthermore, most single-parent and two-parent families do participate in the labor market, often on a year-round, full-time basis. Clearly, the Flawed Character stereotypes won't easily fit the entire poverty population.

The Flawed Character generalization suffers not only from a narrowed focus but also from shortsightedness. Even those poor families who manifest distinctive demographic traits, such as broken homes, are not necessarily poor because of those traits. On the contrary, most of the aged poor were poor before they became aged, many broken poor families were poor before they were fragmented, large poor families were poor when they were smaller, and sick poor families were poor even when they were well. Thus, theories of poverty causation that are based only on observations at a single point in time fail to perceive the dynamics of impoverishment. They confuse association with causality.

Correlation between demographic characteristics and poverty status lose more causal significance in a dynamic context. As we have observed, incomes vary greatly from year to year and over longer stretches of time. People who fall into poverty one year are likely to move out of poverty the next year. As a result, the poverty population is continuously changing; people's income status changes faster than their demographic profile. Hence, demographic characteristics are better understood as indicators of poverty *risks* than poverty *status*.

The risks of poverty for any individual are largely determined by his or her labor market status. How attached a person is to employment is the critical factor in separating the poor from the nonpoor. In view of this, the paramount questions for poverty policy are: (1) What forces determine how many good income-earning opportunities are available? and (2) What forces determine who will obtain those opportunities? The myopic perspective of demographic theories of poverty encompasses only the second question. It assumes that good jobs are always available in sufficient quantity. But they are not, as history has repeatedly shown, and as we witnessed in the high unemployment rates of the early 1980s, in 1990–1992, and again in 2001–2002. To understand why so much poverty exists at any point in time, we must consider and resolve the first question. The answer to the second question tells us primarily how that poverty will be distributed.

In seeking to resolve the first question, we have put a heavy stress on the importance of aggregate (macro) economic policies in determining the extent of poverty. The number of available jobs is a phenomenon over which individual members of society have very little control. Similarly, they have little control over what kinds of jobs will be available or where they will be located. These decisions are made, instead, by the interplay of labor-market forces, among which government fiscal and monetary decisions are often decisive. Accordingly, we conclude that collective social decisions in the area of economic policy—especially those concerning the extent and structure of the demand for labor—are responsible for much poverty.

We should not conclude, however, that all available income-earning opportunities are taken. Even in relatively prosperous times, some families break up, others become sick or disabled, and some may even choose not to work. Still more children will be born to unwed teenagers and face a high probability of poverty regardless of labor-market conditions. Hence, even with prolonged full employment, not all families will participate fully in the economy. Sometimes the mismatch between the number of available jobs and potential workers originates in demographic forces, and we must include them as independent causes of poverty where appropriate. In this regard, the alarming increase in the number of unwed teenage mothers stands out as an independent cause of poverty and long-term dependency. Increasing rates of marital dissolution also increase the number of poor people in any given macroeconomic environment. Finally, age and disability tend to increase the incidence of poverty as well.

The third general set of causes are those related to discrimination, both in the schools and in the labor market. Minority groups, the offspring of the poor, and women are still deprived of an equal chance to acquire productive skills and to use those skills in the labor market. Racial, class, and sex discrimination has significant impact on both the distribution and extent of poverty. As long as discrimination persists, the children of the poor, blacks, Hispanics, and female-headed families will dominate the ranks of the poverty population. Even in a relatively prosperous economy, discrimination creates artificial barriers between workers and jobs, leaving more individuals poor than necessary.

Finally, we have recognized that government efforts to assist the poor may also play a role in perpetuating poverty. Although the welfare system is an essential source of income support, it also creates moral hazards that "reward" undesirable behavior. Welfare benefits and eligibility rules still create financial incentives for unwed parenthood and discourage work effort. But less than half of the poverty population has ever been on (cash) welfare at any time. And even among welfare recipients the evidence suggests that these perverse incentives have played an important but not major role in employment and marital behavior.

No one can disentangle all of the overlapping forces that cause poverty. At best, the evidence allows us to reject some explanations and draw broad conclusions about others. In that regard, it appears reasonable to conclude that (1) labor-market forces are primarily responsible for the extent of poverty, with demographic handicaps and discrimination of secondary importance; and (2) the distribution of poverty is determined by changing demographic patterns (especially unwed mothers, family breakups, and ill health) and discrimination. Public programs to alleviate poverty and discrimination, while successful in many respects, also contribute to the problem by distorting family and work incentives. This is a reflection of the goal conflicts inherent in all such programs.

POLICY DIRECTIONS

An understanding of the causes of poverty gives direction to the formulation of required public policy. To eliminate poverty, we must first expand the number of decent job opportunities and their availability. Harry Johnson of the University of Chicago summarized the point well: ". . . in the absence of a policy of raising the demand for labor to the stretching point, ad hoc policies for remedying poverty by piecemeal assaults on particular poverty-associated characteristics are likely to prove both ineffective and expensive. The most effective way to attack poverty is to attack unemployment, not the symptoms of it."[1]

A strong economy not only creates more job opportunities but also reduces discrimination barriers.[2] In a sluggish economy, the competition for available jobs fosters an "us versus them" mentality that resists *equal* opportunity, not to mention *preferential* opportunity for minority groups. When jobs are plentiful, white males are less threatened by the advancement of minorities and women and are more receptive to affirmative action.

To promote a stronger economy, the government has several options available. First and foremost, it must seek to maintain a high level of aggregate demand by the judicious use of fiscal and monetary tools. In addition, it must give special consideration

[1]Harry G. Johnson, "Poverty and Unemployment," in *The Economics of Poverty,* ed. Burton Weisbrod (Englewood Cliffs, NJ: Prentice-Hall, 1965), p. 170. Rebecca Blank echoes this theme in her assessment of the 1990s, declaring that "a strong macroeconomy matters more than anything else" is "lesson 1"; see her "Fighting Poverty: Lessons from Recent U.S. History," *Journal of Economic Perspectives* (Spring 2000), pp. 3–19; also Hilary Hoynes, Marianne Page, and Ann Huff Stevens, "Poverty in America: Trends and Explanation," *Journal of Economic Perspectives* (Winter 2006), pp. 47–68; also John Ireland, "Why Poverty Remains High: The Role of Income Growth, Economic Inequality, and Changes in Family Structure, 1949–1999," *Demography* (August 2003), pp. 499–519.

[2]See Judith Fields and Edward N. Wolff, "The Decline of Sex Segregation and the Wage Gap, 1970–80," *Journal of Human Resources* (Fall 1991), pp. 608–622.

to the structure of demand those tools stimulate. Aggregate economic policies have identifiable impact on different areas, industries, and labor-market groups. Accordingly, government policy makers may strive to select that mix of public actions that maximizes impact on the unemployed and poor, while minimizing dislocations, such as inflation, elsewhere.

Aggregate economic policies must also incorporate clear supply-side incentives for employment and training of the poor. Tax, spending, or regulatory policies that raise the cost of hiring the poor will not reduce poverty. In principle, employer tax credits that reduce the cost of hiring should bolster employment prospects for targeted workers. Their impact has been minimal, however. Employee tax credits have been much more successful in raising *incomes,* if not *employment.* As we observed in Chapter 15, the wage subsidy provided by the Earned Income Tax Credit has lifted millions of low-wage workers above the poverty line. It's had little impact on net employment levels, however,

In addition to seeking full employment, government agencies must make a determined effort to equalize educational opportunities. This will not only further reduce poverty and inequity, it will also make the attainment of full employment easier and less expensive. Experience suggests that the goal of equal opportunity will be easier to achieve by *adding* resources to school systems than by *reallocating* them (e.g., through busing, quotas, etc.).

Finally, the public must assume responsibility for those who are temporarily or permanently unable to participate in the labor market. Adequate income support must be available, both to alleviate hardship and to reduce intergenerational deprivation. Greatest priority should be placed, however, on reducing the need for public assistance to a minimum.

Viewed against this policy framework, the history of antipoverty policy has been inconsistent and often incidental. All too often, macroeconomic policy has stopped short in the pursuit of full employment. Billions of dollars have been spent on employment training programs that generated few marketable skills and little net employment gains. Communities across the country have been wrenched by affirmative action programs that focused too much on reallocating resources than on increasing resources that would raise educational quality. For far too long, welfare policy has also been developed in a vacuum, separate and apart from employment policy. This disconnected approach was rooted in the mistaken belief that poverty can be eliminated without full employment. As a consequence, public antipoverty activities often have had the aura of a bread and circus kind of gesture. We allotted—grudgingly, to be sure—huge sums of money to feed, clothe, and house the poor, in the hope, perhaps, of achieving social tranquility. At the same time, we subjected the poor to a kaleidoscope of training and educational activities, holding out false promises of job opportunity. Yet we have too often failed to create the job opportunities that are critical to poverty reduction. Finally, the shared responsibilities of local, state, and federal governments have often created bureaucratic gridlock rather than effective synergy.

WELFARE REFORM

The welfare reforms of the 1990s represented a radical departure in policy strategies. In effect, the Personal Responsibility and Work Opportunity Reconciliation Act (PRWORA) of 1996 legislated permanent dependency out of existence. Acting as a moral tutor, the government compelled welfare recipients to make a greater personal effort to acquire skills and a job. The PRWORA also set strict limits on the duration of dependency. In effect, these provisions proclaimed, "We'll help you, but only for a while and only if you also help yourself at the same time." This was a dramatically different position than the "We're always here if you need us" foundation of prior welfare programs.

The welfare reforms of 1996 were not entirely driven by Flawed Character biases. The reforms also addressed obstacles that restricted employment opportunities, especially for low-income mothers. To this end, resources for child care were significantly increased and more transitional assistance (e.g., continued Medicaid coverage) was made available for individuals leaving welfare to take a job. The EITC tax credit was also enhanced, further increasing the financial incentive to work.

Another dramatic change in strategy was the shift of program responsibility to the states. The decision of federal lawmakers to turn more welfare responsibilities over to the states was an admission that Congress didn't know how to solve the larger welfare problem. Since July 1997 the states have taken much greater control over who gets welfare, for how long, and under what conditions. As a consequence, cash welfare is now much less of a national program. Despite this fragmentation, however, welfare reform has been a dramatic national success. Not only have welfare caseloads plummeted, but millions of former welfare recipients have developed stronger attachments to the labor force and attained higher incomes in the process.

SOCIAL INSURANCE

Although the 1996 welfare reforms are undoubtedly the most visible policy intervention of the last twenty years, the most powerful antipoverty programs have been broader social insurance policies. While not designed as antipoverty mechanisms, Social Security and Medicare transfer so much income that they greatly reduce poverty among the aged, the disabled, and survivors of deceased workers. The explicit redistributive emphasis of Social Security is also vital to its antipoverty effectiveness.

Unemployment insurance is currently less of an antipoverty mechanism than a middle-class safety net. To increase its poverty impact, benefits would have to be available to a broader spectrum of unemployed workers. Such an expansion would be very costly, however, especially in relation to its poverty impact.

Child-support enforcement is virtually a failsafe policy option as it not only reduces poverty and welfare but also appeals to a broader social consensus on parental obligation. Its antipoverty impact is not likely to be large, however, unless tougher enforcement reduces the rate of illegitimate births, particularly among teenagers. A child-support assurance program could have much greater poverty impact but faces substantial budgetary and social opposition.

EDUCATION AND TRAINING

Education and training initiatives typically rank high in most antipoverty agendas. Administrative and congressional spokespersons exhort the young to stay in school and the unemployed—especially those on welfare—to undertake further training. There are always suggestions to expand government training programs and political support for educational outlays is easy to muster.

No general case against educational and training expenditures has been presented here. Again, the focus is only on the effectiveness of those expenditures as antipoverty tools. The issue is important because educational and training programs gather much of their support on the basis of their reputed antipoverty effectiveness. What we have sought to demonstrate is that this belief bears very little resemblance to the causal roots of poverty. Lack of formal training or education, by itself, is not a very significant cause of poverty. Thus, programs to provide more education and training are not particularly well suited to reduce the incidence of poverty. What impact they have is dependent on general economic conditions. Ironically, they are most effective when least needed (in a strong economy) and least effective when the need for them seems most apparent (in a weak economy with high rates of unemployment). Low skill levels are a major concern for broader issues of inequality but by themselves are not very compelling explanations for poverty.

Even if skill deficiencies were identified as a basic cause of poverty, it is not evident that expanded government programs would remedy the problem. Public training programs have rarely attained noteworthy net impact, much less cost-effectiveness. Most training takes place on the job. Hence, it is more important to get people into real job settings than into formal training programs. Once individuals have some job experience, they can make better training decisions.

Training and education programs can still be improved, of course. Of particular interest is the potential to target training services more directly on the poor. CETA did this by focusing almost exclusively on the disadvantaged, and most JTPA expenditures were similarly targeted. Available evidence suggests that mandatory participation requirements help bring these services to those who need them but might otherwise not participate. Early exposure to real-world job situations—via job-search or workfare-type programs—can also increase the efficiency of training decisions and outcomes. Tax credits can also encourage low-skill workers to take low-wage jobs.

MACROECONOMIC POLICY

The single most important observation of this book is the causal significance of aggregate demand policies for the incidence of poverty. High unemployment and sluggish economic growth are the most certain and forceful agents in perpetuating poverty. Nevertheless, public policy in the mid-1970s and early 1980s can be characterized as a deliberate return to the slower growth and higher unemployment rates that characterized much of the 1950s. The recovery from the 1990–1991 recession was also deliberately slowed to avoid any increase in actual or expected inflation. Only after the economy again approached full employment in the late 1990s did poverty rates begin to recede once more. Then concern about inflation again dominated the policy agenda. Even before the terrorist attacks of September 11, 2001, the U.S. economy—and progress against poverty—was slowing.

The lesson of these repeated experiences is clear: Fighting inflation is politically more important than fighting poverty. Whenever a trade-off between full employment and inflation is apparent or imagined, our employment goals are quickly abandoned. Only sustained full employment will materially reduce poverty.

EQUAL OPPORTUNITY

Recent activity in the area of civil rights has largely been a retreat from aggressive affirmative action. It is important to realize, however, that even complete enforcement of civil rights legislation will not lead to equal status for all Americans. The desegregation and affirmative action activities of the last several decades have narrowed the gap between white and minority Americans, but the results are agonizingly slow to appear. Even if all racially based barriers to achievement fell tomorrow, blacks would continue to be handicapped by past discrimination. Black and Hispanic schoolchildren would still be far behind their white peers in educational attainments. Equal opportunity to attend college would thus still exclude most minorities. In the labor market, too, the enforcement of nondiscrimination would be of relatively little use to a person who has been denied 20 years of training and experience.

To achieve equal economic status between whites and minority groups, we must do more than enforce equal opportunity; we must also compensate for the heritage of previous discrimination. This means providing compensatory education and training. It also means providing preferential opportunities in some situations. Minority schoolchildren with fewer attainments will have to receive special consideration, while job requirements, in terms of qualifications, experience, and credentials, will have to be set aside for many black workers. As we noted in Chapter 16, such extreme affirmative action inevitably conflicts with the claims of those whites who feel they have "earned" admission to desired schools or jobs and thus necessitates difficult and delicate compromises. Defining preferences in terms of socioeconomic class may achieve anti-poverty goals more efficiently and with less social tension.

CAUSES, ATTITUDES, AND POLICY

Although no policy initiative is likely to achieve equality or eliminate poverty, there is some prospect for future change. Both the nonpoor and the poor are becoming increasingly frustrated with policies that provide more income maintenance and fewer opportunities. While nearly two out of three Americans feel that "we are spending too little on assistance to the poor," only one out of five thinks we are spending too little on welfare.

Although public demands for less welfare and more jobs are persistent, an undercurrent of hostility and distrust remains. Over 80 percent of the public agrees that "too many people on welfare could be working" and that "too many people on welfare cheat by getting money they are not entitled to." With respect to minority concerns, 41 percent of white America believes that black unemployment rates are high because blacks don't want jobs. In addition, one out of four whites believes blacks have less native intelligence. Only 4 percent of all whites believe that job discrimination is a major barrier to black employment. White perceptions of Hispanic minorities are comparable. Finally, a majority of Americans opposes preferential access to jobs or schools for either poor people or minorities, preferring to let "merit" determine access to schools and jobs.

These perceptions of poverty and discrimination are major determinants of public policy. If we are going to eliminate either poverty or discrimination, public perceptions must reflect reality more closely. Then those perceptions must be reflected in public policy.

INDEX

❧